谨以此书献给伟大的祖国

This book is dedicated to our great motherland

北京 2022 年 冬奥会和冬残奥会
Beijing 2022 Olympic and Paralympic Winter Games

场馆设施手册
Overlay Book

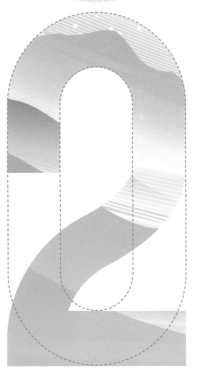

北京市建筑设计研究院有限公司
中国建筑设计研究院有限公司　　编著
清华大学建筑设计研究院有限公司
中国城市发展规划设计咨询有限公司

中国建筑工业出版社

图书在版编目（CIP）数据

北京2022年冬奥会和冬残奥会场馆设施手册 =
Beijing 2022 Olympic and Paralympic Winter Games
Overlay Book：英汉对照 / 北京市建筑设计研究院有限
公司等编著. — 北京：中国建筑工业出版社，2022.6
　　ISBN 978-7-112-27367-6

　　Ⅰ.①北… Ⅱ.①北… Ⅲ.①冬季奥运会—体育场—
设备—北京—手册—英、汉②世界残疾人运动会—冬季奥
运会—体育场—设备—北京—手册—英、汉 Ⅳ.
①G811.212-62②G818-62

中国版本图书馆CIP数据核字（2022）第079851号

责任编辑：何楠　徐冉　易娜　段宁
责任校对：王烨

北京2022年冬奥会和冬残奥会场馆设施手册
Beijing 2022 Olympic and Paralympic Winter Games Overlay Book
北京市建筑设计研究院有限公司
中国建筑设计研究院有限公司　　编著
清华大学建筑设计研究院有限公司
中国城市发展规划设计咨询有限公司

*

中国建筑工业出版社出版、发行（北京海淀三里河路9号）
各地新华书店、建筑书店经销
北京锋尚制版有限公司制版
北京富诚彩色印刷有限公司印刷

*

开本：965毫米×1270毫米　1/16　印张：23　字数：1103千字
2022年8月第一版　2022年8月第一次印刷
定价：240.00元
ISBN 978-7-112-27367-6
（39552）

编委会

2022年2月4日，正逢中国的立春，在北京国家体育场"鸟巢"内，第24届冬季奥林匹克运动会拉开帷幕！

从1999年申办夏奥会到2008年夏奥会成功举办，从2014年申办冬奥会到2022年冬奥会圆满落幕，两届奥运会的筹办前后近18年，北京发生了很大的变化：开放、包容、高科技、可持续，城市建设更加优异，奥林匹克运动发展更为广阔。

2008年夏奥会，北京建设了一批现代化大型体育场馆：国家体育场"鸟巢"、国家游泳中心"水立方"、国家体育馆、五棵松体育中心……2022年冬奥会，它们作为夏奥会遗产被再次使用，成为"冰立方""冰之帆""冰上运动中心"，成为"双奥遗产"。

延庆赛区和张家口赛区，在原本偏僻的山地上，建设了国家高山滑雪中心"雪飞燕"、国家雪车雪橇中心"雪游龙"、国家跳台滑雪中心"雪如意"等户外场馆，并将京张高铁和京礼高速毗邻场馆核心区设置，带动了区域的全面发展。

北京冬奥组委办公区和滑雪大跳台"雪飞天"落户首钢，让停产近10年的首钢园区，实现了全面复兴，成为世界知名的工业遗址再利用示范园区。

在场馆的绿色可持续方面，北京2022年冬奥会和冬残奥会成绩卓越。新建改建的7座冰上场馆，均使用了环保型制冷系统和制冷剂。特别是国家速滑馆等4个场馆，采用了二氧化碳跨临界直接制冷系统，该系统是目前世界上最先进、最环保、最节能的制冷技术，为世界环保事业作出了贡献。雪上场馆则全面践行了"源于自然而生，返璞自然而行"的设计理念。

北京冬奥会所有新建室内场馆，全部达到绿色建筑三星级标准，还为雪上项目研究制订了《绿色雪上运动场馆评价标准》，为奥林匹克留下了宝贵的可持续遗产。

所有场馆在规划建设之初，就同步考虑了赛时使用和赛后运营的双重需要，并将中国的传统文化融入到场馆中，讲述了温暖而流长的"中国故事"。而这些丰厚的场馆建设成果，均作为《场馆设施手册》这一赛时最重要的空间运行文件载体，成为冬奥会和冬残奥会顺利举办的基石。

作为两届奥运会的参与者，我们见证了北京作为"双奥之城"，推动城市建设发展的同时，更为奥林匹克运动在中国乃至世界的发展带去了动力！这是北京2008和北京2022贡献给世界奥林匹克运动的初心所在，更是中国作为一个大国的胸怀和格局所在。

2022年3月13日，第13届冬季残疾人奥林匹克运动会的火炬轻轻熄灭，两场冰雪盛宴结束了，但北京2022所传承的"共向未来"的信念和使命，不会结束！

苍松迎远客，折柳寄深情。感谢这个伟大的时代所赋予我们的责任和荣光，必将在这历史的长河中，奔涌向前、湍流不息！

On 4th February 2022, the day coinciding with the Beginning of Spring, the first solar term in the Chinese lunar calendar, the Olympic Winter Games Beijing 2022 held a grand opening ceremony at the National Stadium, also known as the Bird's Nest, in Beijing.

From 1999 when Beijing bid for hosting the 2008 Olympic Games to 2008 when the XXIX Olympic Summer Games took place, then to 2014 when the city again bid for hosting the 2022 Olympic Winter Games and to 2022 the year of XXIV Olympic Winter Games, in the timespan of 18 years, the city underwent profound changes and became more open, inclusive, high-tech and sustainable, with upgraded facilities and an improved environment, and a more promising future for the Olympic Movement.

To host the Beijing 2008 Games, Beijing built an array of large-scale modern venues including the National Stadium (the Bird's Nest), the National Aquatics Centre (the Water Cube), the National Indoor Stadium, and the Wukesong Sports Centre. These legacies of Beijing 2008 were retrofit for the Beijing 2022 Games into the "Ice Cube", "Sail of Ice" and Wukesong Ice Hockey Training Hall, etc., thus becoming the legacies for both the Olympic Summer and Winter Games.

The National Alpine Skiing Centre (the "Snow Swallow"), the National Sliding Centre (the "Snow Dragon"), the National Ski Jumping Centre (the "Snow Ruyi") and other outdoor venues were erected on the remote mountainous area in the Yanqing and Zhangjiakou Zones, and the Beijing-Zhangjiakou High speed Railway and the Beijing-Chongli Expressway run through the core area of the competition zones, driving the comprehensive development in the region.

Shougang Park, where production has been suspended for nearly a decade, welcomes its revival after it became home to the Beijing 2022 headquarters and the Big Air Shougang (the "Snow Flying Ribbon"). It has become a world-renowned paradigm for its reuse of industrial heritage.

The Beijing 2022 Games has stood out in enabling green, sustainable venues. Environmentally friendly refrigeration systems and refrigerants were used in all seven newly-built or renovated ice venues. In particular, four venues including the National Speed Skating Oval use the carbon dioxide trans-critical refrigeration technology, the most advanced, eco-friendly, and energy-saving refrigerating technology in the world, contributing greatly to the global endeavour in environmental protection. Besides, the principle of respecting and preserving nature was practised in the design of snow venues.

All newly-built indoor venues for the Beijing 2022 Games are up to the 3-star standards of green buildings. Also, efforts have been made to lay down Evaluation Standards for Green Snow Sports Venues. All these have become precious and enduring Olympic legacies.

The requirements for Games-time usage and post-Games operation were considered in the early stage of venue planning and construction, and China's traditional culture is incorporated in venue designs to tell China's stories in a warm, long-lasting way. The rich achievements in venue construction underlie the Overlay Books, which is the most important guide for Games-time space operation, laying the cornerstone for the success of the Beijing 2022 Games.

Having participated in both the Beijing 2008 Games and the Beijing 2022 Games, We have witnessed how Beijing, as a host city of both the Olympic Summer and Winter Games, has been promoting urban development and injecting momentum into the Olympic Movement in China and even worldwide. This is what Beijing aspired to in hosting the two editions of the Games, and an endeavour China took up as a responsible, visionary major country.

When the Flame was extinguished at the Beijing 2022 Paralympic Winter Games on 13th March 2022, the grand feasts on ice and snow were wrapped up, but not the pursuit of "Together for a Shared Future."

We welcome our guests with fireworks resembling Guest Greeting Pine and bid farewell to them by waving willow twigs. We are grateful and honoured to take up the responsibility in this great era, and we will continue to make new headway as the river of time rolls on.

《场馆设施手册》最早是国际奥委会在1996年亚特兰大奥运会首次提出的,当时命名为"场馆运行设计"。此后经过历届奥运会扩充、完善,形成了目前各主办城市普遍使用的《场馆设施手册》。

奥运会赛事运行需要一套完整的场馆"运行设计图纸",标示出所有在场馆内运行的空间和设施,如赛道、出发门、结束门、缆车、打蜡房、运动员休息室、转播、计时计分、媒体席位、大家庭休息室等,这些图纸连同对应的空间、面积、位置等全要素表格,共同形成了《场馆设施手册》。

2016~2019年,北京冬奥组委规划建设部主责的场馆和基础设施业务领域(简称VNI业务领域),其工作重点是梳理场馆基本需求,按照赛时运行初步设想进行永久性设施的建设和改造,并牵头编制了《场馆设施手册》编制标准和《场馆设施手册》1.0~3.0版。

2019~2021年,北京冬奥组委场馆管理部、奥运村部、媒体运行部等部门相继成立,VNI业务领域和相关部门紧密配合,继续深化、细化《场馆设施手册》,并同步完成场馆永久性设施和临时设施的建设。

2021年10月,在北京市建筑设计研究院有限公司、中国建筑设计研究院有限公司、清华大学建筑设计研究院有限公司、中国城市发展规划设计咨询有限公司的鼎力支持下,最终版《场馆设施手册》OB7.0版编制完成。

2021年12月~2022年3月,四家编制单位将《场馆设施手册》的主要图纸进行了筛选,增加了场馆总体布局、场馆设计简介等内容,形成了《北京2022年冬奥会和冬残奥会场馆设施手册》一书。

场馆运行图纸共有几千张,本书只精选了34个场馆的主要图纸约300张、场馆照片约90张,另外,为展示场馆运行方案的变化,本书还收录了场馆典型图纸从1.0到7.0的演变历程。场馆图纸作为赛时几千人同步运行的唯一空间文件,赛前几年每天都有大量讨论修改,且图中所有信息均为中英文对照,因此图纸绘制和校核同步性的难度非常大,图中难免会出现英文大小写不精准、房间全称简称不统一等情况,但并不影响场馆运行使用。

为践行环保可持续的理念,场馆图纸的发布均以电子文件的形式进行。为保证每个房间都有中英文标注,图中文字尺寸普遍较小、只保证了电子文件阅读条件下的清晰可见。

本书作为冬奥会场馆运行设计的记录,并未对以上内容进行全面修订,旨在还原其真实历程和辗转足迹。

另外,鉴于版面有限,文字内容的英译文有少量删减,但主要内容与中文一致。

《场馆设施手册》是国际奥委会开创的一种场馆设计模式,但在中国的规划设计体系中,并没有这个环节。随着北京乃至中国举办大型赛事的逐步增多、特别是在解决"如何提供一个多领域无缝衔接平台,如何绘制一套让所有利益相关方都'用得上、看得懂'的图纸,如何让设计和建设更加精准、简约"等方面,《场馆设施手册》都是最好的方式之一。

为此,《场馆设施手册》编制单位,编著了本书,旨在记录过去8年冬奥会和冬残奥会场馆规划建设的历程,也为未来北京乃至中国举办大型赛事、大型活动,提供一种高水准、国际化的、经实践检验成功的场馆运行组织模式,并借此机缘,推动后续运行设计体系的形成,这是所有编写者的责任与希望,也是我们共同的使命。

The Overlay Book (OB) was firstly proposed by the International Olympic Committee (IOC) for the Olympic Games Atlanta 1996 with the name Venue Operational Design. It is based on the contribution and improvement by subsequent Organising Committees that the OB has finally evolved into the current version that is widely used today.

Sport operation of the Olympic Games requires a set of venue operational design drawings, with all the operating space and facilities marked out, such as courses, start gates, finish gates, gondolas, wax cabins, athlete lounges, broadcasting, timing & scoring, media tribunes, and Olympic Family Lounge. An OB should include these drawings and corresponding sheets covering space, area and location.

From 2016 to 2019, Venues and Infrastructure (VNI) under the Venue Planning and Construction Department of Beijing 2022, based on analysis of basic requirements for Games venues, built and renovated permanent facilities according to the preliminary vision for Games-time operation and took the lead in compiling the OB preparation standards and the Version 1.0 to 3.0 of OBs.

From 2019 to 2021, Beijing 2022 set up the Venue Management Department, Village Planning and Operation Department and Media Operations Department successively. VNI, in cooperation with relevant authorities, continued to refine the OBs and finished the construction of permanent and temporary facilities in venues.

With the support of Beijing Institute of Architectural Design, China Architecture Design & Research Group, the Architectural Design & Research Institute of Tsinghua University, and China Urban Development Planning & Design Consulting Co., Ltd, the OB (Version 7.0) was finalised and completed in October 2021.

From December 2021 to March 2022, worked to compile Beijing 2022 Olympic and Paralympic Winter Games Overlay Book by selecting some main drawings of the OBs, and adding the overall layout of the venues, the introduction of the venue design, etc.

There are thousands of venue operational design drawings for the Beijing 2022 Games, and only about 300 for 34 venues are included in this book. Besides, this book covers the updates on typical venue drawings to display the changes from Version 1.0 to Version 7.0. As the only space planning document guiding the work of thousands of people at the same time during the Games, the venue drawings went through a lot of modifications based on discussions almost every day for several years before the Games. With all the information in the drawings in both Chinese and English, it was very difficult to ensure synchronisation when making and reviewing the drawings. Therefore, capitalisation errors and inconsistent abbreviations or full names of the rooms in the drawings were inevitable, but the use of the drawings in venue operations was not affected.

The drawings were all electronic documents as an effort to protect the environment and promote sustainability. Smaller font sizes were used to ensure complete information for each room in both Chinese and English, so the text was more suitable for reading in an electronic format.

This book, as a record of our efforts in venue design and operations, did not make changes to the drawings regarding the above-mentioned problems, so that it tells an authentic story about our journey together to a successful Beijing 2022 Games.

The OBs initiated by the IOC are guidelines for the design of Olympic venues. While there were no such guidelines in China's planning and designing system, it would be wise to compile OBs as Beijing and other Chinese cities are hosting more and more major international sports events. OBs help provide a platform that seamlessly connects multiple sectors, and formulate a set of drawings that are accessible and easy-to-use for all stakeholders so that efforts in venue design and construction will be done in a more targeted and simpler manner.

To this end, the OB compilation authorities to produce this book to document our efforts in venue planning and construction for the Olympic and Paralympic Winter Games Beijing 2022 over the past eight years. For future large events hosted in Beijing and other cities in China, it provides a world-class venue operational pattern that has proved effective. Also, the editorial team believes that it is our hope and responsibility for this book to play its due part in facilitating the shaping of operation and design systems for future sport events.

目录

Contents

序
Preface

前言
Foreword

北京奥林匹克公园
Beijing Olympic Park

北京冬奥组委 提供
Provide by BOCOG

北京冬奥组委总部
Beijing 2022 Headquarter

北京冬奥组委 提供
Provide by BOCOG

国家高山滑雪中心
Yanqing National Alpine Skiing Centre
场馆业主 提供
Provide by Venue Owner

张家口赛区古杨树场馆群
Zhangjiakou Guyangshu Cluster

清华院 提供
Provide by THAD

张家口赛区太子城冰雪小镇
Zhangjiakou Taizicheng ice and snow town

清华院 提供
Provide by THAD

京张高铁
Beijing-Zhangjiakou Highspeed Railway

清华院 提供
Provide by THAD

京礼高速
Beijing-Chongli Expressway

清华院　提供
Provide by THAD

场馆概览
Venue Overview

北京2022年冬奥会和冬残奥会场馆总体布局
Olympic and Paralympic Winter Games Beijing 2022 Generic Venue Layout

1. 场馆规划总体布局

北京2022年冬奥会和冬残奥会共使用41个场馆，其中冬奥会使用了其中的39个、冬残奥会使用了其中的28个。场馆分布在3个赛区，分别是北京赛区、延庆赛区和张家口赛区。

冬奥会的39个场馆包括12个竞赛场馆、3个训练场馆和24个非竞赛场馆。冬残奥会的28个场馆包括5个竞赛场馆和23个非竞赛场馆。

北京2022年冬奥会共有109个小项、产生109项金牌，其中北京赛区37项、延庆赛区21项、张家口赛区51项。

北京2022年冬奥会共使用14个2008年夏奥会遗产，其中10个为场馆遗产、4个为土地遗产，全部位于北京赛区。

2. 赛区间交通

（1）高速铁路

连接三个赛区的京张高铁和崇礼线已于2019年年底建成通车，全长174km，最高速度为350km/h。冬奥会期间，从北京清河站到延庆站的运行时间约20min，到张家口赛区太子城高铁站的运行时间约50min。

（2）高速公路

京礼高速：连接三个赛区的第一高速路是京礼高速，京礼高速在冬奥会期间设置了双向奥运专用道，从北京冬奥村到延庆冬奥村大约90km，行车时间约1小时；从延庆冬奥村到张家口冬奥村大约85km、行车时间约1小时。

第二高速路：连接三个赛区的第二高速路是G6京藏高速+张承高速，这条高速公路已经建成通车12年。

3. 北京赛区冬奥会场馆规划布局

北京赛区位于北京中心城范围内，冬奥会共有25个场馆，包括6个竞赛场馆、3个训练场馆和16个非竞赛场馆（冬残奥会共有2个竞赛场馆和15个非竞赛场馆）。北京赛区共承担4个大项（冰壶、冰球、滑冰、滑雪）、7个分项（冰壶、冰球、短道速滑、花样滑冰、速度滑冰、单板滑雪、自由式滑雪）、37个小项的比赛。

北京赛区的场馆主要分布在4个区域，分别是：北京奥林匹克公园、首都体育馆场馆群、五棵松体育中心和首钢/京能园区。

2022年北京冬奥会包含10个场馆，其中竞赛场馆3个，分别是国家速滑馆（冰丝带）、国家游泳中心（冰立方）和国家体育馆（冰之帆）；非竞赛场馆7个，分别是国家体育场（鸟巢）、北京冬奥村/冬残奥村、北京颁奖广场、主媒体中心、奥林匹克大家庭酒店/残奥大家庭酒店、北京奥林匹克公园公共区和北京冬奥会兴奋剂检测中心。冬残奥会期间不使用北京颁奖广场。

首都体育馆场馆群共有首都体育馆1个竞赛场馆和首体花样滑冰训练馆、首体短道速滑训练馆2个训练场馆。

五棵松体育中心包含1个竞赛场馆和1个冰球训练馆。

首钢及京能园区包含1个竞赛场馆和5个非竞赛场馆，竞赛场馆是首钢滑雪大跳台，非竞赛场馆是运行指挥部调度中

1. Venue Planning and Generic Layout

A total of 41 venues were used during the Olympic and Paralympic Winter Games Beijing 2022, 39 for the Olympic Winter Games and 28 for the Paralympic Winter Games. The venues are located in three zones, namely Beijing, Yanqing and Zhangjiakou.

The 39 venues for the Olympic Winter Games include 12 competition venues, 3 training venues, and 24 non-competition venues. The 28 venues for the Paralympic Winter Games include 5 competition venues and 23 non-competition venues.

There were 109 events held and 109 gold medals won during the Olympic Winter Games Beijing 2022. Among them, 37 events were held in Beijing Zone, 21 events in Yanqing Zone and 51 events in Zhangjiakou Zone.

A total of 14 legacies of the Beijing 2008 Games were used during the Beijing 2022 Games, including 10 venues and 4 land legacies. All of them are located in Beijing Zone.

2. Inter-Zone Transport

(1) High-speed railway

The Beijing-Zhangjiakou High-speed Railway and its Chongli branch line were opened to traffic by the end of 2019. The railway stretches for 174 kilometres and is designed for trains running at up to 350 kilometres per hour. It takes about 20 minutes to travel from Qinghe Station in Beijing to Yanqing Station and about 50 minutes to Taizicheng Railway Station in Zhangjiakou Zone.

(2) Expressways

Beijing-Chongli Expressway: This is the primary expressway connecting the three zones, with two-way Olympic lanes. It takes about one hour to drive from the Beijing Olympic Village to the Yanqing Olympic Village (about 90 kilometres), or from the Yanqing Olympic Village to the Zhangjiakou Olympic Village (about 85 kilometres).

The second expressway: The second expressway connecting the three zones includes the Beijing-Tibet Expressway (G6) and the Zhangjiakou-Chengde Expressway, both of which have been open to traffic for 12 years.

3. Venue Planning in Beijing Zone

Located in downtown Beijing, Beijing Zone contains 25 venues, including 6 competition venues, 3 training venues, and 16 non-competition venues. It hosted 37 events in 7 disciplines (Curling, Ice Hockey, Short Track Speed Skating, Figure Skating, Speed Skating, Snowboard, and Freestyle Skiing) across 4 sports (Curling, Ice hockey, Skating, and Skiing).

Venues in this zone are categorised into 4 groups, namely the Beijing Olympic Park, the Capital Indoor Stadium venue cluster, Wukesong Sports Centre, and the Shougang/Jingneng Park.

The Beijing Olympic Park houses 10 venues for the Beijing 2022 Games, including 3 competition venues and 7 non-competition venues.

The Capital Indoor Stadium venue cluster contains 1 competition venue and 2 training venues: CTS Figure Skating Training Hall and CTS Short Track Speed Skating Training Hall.

Wukesong Sports Centre contains 1 competition venue and 1 Ice

心（MCC）、注册与制服发放中心（UAC）、技术运行中心（TOC）、电力运行中心（EOC）、交通运行中心（OTC），均利用现有工业厂房改造而成。

4. 延庆赛区冬奥会场馆规划布局

延庆赛区位于北京赛区的西北方向，冬奥会共有5个场馆，其中竞赛场馆2个、非竞赛场馆3个（冬残奥会只使用1个竞赛场馆，另外增加了1个非竞赛场馆——延庆颁奖广场）。赛区核心区位于小海坨山区域，包含国家高山滑雪中心、国家雪车雪橇中心2个竞赛场馆和延庆冬奥村1个非竞赛场馆，共承担3个大项（高山滑雪、雪车、雪橇）、4个分项（高山滑雪、雪车、钢架雪车、雪橇）、21个小项的比赛。

延庆残奥颁奖广场和延庆制服和注册分中心位于延庆城区内。阪泉综合服务中心位于京礼高速上。

5. 张家口赛区冬奥会场馆规划布局

张家口赛区位于张家口市崇礼区太子城区域，冬奥会共有9个场馆，其中竞赛场馆4个、非竞赛场馆5个（冬残奥会共有竞赛场馆2个、非竞赛场馆4个）。张家口赛区共承担2个大项（滑雪、冬季两项）、6个分项（单板滑雪、自由式滑雪、越野滑雪、跳台滑雪、北欧两项、冬季两项）、51个小项的比赛。

张家口赛区的场馆布局十分紧凑，集中分布在3个区域：北部的云顶滑雪公园场馆群、中部太子城冰雪小镇和南部的古杨树场馆群。

云顶滑雪公园场馆群包含云顶滑雪公园1个竞赛场馆和张家口新闻中心1个非竞赛场馆。太子城冰雪小镇包含张家口冬奥村/冬残奥村、张家口颁奖广场、张家口制服和注册分中心3个非竞赛场馆。古杨树场馆群包含国家跳台滑雪中心、国家冬季两项中心、国家越野滑雪中心3个竞赛场馆和张家口山地转播中心1个非竞赛场馆。

6. 冬残奥会场馆规划布局

北京2022年冬残奥会共使用28个场馆，包括5个竞赛场馆和23个非竞赛场馆。5个竞赛场馆分别是国家体育馆、国家游泳中心、延庆国家高山滑雪中心、张家口云顶滑雪公园和国家冬季两项中心，承担的比赛项目为6项，分别是残奥冰球、轮椅冰壶、残奥高山滑雪、残奥单板滑雪、残奥越野滑雪和残奥冬季两项。

为保证"两个奥运、同样精彩"，北京2022所有的场馆均遵循了冬奥会和冬残奥会"同步规划、同步实施"的原则，无障碍设施在冬奥会前一次性建成。

结语

2019年到2021年，国际单项体育组织对所有12个竞赛场馆和3个训练场馆均进行了现场踏勘，并对比赛场地、比赛赛道、训练场地进行了验收和认证。

冬奥会和冬残奥会已经落下帷幕，所有场馆均出色完成竞赛任务，并得到了运动员、国际奥委会、国际单项体育组织和国内外媒体的好评，冬奥会前后8年场馆和基础设施的规划建设，为国际奥林匹克运动再次抒写了北京的篇章！

Hockey Training Hall.

The Shougang/Jingneng Park contains 1 competition venue (Big Air Shougang) and 5 non-competition venues: MOC Coordination Centre (MCC), Uniform Distribution and Accreditation Centre (UAC), Technology Operation Centre (TOC), Olympic Energy Operation Centre (EOC), and Olympic Transport Command Centre (OTC). All of these venues were converted from existing factories.

4. Venue Planning in Yanqing Zone

Situated in the northwest of Beijing Zone, Yanqing Zone contains 5 venues, including 2 competition venues and 3 non-competition venues. The core area in the Xiaohaituo Mountain contains 2 competition venues, namely the National Alpine Skiing Centre and National Sliding Centre, and 1 non-competition venue (the Yanqing Olympic Village). A total of 21 events in 4 disciplines (Alpine Skiing, Bobsleigh, Skeleton, and Luge) across 3 sports (Alpine Skiing, Bobsleigh, Luge) are held in the zone.

Yanqing Paralympic Medals Plaza and Yanqing Uniform Distribution and Accreditation Centre are situated in the urban area of Yanqing. Yanqing Banquan Service Centre Area sits on the Beijing-Chongli Expressway.

5. Venue Planning in Zhangjiakou Zone

Located in the Taizicheng region in Chongli District, Zhangjiakou Zone contains 9 venues, including 4 competition venues and 5 non-competition venues. It hosted 51 events in 6 disciplines (snowboard, freestyle skiing, cross-country skiing, ski jumping, Nordic combined, and biathlon) across 2 sports (skiing and biathlon).

Venues are concentrated in 3 areas: the Genting Snow Park venue cluster in the northern region, the Taizicheng Snow Town venue cluster in the central region, and the Guyangshu venue cluster in the southern region.

The Genting Snow Park venue cluster contains 1 competition venue (Genting Snow Park) and 1 non-competition venue (Zhangjiakou Mountain Press Centre). Taizicheng Snow Town contains 3 non-competition venues, including Zhangjiakou Olympic Village/ Zhangjiakou Paralympic Village, Zhangjiakou Medals Plaza, and Zhangjiakou Uniform Distribution and Accreditation Centre. The Guyangshu venue cluster contains 3 competition venues, namely National Ski Jumping Centre, National Biathlon Centre, National Cross-Country Skiing Centre, and 1 non-competition zone, Zhangjiakou Mountain Broadcast Centre.

6. Venue Planning for the Paralympic Winter Games

A total of 28 venues were used for Beijing 2022 Paralympic Winter Games, including 5 competition venues and 23 non-competition venues. The 5 competition venues are National Indoor Stadium, National Aquatics Centre, National Alpine Skiing Centre, Genting Snow Park, and National Biathlon Centre, hosting 6 sports: Para ice hockey, wheelchair curling, Para alpine skiing, Para snowboard, Para cross-country skiing, and Para biathlon.

To host "two Games of equal splendour", synchronised efforts were made in the planning and implementation of all venues for the Olympic and Paralympic Winter Games Beijing 2022, with all accessible facilities ready before the Olympic Winter Games Beijing 2022.

N

北五环路 North Fifth Ring Road

林萃路 Lincui Road

安立路 Anli Road

G6 Beijing–Tibet Expressway

大屯路 Datun Road

北辰西路 Beichen West Road

慧忠路 Huizhong Road

北辰东路 Beichen East Road

安定路 Anding Road

北四环路 North Fourth Ring Road

1 国家速滑馆/National Speed Skating Oval
2 主媒体中心/Main Media Centre
3 奥林匹克大家庭酒店/Olympic Family Hotel
4 国家体育馆/National Indoor Stadium
5 国家游泳中心/National Aquatics Centre
6 北京颁奖广场/Beijing Medals Plaza
7 国家体育场/National Stadium
8 北京冬奥村/北京冬残奥村
  Beijing Olympic Village/Beijing Paralympic Village

北京奥林匹克公园总图
Beijing Olympic Park Master Plan

北土城东路 Beitucheng East Road

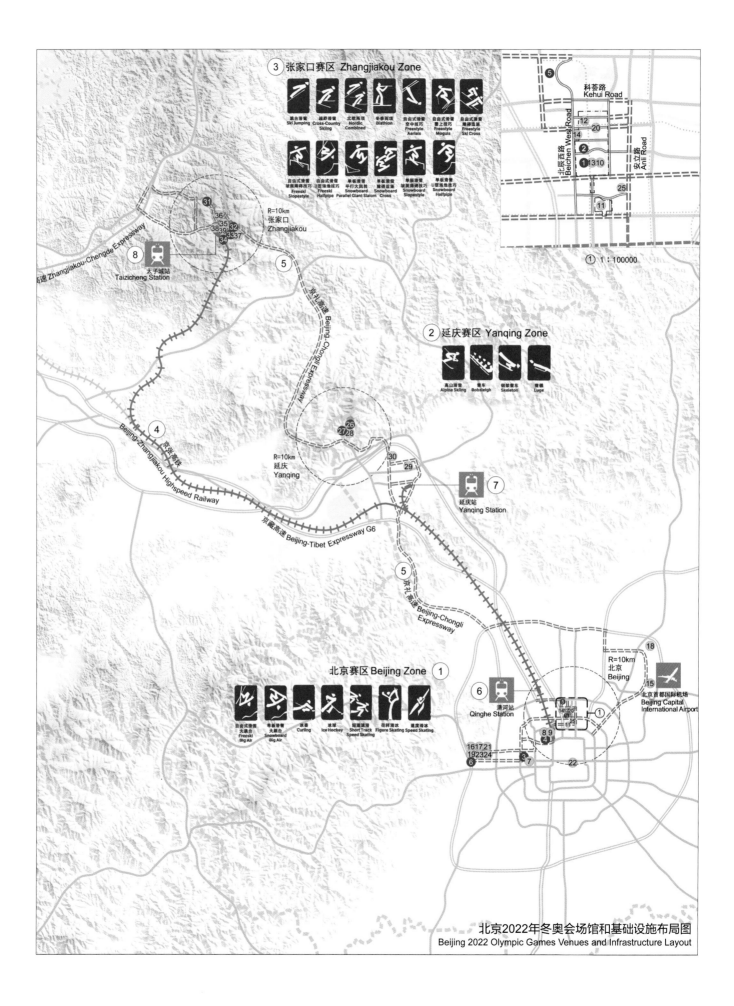

③ 张家口赛区 Zhangjiakou Zone

跳台滑雪 Ski Jumping | 越野滑雪 Cross-Country Skiing | 北欧两项 Nordic Combined | 冬季两项 Biathlon | 自由式滑雪空中技巧 Freestyle Aerials | 自由式滑雪雪上技巧 Freestyle Moguls | 自由式滑雪障碍追逐 Freestyle Ski Cross

自由式滑雪坡面障碍技巧 Freeski Slopestyle | 自由式滑雪U型场地技巧 Freeski Halfpipe | 单板滑雪平行大回转 Snowboard Parallel Giant Slalom | 单板滑雪障碍追逐 Snowboard Cross | 单板滑雪坡面障碍技巧 Snowboard Slopestyle | 单板滑雪U型场地技巧 Snowboard Halfpipe

② 延庆赛区 Yanqing Zone

高山滑雪 Alpine Skiing | 雪车 Bobsleigh | 钢架雪车 Skeleton | 雪橇 Luge

北京赛区 Beijing Zone ①

自由式滑雪大跳台 Freeski Big Air | 单板滑雪大跳台 Snowboard Big Air | 冰壶 Curling | 冰球 Ice Hockey | 短道速滑 Short Track Speed Skating | 花样滑冰 Figure Skating | 速度滑冰 Speed Skating

科荟路 Kehui Road

北辰西路 Beichen West Road

安立路 Anli Road

① 1:100000

R=10km 张家口 Zhangjiakou

延庆赛区 Yanqing Zone

京礼高速 Beijing-Chongli Expressway

京张高铁 Beijing-Zhangjiakou Highspeed Railway

京藏高速 Beijing-Tibet Expressway G6

京礼高速 Beijing-Chongli Expressway

崇礼高速 Zhangjiakou-Chengde Expressway

太子城站 Taizicheng Station

延庆站 Yanqing Station

清河站 Qinghe Station

R=10km 延庆 Yanqing

R=10km 北京 Beijing

北京首都国际机场 Beijing Capital International Airport

北京2022年冬奥会场馆和基础设施布局图
Beijing 2022 Olympic Games Venues and Infrastructure Layout

028

功能设施 Functional Facilities

(1) 北京赛区
Beijing Zone

(2) 延庆赛区
Yanqing Zone

(3) 张家口赛区
Zhangjiakou Zone

(4) 京张高铁
Beijing-Zhangjiakou Highspeed Railway

(5) 京礼高速
Beijing-Chongli Expressway

(6) 清河高铁站
Qinghe Station

(7) 延庆高铁站
Yanqing Station

(8) 太子城高铁站
Taizicheng Station

北京赛区 Beijing Zone

1 国家游泳中心（冰壶）
National Aquatics Centre (Curling)

2 国家体育馆（冰球Ⅰ）
National Indoor Stadium (Ice Hockey Ⅰ)

3 五棵松体育中心（冰球Ⅱ）
Wukesong Sports Centre (Ice Hockey Ⅱ)

4 首都体育馆（短道速滑／花样滑冰）
Capital Indoor Stadium
(Short Track Speed Skating/Figure Skating)

5 国家速滑馆（速度滑冰）
National Speed Skating Oval (Speed Skating)

6 首钢滑雪大跳台（单板滑雪／自由式滑雪）
Big Air Shougang (Snowboard/Freestyle Skiing)

7 五棵松冰球训练馆
WKS Ice Hockey Training Hall

8 首体花样滑冰训练馆
CIS Figure Skating Training Hall

9 首体短道速滑训练馆
CIS Short Track Speed Skating Training Hall

10 国家体育场
National Stadium

11 北京冬奥村／北京冬残奥村
Bejing Olympic/Paralympic Village

12 主媒体中心
Main Media Centre

13 北京颁奖广场
Beijing Medals Plaza

14 奥林匹克大家庭酒店
Olympic Family Hotel

15 北京首都国际机场
Bejing Capital International Airport

16 运行指挥部调度中心
MOC Coordination Centre

17 北京冬奥组委总部
Beijing 2022 Headquarter

18 主物流中心
Main Distribution Centre

19 制服和注册中心
Uniform Distribution and Accreditation Centre

20 北京奥林匹克公园公共区
Bejing Olympic Park

21 技术运行中心
Technology Operation Centre

22 冬奥安保指挥中心
Olympic Security Command Centre

23 冬奥交通指挥中心
Olympic Transport Command Centre

24 冬奥电力运行中心
Olympic Energy Operation Centre

25 北京冬奥会兴奋剂检测中心
Beijing Olympic Anti-doping Centre

延庆赛区 Yanqing Zone

26 国家高山滑雪中心（高山滑雪）
Yanqing National Alpine Ski Centre (Alpine Skiing)

27 国家雪车雪橇中心（雪车／雪橇）
Yanqing National Sliding Centre (Bobsleigh/Luge)

28 延庆冬奥村／延庆冬残奥村
Yanqing Olympic/Paralympic Village

29 延庆制服和注册分中心
Yanqing Uniform Distribution and Accreditation Centre

30 延庆阪泉综合服务中心
Yanqing Banquan Service Centre

张家口赛区 Zhangjiakou Zone

31 云顶滑雪公园（自由式滑雪／单板滑雪）
Zhangjiakou Genting Snow Park (Freestyle
Skiing/ Snowboard)

32 国家冬季两项中心（冬季两项）
Zhangjiakou National Biathlon Centre (Biathlon)

33 国家跳台滑雪中心（跳台滑雪／北欧两项）
Zhangjiakou National Ski Jumping Centre (Ski
Jumping/Nordic Combined)

34 国家越野滑雪中心（越野滑雪／北欧两项）
Zhangjiakou National Cross-Country Skiing
Centre (Cross-Country Skiing / Nordic Combined)

35 张家口冬奥村／张家口冬残奥村
Zhangjiakou Olympic/Paralympic Village

36 张家口山地新闻中心
Zhangjiakou Mountain Press Centre

37 张家口山地转播中心
Zhangjiakou Mountain Broadcasting Centre

38 张家口颁奖广场
Zhangjiakou Medals Plaza

39 张家口制服和注册分中心
Zhangjiakou Uniform Distribution and
Accreditation Centre

图例 LEGEND

铁路
Railway

双向奥运会／残奥会专用道
Two-way Olympic/Paralympic Lanes

奥运会／残奥会专用道
Olympic/Paralympic Lanes

奥运会／残奥会优先道
Olympic/Paralympic Priority Lanes

奥运会／残奥会专用道（连接线路）
Olympic/Paralympic Connecting Lanes

城市道路
Urban Road

城市高速路
Urban Expressway

竞赛场馆
Competiton Venues

非竞赛场馆
Non-competition Venues

水域
Water

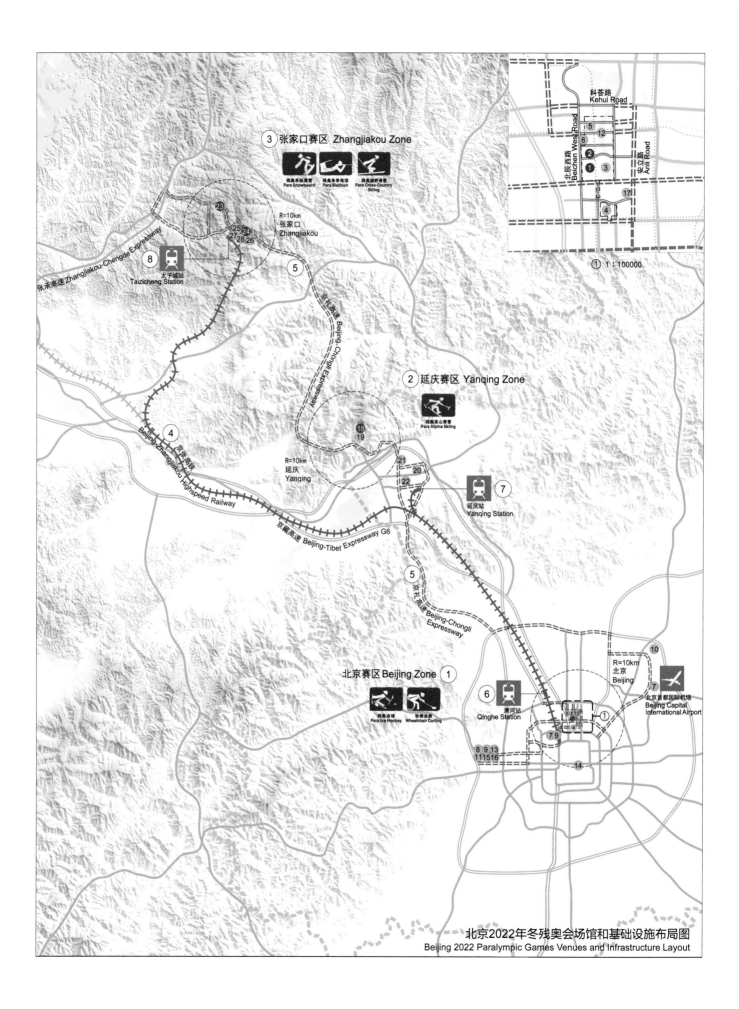

北京2022年冬残奥会场馆和基础设施布局图
Beijing 2022 Paralympic Games Venues and Infrastructure Layout

功能设施 Functional Facilities

1 北京赛区
   Beijing Zone

2 延庆赛区
   Yanqing Zone

3 张家口赛区
   Zhangjiakou Zone

4 京张高铁
   Beijing-Zhangjiakou Highspeed Railway

5 京礼高速
   Beijing - Chongli Expressway

6 清河高铁站
   Qinghe Station

7 延庆高铁站
   Yanqing Station

8 太子城高铁站
   Taizicheng Station

北京赛区 Beijing Zone

1 国家游泳中心（轮椅冰壶）
   National Aquatics Centre (Wheelchair Curling)

2 国家体育馆（残奥冰球）
   National Indoor Stadium (Para Ice Hockey)

3 国家体育场
   National Stadium

4 北京冬奥村 / 北京冬残奥村
   Beijing Olympic/Paralympic Village

5 主媒体中心
   Main Media Centre

6 残奥大家庭酒店
   Paralympic Family Hotel

7 北京首都国际机场
   Bejing Capital International Airport

8 运行指挥部调度中心
   MOC Coordination Centre

9 北京冬奥组委总部
   Beijing 2022 Headquarter

10 主物流中心
   Main Distribution Centre

11 制服和注册中心
   Uniform Distribution and Accreditation Centre

12 北京奥林匹克公园公共区
   Beijing Olympic Park

13 技术运行中心
   Technology Operation Centre

14 冬奥安保指挥中心
   Olympic Security Command Centre

15 冬奥交通指挥中心
   Olympic Transport Command Centre

16 冬奥电力运行中心
   Olympic Energy Operation Centre

17 北京冬奥会兴奋剂检测中心
   Beijing Olympic Anti-doping Centre

延庆赛区 Yanqing Zone

18 国家高山滑雪中心（残奥高山滑雪）
   Yanqing National Alpine Ski Centre
   (Para Alpine Skiing)

19 延庆冬奥村 / 延庆冬残奥村
   Yanqing Olympic/Paralympic Village

20 延庆制服和注册分中心
   Yanqing Uniform Distribution and
   Accreditation Centre

21 延庆阪泉综合服务中心
   Yanqing Banquan Service Centre

22 延庆残奥颁奖广场
   Yanqing Paralympic Medals Plaza

张家口赛区 Zhangjiakou Zone

23 云顶滑雪公园（残奥单板滑雪）
   Zhangjiakou Genting Snow Park (Para Snowboard)

24 国家冬季两项中心（残奥冬季两项 / 残奥越野滑雪）
   Zhangjiakou National Biathlon Centre (Para Biathlon/Para
   Cross-Country Sking)

25 张家口冬奥村 / 张家口冬残奥村
   Zhangjiakou Olympic/Paralympic Village

26 张家口山地转播中心
   Zhangjiakou Mountain Broadcasting Centre

27 张家口颁奖广场
   Zhangjiakou Medals Plaza

28 张家口制服和注册分中心
   Zhangjiakou Uniform Distribution and Accreditation Centre

图例 LEGEND

+++++++ 铁路
         Railway

- - - - - 双向奥运会 / 残奥会专用道
         Two-way Olympic/Paralympic Lanes

━━━━━━ 奥运会 / 残奥会专用道
         Olympic/Paralympic Lanes

- - - -   奥运会 / 残奥会优先道
         Olympic/Paralympic Priority Lanes

- - - - - 奥运会 / 残奥会专用道（连接线路）
         Olympic/Paralympic Connecting Lanes

─────   城市道路
         Urban Road

━━━━━   城市高速路
         Urban Expressway

●   竞赛场馆
         Competiton Venues

●   非竞赛场馆
         Non-competition Venues

▭   水域
         Water

北京2022年冬奥会场馆布局一览表
Beijing 2022 Olympic Games Venues List

赛区	Zone	场馆类型	Venue Type	编号	No.	场馆/场地名称		Venue		代码	
北京赛区	Beijing Zone	竞赛场馆	Competition Venue	1	1	国家游泳中心		National Aquatics Centre		NAC	
				2	2	国家体育馆		National Indoor Stadium		NIS	
				3	3	五棵松体育中心		Wukesong Sports Centre		WKS	
				4	4	首都体育馆		Capital Indoor Stadium		CTS	
				5	5	国家速滑馆		National Speed Skating Oval		NSS	
				6	6	首钢滑雪大跳台		Big Air Shougang		BAS	
		训练场馆	Training Venue	7	7	五棵松冰球训练馆		WKS Ice Hockey Training Hall		WIT	
				8	8	首体花样滑冰训练馆		CTS Figure Skating Training Hall		CFT	
				9	9	首体短道速滑训练馆		CTS Short Track Speed Skating Training Hall		CST	
		非竞赛场馆	Non-competition Venue	10	10	国家体育场		National Stadium		NST	
				11	11	北京冬奥村/北京冬残奥村		Beijing Olympic Village/Beijing Paralympic Village		BVL	
				12	12	主媒体中心		Main Media Centre		MMC	
				13	13	北京颁奖广场		Beijing Medals Plaza		BMP	
				14	14	奥林匹克大家庭酒店		Olympic Family Hotel		OFH	
				15	15	北京首都国际机场		Beijing Capital International Airport		PEK	
				16	16	运行指挥部调度中心		MOC Coordination Centre		MCC	
				17	17	技术运行中心		Technology Operation Centre		TOC	
				18	18	冬奥安保指挥中心		Olympic Security Command Centre		SCC	
				19	19	冬奥交通指挥中心		Olympic Transport Command Centre		OTC	
				20	20	冬奥电力运行中心		Olympic Energy Operation Centre		EOC	
				21	21	北京冬奥组委总部		Beijing 2022 Headquarter		BHQ	
				22	22	主物流中心		Main Distribution Centre		MDC	
				23	23	制服和注册中心		Uniform Distribution and Accreditation Centre		UAC	
				24	24	北京冬奥会兴奋剂检测中心		Beijing Olympic Anti-doping Labotory		BAL	
				25	25	北京奥林匹克公园公共区		Beijing Olympic Park		BOP	
延庆赛区	Yanqing Zone	竞赛场馆	Competition Venue	26	26	国家高山滑雪中心	高山滑雪速度场地	Yanqing National Alpine Skiing Centre	Alpine Skiing Speed Stadium	YAS	AS
							高山滑雪技术场地		Alpine Skiing Technical Stadium		AS
				27	27	国家雪车雪橇中心		Yanqing National Sliding Centre		YSC	
		非竞赛场馆	Non-competition Venue	28	28	延庆冬奥村/延庆冬残奥村		Yanqing Olympic Village/Yanqing Paralympic Village		YVL	
				29	29	延庆制服和注册分中心		Yanqing Uniform Distribution and Accreditation Centre		YUA	
				30	30	延庆阪泉综合服务中心		Yanqing Banquan Service Centre		YBS	
张家口赛区	Zhangjia-kou Zone	竞赛场馆	Competition Venue	31	31	云顶滑雪公园	平行大回转和障碍追逐场地	Zhangjiakou Genting Snow Park	Genting Snow Park P&X Stadium	ZSP	GP
							U型场地和坡面障碍场地		Genting Snow Park H&S Stadium		GH
							空中技巧和选上技巧场地		Genting Snow Park A&M Stadium		GA
				32	32	国家越野滑雪中心		Zhangjiakou National Cross-Country Skiing Centre		ZCC	
				33	33	国家跳台滑雪中心		Zhangjiakou National Ski Jumping Centre		ZSJ	
				34	34	国家冬季两项中心		Zhangjiakou National Biathlon Centre		ZBT	
		非竞赛场馆	Non-competition Venue	35	35	张家口冬奥村/张家口冬残奥村		Zhangjiakou Olympic Village / Zhangjiakou Paralympic Village		ZVL	
				36	36	张家口山地新闻中心		Zhangjiakou Mountain Press Centre		ZPC	
				37	37	张家口山地转播中心		Zhangjiakou Mountain Broadcast Centre		ZBC	
				38	38	张家口颁奖广场		Zhangjiakou Medals Plaza		ZMP	
				39	39	张家口制服和注册分中心		Zhangjiakou Uniform Distribution and Accreditation Centre		ZUA	

Venue Code	冬奥/冬残奥使用	Olympic/ Paralympic	用途 (大项)	用途 (分项/小项)	Sport / Use of Venue Sport	Sport / Use of Venue Discipline	08年遗产	Legacy
AC	冬奥&冬残奥	O&P	冰壶	冰壶	Curling	Curling	是（场馆遗产）	Y (Venue Legacy)
NIS	冬奥&冬残奥	O&P	冰球	冰球（Ⅰ）	Ice Hockey	Ice Hockey（Ⅰ）	是（场馆遗产）	Y (Venue Legacy)
KS	仅冬奥	O	冰球	冰球（Ⅱ）	Ice Hockey	Ice Hockey（Ⅱ）	是（场馆遗产）	Y (Venue Legacy)
TS	仅冬奥	O	滑冰	花样滑冰、短道速滑	Skating	Short Track/Figure Skating	是（场馆遗产）	Y (Venue Legacy)
SS	仅冬奥	O	滑冰	速度滑冰	Skating	Speed Skating	是（土地遗产）	Y (Land Legacy)
AS	仅冬奥	O	滑雪	单板滑雪、自由式滑雪	Skiing	Snowboard/Freestyle Skiing	是（土地遗产）	Y (Land Legacy)
IT	仅冬奥	O		冰球（训练）	Ice Hockey (Training)		是（土地遗产）	Y (Land Legacy)
FT	仅冬奥	O		花样滑冰（训练）	Figure Skating (Training)		是（场馆遗产）	Y (Venue Legacy)
ST	仅冬奥	O		短道速滑（训练）	Short Track Speed Skating (Training)		否	N
ST	冬奥&冬残奥	O&P		开、闭幕式	Opening and Closing Ceremonies		是（场馆遗产）	Y (Venue Legacy)
VL	冬奥&冬残奥	O&P		运动员及随队官员居住	Residence of athletes and team officials		是（土地遗产）	Y (Land Legacy)
MC	冬奥&冬残奥	O&P		媒体运行、转播服务	Press Operations/Broadcast Services		是（土地遗产）	Y (Land Legacy)
MP	仅冬奥	O		颁奖	Medals Plaza		是（场馆遗产）	Y (Venue Legacy)
FH	仅冬奥	O		奥林匹克大家庭住宿	Hospitality, Olympic Family		是（场馆遗产）	Y (Venue Legacy)
PEK	冬奥&冬残奥	O&P		抵离	Arrivals and Departures		否	N
CC	冬奥&冬残奥	O&P		运行指挥	Operation Command		否	N
OC	冬奥&冬残奥	O&P		技术运行指挥	Technology Operation Command		否	N
CC	冬奥&冬残奥	O&P		安保指挥	Security Command		否	N
TC	冬奥&冬残奥	O&P		交通指挥	Transport Command		否	N
OC	冬奥&冬残奥	O&P		电力运行指挥	Energy Operation Command		否	N
HQ	冬奥&冬残奥	O&P		总部	Headquarters		否	N
DC	冬奥&冬残奥	O&P		仓储物流	Warehousing and Logistics		否	N
AC	冬奥&冬残奥	O&P		制服和注册	Uniform Distribution and Accreditation		否	N
AL	冬奥&冬残奥	O&P		兴奋剂检测	Doping Control		是（场馆遗产）	Y (Venue Legacy)
OP	冬奥&冬残奥	O&P		奥林匹克公园公共区	Common Domain		是（场馆遗产）	Y (Venue Legacy)
ASP / AST	冬奥&冬残奥	O&P	滑雪	高山滑雪	Skiing	Alpine Skiing	否	N
SC	仅冬奥	O	雪车、雪橇	雪车、钢架雪车、雪橇	Bobsleigh/Luge	Bobsleigh//Skeleton/Luge	否	N
VL	冬奥&冬残奥	O&P		运动员及随队官员居住	Residence of athletes and team officials		否	N
UA	冬奥&冬残奥	O&P		制服和注册	Uniform Distribution and Accreditation		否	N
BS	冬奥&冬残奥	O&P		综合服务枢纽	Transportation hub		否	N
GPX / GHS / GAM	冬奥&冬残奥	O&P	滑雪	平行大回转、障碍追逐 U型场地技巧、坡面障碍技巧 空中技巧、雪上技巧	Skiing	Freestyle Skiing/Snowboarding Freestyle Skiing/Snowboarding Freestyle Skiing	否	N
CC	仅冬奥	O	滑雪	越野滑雪、北欧两项	Skiing	Cross Country/Nordic Combined	否	N
SJ	仅冬奥	O	滑雪	跳台滑雪、北欧两项	Skiing	Ski Jumping/Nordic Combined	否	N
BT	冬奥&冬残奥	O&P	冬季两项	冬季两项	Biathlon	Biathlon	否	N
VL	冬奥&冬残奥	O&P		运动员及随队官员居住	Residence of athletes and team officials		否	N
PC	仅冬奥	O		媒体运行	Press Operations		否	N
BC	冬奥&冬残奥	O&P		转播服务	Broadcast Services		否	N
MP	冬奥&冬残奥	O&P		颁奖	Medals Plaza		否	N
UA	冬奥&冬残奥	O&P		制服和注册	Uniform Distribution and Accreditation		否	N

北京2022年冬残奥会场馆布局一览表
Beijing 2022 Paralympic Games Venues List

赛区	Zone	场馆类型	Venue Type	编号	No.	场馆/场地名称		Venue		代码	
北京赛区	Beijing Zone	竞赛场馆	Competition Venue	1	1	国家游泳中心		National Aquatics Centre		NAC	
				2	2	国家体育馆		National Indoor Stadium		NIS	
		非竞赛场馆	Non-competition Venue	3	3	国家体育场		National Stadium		NST	
				4	4	北京冬奥村/北京冬残奥村		Beijing Olympic Village/Beijing Paralympic Village		BVL	
				5	5	主新闻中心		Main Media Centre		MMC	
				6	6	残奥大家庭酒店		Paralympic Family Hotel		PFH	
				7	7	北京首都国际机场		Beijing Capital International Airport		PEK	
				8	8	运行指挥部调度中心		MOC Coordination Centre		MCC	
				9	9	技术运行中心		Technology Operation Centre		TOC	
				10	10	冬奥安保指挥中心		Olympic Security Command Centre		SCC	
				11	11	冬奥交通指挥中心		Olympic Transport Command Centre		OTC	
				12	12	冬奥电力运行中心		Olympic Energy Operation Centre		EOC	
				13	13	北京冬奥组委总部		Beijing 2022 Headquarter		BHQ	
				14	14	主物流中心		Main Distribution Centre		MDC	
				15	15	制服和注册中心		Uniform Distribution and Accreditation Centre		UAC	
				16	16	北京冬奥会兴奋剂检测中心		Beijing Olympic Anti-doping Labotory		BAL	
				17	17	北京奥林匹克公园公共区		Beijing Olympic Park		BOP	
延庆赛区	Yanqing Zone	竞赛场馆	Competition Venue	18	18	国家高山滑雪中心	高山滑雪速度场地	Yanqing National Alpine Skiing Centre	Alpine Skiing Speed Stadium	YAS	AS
							高山滑雪技术场地		Alpine Skiing Technical Stadium		AS
		非竞赛场馆	Non-competition Venue	19	19	延庆冬奥村/延庆冬残奥村		Yanqing Olympic Village/Yanqing Paralympic Village		YVL	
				20	20	延庆制服和注册分中心		Yanqing Uniform Distribution and Accreditation Centre		YUA	
				21	21	延庆残奥颁奖广场		Yanqing Paralympic Medals Plaza		YMP	
				22	22	延庆阪泉综合服务中心		Yanqing Banquan Service Centre		YBS	
张家口赛区	Zhangjia-kou Zone	竞赛场馆	Competition Venue	23	23	云顶滑雪公园	平行大回转和障碍追逐场地	Zhangjiakou Genting Snow Park	Genting Snow Park P&X Stadium	ZSP	G
				24	24	国家冬季两项中心		Zhangjiakou National Biathlon Centre		ZBT	
		非竞赛场馆	Non-competition Venue	25	25	张家口冬奥村/张家口冬残奥村		Zhangjiakou Olympic Village/Zhangjiakou Paralympic Village		ZVL	
				26	26	张家口山地转播中心		Zhangjiakou Mountain Broadcast Centre		ZBC	
				27	27	张家口颁奖广场		Zhangjiakou Medals Plaza		ZMP	
				28	28	张家口制服和注册分中心		Zhangjiakou Uniform Distribution and Accreditation Centre		ZUA	

Venue Code	冬奥/冬残奥使用	Olympic / Paralympic	用途	用途	08年遗产	08年遗产
AC	冬奥&冬残奥	O&P	轮椅冰壶	Wheelchair Curling	是（场馆遗产）	Y (Venue Legacy)
IS	冬奥&冬残奥	O&P	残奥冰球	Para Ice Hockey	是（场馆遗产）	Y (Venue Legacy)
ST	冬奥&冬残奥	O&P	开、闭幕式	Opening/Closing Ceremonies	是（场馆遗产）	Y (Venue Legacy)
VL	冬奥&冬残奥	O&P	运动员及随队官员居住	Residence of athletes and team officials	是（土地遗产）	Y (Land Legacy)
MC	冬奥&冬残奥	O&P	媒体运行、转播服务	Press Operations/Broadcast Services	是（土地遗产）	Y (Land Legacy)
FH	仅冬残奥	P	残奥大家庭	Hospitality, Olympic Family	是（场馆遗产）	Y (Venue Legacy)
EK	冬奥&冬残奥	O&P	抵离	Arrivals and Departures	否	N
CC	冬奥&冬残奥	O&P	运行指挥	Operation Command	否	N
DC	冬奥&冬残奥	O&P	技术运行指挥	Technology Operation Command	否	N
CC	冬奥&冬残奥	O&P	安保指挥	Security Command	否	N
TC	冬奥&冬残奥	O&P	交通指挥	Transport Command	否	N
DC	冬奥&冬残奥	O&P	电力运行指挥	Energy Operation Command	否	N
HQ	冬奥&冬残奥	O&P	总部	Headquarters	否	N
DC	冬奥&冬残奥	O&P	仓储物流	Warehousing and Logistics	否	N
AC	冬奥&冬残奥	O&P	制服和注册	Uniform Distribution and Accreditation	否	N
AL	冬奥&冬残奥	O&P	兴奋剂检测	Doping Control	是（场馆遗产）	Y (Venue Legacy)
DP	冬奥&冬残奥	O&P	奥林匹克公园公共区	Common Domain	是（场馆遗产）	Y (Venue Legacy)
ASP AST	冬奥&冬残奥	O&P	残奥高山滑雪	Para Alpine Skiing	否	N
VL	冬奥&冬残奥	O&P	运动员及随队官员居住	Residence of athletes and team officials	否	N
JA	冬奥&冬残奥	O&P	制服和注册	Uniform Distribution and Accreditation	否	N
MP	仅冬残奥	P	颁奖	Medals Plaza	否	N
BS	冬奥&冬残奥	O&P	综合服务枢纽	Transportation hub	否	N
GPX	冬奥&冬残奥	O&P	残奥单板滑雪	Para Snowboard	否	N
BT	冬奥&冬残奥	O&P	残奥冬季两项、残奥越野滑雪	Para Biathlon, Para Cross-Country Skiing	否	N
VL	冬奥&冬残奥	O&P	运动员及随队官员居住	Residence of athletes and team officials	否	N
BC	冬奥&冬残奥	O&P	转播服务	Mountain Broadcast Centre	否	N
MP	冬奥&冬残奥	O&P	颁奖	Medals Plaza	否	N
JA	冬奥&冬残奥	O&P	制服和注册	Uniform Distribution and Accreditation	否	N

北京2022年冬奥会和冬残奥会
《场馆设施手册》编制标准与历程
Olympic and Paralympic Winter Games Beijing 2022
Compilation Standards and Process of Overlay Books

1.《场馆设施手册》编制背景

（1）《场馆设施手册》编制缘起

《场馆设施手册》（"Overlay Book"，简称OB）是指导奥运会赛前场馆建设、赛时场馆运行和赛后恢复工作的重要指南文件，是指导各业务领域在场馆内开展建设和运行工作的唯一空间技术文件。

《场馆设施手册》最早源于"运行设计"，在1996年亚特兰大奥运会首次提出并开始使用，此后历届奥运会逐渐扩充，2012年伦敦奥运会后，国际奥委会在各主办城市全面推行《场馆设施手册》的编制和使用，要求各主办城市按照7个时间点、每隔半年更新、递交一次《场馆设施手册》。

（2）《场馆设施手册》涵盖范围

国际奥委会的场馆设施指南中，将场馆分为三个层次：分别是：场馆群（如古杨树场馆群，群内有4个独立的场馆），场馆区（如云顶滑雪公园，场馆比赛区域分别独立，但后院很多设施是共用的），独立场馆（如国家速滑馆）。

国际奥委会将场馆分为竞赛场馆和非竞赛场馆两种类型。竞赛场馆是直接进行比赛的场馆，比如国家高山滑雪中心、首钢滑雪大跳台等；非竞赛场馆是为比赛提供支撑服务的场馆，如冬奥村、媒体中心、颁奖广场、奥运大家庭酒店等。

以上所有场馆、场馆群，均需编制《场馆设施手册》。

（3）《场馆设施手册》主要内容

《场馆设施手册》成果主要包含两方面，一是场馆空间面积分配表（Area Allocation Matrix，简称AAM表格），二是场馆赛时运行系列图纸。旨在通过AAM表格和系列图纸的编制，指导场馆建设和运行的全过程。其中，AAM表格是各业务领域对场馆空间和设施需求的清单列表，是《场馆设施手册》编制的基础。场馆系列图纸是各类规划设计图纸的集合，体现了从区域空间布局到详细房间布局的各类图纸内容。

AAM表格是场馆运行相关的空间表格，主要包括房间、场地、位置以及装修交付标准等。比如，冰球场馆需要14套运动员更衣室，每套更衣室包含厕所、沐浴间、按摩室、领队室、会议室、烘干室等，面积约200m²等。这些需求在AAM表格中会有详细描述，并会体现在图纸中。

《场馆设施手册》图纸涵盖场馆内所有和赛时运行相关的永久性设施、临时设施和临时工程，"所见即所得"，即在赛时，现场所有和运行相关的设施，如建筑、门、坡道、楼电梯、停车位、家具、转播所需要的线缆路由等内容，均需在图纸中体现。

1. Background

(1) Origin

The Overlay Book (OB) is a major guide on pre-Games venue construction, Games-time venue operations and post-Games restoration for the Olympic Games. It serves as the only technical document in this respect for Functional Areas (FAs).

Originating from operational design, the OB was first proposed and put into use at the Olympic Games Atlanta 1996 and has been enriched by subsequent Organising Committees. After the Olympic Games London 2012, the preparation and use of OB has been promoted across host cities. The International Olympic Committee (IOC) demands each host city to update and submit its OBs on a semi-annual basis by seven key dates.

(2) Scope

According to the IOC's Olympic Games Guide on Venues and Infrastructure, venues fall into 3 categories: venue clusters (e.g., Guyangshu Venue Cluster, which consists of 4 stand-alone venues), precincts (e.g., Genting Snow Park, in which competition areas are stand-alone while many BOH facilities are for common use), and stand-alone venues (e.g., National Speed Skating Oval).

The IOC divides venues into competition venues and non-competition venues. Competition venues are those that host competitions, such as National Alpine Skiing Centre and Big Air Shougang, while non-competition venues provide support services for competitions, such as the Olympic villages, media centres, medals plazas, and Olympic Family hotels.

Each venue or venue cluster is required to prepare its own OB.

(3) Main Contents

Each OB includes two parts: the Area Allocation Matrix (AAM) and drawings for Games-time venue operations, to guide the whole process of venue construction and operations. The AAM lists each FA's requirements for venue spaces and facilities, and is thus the basis for the OB. Venue drawings comprise all types of drawings for planning and design, presenting the layouts of both spaces and specific rooms.

Developed for venue operations, the AAM includes standards for rooms, fields of play (FOP), locations, fit-out and delivery. For example, the AAM provides that an ice hockey venue requires 14 athletes' dressing rooms, each equipped with a toilet room, a shower room, a message room, a team leader's office, a meeting room and a drying room, with an area of some 200 square metres, which is presented in drawings.

Drawings in OBs cover all the permanent/temporary facilities and temporary projects in venues that operate during Games-time. Development of the drawings follow the principle of "what you see is what you get", i.e., presenting all the operating facilities on site during Games-time, such as buildings, gates, ramps, elevators, parking spaces, furniture, and broadcasting containments.

2. 北京2022《场馆设施手册》编制概况

（1）编制范围

北京冬奥会和冬残奥会《场馆设施手册》的编制范围包含北京冬奥会使用的竞赛场馆、训练场馆、非竞赛场馆、部分服务设施以及三个赛区总体运行设计，共计47项。

（2）编制版本

北京2022《场馆设施手册》编制工作于2018年启动，2021年底完成，基本上按照计划半年更新一版，总共完成了七个正式版本的编制工作。此外，为了配合电视转播、冬残奥会、临时设施建设等相关工作，还完成了五个更新版本的编制和提交工作（表1）。

表1 《场馆设施手册》提交时间/Table 1 Time of Submission

提交时间 Time of Submission	正式版本 Official Version	更新版本 Revised Version
2018.09	OB1.0	OB1.2
2019.03	OB2.0	OB2.1
2019.09	OB3.0	OB3.1
2020.05	OB4.0	OB4.1
2020.10	OB5.0	—
2021.05	OB6.0	OB6.1
2021.11	OB7.0	—

（3）编制历程

2018年9月，北京冬奥组委规划建设部在国际奥委会专家的指导下，编制了《北京2022年冬奥会设施手册编制标准》第一版，并完成了《场馆设施手册》1.0版的编制工作。

2018年11月至2019年1月，规划建设部根据国际奥委会专家意见，借鉴伦敦、里约、平昌、东京奥运会《场馆设施手册》编制经验，整合此前制定的绘图标准，更新完成了《北京2022年冬奥会设施手册编制标准V2.0版》。

北京冬奥组委规划建设部牵头完成了OB1.0、2.0和3.0三个版本的编制和提交工作，编制范围包括12个竞赛场馆、3个训练场馆、3个冬奥村、4个媒体运行相关场馆以及2个颁奖广场，涉及场馆24个。

2019年下半年，随着场馆管理部、媒体运行部、奥运村部、开闭幕式工作部等部门的成立，《场馆设施手册》开始由规划建设部会同各场馆主责部门共同编制，截至2021年底，陆续完成了所有场馆OB4.0-7.0的编制工作。

每一轮OB编制完成后，均会向国际奥委会（IOC）、奥林匹克广播服务公司（OBS）、北京冬奥组委、北京市和河北省相关部门发布。

（4）冬残奥会和无障碍设施

《场馆设施手册》图纸中包含所有的无障碍设施内容，包括残疾人坡道、无障碍卫生间、无障碍电梯、无障碍坐席、无障碍摄影机位等。

北京冬残奥会使用的5个竞赛场馆：国家游泳中心、国家体育馆、国家高山滑雪中心、国家冬季两项中心和云顶滑雪公园，以及3个冬残奥村：北京冬残奥村、延庆冬残奥村和张家口冬残奥村，在《场馆设施手册》里特别增加了冬残奥会相关的内容和无障碍流线等内容。

2. Overview of OB Compilation for the Beijing 2022 Games

(1) Scope

The OBs of the Beijing 2022 Games cover the operational design of a total of 47 items, ranging from competition/non-competition venues, training venues and part of the service facilities to the 3 competition zones.

(2) Version History

The compilation of OBs for the Beijing 2022 Games spanned from 2018 to the end of 2021, with 7 versions released on a semi-annual basis as scheduled. Besides, 5 revised revisions were developed and submitted to support broadcasting, the Beijing 2022 Paralympic Winter Games, and construction of temporary facilities (Table 1).

(3) Process

In September 2018, under the guidance of IOC experts, the Venue Planning and Construction Department of Beijing 2022 prepared the OB Compilation Standards for the Beijing 2022 Games (V 1.0), and completed the OB1.0.

Between November 2018 and January 2019, the Venue Planning and Construction Department completed the OB Compilation Standards (V2.0), based on opinions from IOC experts and the established drawing standards. It also drew on the experience in OB compilation from London, Rio de Janeiro, PyeongChang and Tokyo.

The Venue Planning and Construction Department led the compilation and submission of OB1.0, OB2.0 and OB3.0, covering 24 venues in total, including 12 competition venues, 3 training venues, 3 Olympic Villages, 4 venues for media operations, and 2 medals plazas.

In the second half of 2019, Beijing 2022 set up the Venue Management Department, Media Operations Department, Village Planning and Operation Department and the Department of Opening and Closing Ceremonies, and the Venue Planning and Construction Department began to join hands with departments responsible for each venue to develop the OBs. As of the end of 2021, OB4.0–OB7.0 for all the venues were finished successively.

Each version of OBs, once completed, was submitted to the IOC, OBS, Beijing 2022, and related government departments in Beijing Municipality and Hebei Province.

(4) The Paralympic Winter Games and accessible facilities

Drawings in OBs represent all the accessible facilities, including wheelchair ramps, accessible toilets, accessible elevators, accessible seating and accessible photo positions.

In particular, the OBs show that contents related to the Beijing 2022 Paralympic Winter Games and accessible flows were added to Paralympic venues, i.e., 5 competition venues (National Aquatics Centre, National Indoor Stadium, National Alpine Skiing Centre, National Biathlon Centre and Genting Snow Park) and 3 Paralympic Villages in Beijing, Yanqing and Zhangjiakou.

3. OB Compilation Standards for the Beijing 2022 Games

(1) The Area Allocation Matrix (AAM)

1) Introduction

The Area Allocation Matrices (AAMs) are programmatic documents developed for OBs. Each FA fills in an AAM with its requirements for room areas, layouts, and functions and submit it to the lead FA for review. The reviewed AAMs are then presented to the unit responsible for OB compilation, which organises them into a Master AAM that contains all the requirements for indoor and outdoor spaces and facilities for Games-time operation. Space demands in each venue are up to several hundreds and even thousands, involving all the departments and 58 FAs of Beijing 2022 (Table 2).

表2　北京冬奥组委各部门业务领域名称一览表/Table 2　Departments and FAs of Beijing 2022

序号/No.	主责部门/Department		业务领域/Functional Area		缩写/Acronym
1	秘书行政部	Department of General Administration	城市运行	City Operations	CTY
2			政府关系	Government Relations	GOV
3	总体策划部	General Planning Department	计划与协调	Planning and Coordination	PNC
4			可持续	Sustainability	SUS
5			遗产	Legacy	LGY
6			风险管理	Risk Management	RSK
7	对外联络部	International Relations Department	奥林匹克/残奥大家庭服务和礼宾	Olympic/Paralympic Family Services and Protocol	OFS/PFS
8			国家（地区）奥委会和残奥委会服务	NOC/NPC Services	NCS
9			语言服务	Language Services	LAN
10	体育部	Sports Department	体育	Sport	SPT
11	新闻宣传部	Media and Communications Department	宣传	Communications	COM
12			教育	Education	EDU
13	规划建设部	Venue Planning and Construction Department	场馆和基础设施	Venues and Infrastructure	VNI
14			电力	Energy	NRG
15			清洁与废弃物	Cleaning and Waste	CNW
16	市场开发部	Marketing Department	市场开发	Business Development	BUS
17			特许经营	Licensing	LIC
18			赞助企业服务	Marketing Partner Services	MPS
19	人力资源部	Human Resources Department	人员管理	People Management	PEM
20			信息和知识管理	Information and Knowledge Management	IKM
21	财务部	Finance Department	财务	Finance	FIN
22	技术部	Technology Department	技术	Technology	TEC
23	法律事务部	Legal Affairs Department	权益保护	Rights Protection	RPP
24			法律	Legal	LGL
25	运动会服务部	Games Services Department	住宿	Accommodation	ACM
26			反兴奋剂	Doping Control	DOP
27			餐饮	Food and Beverage	FNB
28			医疗服务	Medical Services	MED
29			观众体验	Spectator Experience	SPX
30			赛事服务	Event Services	EVS
31			公共卫生	Public Health Services	PHS
32			接待	Hospitality	HOS
33	文化活动部	Culture and Ceremonies Department	品牌、形象和赛事景观	Brand, Identity and Look of the Games	BIL
34			庆典仪式	Ceremonies	CER
35			城市活动与文化广场	City Activities and Live Sites	LIV
36			体育展示	Sport Presentation	SPP
37			文化	Culture	CUL
38			火炬传递	Olympic/Paralympic Torch Relay	OTR/PTR
39	物流部	Logistics Department	物流	Logistics	LOG
40			采购	Procurement	PRC
41	残奥会部	Paralympic Games Integration Department	残奥整合	Paralympic Games Integration	PGI
42			无障碍	Accessibility	ACS
43			分级	Classification	CLA
44	媒体运行部	Media Operations Department	转播服务	Broadcast Services	BRS
45			媒体运行	Press Operations	PRS
46	场馆管理部	Venue Management Department	场馆管理	Venue Management	VEM
47			指挥、控制、通信	Command, Control & Communications	CCC
48			运行就绪	Operational Readiness	OPR
49			引导标识	Signage (Wayfinding)	SIG
50			测试赛管理	Test Events Management	TEM
51	安保部	Security Department	安保	Security	SEC
52	交通部	Transport Department	交通	Transport	TRA
53	开闭幕式工作部	Department of Opening and Closing Ceremonies	开闭幕式	Opening and Closing Ceremonies	OCC
54	奥运村部	Village Planning and Operation Department	奥运村管理	Villages Management	VIL
55	志愿者部	Volunteer Department	志愿者	Volunteers	VOL
56	注册中心	Accreditation Centre	注册	Accreditation	ACR
57	票务中心	Ticketing Centre	票务	Ticketing	TKT
58	抵离中心	Arrival and Departure Centre	抵离	Arrivals and Departures	AND

3. 北京2022《场馆设施手册》编制标准

（1）AAM表格

1）AAM表格概念

AAM表格是《场馆设施手册》编制的纲领性文件。各业务领域将房间面积、区域位置、功能要求等需求信息填写在AAM表格中，提交牵头业务领域汇总审核后，交由《场馆设施手册》编制单位整理成为一个包含场馆赛时运行所有室内外空间和设施需求的总清单。每个场馆使用的空间数量多达几百至数千，涉及冬奥组委所有部门、58个业务领域（表2）。

2）AAM表格构成

AAM表格在《场馆设施手册》中位于封面和图纸目录之后、运行设计系列图纸之前。AAM表格分为三组信息（表3）：

一是基础数据：说明空间所属业务领域、空间代码和中英文房间名称；

二是设计数据：该空间面积、数量、总面积、占地面积以及是永久设施还是临时设施；

三是位置信息：该空间所在的位置和楼层。

3）AAM表格与系列图纸的关系

各业务领域的空间需求在一开始的时候也是不确定的，是随着工作的推进逐渐明晰的。各业务领域内部需事先整合协调各专业需求，整合后形成自己业务领域的AAM表格。

为了各项工作顺利推进，各个业务领域要在OB节点提出各自需求，整合到AAM表格中，运行设计团队会根据各业务领域的需求进行统筹调整落图之后，并将发现的问题反映到AAM表中进而反馈给各业务l领域。若某个业务领域需求的提出错过了某个OB节点，那相应需求的反馈只能表现在下一版OB图中。

2) Structure

An AAM follows the cover and contents of an OB and is prior to the drawings for operational design. It comprises three types of information concerning each space (Table 3):

i) Generic program data, i.e. related FA, space code and space name (in Chinese and English);

ii) Design data, i.e. area, quantity, total area, site area, and whether it is permanent or temporary;

iii) Location data: zone and floor number.

3) Relation between AAMs and drawings

FAs were not sure about their space demands at the beginning, which only became clear as their work proceeded. Each FA shall gather and coordinate internal demands in advance and consolidate them to produce its AAM.

To ensure smooth progress of work, at each time point of the OB timeline, each FA shall put forth its own requirements and add them to the AAM. Based on these requirements, the operational design team shall adjust the matrix on a coordinated manner and report problems to FAs via the AAM. If a FA misses the submission date, its requirements can only be included in the next version of the OB.

表3　AAM表格样式/Table 3　Sample AAM

国家游泳中心—奥运会冰壶/National Aquatics Centre—OCU									
基础数据/Generic Program Data		设计数据/Design Data						位置/Location	
FA or Sport Discipline Code	Space Name	Commodity Size (m)	Area (m²)	Quantity	Total Area (m²)	Site Area (m²)	Design Description（Permanent / Temporary）	Zone	Number Of Stories
业务领域或体育大项、分项代码	空间名称	尺寸（m）	面积（m²）	数量	总面积（m²）	占地面积（m²）	设计描述（永久/临时）	区域	楼层
ACR	注册认证 Accreditation								
ACR	场馆注册办公室1 Venue Accreditation Office1	180	1	180			临时 Temporary		室外/Outdoor
ACR	卫生间-男 Toilets-Men			1			临时 Temporary		室外/Outdoor
ACR	卫生间-女 Toilets-Women			1			临时 Temporary		室外/Outdoor
ACR	场馆注册办公室2 Venue Accreditation Office 2	17	1	17			永久 Permanent		3层

（2）OB各阶段深度要求

《场馆设施手册》不同版本的内容是逐步详尽、逐步细化的：

OB1.0和OB2.0为区域规划和总平面设计阶段，编制工作以合理划分功能区块为主，将各业务领域的功能空间布局在场馆或用地内。

OB3.0和OB4.0为初步设计阶段，编制工作继续优化功能布局和人群流线，同时细化房间设计和临时设施设计。OB3.0阶段各个业务领域需要提供较为明确的使用要求。

OB5.0和OB6.0为扩初设计/详细设计阶段，编制工作基本确定场馆各类临时设施详细设计，用于实施采购和建设。此阶段之后AAM表不宜有变动，临时设施的采购工作已经开始。

在OB7.0阶段，OB编制完成最终版时《场馆设施手册》内容，将用于指导场馆和各类人群的赛时运行工作（表4）。

(2) In-depth requirements for different versions of OBs

Each version of OBs is more detailed than the previous one. OB1.0 and OB2.0 cover the phase of zoning and master graphic design. They focus on rational functional zoning, specifying FAs' functional areas within venues or spots.

OB3.0 and OB4.0 cover the phase of preliminary design. Efforts are made to further improve functional layouts and flows and refine design of rooms and temporary facilities. During the compilation of OB3.0, FAs shall present specific usage requirements.

OB5.0 and OB6.0 cover the phase of enlarged/detailed design. Detailed design schemes for all types of temporary venue facilities are identified to facilitate procurement and construction. AAMs shall remain unchanged following this phase as procurement for temporaries has begun.

OB7.0 is the final Games-time OBs as a guide on Games-time operations for venues and different client groups (Table 4).

表4　OB各阶段深度要求表/Table 4　In-depth Requirements for Different Versions of OBs

客户群 Client Group	运动员/随队官员/Athletes/Team officials		
	技术官员/Technical officials		
	奥林匹克/残奥大家庭/Olympic/Paralympic Family		
	转播/Broadcasting		
	新闻媒体/Press		
	市场开发合作伙伴/Marketing partners		
	观众/访客/Spectators/Guests		
	工作人员/Staff		
图纸中包含的信息/Information contained in drawings			OB版本/Version
安保/场馆周界 Security/Venue Perimeter	确定周界，包括所有客户群的人员安检口（PSA）及所有车辆安检口（VSA）/ Identifying perimeters, including all the pedestrian screening areas (PSA) and vehicle screening areas (VSA) for all the client groups		1.0-4.0
	确定周界，包括所有的界墙类型和大门及相关的尺寸/类型/ Identifying perimeters, including all types of rink board and gate, and their sizes/types		5.0-6.0
	面向所有客户群的人员安检口（PSA）——布局、队列等/ PSAs for all the client groups – layout and queue		
	车辆安检口（VSA）——布局、队列等/VSAs – layout and queue		
交通区域 Transport Area	确定下车/上车站点和停车位置/Identifying load zones and parking areas		1.0-2.0
	确定所有客户群的下车/上车站点和停车位置，包括持权转播组织（RHB）停车位置的分配/ Identifying load zones and parking areas for all the client groups, including parking areas for rights holding broadcasters (RHBs)		3.0-4.0
	确定所有客户群的下车/上车站点和停车的具体数量和规模，包括持权转播组织（RHB）停车位置的分配/ Identifying load zones for all client groups and specific quantity and scale of their parking, including parking areas for RHBs		5.0-6.0
通行路线 Access Route	确定面向所有客户群的车辆通行路线/ Identifying access routes for all the client groups		1.0-2.0
	确定面向所有客户群的主要步行通行路线，包括观众/访客的"最后一英里"/ Identifying major pedestrian routes for all the client groups, including the "last mile" for speculators/guests		3.0-4.0
	场馆周边的急救车出入口/通行路线/ Entry & Exit/Access routes around the venue for ambulances		
	确定面向所有客户群的步行通行路线和排队区/ Identifying pedestrian routes and queueing areas for all the client groups		5.0-6.0
后院内外部空间 Internal/External BOH Space	业务领域综合区/FA compounds		1.0-2.0
	确定临时设施（围栏、帐篷、临时室内场所、发电机组等）/ Identifying temporary facilities (fences, tents, temporary indoor areas, power generators, etc.)		3.0-4.0
	实施总体布局——特定场馆/Implementing the overall layouts—certain venues		
	热身场地/Warm-up spaces		
	添加内墙、表面、家具、固定装置和设备（FF&E）及其他特殊项目的信息/ Adding information about interior walls; surfaces; furniture, fixtures and equipment (FF&E); and other special items		5.0-6.0

前院内外部空间 Internal/External FOH Space	业务领域空间，重点核心业务领域包括：场馆管理、体育、转播、新闻媒体、安保和技术/ FA spaces. Major core FAs include Venue Management, Sport, Broadcast Services, Press Operations, Security and Technology	1.0-2.0
	确定临时设施（围栏、帐篷、临时室内场所、发电机组等）/ Identifying temporary facilities (fences, tents, temporary indoor areas, power generators, etc.)	3.0-4.0
	完成大体布局——让场馆更加明确具体/ Completing the rough layouts — so that venue functions are clearer and more specific	
	添加内墙、表面、家具、固定装置和设备（FF&E）及其他特殊项目的信息/ Adding information about interior walls, surfaces, FF&E and other special items	5.0-6.0
比赛场地 FOP	确定竞赛区和第一排坐席前的运行区/ Identifying competition areas and operational zones in front of the first row of seating area	1.0-2.0
	业务领域空间/元素大体确定——体育；转播；摄影师/ Roughly identifying FA spaces/elements — Sport, Broadcast Services, photographers	3.0-4.0
	确认颁奖仪式台的位置（但不以图形方式显示）/Identifying locations of podiums (not by symbol)	
	指定混合采访区的位置/Specifying locations of mixed zones	
	视频板/记分牌/Videoboards/Scoreboards	
	确定竞赛比赛场地区域细节/Identifying details of competition areas	5.0-6.0
	确定比赛场地（FOP）外至第一排坐席的运行区，包括运动员区、技术台等/ Identifying operational zones from outside the FOP to the first row of seating area, including athlete areas and technology services desk	
	确定比赛场地（FOP）时，需要确定以下业务领域的特定位置/ Locations of following FAs shall be identified while determining FOPs	
	体育；体育展示；技术；转播；新闻媒体（摄影师）；医疗；兴奋剂检查；仪式典礼/ Sport; Sport Presentation, Technology, Broadcast Services, Press Operations (photographers), Medical Services, Doping Control, Ceremonies	
	混合采访区布局/Layouts of mixed zones	
	摄像机平台或其他特殊项目/Photo platforms or other special items	
	吊顶设计计划/Design planning for suspended ceilings	
坐席区和保留看台 Seating Area & Reserved Stand	模块化坐席区总体布局/Modular layouts of seating areas	1.0-2.0
	区块式划分注册人群的保留看台布局/ Dividing the reserved stands for accredited groups into different blocks	
	视频板/记分牌/Videoboards/Scoreboards	
	符合规范/Compliance with standards	3.0-4.0
	无障碍坐席/Accessible seats	
	确定所有客户群的保留看台/Identifying reserved stands for all the client groups	5.0-6.0
	确定所有客户群相关的事宜，包括保留看台布局/ Identifying matters related to all the client groups, including the layouts of reserved stands	
	奥林匹克大家庭——确定坐席位置和数量/Olympic Family — specifying seat locations and quantity	
	转播——确定摄像机平台、评论员席、评论员摄像机机位、播报位置和观察员坐席的位置和数量/ Broadcasting — specifying locations and quantity of photo platforms, commentary positions, photo positions for commentators, announce positions, and observer seat	
	新闻媒体——确定带桌记者、不带桌记者和摄影师的位置和数量/ Press — specifying seat locations and quantity for tabled/non-tabled journalists and photographers	
	运动员——确定同一体育项目和不同体育项目运动员的位置和数量/ Athletes — specifying seat locations and quantity for same/different discipline athletes	
	观众/访客/市场开发合作伙伴——确定观众/访客的位置和数量/ Speculators/Guests/Marketing partners — specifying seat locations and quantity for speculators/guests	
	（票务将分配市场开发合作伙伴的位置和数量——不在图纸上显示）/ (Seat locations and quantity for marketing partners are allocated by Ticketing — not presented in drawings)	
	无障碍坐席——确定无障碍座位的位置和数量——轮椅、礼仪坐席和肥胖人员坐席/ Accessible seats (wheelchair spaces/courtesy seats/seats for people with obesity) — specifying locations and quantity	
	视频板/记分牌——确定视频板和记分牌位置，包括结构支撑/ Videoboards/Scoreboards — specifying locations, including the supporting structure	
残奥会设计要求 Design Requirements for Paralympics	—	1.0-2.0
	比赛场地/FOPs	3.0-4.0
	坐席区/Seating areas	5.0-6.0
	运动员区——与奥运会有重大差异/Athlete areas — greatly different from those of the Olympic Games	
临时设施 Temporary Facility	所有临时设施/All temporary facilities	5.0-6.0

（3）图纸系列和内容

《场馆设施手册》的图纸内容，从宏观到微观，共分为9个系列，其中，100系列是区域位置图，200系列是规划设计总平面图，300系列是场馆及周边平面图，400系列是核心设施平面图，500系列是配套设施平面图，600系列是FOP平面图和吊顶平面图（雪上场馆无吊顶平面图），700系列是场馆详细平面图，800系列是场地及建筑立面和剖面图，900系列是临时设施施工详图等内容（表5）。

(3) Drawings

Drawings in OBs fall into 9 series, ranging from macro level to micro level. Among them, Series 100 are drawings on locations of zones, Series 200 master plans for planning and design, Series 300 plans of venues and their surrounding areas, Series 400 plans of core facilities, Series 500 plans of supporting facilities, Series 600 plans of FOPs and suspended ceilings (no suspended ceiling plan for snow sport venues), Series 700 enlarged plans of venues, Series 800 elevations and sections of site areas and buildings, and Series 900 enlarged drawings for temporary facility construction (Table 5).

表5 系列图纸绘制内容/Table 5 Contents of Drawings

图纸系列 Series	绘制内容 Content	涵盖范围 Scope
100系列 Series 100	区域位置图，包括北京、延庆、张家口三个赛区总图和每个赛区分图/ Drawings on locations of zones, including the master drawing of Beijing, Yanqing and Zhangjiakou zones and sub-drawings of each competition zone	所有场馆 All venues
200系列 Series 200	场馆群总图，包括：北京奥林匹克公园中心区、首都体育场馆群、延庆赛区场馆群、张家口赛区场馆群、张家口赛区古杨树场馆群、张家口赛区云顶场馆群等/ Master plans of venue clusters, including venue clusters of Beijing Olympic Green Centre Zone, Capital Indoor Stadium, Yanqing Zone venue clusters, Zhangjiakou Zone venue clusters, Guyangshu Venue Cluster (Zhangjiakou Zone), Genting Venue Cluster (Zhangjiakou Zone)	部分场馆 Some venues
300系列 Series 300	场馆及近周边总平面图，表达本场馆及周边使用区域场地信息，所有场馆均需绘制/ Master plans of venues and their surrounding areas, representing information of areas for use (required for all the venues)	所有场馆 All venues
400系列 Series 400	核心设施平面图，主要包括场馆各层平面图，所有场馆均需绘制/ Plans of core facilities, including plans of each floor of the venue (required for all the venues)	所有场馆 All venues
500系列 Series 500	配套设施平面图/ Plans of supporting facilities	部分场馆 Some venues
600系列 Series 600	FOP及近周边平面图、吊顶平面图，吊顶平面图从650开始编制/ Plans of FOPs and their surrounding areas and suspended ceilings. Suspended ceiling plans start from 650	竞赛场馆 训练场馆 Competition/Training venues
700系列 Series 700	场馆详细平面图，包括注册席位区、混采区等，混采区从750开始编制/ Enlarged plans of venues, including plans of accredited seating areas and mixed zones. Mixed zone plans start from 750.	竞赛场馆 Competition venues
800系列 Series 800	场地及建筑剖面图、立面图，主要表达坐席视线分析/ Sections and elevations of venues and buildings, presenting sightline analysis for seats	竞赛场馆 Competition venues
900系列 Series 900	临时设施施工详图，由临时设施承包商绘制/ Enlarged drawings for temporary facility construction (by contractors of temporary facilities)	所有场馆 All venues

4. 北京2022《场馆设施手册》制图标准

（1）文件命名标准

《场馆设施手册》编制的工作模式是以场馆图纸作为基础参照到工作文件中，由运行设计单位在工作文件中进行绘制。在这样的工作模式下，除AAM表格外，产生了DWG和PDF两种类型文件，其中DWG文件是进行运行设计时绘制的工作文件，PDF文件是完成绘图后导出的成果文件。

由于《场馆设施手册》的成果文件众多，对文件进行标准化命名十分重要。结合往届奥运会运行设计经验，北京冬奥会《场馆设施手册》文件名称由场馆代码、模式、体育项目代码、专业代码、图纸深度编号、版本号、文件格式等一系列元素组成。

1）文件名称构成元素

① 场馆代码

根据奥运会惯例，北京冬奥组委为每个场馆制定了由三位大写英文字母组成的场馆代码。

4. Standards of OB Drawings for the Beijing 2022 Games

(1) Document naming

The pattern for OB compilation is as follows. The operational design unit draws in work files, with venue drawings as basic reference. Accordingly, aside from AAMs, two formats of files, i.e. DWG and PDF are produced: DWG files, the work files drawn for operational design; and PDF files, the result files exported when the drawing is done.

The large quantity of OB-related files highlights the importance of standardised file naming. Based on experience drawn from operational design for previous editions of the Olympic Games, files in OBs for the Beijing 2022 Games are named as "Venue Code-Mode-Sport Code-Drawing Agent Code-Sheet Number-Version Number-File Format".

1) Components

① Venue code

By conventions of the Olympic Games, Beijing 2022 developed for each venue a code in 3 capital letters.

② 模式

根据场馆举办赛事的类型，共有四种模式，分别为：测试赛（T）、奥运会（O）、残奥会（P）、遗产（L）。

③ 体育项目代码

体现场馆所举办体育赛事项目代码（表6）。

② Mode

Based on events hosted, there are 4 venue modes: T/Test Events, O/Olympic Games, P/Paralympic Games, and L/Legacy.

③ Sport code

It represents the sport code of the events hosted in the venue:

表6 体育项目代码/Table 6 Sport Codes

代码 Code	体育项目 Sport/Discipline		代码 Code	体育项目 Sport/Discipline		代码 Code	体育项目 Sport/Discipline	
AS	高山滑雪	Alpine Skiing	LG	雪橇	Luge	FR	自由式滑雪	Freestyle Skiing
BS	雪车	Bobsleigh	NC	北欧两项	Nordic Combined	FS	花样滑冰	Figure Skating
BT	冬季两项	Biathlon	SB	单板滑雪	Snowboard	IH	冰球	Ice Hockey
CC	越野滑雪	Cross-Country Skiing	SJ	跳台滑雪	Ski Jumping	SS	速度滑冰	Speed Skating
CU	冰壶	Curling	SN	钢架雪车	Skeleton	ST	短道速滑	Short Track Speed Skating

注：非竞赛场馆体育项目代码为XX
Note: Sport code for non-competition venues is XX

④ 专业代码

根据图纸的类型或用途，为每张图纸添加专业代码。分别为：建筑（A）、线缆路由图（CT）、注册分区（ZN）。

⑤ 图纸深度编号

对于《场馆设施手册》的系列图纸，每张图纸有唯一对应的深度编号。每系列图纸内从X01开始排列，如核心设施平面图从401开始编号命名。

⑥ 版本号

根据《场馆设施手册》编制提交情况，OB成果分正式版本和更新版本两种。OBX.0为正式版本成果，OBX.X为在某一版本后的更新版本，如OB4.1指在OB4.0之后OB5.0之前第1次修订更新版。

2）DWG文件命名标准

DWG工作文件按照以下原则命名：场馆代码-模式-体育项目代码-专业代码-图纸深度编号-版本号-BIND-文件格式（.dwg）。

示例：NAC-OCU-A-401-OB1.2-BIND.DWG，为国家游泳中心奥运冰壶图纸深度编号401，OB1.2版的建筑BIND图纸（表7）。

④ Drawing agent code (Table 6)

Each drawing is given a drawing agent code for its type or use: A/Architecture, CT/Cable Pathway, and ZN/Zoning.

⑤ Sheet number

Every drawing in each series has a unique sheet number starting from X01. For example, the number of core facility plans start from 401.

⑥ Version number

Considering the status of OB compilation and submission, OB outcomes are divided into 2 types: official versions and revised versions. OBX.0 refers to an official version. While OBX.X refers to a revision released following a certain official version. For example, OB4.1 refers to the first revision to OB4.0, published in prior to OB5.0.

2) Naming of DWG files

DWG files are named as follows: Venue Code-Mode-Sport Code-Drawing Agent Code-Sheet Number-Issue Number-BIND-File Format (.dwg).

Sample: NAC-OCU-A-401-OB1.2-BIND.DWG refers to the BIND file 401 in OB1.2 for the architecture of curling at National Aquatics Centre (Table 7).

表7 DWG文件命名示例/Table 7 Naming of DWG files

场馆代码/Venue	NAC	国家游泳中心/National Aquatics Centre
模式/Mode	O	奥运会/Olympic Games
体育项目代码/Sport Code	CU	冰壶/Curling
专业代码/Drawing Agent Code	A	建筑/Architecture
图纸深度编号/Sheet Number OB Version	401	详细场地平面图 1/Enlarged Site Plan 1
OB阶段版本号/OB Version	OB1.2	OB1.0 之后的第2次修改/Second revision to OB1.0
BIND	BIND	绑定文件/BIND file
文件格式/File Format	DWG	DWG文件格式/CAD file format

表8　PDF文件命名示例/Table 8　Naming of PDF files

场馆代码/Venue	NAC	国家游泳中心/National Aquatics Centre
模式/Mode	O	奥运会/Olympic Games
体育项目代码/Sport Code	CU	冰壶/Curling
专业代码/Drawing Agent Code	A	建筑/Architecture
图纸深度编号/Sheet Number OB Version	401	详细场地平面图 1/Enlarged Site Plan 1
OB 阶段版本号/OB Version	OB1.2	OB1.0 之后的第2次修改/Second revision to OB1.0
文件格式/File Format	PDF	PDF文件格式/PDF file

3）PDF文件命名标准

PDF 成果文件按照以下原则命名：场馆代码-模式-体育项目代码-专业代码-图纸深度编号-版本号-文件格式（.pdf）。

示例：NAC-OCU-A-401-OB1.2.PDF，为国家游泳中心奥运冰壶图纸深度编号 401 OB1.2 版的建筑PDF图纸（表8）。

（2）绘图标准

1）《场馆设施手册》封面

《场馆设施手册》封面包含场馆中英文名称、场馆代码、举办体育项目、北京2022年冬奥会和冬残奥会会徽、当前OB版本号以及历史版本信息等内容（图1）。

3) Naming of PDF files

PDF files are named as follows: Venue Code-Mode-Sport Code-Drawing Agent Code-Sheet Number-Version Number-File Format (.pdf).
Sample: NAC-OCU-A-401-OB1.2.PDF refers to PDF file 401 in OB1.2 for the architecture of curling at National Aquatics Centre (Table 8).

(2) Drafting

1) Cover

An OB cover contains the venue name (both in Chinese and English), venue code, sport, emblems of the Olympic Winter Games Beijing 2022 and the Beijing 2022 Paralympic Winter Games, and current OB version and version history (Image 1).

国家高山滑雪中心

（高山滑雪）

Yanqing National Alpine Skiing Centre [YAS]

Overlay Design 7.0

NO.	DATE	OB VERSION	DESCRIPTION		DRAWING ISSUED	NOTE
1.	20180915	OB1.0	《设施手册》1.0版	General OB 1.0 Design	All Drawing	-
2.	20190315	OB2.0	《设施手册》2.0版	General OB 2.0 Design	All Drawing	-
3.	20190531	OB2.1	《设施手册》2.1版（提供给OBS）	Overlay Book 2.1 (for OBS)	All Drawing	-
4.	20190915	OB3.0	《设施手册》3.0版	General OB 2.0 Design	All Drawing	-
5.	20200315	OB4.0	《设施手册》4.0版	General OB 4.0 Design	All Drawing	-
6.	20200828	OB4.1	《设施手册》4.1版（提供给IPC）	Overlay Book 4.1 (for IPC)	All Drawing	-
7.	20201016	OB5.0	《设施手册》5.0版	General OB 5.0 Design	All Drawing	-
8.	20210520	OB6.0	《设施手册》6.0版	General OB 6.0 Design	All Drawing	-
9.	20210831	OB6.1	《设施手册》6.1版	General OB 6.1 Design	All Drawing	-
10.	20211215	OB7.0	《设施手册》7.0版	General OB 7.0 Design	All Drawing	-

图1　封面示意图/Image 1　The cover

2）图框

① 架构

《场馆设施手册》的图幅标准为A3横板图纸，标准图框由两部分组成，左侧为图纸内容，右侧为图签（图2）。

图签自上而下由会徽及版权标记、图例、OB阶段版本更新信息、索引图、图纸基础信息栏五部分组成。

2) Frame

① Structure

A standard OB drawing is an A3 paper in horizontal, on which a frame consists of two parts: content on the left and the title block on the right (Image 2).

The title block comprises 5 parts from top to bottom, including emblems and copyright marks, legends, updates on OB versions, key map, and basic information.

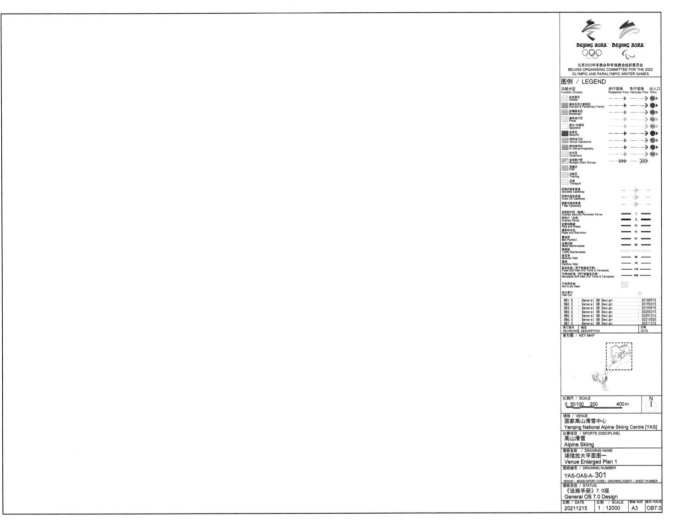

图2　标准A3图框示意/Image 2　A Standard A3 Drawing Frame

② 会徽及版权标记

包含北京2022年冬奥会会徽、北京2022年冬残奥会会徽，以及北京冬奥组委中英文名称（图3）。

② Emblems and copyright marks

This section includes emblems of the Olympic and Paralympic Winter Games Beijing 2022, as well as the Chinese and English names of Beijing 2022 (Image 3) .

北京2022年冬奥会和冬残奥会组织委员会
BEIJING ORGANISING COMMITTEE FOR THE 2022
OLYMPIC AND PARALYMPIC WINTER GAMES

图3　图签放大图 会徽及版权标记
Image 3　The Enlarged Title Block － Emblems and Copyright Marks

图例 / LEGEND

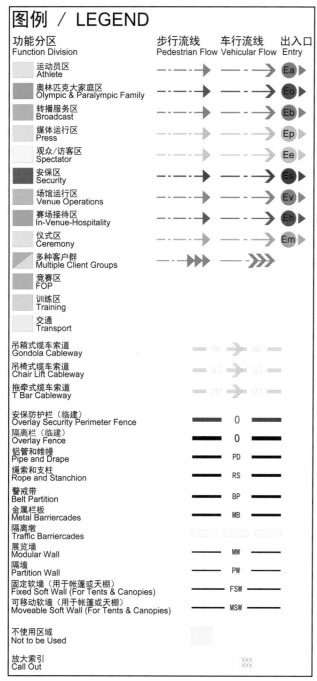

功能分区 / Function Division

		步行流线 / Pedestrian Flow	车行流线 / Vehicular Flow	出入口 / Entry
	运动员区 Athlete			Ea
	奥林匹克大家庭区 Olympic & Paralympic Family			Eo
	转播服务区 Broadcast			Eb
	媒体运行区 Press			Ep
	观众/访客区 Spectator			Ee
	安保区 Security			Es
	场馆运行区 Venue Operations			Ev
	赛场接待区 In-Venue-Hospitality			Eh
	仪式区 Ceremony			Em
	多种客户群 Multiple Client Groups			
	竞赛区 FOP			
	训练区 Training			
	交通 Transport			

吊箱式缆车索道 Gondola Cableway — [G]
吊椅式缆车索道 Chair Lift Cableway — [L]
拖牵式缆车索道 T Bar Cableway — [T]

安保防护栏（临建）Overlay Security Perimeter Fence — O
隔离栏（临建）Overlay Fence — O
铝管和帷幔 Pipe and Drape — PD
绳索和支柱 Rope and Stanchion — RS
警戒带 Belt Partition — BP
金属栏板 Metal Barriercades — MB
隔离墩 Traffic Barriercades
展览墙 Modular Wall — MW
隔墙 Partition Wall — PW
固定软墙（用于帐篷或天棚）Fixed Soft Wall (For Tents & Canopies) — FSW
可移动软墙（用于帐篷或天棚）Moveable Soft Wall (For Tents & Canopies) — MSW

不使用区域 Not to be Used
放大索引 Call Out — XXX XXX

图4　图签放大图 图例
Image 4　The Enlarged Title Block – Legends

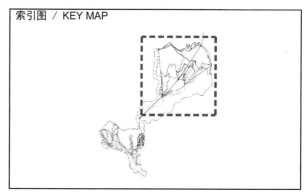

OB1.0	General OB Design		20180915
OB2.0	General OB Design		20190315
OB3.0	General OB Design		20190915
OB4.0	General OB Design		20200315
OB5.0	General OB Design		20201016
OB6.0	General OB Design		20210520
OB7.0	General OB Design		20211215
修订版本 REVISIONS	描述 DESCRIPTION		日期 DATE

图5　图签放大图 OB阶段版本更新信息
Image 5　The Enlarged Title Block – Updates on OB Versions

索引图 / KEY MAP

图6　图签放大图 索引图
Image 6　The Enlarged Title Block – Key Map

比例尺 / SCALE
0 50 100 200 400m
N

场馆 / VENUE
国家高山滑雪中心
Yanqing National Alpine Skiing Centre [YAS]

比赛项目 / SPORTS (DISCIPLINE)
高山滑雪
Alpine Skiing

图纸名称 / DRAWING NAME
场馆放大平面图一
Venue Enlarged Plan 1

图纸编号 / DRAWING NUMBER
YAS-OAS-A-301
VENUE / MODE-SPORT CODE / DRAWING AGENT / SHEET NUMBER

图纸状态 / STATUS
《设施手册》7.0版
General OB 7.0 Design

日期 / DATE	比例 / SCALE	图幅/SIZE	版本/ISSUE
20211215	1：12000	A3	OB7.0

图7　图签放大图 图纸基础信息栏
Image 7　The Enlarged Title Block – Basic Information

③ 图例
作为本图纸绘制内容及表达方式的说明（图4）。
④ OB阶段版本更新信息
包含当前及历史版本号、更新内容描述、版本日期（图5）。
⑤ 索引图
用于较大范围的场馆，索引本张图纸在整个场馆总平面中所处的范围（图6）。
⑥ 图纸基础信息栏
包含场馆名称、比赛项目、图纸名称、图纸编号等内容信息，以及图纸状态、出图时间、图幅、版本等制图信息（图7）。

③ Legends
The legend section lists drawing contents and their symbols (Image 4).
④ Updates on OB versions
The section contains the numbers of current and previous OB versions, as well as their description and date (Image 5).
⑤ Key map
A key map is developed for a large venue, indicating where the drawing locates among the master venue plan (Image 6).
⑥ Basic information
This section contains the venue name, sport (discipline), drawing name, drawing number, and drafting information such as status, completion time, size and version (Image 7).

3）《场馆设施手册》目录

《场馆设施手册》目录位于封面之后，由三列信息构成。列包含图纸编号、图纸名称（中英文）、图纸比例。行按照封面、目录、AAM表格、系列图纸顺序排列。第一条是000封面，第二条001目录，AAM表格从011开始排序。图纸系列之间空一行（图8）。

4）图例

① 客户群相关图例

对客户群分区、步行流线、车行流线、出入口及主要功能区色块、箭头形状及绘图线型制定了标准。此外还制定了不同类型临时隔离措施的图例；针对雪上场馆缆车流线制定了单独的线型；对场馆无障碍设施和流线制定了单独的图例（图9、图10）。

3) Table of contents

Following the cover, the table of contents consists of 3 columns, containing drawing numbers, drawing titles (both in Chinese and English) and scales, respectively. The lines are in the order of "cover – contents – AAM – drawings". Number 000 at the first line refers to the cover. Number 001 at the second line refers to the table of contents. AAMs start from 011. A line is left between every two drawing series (Image 8).

4) Legends

① Legends for client groups

Standards have been developed for colours, arrow shapes and line types representing client group zoning, pedestrian flow, vehicle flow and major functional zones. In addition, efforts have been made to develop legends for different types of temporary isolation measures, special line types for cableways at snow sport venues, and special legends for accessible facilities and flows (Image 9, Image 10).

图纸编号 DRAWING NUMBER	图纸名称 DRAWING TITLE	图纸比例 SCALE	图纸编号 DRAWING NUMBER	图纸名称 DRAWING TITLE	图纸比例 SCALE
YAS-OAS-A-000	封面 Cover	NTS	YAS-OAS-A-305	场馆放大平面图五 Venue Enlarged Plan-5	1/2000
YAS-OAS-A-001	图纸目录 Content	NTS	YAS-OAS-A-411	山顶出发区一层平面图 Top Starting Area L1 Plan	1/500
YAS-OAS-A-002	图纸目录 Content	NTS	YAS-OAS-A-412	山顶出发区二层平面图 Top Starting Area L2 Plan	1/500
YAS-OAS-A-003	图纸目录 Content	NTS	YAS-OAS-A-413	山顶出发区三层平面图 Top Starting Area L3 Plan	1/500
YAS-OAS-A-004	图纸目录 Content	NTS			
YAS-OAS-A-005	图纸目录 Content	NTS	YAS-OAS-A-421	中间平台地下一层平面图 Middle Platform B1 Plan	1/500
			YAS-OAS-A-422	中间平台一层平面图 Middle Platform L1 Plan	1/500
YAS-OAS-A-011	房间矩阵表1 Area Allocation Matrix 1	NTS	YAS-OAS-A-423	中间平台二层平面图 Middle Platform L2 Plan	1/500
YAS-OAS-A-012	房间矩阵表2 Area Allocation Matrix 2	NTS			
YAS-OAS-A-013	房间矩阵表3 Area Allocation Matrix 3	NTS	YAS-OAS-A-431	集散广场一层平面图 Concoures L1 Plan	1/500
YAS-OAS-A-014	房间矩阵表4 Area Allocation Matrix 4	NTS	YAS-OAS-A-432	集散广场二层平面图 Concoures L2 Plan	1/500
YAS-OAS-A-015	房间矩阵表5 Area Allocation Matrix 5	NTS	YAS-OAS-A-433	集散广场三层平面图 Concoures L3 Plan	1/500
YAS-OAS-A-016	房间矩阵表6 Area Allocation Matrix 6	NTS	YAS-OAS-A-434	集散广场四层及竞速结束区一层平面图 Concoures L4 & Speed Finish Area L1 Plan	1/600
YAS-OAS-A-017	房间矩阵表7 Area Allocation Matrix 7	NTS	YAS-OAS-A-435	竞速结束区二层平面图、三层平面图 Speed Finish Area L2 Plan and L3 Plan	1/500
YAS-OAS-A-018	房间矩阵表8 Area Allocation Matrix 8	NTS	YAS-OAS-A-436	竞速结束区四层平面图、六层平面图 Speed Finish Area L4 Plan and L6 Plan	1/500
YAS-OAS-A-019	房间矩阵表9 Area Allocation Matrix 9	NTS	YAS-OAS-A-437	竞速结束区五层平面图 Speed Finish Area L5 Plan	1/500
YAS-OAS-A-020	房间矩阵表10 Area Allocation Matrix 10	NTS	YAS-OAS-A-438	竞速结束区看台及比赛场地平面图 Speed Finish Area Stand And FOP Plan	1/750
YAS-OAS-A-021	房间矩阵表11 Area Allocation Matrix 11	NTS	YAS-PAS-A-438	竞速结束区看台及比赛场地平面图 Speed Finish Area Stand And FOP Plan	1/750
YAS-OAS-A-022	房间矩阵表12 Area Allocation Matrix 12	NTS			
YAS-OAS-A-023	房间矩阵表13 Area Allocation Matrix 13	NTS	YAS-OAS-A-440	竞技结束区地下一层平面图 Technical Finish Area B1 Plan	1/500
YAS-OAS-A-024	房间矩阵表14 Area Allocation Matrix 14	NTS	YAS-OAS-A-441	竞技结束区一层平面图 Technical Finish Area L1 Plan	1/500
YAS-OAS-A-025	房间矩阵表15 Area Allocation Matrix 15	NTS	YAS-OAS-A-442	竞技结束区二层平面图 Technical Finish Area L2 Plan	1/500
YAS-OAS-A-026	房间矩阵表16 Area Allocation Matrix 16	NTS	YAS-OAS-A-443	竞技结束区三层平面图 Technical Finish Area L3 Plan	1/500
YAS-OAS-A-027	房间矩阵表17 Area Allocation Matrix 17	NTS	YAS-OAS-A-444	竞技结束区看台及比赛场地平面图 Technical Finish Area Stand And FOP Plan	1/800
YAS-OAS-A-028	房间矩阵表18 Area Allocation Matrix 18	NTS	YAS-PAS-A-444	竞技结束区看台及比赛场地平面图 Technical Finish Area Stand And FOP Plan	1/800
YAS-OAS-A-029	房间矩阵表19 Area Allocation Matrix 19	NTS			
YAS-OAS-A-030	房间矩阵表20 Area Allocation Matrix 20	NTS	YAS-OAS-A-451	场馆群放大平面图-2号上落客区 Cluster Enlarged Plan - YMC Hub No.2 Land And Drop Area	1/600
YAS-OAS-A-031	房间矩阵表21 Area Allocation Matrix 21	NTS			
YAS-OAS-A-032	房间矩阵表22 Area Allocation Matrix 22	NTS	YAS-OAS-A-452	场馆群放大平面图-运营广场 Cluster Enlarged Plan - Operation Plaza	1/600
			YAS-OAS-A-453	场馆群放大平面图-打蜡房、1号上落客区 Cluster Enlarged Plan - Wax Cabin Area & No.1 Land And Drop Area	1/600
YAS-OAS-A-101	延庆赛区区域位置图 Yanqing Zone Wide Area Map	1/90000	YAS-OAS-A-454	高山滑雪领队会会议室平面图 YAS TCM Plan	1/500
YAS-OAS-A-201	赛区总平面图 Competition Area Master Plan	1/20000			
			YAS-OAS-A-501	集散广场一层放大平面图 Concourse L1 Enlarged Plan	1/200
YAS-OAS-A-301	场馆放大平面图一 Venue Enlarged Plan-1	1/12000	YAS-OAS-A-502	竞速结束区VMC放大平面图 Speed Finish Area VMC Enlarged Plan	1/200
YAS-OAS-A-302	场馆放大平面图二 Venue Enlarged Plan-2	1/7000	YAS-OAS-A-503	竞速结束区大家庭休息室放大平面图 Speed Finish Area Family Lounge Enlarged Plan	1/200
YAS-OAS-A-303	场馆放大平面图三 Venue Enlarged Plan-3	1/3000	YAS-OAS-A-504	竞速结束区竞赛用房放大平面图 Speed Finish Area SPT Room Enlarged Plan	1/200
YAS-OAS-A-304	场馆放大平面图四 Venue Enlarged Plan-4	1/3000	YAS-OAS-A-505	竞速结束区看台后部评论员席放大平面 Speed Finish Area CP Enlarged Plan	1/200

图8 目录示意图
Image 8 The Table of Contents

图例 / LEGEND

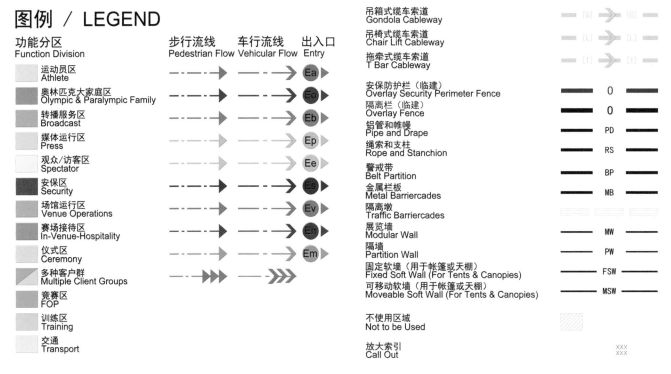

功能分区
Function Division

运动员区
Athlete

奥林匹克大家庭区
Olympic & Paralympic Family

转播服务区
Broadcast

媒体运行区
Press

观众/访客区
Spectator

安保区
Security

场馆运行区
Venue Operations

赛场接待区
In-Venue-Hospitality

仪式区
Ceremony

多种客户群
Multiple Client Groups

竞赛区
FOP

训练区
Training

交通
Transport

步行流线
Pedestrian Flow

车行流线
Vehicular Flow

出入口
Entry

Ea
Eo
Eb
Ep
Ee
Es
Ev
En
Em

吊箱式缆车索道
Gondola Cableway

吊椅式缆车索道
Chair Lift Cableway

拖牵式缆车索道
T Bar Cableway

安保防护栏（临建）
Overlay Security Perimeter Fence   0

隔离栏（临建）
Overlay Fence   0

铝管和帷幔
Pipe and Drape   PD

绳索和支柱
Rope and Stanchion   RS

警戒带
Belt Partition   BP

金属栏板
Metal Barriercades   MB

隔离墩
Traffic Barriercades

展览墙
Modular Wall   MW

隔墙
Partition Wall   PW

固定软墙（用于帐篷或天棚）
Fixed Soft Wall (For Tents & Canopies)   FSW

可移动软墙（用于帐篷或天棚）
Moveable Soft Wall (For Tents & Canopies)   MSW

不使用区域
Not to be Used

放大索引
Call Out   XXX
XXX

图9　客户群相关图例放大图 含缆车
Image 9　Enlarged Legends for Client Groups, Including Cableways

无障碍空间设施标识
Accessible Space
Facilities Legend

无障碍步行流线标识
Accessible Pedestrian
Flow Legend

图10　无障碍图例放大图
Image 10　Enlarged Legends for Accessibility

连至上层
See level up

连至下层
See level down

转播线缆
Broadcast Pathway   BRS   BRS

电力线缆
Power Pathway   NRG   NRG

技术线缆
Technology Pathway   TEC   TEC

电缆桥架
Cable Bridge

电缆线在管道中
Cable line in the pipe

电缆分支点
Separation marker   BRS   BRS

图11　线缆综合图例放大图
Image 11　Enlarged Legends for Pathways

② 线缆综合图例

根据临时设施工作要求，需要在《场馆设施手册》中绘制转播（BRS）、技术（TEC）和电力（NRG）三个业务领域在场馆中的临时线缆路由图，核实各段路由的实现方式和架设标准，并绘制临时管沟、临时桥架图（图11）。

③ 注册分区及防疫分区图例

根据注册卡运行系统要求，不同客户群可通行区域权限不同，需绘制竞赛场馆和主要非竞赛场馆的注册分区图。同时为满足新冠肺炎疫情防控要求，对注册分区需要进行闭环内、闭环外区域的划分（图12）。

② Legends for containments

In accordance with the requirements for temporary facilities, containments installed in venues by Broadcast Services, Technology and Energy are included in OBs, so as to confirm the implementation and set-up standard for each containment section. Drawings for temporary pipes and bridges are also developed (Image 11).

③ Legends for accreditation zoning and anti-epidemic zoning

According to the requirements for accreditation card operation system, accessible areas vary among different client groups, leading to a need for accreditation zoning in competition and non-competition venues. Meanwhile, in response to epidemic countermeasures, accreditation zones shall be divided by the closed-loop management system into areas inside and outside it (Image 12).

图例 / LEGEND

注册分区
Venue Accreditation Zoning

R	运行管理区 Operational Areas
W	公共活动区 General Circulation Areas
B	竞赛活动区 Field of Play
2	运动员准备区 Athlete Preparation Areas
4	媒体工作区 Press Areas
5	转播工作区 Broadcast Areas
6	大家庭接待服务区 Olympic/Paralympic Family Areas
R	奥运村居住区 Residential Zone

闭环内
In-Bubble

闭环外
Outside-Bubble

验证点
Access Control Point (ACP)

SPT
DOP
EVS
OFS
PRS
BRS
SEC

图12　注册分区防疫分区图例放大图
Image 12 Enlarged Legends for Accreditation Zoning and Anti-epidemic Zoning

5）标准图块

除图例外，在图纸内容部分，还有一些诸如检票亭、安检篷等采用了标准尺寸设计；由组委会提供团队使用的家具白电物资；为外方提供的收费卡业务相关等规格已确定的设备设施；属于临时设施的各类篷房、集装箱房、打包箱式房、各式围栏等临设标准单元。为此制定了相应的标准图块。

① 票检亭、安检篷房标准图块

根据不同使用功能的空间需求，通过调研市场上篷房等不同类型临时设施的模数，设计了标准尺寸的图块，方便设计师在《场馆设施手册》的总平面规划设计中组合使用（图13）。

② 家具白电标准图块

根据《场馆设施手册》编制要求，需要在主要的空间（房间）内布置落地的家具和重点设施设备，如桌椅、沙发、柜子、衣架、落地饮水机、落地打印机、电视屏幕等（图14）。

③ 媒体租用空间标准图块

用于组委会为媒体提供的租用空间的平面布置，包含电力、技术、物流、医疗等业务领域提供的设备设施（图15）。

④ 临设标准单元

临时设施类型包括篷房、集装箱房、打包箱式房、摄影平台、临时看台、安保围栏等，这些临时设施由组委会组织制定了相关技术要求标准，结合各类型临设技术标准，制定了相应的标准单元图块，编制在《场馆设施手册》后，由临时设施供应商进行深化实施（图16～图20）。

5) Standard modules

Aside from those that are represented by legends, such contents on drawings as ticket check peak tents and PSA/VSA gable tents are also designed in standard size. Standard modules are also developed for FF&E for teams provided by Beijing 2022; Rate Card equipment and facilities with established specifications offered to international participants; and standard units of temporary facilities, including various types of tents, containers, boxes and fences.

① Ticket check peak tents and PSA/VSA gable tents

To meet spatial requirements for different functions, we have surveyed modules of tents and other temporary facilities available on the market and designed standard modules, so as to facilitate combined use of these modules in master planning and design (Image 13).

② FF&E

According to the requirements for OB compilation, floor-standing furniture and key facilities and equipment shall be installed in major spaces (rooms), such as tables and chairs, sofas, cabinets, hangers, floor-standing drinking fountains, floor-standing printers, and TV screens (Image 14).

③ Rental space for press

These modules are used for plans of rental spaces for press provided by Beijing 2022, including equipment and facilities offered by Energy, Technology, Logistics and Medical Services (Image 15).

④ Standard units of temporary facilities

Temporary facilities include tents, containers, boxes, platforms, temporary stands and security fences. Based on related technical standards developed by Beijing 2022 and technical standards for all types of temporary facilities, we have developed relevant standard unit modules and included them in OBs, which have been implemented by temporary facility suppliers (Image 16, Image 17, Image 18, Image 19, Image 20).

屋顶平面
Roof Plan

VSA 150m²

15m×10m车行流线安检帐篷VSA（双排车道低安检级别或单排车道加步行人员安检口PSA高安检级别）
15m×10m VSA Gable Tent (double line of Vehicle, low level of security or one line of Vehicle plus one line of PSA, high level of security)

屋顶平面
Roof Plan

3m×3m票检亭TKT（单排）
3m×3m Ticket Check Peak Tent TKT (one line)

墙体平面
Floor Plan

VSA 225m²

15m×15m车行流线安检帐篷VSA（三排车道低安检级别或双排车道加步行人员安检口PSA高安检级别）
15m×10m VSA Gable Tent (three line of Vehicle, low level of security or two line of Vehicle plus one line of PSA, high level of security)

3m×3m票检亭TKT（单排）
3m×3m Ticket Check Peak Tent TKT (one line)

图13 票检亭、安检篷房标准图块放大图
Image 13 Enlarged Standard Modules of Ticket Check Peak Tents and PSA/VSA Gable Tents

办公桌、椅类产品
及其他家具类产品

Desk	Small folding table (Steel wood)	Small folding table (Steel plastic)	Medium folding table (Steel wood)	Large folding table (Steel wood)	Large folding table (Steel plastic)	Round table	tea table	Double deck table	Hot pressing table
办公桌1600×800×760	小型折叠条桌1200x600x760钢木	小型折叠条桌1200x600x740钢塑	中型折叠条桌1600x700x760钢木	大型折叠条桌1800x600x760钢木	大型折叠条桌1830x760x740钢塑	圆桌 口900x760	茶几 1200x600x450	双层条桌 1400x800x1500	热压桌1500x800x940
Square table	Round table	High chair	Folding chair	folding chair	Dining chair	Office chair	Simple office chair	Armchair	Office chair
方桌1000×1000×760	高脚圆桌 台面直径600-800	高脚椅 470x520x890	软塑折叠椅450x450x780	硬质折叠椅 500x580x880	餐椅 495x530x815	办公椅 580x570x1100	简易办公椅 525x525x890	靠背椅 540x570x950	写字板办公椅600x610x850
Bench	Small round stool	Three-seat sofa	Two-person sofa	Single sofa	Folding bed	Bunk bed			Vertical hanger
长条凳1800x450x450	小圆凳320x440	三人沙发 2000x880x940	双人沙发 1830x730x660	单人沙发 730x730x660	折叠床 1900x800x400	上下铺床 2000x900x2000			立式衣架 底座直径350x1800
Gantry hanger	Athlete changing hanger (with hook)		Results bulletin cabinet	Small file cabinet	Double door wardrobe	Athlete wardrobe	4-door locker	8-door locker	Open cabinet
龙门衣架 1200x400x1800	运动员更衣架（带挂钩）2000x670x460/1850		成绩公报柜 600x375x2000	小型文件柜900x400x900	双门衣柜900x550x1850	运动员衣柜800x650x2160	4门储物柜 1280x500x1750	8门储物柜 900x500x1850	敞口柜1000x400x2000
Small storage rack		Removable screen	Storage box	Storage basket	Makeup mirror (large)	Makeup mirror (small)	Vertical dressing mirror	wall clock	
小型储物架 1800x600x2000		可移动屏风500 (w) x1800 (d)	收纳箱	收纳篮350x260x80	化妆镜(大) 1000x650	化妆镜(小) 360x470	立式更衣镜 380x1500	挂钟350 (di)	

白电类产品

5HP Cabinet Air Conditioner	3HP Cabinet Air Conditioner	2HP Wallmounted airconditioner	Small refrigerator	Medium-sized refrigerator	Hot water bucket	Drinking fountain	Vertical table lamp
5匹柜式空调600x350x1880	3匹柜式空调540x357x1880	2匹壁挂空调	小型电冰箱50L	中型电冰箱600X650X1900	热水桶350X345X570	饮水机310X307X980	立式台灯

设备类产品

Multifunctional Printer	55 Inch TV + Bracket
多功能一体打印机	55寸电视+支架

图例说明：
图例绘制方式：以仿形为主，以便识别。
图块设置方式：以图例名设置，以便查找。
图层设置方式：以固有家具图层00D_Furniture为家具及白电等活动产品的图层，方便统一标准。

图14 家具白电标准图块放大图
Image 14 Enlarged Standard Modules of FF&E

NRG LEGEND

PCB1001	PCB1002
220V 16A 1PH circuit (max. Load 3KVA)	220V 32A 1PH circuit (max. load6KVA)
PCB1003	PCB1004
380V 16A 3PH circuit (max. load10KVA)	380V 32A 3PH circuit (max. load20KVA)

MED LEGEND

MED1001	MED1002
AED (Automatic External Defibrillator)	Examination bed
MED1003	MED1004
Examination Light	Portable medical massage table
MED1005	MED1006
Electronic scales	Movable screen
MED1007	
Trolley	

LOG LEGEND

FF01001	FF01002	FF01003	FF01004
Office desk including a drawer 1800(w)×800(d)×760(h)mm	Steel-wooden folding table-medium 1800(w)×700(d)×760(h)mm	Steel-wooden folding table-small 1200(w)×600(d)×760(h)mm	Office chair with arms Fixed armrests, wheeled base rotatable seat 650(w)×650(d)×1000(h)mm
FF01005	FF01006	FF01007	FF01008
Office chair with tablet	Folding chair with cusion 470(w)×610(d)×850(h)mm	Coffee table 1200(w)×600(d)×460(h)mm	Round table 900(d)×760(h)mm
FF01009	FF01010	FF01011	FF01012
3 seater sofa 2000(w)×790(d)×800(h)mm	2 seater sofa 1400(w)×790(d)×800(h)mm	One seater sofa 780(w)×790(d)×800(h)mm	Lockable safe-large 460(w)×510(d)×600(h)mm
FF01013	FF01014	FF01015	FF01016
Lockable safe-small 410(w)×360(d)×210(h)mm	Book case 800(w)×280(d)×1200(h)mm	Luggage trolley 420(w)×600(d)×750(h)mm	Filing cabinet-Small 900(w)×600(d)×600(h)mm
FF01017	FF01018	FF01019	FF01020
Filing cabinet-Large 900(w)×450(d)×1860(h)mm	Drawers 420(w)×520(d)×620(h)mm	Side by side wardrobe 900(w)×650(d)×1860(h)mm	Steel stocking shelf 1800(w)×600(d)×2000(h)mm
FF01021	FF01022	FF01023	FF01024
Coat stand 300（d)×1800	Portable partition wall Each 600(w)×1800(h) Four in tolle	Wall clock-quartz 300(d)	Dry erase board Both side white, removable 900(w)×1800（h)
FF01025	FF01026	FF01027	FF01028
6-outlet power strip 5 meters	3-outlet power strip 10 meters	Electric kettle 1.7L	Coffee maker
FF01029	FF01030	FF01031	FF01032
Desk lamp	Floor lamp	Microwave oven 23Lg	Fan Heater 260（di）x690(h)mm
FF01033	FF01034	FF01035	FF01036
Space heater 570(w)×310(d)×660(h)mm	Shoe dryer 211(w)X 117(d)X280(h)mm	Refrigerator-small 95L 430(w)X450(d)X820(h)mm	Refrigerator-medium 303L 600(w) X 660 (d) X 1900 (h) mm

TEC LEGEND

TE01201	TE01202	TE01301	TE01302
Private Socket (Private Dynamic IP Address)	Private Socket (Private Static IP Address)	Private socket plus dedicated access 10 Mbps	Private socket plus dedicated access 20 Mbps
TE01303	TE01304	TE01401	TE02201
Private socket plus dedicated access 50 Mbps	Private socket plus dedicated access 100 Mbps	Additional Public Static IP address (Optional)	Olympic Data Feed
TE03101	TE03102	TE03201	TE04101
Info workstation	Info printer	CIS workstation	Laptop computer
TE04102	TE04103	TE05101	TE05201
Desktop Computer	23" monitor	Floor standing color multifunction printer	Desktop monochrome multifunction printer
TE05301	TE05401	TE06101	TE06102
Desktop monochrome laser printer	Desktop color laser printer	Olympic/Paralympic Fixed Telephone with handset (Ordinary)	Olympic/Paralympic Fixed Telephone with handset (Chinese Mainland)
TE06103	TE06104	TE06201	TE06202
Olympic/Paralympic Fixed Telephone with handset(Hong Kong SAR, Macao SAR, Taiwan region access)	Olympic/Paralympic Fixed Telephone with handset (International access)	Hearing impairment device for fixed telephones	Flash phone bell for fixed telephones
TE08101	TE08102	TE08103	TE08201
Small: 17" LCD television without CATV service	Medium: 43" LCD television without CATV service	Large: 55" LCD television without CATV service	Small: 17" LCD television with CATV service
TE08202	TE08203	TE08301	
Medium: 43" LCD television with CATV service	Large: 55" LCD television with CATV service	CATV connection only for user provided TV	

图15 媒体租用空间标准图块放大图
Image 15 Enlarged Modules of Rental Spaces for Press

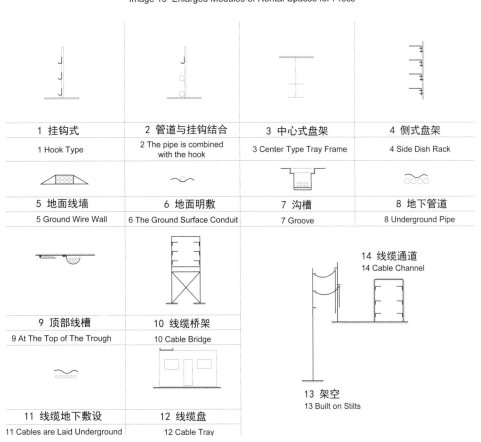

1 挂钩式	2 管道与挂钩结合	3 中心式盘架	4 侧式盘架
1 Hook Type	2 The pipe is combined with the hook	3 Center Type Tray Frame	4 Side Dish Rack
5 地面线墙	6 地面明敷	7 沟槽	8 地下管道
5 Ground Wire Wall	6 The Ground Surface Conduit	7 Groove	8 Underground Pipe
9 顶部线槽	10 线缆桥架		
9 At The Top of The Trough	10 Cable Bridge		
11 线缆地下敷设	12 线缆盘		
11 Cables are Laid Underground	12 Cable Tray		

13 架空
13 Built on Stilts

14 线缆通道
14 Cable Channel

图16 临设标准单元 1/Image 16 Standard Units of Temporary Facilities 1

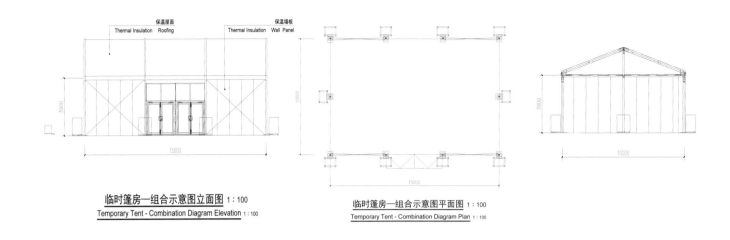

临时篷房—组合示意图立面图 1:100
Temporary Tent - Combination Diagram Elevation 1:100

临时篷房—组合示意图平面图 1:100
Temporary Tent - Combination Diagram Plan 1:100

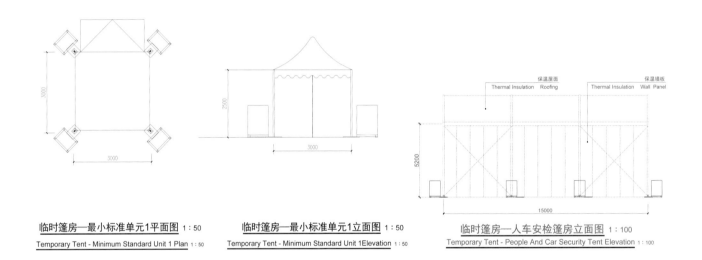

临时篷房—最小标准单元1平面图 1:50
Temporary Tent - Minimum Standard Unit 1 Plan 1:50

临时篷房—最小标准单元1立面图 1:50
Temporary Tent - Minimum Standard Unit 1Elevation 1:50

临时篷房—人车安检篷房立面图 1:100
Temporary Tent - People And Car Security Tent Elevation 1:100

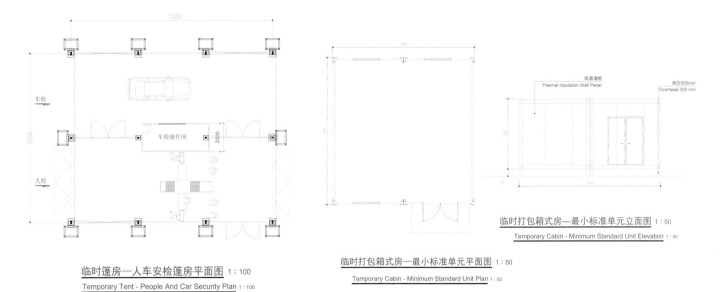

临时篷房—人车安检篷房平面图 1:100
Temporary Tent - People And Car Security Plan 1:100

临时打包箱式房—最小标准单元平面图 1:50
Temporary Cabin - Minimum Standard Unit Plan 1:50

临时打包箱式房—最小标准单元立面图 1:50
Temporary Cabin - Minimum Standard Unit Elevation 1:50

图17 临设标准单元 2/Image 17 Standard Units of Temporary Facilities 2

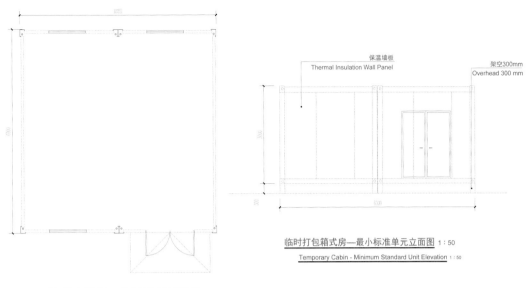

临时打包箱式房—最小标准单元平面图 1:50

Temporary Cabin - Minimum Standard Unit Plan 1:50

保温墙板
Thermal Insulation Wall Panel

架空300mm
Overhead 300 mm

临时打包箱式房—最小标准单元立面图 1:50

Temporary Cabin - Minimum Standard Unit Elevation 1:50

集装箱卫生间组合示意图
Container Toilet Combination Schematic Diagram

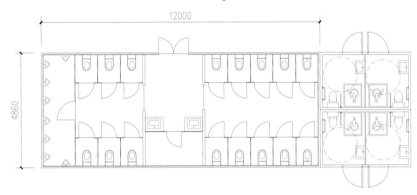

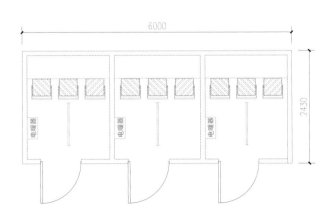

其他临时设施—评论员间平面图 1:50

Other Temporary Facilities - Comment Booth Plan 1:50

图18　临设标准单元 3/Image 18　Standard Units of Temporary Facilities 3

可移动围栏
Movable Fence
1.2m围栏(配重式)
1.2 m Fence
(Counterweight fencing)

其他临时设施—临时隔离设施隔离支座 1：30
Isolation Bearing 1：30

其他临时设施—临时隔离设施立面图 1：30
Other Temporary Facilities - Temporary Isolation Facility Elevation 1：30

固定式围栏
Fixed Fence
2.5m围栏(预埋式)
2.5m Fence
(Embedded Fencing)

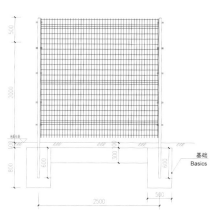

其他临时设施—临时隔离设施立面图 1：30
Other Temporary Facilities - Temporary 1：30
Isolation Facility Elevation

其他临时设施—临时隔离设施剖面图 1：30
Other Temporary Facilities - Temporary 1：30
Isolation Facility Cross-section Drawn

固定式围栏
Fixed Fence
1.8m围栏(配重式)
1.8m Fence
(Counterweight fencing)

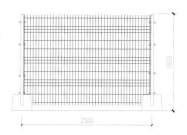

其他临时设施—临时隔离设施立面图 1：30
Other Temporary Facilities - Temporary 1：30
Isolation Facility Elevation

其他临时设施—临时隔离设施剖面图 1：30
Other Temporary Facilities - Temporary 1：30
Isolation Facility Cross-section Drawn

固定式围栏
Fixed Fence
2.5m围栏(配重式)
2.5 m Fence
(Counterweight fencing)

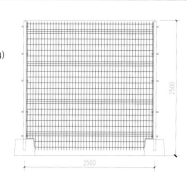

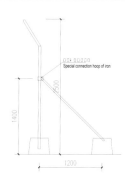

其他临时设施—临时隔离设施立面图 1：30
Other Temporary Facilities - Temporary 1：30
Isolation Facility Elevation

其他临时设施—临时隔离设施剖面图 1：30
Other Temporary Facilities - Temporary 1：30
Isolation Facility Cross-section Drawn

图19　临设标准单元 4/Image 19　Standard Units of Temporary Facilities 4

摄像平台四
Camera Platform 4

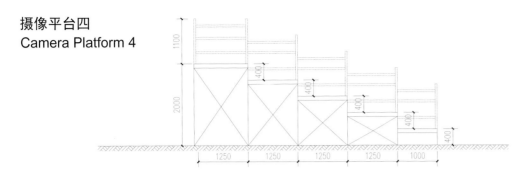

其他临时设施—摄像平台立面图 1：50
Other Temporary Facilities - Camera Platform Elevation 1：50

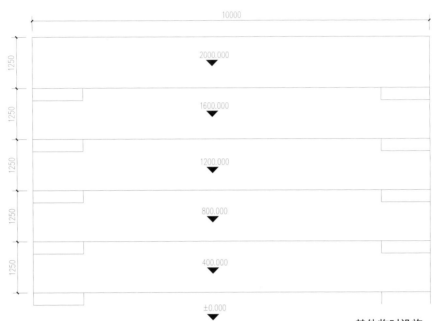

其他临时设施—摄像平台平面图 1：50
Other Temporary Facilities - Camera Platform Plan 1：50

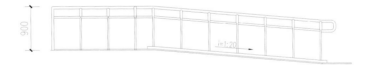

其他临时设施—无障碍坡道立面图 1：30
Other Temporary Facilities - Wheelchair Accessible Ramp Elevation 1：30

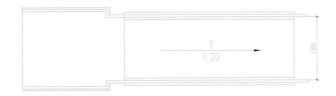

其他临时设施—无障碍坡道平面图 1：30
Other Temporary Facilities - Wheelchair Accessible Ramp Plan 1：30

图20　临设标准单元 5/Image 20　Standard Units of Temporary Facilities 5

《场馆设施手册》问答录
Q&A on Overlay Books

1. 为什么要编制《场馆设施手册》？谁来编制、谁来使用？

冬奥会场馆的赛时运行是一套非常复杂的系统，仅一个竞赛场馆赛时就涉及国内外几千名工作人员、几百辆车的进出和工作，需保障建筑、缆车、制冰、造雪、比赛、训练、计时计分、新闻报道、媒体转播、电力、光纤等所有设施的同时运行，不可有任何闪失，所有的人、车和设备在场馆内的空间布局需要一套完整而统一的图纸平台供大家共同遵守和使用，《场馆设施手册》就提供了这样的图纸系统。

《场馆设施手册》原则上是场馆赛时的使用方来进行需求的整理和运行方案的确认，由建筑设计院的设计师来完成图纸落位工作。

北京2022年冬奥会和冬残奥会的《场馆设施手册》，前期主要由北京冬奥组委规划建设部牵头编制；后期，随着场馆管理部、奥运村部、媒体运行部以及场馆（群）运行团队的成立，《场馆设施手册》由规划建设部会同相关部门共同编制完成。

2.《场馆设施手册》的主要内容是什么？和运行设计的关系是什么？和建筑设计有什么不同？

《场馆设施手册》总体来说分为两部分，一是场馆空间面积分配表（AAM表），二是运行设计图纸。

AAM表是场馆空间的面积对应表格，早期是运行设计的任务书，后期转为运行设计的成果空间汇总表。

运行设计图纸是场馆赛时建筑空间和主要设备设施的"所见即所得"，包括场馆封闭线范围内和部分临近区域所有参与赛时运行的永久性设施和临时性设施，如建筑、缆车、道路、看台、楼梯、电梯、坡道、广场、停车场、停车位、保障车辆、家具白电、栅栏等所有放置在地面或楼面上的设施，以及各类人群、车辆的流线。

对于新建的场馆和需要建筑改造的场馆，运行设计和永久性建筑设计是密不可分、合并进行的。前期，赛时运行的内容主要体现在建筑设计方案中；后期，待永久建筑方案稳定后，运行设计的内容会独立出来，在涵盖永久性设施和临时设施的基础上，成为赛时专用的"运行设计方案"。

对于不需要建筑改造的现有场馆，如冬奥交通指挥中心，不需再进行建筑设计，而是以原有建筑空间为基底，增画临时设施内容、运行空间分配和人车流线，即可成为"运行设计方案"。

3. 场馆设计过程中，中外方团队是怎样合作的？

2016年前，无论冰上项目还是雪上项目，国内从未建设过冬奥级别的场馆，特别是雪上场馆，设计经验极度缺乏。有的项目，如雪车雪橇，国际上冬奥级别赛道只有16条，国内建设、设计行业几乎没有人见过。针对这种情况，北京冬奥组委规划建设部会同地方政府和场馆业主，采取了中外力量高度融合的工作方法，发挥中方单位熟悉国内情况、各专业力量充足、工作效率高的特点，吸收国外相关领域权威和专家的丰富经验和专业优势，紧密协同开展工作。

在场馆选址确认阶段，邀请国外专家来华到现场勘查调研，对可行性方案比对优选，及时和国际雪联、国际冬季两项联盟、国际雪车协会、国际雪橇协会、国际滑冰联合会、国际冰球联合会和世界冰壶联合会等国际单项体育组织积极沟通，高效对接，稳健决策。

在场馆设计阶段，由国内设计单位和国外有经验的专家团队组成联合体进行场馆设计，外方主要在方案和关键技术节点上把关，中方设计团队负责完善、整合和落地实施。

在场馆建造阶段，北京冬奥组委、业主单位、施工单位分别聘请了不同层面的国际专家上百位，包括赛道设计、转播照明、山地运行、赛道塑型、赛道防风、制冰系统、造雪系统、缆车系统等方面的专家，全面覆盖场馆建设的重点难点、关键时间和工作节点，以保证场馆建设既符合冬奥会和冬残奥会赛事需要、也符合场馆的赛后利用需要。

在发挥国外专家优势的同时，中方团队也积极学习、快速成长，深入了解设计原理、提出改进提升方案、创新填补国内技术空白，培养了一大批具备国际水准冬季项目场馆设计和建设能力的中国团队。在制冰系统的高效环保、冬奥村的智能化等领域，中方团队还引领了世界的设计和建造方向。

4. 大型赛事、大型活动为什么需要编制《场馆设施手册》？

尽管《场馆设施手册》是国际奥委会组织运行奥运会专用的图纸系列，但它也同样适用于其他大型赛事、大型活动。越是涉及国内国外多重利益相关方、涉及人群越多、运行越复杂的赛事和活动，越是需要《场馆设施手册》和运行设计。

通过运行设计的全面统领，可实现赛事前所有的永建改造、临设搭建都有明确的依据；赛事运行时人员、车辆、设备有条不紊、安全有序；赛后临时设施的拆除清晰明确、迅速无痕。

因此，推荐国内各种赛事/活动可参照北京冬奥会《场馆设施手册》的工作理路，组织本赛事/活动的运行设计，在促进赛事组织水平达到国际一流的同时，推进赛事组织的专业化、临时设施建设租赁的常态化，以及搭建撤除的可持续性，实现资源共享、环保节约。

5.《场馆设施手册》为什么分为7个版本？为什么要分100-900系列？版本和系列是什么关系？

从伦敦奥运会以来，国际奥委会要求各主办城市按照7个时间点递交7个版本的《场馆设施手册》，分别是1.0、2.0、3.0、4.0、5.0、6.0和7.0版，约半年更新一次，随着版本的推进，赛时运行所涉及的要素逐步叠加、细化、丰富、全面，最终形成场馆运行要素和各类设施的总成。有时，主办城市根据工作需要会增加中间版本，如北京冬奥会因OBS（奥林匹克广播服务公司）对于转播设施的需求增补，增加了2.1版；因临时设施需求确认、临设招标的需要，增加了6.1版等。

《场馆设施手册》100～900系列图纸是场馆运行设计从宏观到微观的反映，随着数字的增大，图纸深度逐级递进、内容更加微观。其中100～300系列反映的是从赛区到场馆群再到场馆近周边区域的总平面图；400～700系列体现的是场馆内部核心设施及附属后勤空间信息，并逐级放大至详细平面图；800

系列包含场馆立剖面图以及坐席视线分析；900系列是临时设施施工详图。

《场馆设施手册》的7个版本图纸内容都包含从宏观到微观的100~900系列，随着时间的推移、赛事的临近、版本的更新，其图纸内容会越来越精细、更无限接近最终赛时的运行实景。

6.《场馆设施手册》运行设计的制图标准是如何制定的？各项图例都代表什么？

《场馆设施手册》运行设计的制图标准是依据国际奥委会的通用标准，参考了里约、平昌、东京三届奥运会的制图标准，并结合北京冬奥会的实际情况编制而成。

《场馆设施手册》的图例包含"客户群空间和流线表达""通用临时设施表达""特殊临时设施表达""其他图例表达"等几种类型。

"客户群空间和流线表达"规范了客户群主要功能区、步行流线、车行流线及出入口的图例画法，将客户群按照运动员（浅蓝）、奥林匹克大家庭（紫）、转播服务（深绿）、媒体运行（浅绿）、观众（黄）、安保（红）、场馆运行（橙）、接待（深粉）、仪式（浅粉）、比赛场地（湖蓝）等区域使用不同的颜色进行区分，并对步行、车行等不同交通方式通过不同的箭头形式进行了区分。

"通用临时设施表达"主要包含安保防护栏、隔离栏、警戒带、金属栏板、隔离墩、可移动软墙等不同的隔断，棚房、板房、无障碍坡道等临时建筑，防护网、缆车索道等室外基础设施。

"特殊临时设施表达"主要包含室外常规照明灯杆、室外转播照明灯杆、电线杆、雪炮、气象站等内容。

不同深度的图纸使用的图例在数量上略有区别，但图例的类型和标准是统一的。

7. 冰上场馆和雪上场馆运行设计的主要差异是什么？

由于举办项目类型的差异，冰上场馆和雪上场馆在运行设计中也存在很大的不同。在空间布局方面，冰上场馆往往采用集中式室内空间布局，以冰面为核心，四周布置观众看台及各类后勤空间；雪上场馆往往以户外赛道为核心，场馆范围大且高程复杂多变，在赛道出发区或结束区布置各类功能用房及综合区，由赛道和道路串联各功能空间。在功能差异方面，雪上场馆往往需要更大量的临时设施，如临时观众看台、各类长距离临时线缆路由，此外雪上场馆还需要设置几十甚至上百间打蜡房。雪上场馆运行对内部交通依赖很大，在运行设计中还要体现缆车、道路、技术雪道等流线路径。

8. 为什么要设置场馆封闭线？如何设置？为什么有的场馆需要远端安检？

场馆封闭线主要包括外围安保围栏以及划分内部运行区域的围栏。外围安保围栏主要是为了保证场馆安全运行设置的，在场馆主要出入口需要设置人车安检大篷，作为赛时进出场馆的唯一路径，在安检线内有安保人员值守，保证场馆与城市界面的安全。内部的围栏主要为了划分各运行区域通行权限，需要结合注册分区和防疫分区进行设置，并设置相应的验证点。

部分场馆在运行期间，存在瞬时大量人流和物流进入场馆的需求，场馆本身的安检设施不足或场地局促，无法满足如此大量的安检需求，因此采用了远端安检措施，以确保人员和物资进入场馆的速度和效率。

北京冬奥会三个赛区还分别建设了远端物流安检场，场馆内需求的大量物资在远端物流安检场安检后，可直接进入场馆相应的综合区卸货。此外，考虑防疫和天气温度、减少观众在场馆外等待的时间，北京冬奥会的场馆观众也是通过远端安检集结后，直接乘坐车辆抵达进入场馆。

9. 如何划分场馆的前后院？

所有的竞赛场馆和部分非竞赛场馆都需要设置前院和后院。场馆前院是指观众可以到达的区域，场馆后院是指场馆的运行区域，不对观众开放。注册人员可以进入前院区，观众原则上不能进入后院区。前后院之间需要进行物理隔离，在连通处设置验证点。

对场馆进行前后院划分时，要同步考虑注册人群和观众的出入口和流线，可在平面上划分，也可通过地上地下进行划分。观众流线需考虑瞬时大量人流的进出安全，以及和场馆外公共交通的联系便捷，注册人群要兼顾车辆的出入口和各类室外保障空间的充足。

10. 运行设计的主要客户群都有哪些，设计要点分别是什么？

运行设计包含以下几种主要客户群：运动员及随队官员、技术官员、奥林匹克大家庭成员、媒体人员、场馆运行工作人员（包括持证赞助商和安保人员）和观众（包括持票赞助商）。

运动员及随队官员是赛时最重要的客户群体，运行设计需要优先保证该群体的需求。运动员及随队官员从到达场馆开始，训练热身、赛前准备、竞赛、接受采访直至赛后离开，都需要通过最便捷的流线往返FOP和所属区域。

技术官员也是赛时最重要的客户群体之一，该客户群体的工作区域需要靠近FOP区域，便于技术官员快捷地进入比赛场地进行工作，但需要与运动员区域各自独立，流线也尽量不发生交叉。

奥林匹克大家庭成员在赛时也需要全程保持相对独立的运行空间和流线，该客户群体的停车落客区、休息区、看台区流线需简洁顺畅，休息区临近看台布置。看台一般在场馆内视线较好的位置上。

媒体人员分为转播（摄像、评论员、转播控制等）和新闻媒体（文字媒体、摄影媒体）两类人群，工作区域涵盖前院区和后院区，但需要与运动员区域和奥林匹克大家庭成员区域相对隔离，仅在部分区域如混合采访区、新闻发布厅等连通。位于看台区的转播摄像平台、评论员席是媒体运行的核心之一，需要优先保证落位在合理的位置。

观众通常是场馆中人数最多的群体，从验票、安检、入场观赛直至赛后离场都需要预留足够的集散空间，进行人流引导和疏解。在近几届奥运会中，国际奥委会倡导将看台最佳观赛区域优先提供给观众，紧邻比赛场地的区域提供给"粉丝观众"。雪上场馆除观众坐席外，还会设置一定数量的观众站席，站席一般靠近比赛场地。

场馆运行工作人员为上述客户群提供服务保障，并根据各自业务领域的职责和运行需求进行落位，各业务领域之间通过注册分区进行管控。

11. 场馆室外区域为什么需尽量保证平整、不设高差？

场馆室外区域分为前院和后院，前院主要为观众活动区域，入场和散场瞬时人流量大，场地的平整能够更大程度保证观众的人行安全，特别是要考虑残障人士的无障碍环境建设需求，场地不宜有台阶和过大的高差。

后院是各类设施综合工作区，也是各种工作车辆的停靠区，也同样需要平整的场地，尤其是运载转播设备的车辆尺寸非常大、转弯半径很大，需要场地平整空旷，才适合运行。因此，场馆周边室外空间应尽量减少高差，道路两侧尽量不要设置有高差的"路牙"。

12. 场馆室外为什么要设置多种综合区，都是怎样的功能？

综合区是大型活动中将保障后勤服务的相关设施设置在室外集中的区域。大型赛事的举办往往伴随着转播活动需求，制冷、照明、音响等产生的大量临时电力需求，各类人员产生的物资需求、餐饮需求以及垃圾清运等需求。场馆内往往没有足够的空间容纳这些临时需求，因而在室外设置了各类综合区。北京冬奥会的场馆运行设计，综合区主要包括转播综合区、电力综合区、餐饮综合区、清废综合区、物流综合区等类型。

转播综合区是安置各类转播设备器材、车辆以及信号传输处理工作的区域。电视转播是奥运会最重要的环节之一，在运行设计中，需要优先安排转播运行的空间和设施需求。转播综合区尽量安置在靠近场馆主体的位置，需要考虑大型转播车的停放空间及进出便捷。

电力综合区主要是为场馆提供临时电力负荷以及应急电力保障的区域，包括备用电源、临时供电车以及相应的办公空间。冬奥会的场馆电力一般有三方面的四重保障，一是独立的两路"市电"，二是至少30min的不间断电源（UPS），三是柴油发电机。以上供电方式可实现无缝切换。

餐饮综合区是为场馆内提供餐饮服务的区域，要结合厨房及餐饮售卖点进行设置，需要考虑包括车辆的通道和卸货区域、各类食材储藏空间、冷冻存储区域及餐饮办公空间。

清废综合区是消纳场馆内产生的各种废弃物的空间，作为转运站，场馆内产生的所有废弃物均要集中到清废综合区进行处置。主要空间包括垃圾存储、分类及清运空间、车辆回转及停放空间，此外还包括工具存储及一定的办公空间。

物流综合区是为保障场馆内物资存贮、补给、运送和回收设置的区域，通常紧邻道路设置。主要包括车检点、卸货区、停车区、集装箱、叉车等设备存储区以及物流办公空间。

13. 场馆的媒体转播相关区域主要有哪些？OBS在场馆内的运行需求主要是什么？

室内媒体转播区域主要包含：媒体工作区、媒体休息区、媒体储存区、转播信息办公室、评论员控制室、媒体混合采访区、新闻发布厅、节间采访区、带桌媒体席、不带桌媒体席、评论员席、观察员席、主摄像机平台、播报席等。

室外媒体转播区域主要包含：转播综合区、卫星场站等。

OBS（奥林匹克广播服务公司）在场馆内的运行需求主要包含：各类转播摄像机位、临时线缆路由桥架、转播综合区等空间及设备需求，转播所需要的电力供给需求，以及满足持权转播商转播、分发转播信号的光纤技术线路等需求。

14. 混合采访区是什么？设计要点是什么？

混合采访区是在运动员在完成比赛项目或颁发奖牌仪式后接受转播和媒体采访的区域，也是奥运会场馆媒体运行中最有

活力的区域。

混合采访区一般位于比赛区域的完成区，需要设置运动员从比赛场地进入混合区的出口及媒体入口，并为运动员提供2~3m宽的通行空间，同时保证一定数量的持权转播商、非持权转播商和文字记者有充足的空间进行转播及采访工作。运动员和媒体流线平行布置不交叉。

运动员在进入混合采访区后，先经过转播区域，再经过文字媒体区域，接受采访的运动员在相应区域停留接受采访，没有采访的运动员直接经过混合采访区通道返回运动员更衣室。每个转播采访位置宽度约为1.8m，文字媒体宽度约为1m，不同场馆混合采访区长度根据转播商和媒体的预定数量不同而有所变化，一般流线长度在100m左右。

15. 新冠肺炎疫情对场馆运行设计有什么影响？

为应对新冠肺炎疫情，北京冬奥组委出台了一系列指导性政策文件，如《北京2022年冬奥会和冬残奥会防疫手册》《北京2022年冬奥会和冬残奥会新冠肺炎疫情闭环管理指引》等，同时在各场馆团队原有业务领域的基础上增加了公共卫生（PHS）业务领域，来协助团队制定各场馆针对性的运行防疫计划。

运行防疫计划对运行设计主要存在如下几方面的影响：

运行分区。根据防疫政策的要求，所有场馆均被划分为闭环管理区和非闭环管理区，两区域之间采用物理隔离，并保持至少2m宽的隔离距离。各区域的人员、车辆、物资等只能在本区域内活动，并设置完全独立的进出口、交通流线和工作区域。防疫分区需要在注册分区的基础上制定，并尽量使每个注册分区完整地包括在防疫分区之内，减少注册与防疫之间的交叉。

交通流线。外围交通运行采取点到点的方式，各类客户群从驻地到场馆内各工作区都设置了点对点的落客位，保证运动员、大家庭成员、媒体、工作人员等都能乘坐专用班车到达工作区域，尽量减少不同区域的人员交叉，降低新冠肺炎疫情的传播风险。内部流线组织中，为每类客户群体设置独立的出入口，保证从落客点到各工作区域的流线都相互独立。

人员计划。观众采用有组织观赛的模式，考虑防疫距离减少了观众人数。工作人员按照闭环内和闭环外区域进行配置，部分业务领域需要同时配置闭环内和闭环外人员，整体人数相比新冠肺炎疫情前有所增加。人员计划的调整会带来相应的空间、设施、物资的变化。

坐席划分。竞赛场馆的坐席区同样按照防疫要求划分为闭环内坐席区和闭环外坐席区，两类坐席之间采用透明防疫隔板分隔，并保持2m间距。坐席采取间隔落座的方式，赛时场馆实际容量有所减少。

临时设施。面向观众的赛事服务设施，如观众安检篷、售票亭、餐饮售卖点等，由于观众人数减少而有所缩减；面向工作人员的临时设施，尤其是用作区域隔离的铁马、栅栏、防疫隔板、桌面亚克力挡板等，均有增加。

随着新冠肺炎疫情情况不断变化，运行设计也随之调整。在OB6.1版本中通过防疫分区图划分了防疫分区，体现了各类防疫隔离设施；在OB7.0版本中明确了防疫各项内容，并据此实施。

16. 场馆的闭环内外是如何划分的？之间如何交接？

闭环管理是新冠肺炎疫情防控下一种特殊的分区管理方式，涵盖抵离、交通、住宿、餐饮、训练、竞赛、颁奖、开闭幕式、媒体采访等各业务领域及涉冬奥场所，包括闭环内管理和闭环

外管理两部分。其中，闭环内管理是指对场馆、集中驻地等一系列涉冬奥场所指定区域进行封闭管理，各封闭区域通过指定交通工具实现全流程、点对点连接；闭环外管理是指对封闭区域外涉冬奥低风险人员的管理。综合考虑各场馆、集中驻地等具体情况，严格控制不同区域人员跨环活动。闭环内区域和闭环外区域之间应设置至少2m宽的隔离距离。

闭环内外的交接可分为多种情况，闭环外到闭环内输送物资通过在闭环内外的过渡区域设置专门房间，依托无接触配送的方式达成需求；原则上避免从闭环内向闭环外输送物资，有特殊需求时（如闭环内临时卫生间清污等），在场馆团队公共卫生业务领域指导下对闭环内物资进行消杀、静置后输送到闭环外；特殊情况需要闭环外人员到闭环内区域进行工作时，应按照"三区两通道"模式设置过渡区域，闭环外人员在过渡区域按照二级防护标准穿着装备后进入闭环内区域，完成闭环内工作后，按照防疫要求由过渡区域完成消杀后回到闭环外区域。

17. 什么是FOP？运行设计为什么要画FOP专项图纸？

FOP是英文"Field of Play"的缩写，是指竞赛场馆的比赛场地，包含竞赛区、体育缓冲区、所需比赛场地总区域三个部分，冰上场馆一般指竞赛冰面区域，雪上场馆一般指竞赛雪道区域。

FOP是奥运会赛时的核心区域，需要完整表达其中的各种内容。FOP图纸可以清晰地表达比赛场地内的所有信息，包含球门、画线、争球区、运动员席、受罚席、出发门、终点线等；还能表达比赛场地周边各利益相关方的使用区域，包含体育、转播、媒体运行、技术、医疗、清废等；最重要的是可以表达包括运动员、媒体、浇冰车、礼宾颁奖等各类人群的详细运行流线。通过FOP专项图纸的绘制，赛前筹备期可以对各利益相关方的区域和流线做出合理规划，赛事运行期可以配合场馆运行计划对FOP区域的运行做出合理安排。

有的场馆FOP图纸会根据赛事不同，图纸内容有所差异，如首都体育馆针对短道速滑和花样滑冰有不同的FOP图纸；国家高山滑雪中心针对冬奥会和冬残奥会有不同的FOP图纸等。

18. 场馆里为什么要有很多注册坐席？注册坐席主要包括哪些类型？设计的要点是什么？

注册坐席是奥运会期间提供给各类注册人员使用的坐席区，主要包含：奥林匹克大家庭坐席、评论员席、播报席、媒体席、观察员席、观赛运动员坐席等。注册坐席需要结合各利益相关方的流线、人数进行布置，根据不同利益相关方的要求提供差异化的观赛视角，并设置相应的无障碍席位。

奥林匹克大家庭坐席是提供给国际奥委会官员及各单项体联受邀官员使用的坐席，一般位于场馆观赛视角较好的位置，且靠近奥林匹克大家庭休息室。奥林匹克大家庭坐席共分为O、F、H三类坐席，分别提供给不同级别的官员使用。奥林匹克大家庭坐席前方还需设置无障碍坐席，提供给冬奥会及冬残奥会的无障碍人员使用。

评论员席是各国持权转播商进行赛时转播评论的看台工作区域，根据赛前预定数量进行搭建，一般占据2m×2m的空间，可容纳2~3人。由于转播对于奥运会十分重要，因此评论员席需要更好的观赛位置及视线角度，且需靠近评论员控制室及主摄像机平台布置。雪上场馆的评论员席设在看台区的永久或临时建筑内，需能够直接看到比赛比赛场地且视野良好。

播报席主要作为比赛现场采访播报使用，位置一般靠近评论员席，尺寸约为2m×4m，主持人和采访嘉宾以比赛场地作为背景，摄像机架设于播报席后方。

观察员席是国际奥委会观摩人员进行实习观摩的区域，一般利用场馆现有坐席，位置靠近评论员席，观察员包括下一届夏奥会、冬奥会组织委员会的工作人员。

媒体坐席分为带桌媒体席及不带桌媒体席，主要供各国文字记者使用。媒体席需设置于场馆视线较好的坐席区位置，一般带桌媒体席更靠前设置，不带桌媒体席布置在后方区域。媒体席设置的位置取决于媒体的运行流线，能够满足媒体从媒体席更快地到达混合采访区和媒体工作间等区域。雪上场馆鉴于室外温度原因，看台上不设置带桌媒体席。

观赛运动员坐席是为当日没有竞赛的运动员提供观赛的区域，在奥运会及残奥会具有不同的使用要求。奥运会期间运动员坐席一般设置于看台坐席区靠后的位置，不会影响转播及媒体席的工作。冬残奥会期间，乘坐轮椅的观赛运动员一般直接在FOP周边观赛。

19. 冰上场馆为什么要画FOP上空吊顶布局图？

冰上场馆比赛场地上空密布着斗屏、场地照明灯具、扬声器、转播摄像机、摄影相机、升旗系统、万国旗、冰面投影仪等赛时设施，以及连接各类设施的线缆路由。通过绘制FOP上空吊顶布局图，可以将各业务领域在吊顶上的设施、设备以及线缆路由合理、清晰地设计布局，以保证彼此独立运行、相互协作不干扰。

20. 场馆为什么要有单独的线缆路由图？

为保障赛事运行万无一失，场馆内外需敷设相当数量的临时线缆，主要包括电力线缆、技术线缆和转播线缆三类，这三类线缆需要非常安全的路线，因此需要绘制专门的线缆路由图。

线缆由电力、技术和转播（BRS）三个相应业务领域分别敷设。路由特指线缆的敷设方式，包括管道、线槽、线缆钩、桥架、电缆夹、盖板、钢管敷设等方式，一般由场馆和基础设施业务领域实施。

电力线缆路由主要为场馆内外临时设施提供电力供应，包括线缆、柴油发电机、各级箱变、UPS等内容。

技术线缆路由主要为场馆内外各区域提供通信、信息、场馆技术、网络安全和无线电频率管理，包括固定通信、移动通信、集群通信、奥运管理信息系统、办公管理系统、有线电视等内容。

转播线缆路由主要为场馆内外各区域的转播点位提供信号传播，包括转播综合区、摄像机位、评论员席、播报席、评论员控制室等。

线缆路由图为上述三种不同的管线路由提供管线综合，将所有业务领域的管线路由集中在一起，可以判断管线路由敷设是否满足使用要求，各个管线路由之间是否存在冲突，管线路由敷设与主要运行流线是否存在冲突，并最终形成一套同时满足各方运行需求的图纸来指导现场实施和保障工作。

21. 场馆无障碍设施遵循的标准是什么？运行设计的重点主要有哪些？

场馆无障碍设施设计遵循《北京2022年冬奥会和冬残奥会无障碍指南》（下文简称《指南》）的标准。2018年9月，北京冬奥组委向全社会发布了《北京2022年冬奥会和冬残奥会无障碍指南》，该《指南》是基于《国际残奥委会无障碍指南》和中国无障碍现行法规标准，并融合了往届奥运会的无障碍指南编制而成，不仅注重场馆和设施的无障碍建设，还注重形成从城市到场馆的连续无障碍环境。同时，北京冬奥组委还编制了一系列场馆无障碍设施建设技术指导文件，并于2020年9月，发布了《北京2022年冬奥会和冬残奥会无障碍指南技术指标图册》。

北京冬奥会三个赛区的所有场馆和设施，从规划、设计、建设、运行，均严格落实以上技术文件的要求，用统一的标准进行了建设和交付。

为落实"以运动员为核心"的办赛理念，场馆内外运动员所到区域，各项标准会适当提高，根据运动员的身体特点和实际需求，设置自动门、无障碍坐席、无障碍电梯、无障碍卫生间、无障碍淋浴间、无障碍坡道、电梯提示盲道、无障碍更衣室、低位服务台、无障碍标识等，雪上场馆还设置无障碍打蜡房、无障碍缆车系统等。运动员的所到之处均消除细微高差、增设防滑安全措施，以确保通行无障碍。

根据《指南》的要求，冬奥会场馆观众轮椅席位占场馆总席位的比例不低于0.75%，冬残奥会场馆观众轮椅席位不低于1%，有轮椅运动员参加的冬残奥会竞赛场馆，观众轮椅席位不低于1.2%，观众轮椅席位及陪同席位需按照1：1的比例进行设置。运动员轮椅席位不需要设置陪同席位。

22. 冬残奥会的重点场馆，运行设计增补了哪些内容？

北京2022年冬残奥会共使用28个场馆，其中包括5个竞赛场馆（国家游泳中心、国家体育馆、国家高山滑雪中心、国家冬季两项中心、云顶滑雪公园）和23个非竞赛场馆，分布在北京、延庆、张家口三个赛区。除延庆残奥颁奖广场外，其他场馆均沿用了冬奥会的场馆设施。

所有的场馆图纸，均标注了无障碍设施，如无障碍坐席、无障碍卫生间、无障碍电梯、无障碍坡道等内容。此外，针对5个冬残奥会竞赛场馆和3个冬残奥村，图纸中还增加了符合冬残奥会特殊需要的转换图纸，如比赛场地、更衣室转换图纸等。另外，针对这8个场馆，还特别标注了无障碍设施尺寸和轮椅流线等内容。

鉴于场馆图纸内容覆盖了所有无障碍设施，因此，冬残奥会没有编制专门的冬残奥会场馆运行设计，而是和冬奥会共用同一套设计成果。

1. Why is an Overlay Book (OB) being compiled? Who compiled it and who use it?

The Games-time operations of the venues for the Olympic and Paralympic Winter Games Beijing 2022 (Beijing 2022 Games) feature a very complex system and the Games-time operations of only one single competition venue involve the entry, exit, and work or operations of thousands of Chinese and foreign workforce members and hundreds of vehicles. Therefore, it is necessary to guarantee the simultaneous operations of all facilities involving buildings, gondolas, ice and snow making, competitions, training, timing and scoring (T&S), press, broadcasting, energy, and optical cables. A set of complete and unified drawings for common compliance and use is required for the spatial layout of all personnel, vehicles, and equipment in the venues, while such a drawing system is provided in the OB.

In principle, the OB is used by the Games-time users of venues to sort out their requirements and confirm the operation plans and the layout of the drawings is completed by the designers of the architectural design institute.

Beijing 2022 Headquarters took the lead in the compilation of the OBs for the Olympic and Paralympic Winter Games Beijing 2022 in the early phase. In the late phase, the Venue Planning and Construction Department joined hands with relevant departments to compile the OBs after the Venue Management Department, Village Planning and Operation Department, Media Operations Department, and Venue (Cluster) Operations Team were established.

2. What are the main contents of the OBs? What is the relationship between these contents and the operational design? What is the difference between operational design and architectural design?

The OBs mainly involve two parts: Area Allocation Matrices (AAMs) and operational design drawings.

AAMs are tables corresponding to the areas of the venue spaces. In the early phase, they are the task books of the operational design, and in the late phase, they are the summary table of space deliverables of operational design.

Following the principle of "what you see is what you get", operational design drawings cover the Games-time architectural space and major equipment and facilities in venues, including all permanent facilities and overlays used for Games-time operations within the secure perimeters of venues and in some adjacent areas, such as buildings, gondolas, roads, stands, staircases, elevators, ramps, squares, parking lots, parking areas, support vehicles, FF&E, fences, and all other facilities placed on the ground or floor, and the flows of all kinds of groups and vehicles.

For new venues and venues requiring architectural renovation, operational design and permanent architectural design are inseparable and integrated. In the early phase, the contents of Games-time operations are mainly reflected in the architectural design plan. Later, after the architectural design plan is finalised, the contents of the operational design are put into a separate Games-time operational design plan on the basis of covering both permanent facilities and overlays.

For existing venues that do not require architectural renovation, such as the Olympic Transport Command Centre, no architectural design is required and an "operational design plan" can be created by using existing building space as the basis and adding the contents of overlays, allocation of operational space and pedestrian and vehicle flows.

3. How did the Chinese and foreign teams cooperate with each other during venue design?

Before 2016, China had never constructed an Olympic-level venue, no matter for ice sports or snow sports, especially snow venues, and there was a serious lack of design experience. For some sports, such as Bobsleigh and Luge, there were only 16 Olympic-level tracks in the world and few people in the Chinese construction and design industry had seen them. To tackle such a condition, the Venue Planning and Construction Department of Beijing 2022 joined hands with local governments and venue owners, adopted the approach of high integration of Chinese and foreign forces, gave play to the characteristics of Chinese organisations' understanding of China's conditions, sufficient professional strength, and high work efficiency, and drew on the rich experience and professional advantages of foreign authorities and experts in relevant fields to work with them in close collaboration.

In the phase of venue site confirmation, foreign experts were invited to China for field investigation and research, and the feasibility plans were compared and selected. Active communication, efficient connection, and sound decision-making were conducted timely with IFs, such as the International Ski Federation, the International Biathlon Union, the International Bobsleigh & Skeleton Federation, the International Luge Federation, the International Skating Union, the International Ice Hockey Federation, and the World Curling Federation.

In the venue design phase, venues were designed by a consortium of Chinese design institutes and a foreign experienced expert team. While the foreign party was responsible for the overall plan and handling key technical challenges, the Chinese design team was responsible for improvement, integration, and implementation.

In the venue construction phase, Beijing 2022, the venue owners, and the constructors respectively employed hundreds of international experts at different levels, including experts in such fields as track design, broadcast lighting, mountain operations, track shaping, track wind proof, refrigeration system, snowmaking system, and gondola system. Their work covered the key points, difficulties, key dates, and millstones of venue construction and ensured that the venue construction met the needs of the Games as well as the post-Games use of the venues.

While the advantages of foreign experts were exerted, the Chinese teams also actively studied and developed fast, deeply understood the design principles, put forward improvement plans, and made innovations to fill the technical gap in China. Thus, a large number of Chinese teams with international-level design and construction capabilities for winter sports venues were trained. The Chinese teams also led the world in design and construction in fields such as the environmental friendliness of ice making systems and the smart technology in Olympic Villages.

4. Why should an OB be compiled for major events?

An OB is also applicable to other major events through it was originally a series of drawings of the IOC for the organisation and operation of the Games. The more Chinese and foreign stakeholders and other groups of people involved, and more complex the operations, the more the OB and operational design are needed for the events.

Through the overall guidance of the operational design, there is a clear basis for all permanent renovation and installation of overlays before events. The personnel, vehicles, and equipment are orderly and safe during the events. The overlays are clearly and quickly removed after the events.

Therefore, it is recommended to refer to the work ideas in the OBs for the Beijing 2022 Games in Chinese events in the operational design, so as to promote the organisation level to be internationally first-class and push forward the specialisation of event organisation, the standardisation of overlay construction and leasing, and the sustainability of installation and removal, and to realise resource sharing, environmental protection, and resource conservation.

5. Why are there seven official versions of OBs? Why do the OBs fall into Series 100-900? What is the relationship between versions and series?

Since the London 2012 Games, the IOC requires the host city to submit seven versions of OBs (OB1.0, OB2.0, OB3.0, OB4.0, OB5.0, OB6.0, and OB7.0) at seven points, meaning updating its OBs on a semi-annual basis. With the update of the version, the elements involved in Games-time operations will be gradually superimposed, refined, enriched, and comprehensive, and finally, an assembly of venue operation elements and various facilities will be formed. Sometimes, the host city will add intermediate versions according to work needs, for example, in the Beijing 2022 Games, Revision OB2.1 was added due to the requirement of OBS for broadcasting facilities, and Revision OB6.1 was added due to confirmation of overlay requirements and tendering of overlays.

The Series 100-900 drawings in the OBs reflect the venue operational design from macro level to micro level. With the increase of numbers, the details of the drawings are furthered step by step and the contents are more microscopic. Among them, Series 100-300 reflect master plans from zones to venues and their surrounding areas; Series 400-700 embody the information of core facilities and supporting facilities in venues with enlarged plans of venues;

Series 800 includes elevations and sections of venues and sight line analysis of seats; and Series 900 is enlarged drawings for overlay construction.

Each of the 7 versions of drawings in the OBs includes Series 100-900 ranging from macro level to micro level. With the passage of time, the approaching of the Games, and updates of versions, the contents of the drawings become more and more detailed and infinitely closer to the final Games-time operations.

6. How are the drawing standards for the operational design in the OBs developed? What do the legends represent?

The drawing standards for the operational design in the OBs were developed on the basis of general standards of the IOC, with reference to the drawing standards of Rio 2016, PyeongChang 2018, and Tokyo 2020 Games, and in combination with the actual conditions of the Beijing 2022 Games.

The legends in the OBs include such types as "Expression of Client Group Spaces and Flows", "Expression of General Overlays", "Expression of Special Overlays", and "Expression of Other Legends".

The "Expression of Client Group Spaces and Flows" standardises the legend illustration of main functional zones, pedestrian flow, vehicle flow, and entrance/exit of client groups. Different colours are used to distinguish the client groups according to their zones, such as athletes (light blue), Olympic Family (purple), broadcast services (dark green), press operations (light green), spectators (yellow), security (red), venue operations (orange), hospitality (deep pink), ceremonies (light pink), and FOP (turquoise blue). Different traffic modes, such as walking and driving, are distinguished by different arrows.

The "Expression of General Overlays" mainly includes various partitions such as security perimeter fences, fences, belt partitions, metal barricades, traffic barricades and movable soft walls, temporary structures such as shed houses, slab houses and accessible ramps, and outdoor infrastructure such as protective net and gondola ropeway.

The "Expression of Special Overlays" mainly includes outdoor conventional lighting poles, outdoor broadcast lighting poles, electric poles, snow cannons, meteorological stations, etc.

There are slight differences in the number of legends used on drawings of different details, but the types and standards of legends are uniform.

7. What are the main differences between the operational design of ice venues and snow venues?

Due to the differences in the types of events held, the operational design of ice venues is quite different from that of snow venues. In terms of spatial layout, a centralised indoor spatial layout is usually adopted for the ice venues, with the ice surface as the centre and spectator stands and various support spaces arranged around. For snow venues, outdoor tracks are usually taken as the centre and the venues are large, with complex and various elevations.

Various functional rooms and compounds are arranged in the start area or the finish area of the tracks and all functional spaces are connected by tracks and roads. In terms of functional differences, more overlays are often needed in snow venues, such as temporary spectator stands, various types of long-distance containments, and dozens of wax cabins or more are also needed in snow venues. The operations of snow venues rely heavily on internal traffic and the operational design should also reflect the flows such as gondolas, roads, and technical courses.

8. Why should the secure perimeters of venues be set up? How to set up them? Why do some venues require remote security checks?

The secure perimeters of venues mainly include security perimeter fences and fences dividing the internal operation zones. The security perimeter fences are mainly designed to ensure the safe operation of the venues. It is necessary to set up pedestrian/vehicle security check sheds at the main entrances and exits of the venues as the only way in and out of the venues during the Games, with security personnel on duty inside the security perimeter to ensure the security of the interface between the venues and the rest of the city. The internal fences are mainly used to divide the access requirements of each operation zone and should be set in combination with accreditation zoning and COVID-19 prevention zoning, and corresponding accreditation check points should be set.

During the operation of some venues, there is an instantaneous demand for a large number of personnel and materials to enter the venues, and the security check facilities in the venues are insufficient or the security check space is cramped to meet such a large number of security check needs. Therefore, remote security check measures have been adopted to ensure the speed and efficiency of entry of personnel and materials into venues.

Remote material screening areas are respectively built in three zones of the Beijing 2022 Games and a large number of materials required in the venues can be unloaded directly into the corresponding compounds of the venues after being screened in the material screening areas. In addition, the spectators of the Beijing 2022 Games also gather at remote security checkpoints and directly go to the venues by vehicles in consideration of COVID-19 prevention, temperature, and reduction of waiting time of spectators outside venues.

9. How are the FOH and BOH of a venue divided?

FOH and BOH are required in all competition venues and some non-competition venues. The Front of House (FOH) of a venue refers to the area accessible to spectators and the Back of House (BOH) of a venue refers to the operation area of the venue, which is not accessible to spectators. In principle, accredited persons can enter the FOH and spectators cannot access the BOH. The FOH and BOH need to be physically isolated, with an accreditation check point at the connection.

For division of the FOH and BOH of venues, the entrances, exits, and flows of accredited groups and spectators should be considered simultaneously. They can be divided on a plane or by the ground or underground floors. For the spectator flow, the entrance/exit safety of instantaneous pedestrian flow and connection convenience with external public transport should be considered. For accredited groups, both the entrance and exit of vehicles and the adequacy of all kinds of outdoor security space should be taken into consideration.

10. What are the main client groups involved in the operational design and what are the key points of design?

The operational design mainly involves the following main client groups: athletes and team officials, technical officials, Olympic Family members, media personnel, venue operation workforce (including accredited sponsors and security personnel), and spectators (including ticketed sponsors).

Athletes and team officials are the most important client group during the Games and priority in operational design should be given to their needs. Athletes and team officials need to travel to and from the FOP and their areas through the most convenient flow from arriving at the venues, warming up, pre-competition preparation, competition, being interviewed and leaving after the competition.

The technical officials are also one of the most important client groups during the Games. The work area of this client group needs to be close to the FOP area so that they can quickly enter the FOP to work, but their work area needs to be separated from the athlete area, and their flows should avoid crossing as far as possible.

The Olympic Family members also need relatively independent operational space and flow throughout the Games. The flows of the drop-off zone, lounge, and stand area of this client group should be simple and smooth, and the lounge should be arranged near the stands. The stands are usually located in a place with a good line of sight in venues.

Media personnel are divided into broadcast personnel (photographers, commentators, broadcast controllers, etc.) and press personnel (written press personnel and photographic press personnel). The work area covers the FOH and BOH. However, it needs to be relatively isolated from the athlete area and the Olympic Family area and connected only in some areas such as the mixed zone and press conference room. The broadcast camera platform and the commentary positions in the stand area are one of the cores of media operations and should be located in reasonable positions.

Spectators are usually the most populous group in the venues. Sufficient distribution spaces should be reserved for ticket check, security screening, entrance, competition watching, and leaving after the competition, and spectator flow should be guided. In recent Olympic Games, the IOC has advocated providing the best viewing area of the stands to spectators with priority and the area adjacent to the FOP to "fan spectators". In addition to the spectator seats, a certain number of spectator standing positions will be set up in snow venues, which are generally close to the FOP.

Venue operation workforce provide service support for the above-mentioned client groups and these client groups are positioned according to their respective FA responsibilities and operational requirements. And, each FA is managed and controlled through accreditation zoning.

11. Why should the outdoor areas of the venues be as flat as possible without height differences?

The outdoor areas of a venue are divided into FOH and BOH. The FOH is mainly the activity area for spectators, with a large instantaneous flow of people entering and leaving the venue, and the flat site can ensure the safety of spectators to a greater extent. Especially, in consideration of the needs of people with disabilities for an accessible environment, the site should be free of steps and excessive height differences.

The BOH is the comprehensive operation area of various facilities, which is also the parking area of various working vehicles, so a flat site is also needed. In particular, the vehicles carrying the broadcasting equipment are very large and have a large turning radius, so the site needs to be flat and open to be suitable for operation. Therefore, height differences should be minimised in outdoor spaces around the venue, and curbs with height differences should not be set on any side of the roads.

12. Why should multiple compounds be set up outside the venues and what are their functions?

A compound is an area where support service facilities are set up in the outdoor area for major events. Major events are often accompanied by broadcasting activity demands, a large temporary power need is generated from refrigeration, lighting, audio, and the like, and various personnel generates demands for materials, food and beverage, waste removal and transport, and so on. Usually, there is not enough space in the venues to meet these temporary needs, so various types of compounds are set up outdoors. In the venue operational design for the Beijing 2022 Games, main compounds include broadcast compound, energy compound, food and beverage (FNB) compound, cleaning and waste (CNW) compound, and logistics compound.

The broadcast compound is the area where various broadcasting equipment, vehicles, and signal transmission and processing work are arranged. Broadcasting is one of the most important links of the Olympic Games. In the operational design, priority should be given to the space and facilities for broadcasting operations. The broadcast compound should be located close to the main body of the venue and it is necessary to consider the parking space and access convenience of large broadcast vans.

The energy compound mainly provides temporary power load and emergency power support for the venue, including standby power supply, temporary power supply vehicles, and corresponding office space. The venue power supply for the Beijing 2022 Games is generally guaranteed in three aspects and by four means. First, there are two independent "municipal power lines", second, UPS for at least 30min, and third, diesel generators. The above power supply modes can be seamlessly switched.

The FNB compound is the area for providing food and beverage services in the venue, which should be set in combination with the kitchen and the FNB concessions. Considerations should be given to vehicle access and unloading areas, storage space for all types of food ingredients, refrigerated storage areas, and FNB office space.

The CNW compound is a space for disposing of various wastes generated in the venue, as a transfer station. All wastes generated in the venue should be concentrated in the CNW compound for disposal. The main spaces include waste storage, classification, removal and transport spaces, vehicle turning and parking spaces, as well as tool storage and some office spaces.

The logistics compound is an area set up to ensure the storage, supply, transport, and recovery of materials within the venue, which is usually set up close to a road. It mainly includes the vehicle control point, unloading area, parking area, storage area for equipment such as containers and forklifts, and logistics office space.

13. What are the main areas related to broadcasting at venues? What are the main operational requirements of OBS in the venues?

The indoor broadcast compound mainly includes media work area, media lounge, media storage area, broadcast information office, commentary control room, mixed zone, press conference room, between-session interview zone, tabled press tribunes, non-tabled press tribunes, commentary position, observer seats, main camera platform, announce position, etc.

The outdoor broadcast compound mainly includes broadcast compound, satellite station, etc.

The operational demands of Olympic Broadcasting Services (OBS) in the venues mainly include space and equipment demands for various broadcast camera positions, temporary cable pathway trays, and broadcast compound, power supply demands for broadcasting, the needs of rights-holding broadcasters for broadcasting and distributing broadcasting signals, such as optical fibre technology lines.

14. What is a mixed zone? What are its key points of design?

A mixed zone is the area where the athletes receive broadcast and media interviews after completing the competitions or victory ceremonies, and also the most dynamic area in the media operations of the Olympic venues.

It is generally located in the finish area of the competition area. An exit for athletes to enter the mixed zone from the FOP and a media entrance should be provided, and a 2-3m wide passageway space should be provided for athletes. In addition, sufficient spaces should be ensured for a certain number of rights-holding broadcasters, non-rights-holding broadcasters, and journalists to carry out broadcasting and interview work. The athlete and media flows are arranged in parallel without crossing.

After the athletes enter the mixed zone, they pass through the broadcast compound first, and then the written press area. The athletes to be interviewed are stay in the corresponding area to be interviewed. Athletes who are not be interviewed return to the athlete changing room directly through the passageway of the mixed zone. Each broadcast interview position is about 1.8m wide and the written press position is about 1m wide. The length of the mixed zone in different venues varies depending on the number of broadcasters and media scheduled and the general flow length is about 100m.

15. What is the impact of COVID-19 on the venue operational design?

To cope with the COVID-19, Beijing 2022 issued a series of guiding policy documents, such as the Beijing 2022 Playbooks and the Guidelines on Closed-loop COVID-19 Management for the Olympic and Paralympic Winter Games Beijing 2022, and added the Public Health Services (PHS) FA to the original FAs of each venue to help the team in formulating an operational COVID-19 prevention plan for each venue.

The operational COVID-19 prevention plan has the following impacts on the operational design:

Operational zoning. According to the requirements of the COVID-19 prevention policy, all venues are divided into a closed-loop management zone and a non-closed-loop management zone, with physical separation between the two zones and a separation spacing of at least 2m in width. Personnel, vehicles, and materials in each zone can only move within the zone and completely independent entrances, exits, transport flows, and work areas are set up. COVID-19 prevention zoning is established on the basis of accreditation zoning and each accreditation zone should be included in the COVID-19 prevention zone as far as possible to reduce the crossing between accreditation zones and COVID-19 prevention zones.

Transport Flow. Point-to-point drop-off zones have been set up for various client groups from the residence to the work areas within the venues to ensure that athletes, Olympic Family members, media personnel, and the workforce can reach the work areas by dedicated buses, so as to minimise the crossing of personnel of different zones and reduce the risk of transmission of COVID-19. In the organisation of internal flows, independent entrances and exits are set for each type of client group to ensure that the flows from the drop-off zones to each work area are independent.

Personnel Plan. The spectators are organised and the number of spectators is reduced considering social distancing. The workforce is staffed according to the closed-loop management. For some FAs, workforce is needed both in the areas within and outside the closed loop and the total number is increased compared to the planned number before the COVID-19. The adjustment of the personnel plan bring about changes in the corresponding space, facilities, and materials.

Division of seats. The seating areas of a competition venue are also divided into a seating area inside the closed loop and a seating area outside the closed loop according to the COVID-19 countermeasures. The two types of seating areas are separated by transparent COVID-19 prevention partitions, with a spacing of 2m. Seats are used at intervals, so the actual capacity of venues is reduced during the Games

Overlays. Spectator-oriented event service facilities, such as spectator screening sheds, ticket offices, FNB concessions, and so on, are reduced due to the reduced number of spectators. Workforce-oriented overlays are increased, especially iron rails, fences, COVID-19 prevention partitions, and acrylic desk dividers.

As the COVID-19 situation continues to change, the operational design is adapted. In the OB6.1, COVID-19 prevention zoning is made in the COVID-19 prevention zoning drawing, reflecting various COVID-19 prevention separation facilities. The contents of COVID-19 prevention are defined in the OB7.0 and implemented accordingly.

16. How are areas inside and outside the closed loop of venues divided? How do they connect?

The closed-loop management is a special zoning management mode in the case of COVID-19 prevention and control, covering such FAs as Arrivals and Departures, Transport, Accommodation, Food and Beverage, Training, Competition, Victory Ceremonies, Opening and Closing Ceremonies, and Media Interview as well as places involved in the Beijing 2022 Games. The closed-loop management includes management inside the closed loop and management outside the closed loop. Among them, the management inside the closed loop refers to the closed management of a series of designated areas of places involved in the Beijing 2022 Games, such as venues and designated residences, and all the closed areas are connected to each other in a whole-process and point-to-point manner through designated vehicles. The management outside the closed loop refers to the management of low-risk personnel involved in the Beijing 2022 Games outside the closed area. Specific conditions in venues and designated residence are comprehensively considered to strictly control the cross-loop activities of personnel in different areas. A separation spacing of at least 2m in width should be set between the areas inside and outside the closed loop.

The connection between areas inside and outside the closed loop involves multiple conditions. For transport of materials from the area outside the closed loop to the area inside the closed loop, a special room is set in the transition area between the two areas to meet the demands by means of contactless distribution. In principle, it should be avoided to transport materials from the area inside the closed loop to the other area. When there are special needs (such as temporary toilet cleaning in the closed loop), the materials in the closed loop needed to be disinfected, left untouched for predefined periods and then transported outside the closed loop under the guidance of PHS of the venue team. When special conditions require personnel in the area outside the closed loop to work in the closed loop, the transition area should be set according to the model of "three areas and two passageways". The personnel outside the closed loop enter the area inside the closed loop after wearing the equipment according to the Level II protection standard in the transition area, finish the work inside the closed loop, and return to the area outside the closed loop after completing the disinfection and sterilisation in the transition area according to the COVID-19 countermeasures.

17. What is an FOP? Why are special drawings for the FOP included in the operational design?

FOP, the abbreviation of "Field of Play", refers to the field of play of a competition venue, including the competition area, the sports buffer area, and the general area of the required field of play. The FOP generally refers to the competition ice surface area in ice venues and the competition ski course area in snow venues.

The FOP is the core area of the Olympic Games and needs to be fully expressed. The FOP drawings can clearly express all the information in the FOP, including the goal, lines, face-off spot, players' seats, penalty bench, start gate, finish line, etc. They also express the areas used by all stakeholders around the FOP, including Sport, Broadcast Services, Press Operations, Technology, Medical Services, Cleaning and Waste, etc. The most important is that they can express the detailed operational flows of various groups of people and tasks including athletes, media, ice resurfacing machines, protocol, and ceremonies. Through the preparation of FOP drawings, it is possible to reasonably plan the areas and flows of various stakeholders during the pre-Games preparation period and reasonably arrange the operation of FOP areas in cooperation with the venue operation plan during the Games operation period.

The FOP drawings of one venue may vary according to different events. For example, there are different FOP drawings of the Capital Indoor Stadium for short track speed skating and figure skating. There are different FOP drawings of the National Alpine Skiing Centre for the Olympic Winter Games and the Paralympic Winter Games.

18. Why do we need many seats in the accredited seating in the venues? What are the main types of accredited seating? What are the key points of design?

Accredited seating refers to the seating for various accredited personnel, mainly including Olympic Family seats, commentary positions, announce positions, press tribunes, observer seats, spectating athletes' seats, etc. The accredited seating should be arranged according to the flows and numbers of personnel of various stakeholders and provide differentiated viewing angles according to the requirements of different stakeholders, and corresponding accessible seats.

Olympic Family seats are provided for IOC officials and invited IF officials, which are generally located at places with good viewing angles and close to the Olympic Family Lounge. These seats are divided into O, F, and H seats, which are provided for officials at different levels. Accessible seats should be provided in front of the Olympic Family seats during the Olympic Winter Games and the Paralympic Winter Games.

The commentary position is the stand work area of the rights-holding broadcasters of various countries to broadcast the events and give real-time commentary during the Games, which is erected to the pre-set quantity before the Games. It generally occupies a 2m×2m space, and can receive 2 to 3 persons. Due to the importance of broadcasting for the Games, the commentary position requires a better viewing position and viewing angle, and is located close to the commentary control room and the main camera platform. The commentary position in a snow venue is located in a permanent or temporary building in the stand area with a good view, where the competition venue can be viewed directly.

The announce position is mainly used for on-the-spot interviews and broadcasting of the competition, which is usually located close to the commentary position and is about 2m×4m in size. The moderator and interviewed guests take the FOP as the background and the camera is mounted behind the announce position.

The observer seats are an area for the IOC's observers, which are usually the existing seats in the venue and are located close to the commentary position. The observers include the workforce of the organising committees of the next Summer Games and the next Winter Games.

Press tribunes are composed of tabled press tribunes and non-tabled press tribunes, mainly used by journalists of various countries. The press tribunes should be located in the seating area with a good view of the venue. Generally, the tabled press tribunes are located in the front area and the non-tabled press tribunes are located in the rear area. The location of the press tribunes depends on the flow of the media, so that the media personnel can reach the mixed zone and the media workrooms more quickly from the press tribunes. In view of the outdoor temperature, there are no tabled press tribunes on the stands of snow venues.

Spectating athletes' seats are an area for spectators who do not compete on the same day, which have different requirements for use in the Olympic Winter Games and the Paralympic Winter Games. During the Olympic Winter Games, the spectating athletes' seats are usually located in the rear of the seating area, which will not affect the work of the broadcasting and press tribunes. During the Paralympic Winter Games, athletes in wheelchairs usually watch the Games directly around the FOP.

19. Why is it necessary to draw a layout of the suspended ceiling over the FOP?

There are many Games-time facilities such as funnel-shaped displays, venue lighting fixtures, speakers, broadcast cameras, cameras, a flag-raising system, NOC flags, ice projectors, and cable routes for connecting various types of facilities. By drawing the layout of the suspended ceiling over the FOP, the facilities, equipment, and cable pathways on the suspended ceiling of each FA can be reasonably and clearly designed to ensure independent operations and mutual cooperation without interference.

20. Why is it necessary to prepare an independent containment drawing?

In order to ensure the safe operation of the Games, a considerable number of containments, mainly including power pathways, technology pathways, and broadcast pathways, need to be laid inside and outside the venues, and these three types of pathways require very safe routes. Therefore, it necessary to prepare a special containment drawing.

The cables are laid separately by the three respective FAs of Energy, Technology, and Broadcast Services. The containments refer to the cable laying modes, including pipes, cable chases, cable hooks, trays, cable clamps, cover plates, and steel pipes, which are generally implemented by Venues and Infrastructure.

Power pathways mainly provide power supply for overlays inside and outside the venue, including cables, diesel generators, box transformers at all levels, and UPS.

Technology pathways mainly provide communication, information, venue technology, network security, and radiofrequency management for areas inside and outside the venue, including fixed communications, mobile communications, trunked radio, Olympic management information system, office management system, cable TV, etc.

Broadcast pathways mainly provide signal transmission for the broadcast points within and outside the venue, including the broadcast compound, camera position, commentary position, announce position, commentary control room, etc.

The containments drawing provides comprehensive pipelines for the above three different pathways, which shows the pipelines of all FAs. The pathways of all FAs are shown on the drawing to judge whether the pathways can meet the use requirements, whether there is a conflict between the pathways, whether there is a conflict between the pathways and the main operation flow, and finally a set of drawings is developed to meet the operation requirements of all parties to guide the site implementation and support.

21. What are the standards for accessible facilities at venues? What are the main points of operational design?

The accessible facilities at venues are designed in line with the Beijing 2022 Accessibility Guidelines. In September 2018, the Beijing 2022 issued the Beijing 2022 Accessibility Guidelines. The Guidelines was prepared based on the IPC Accessibility Guide and China's existing accessibility regulations and standards, as well as the accessibility guides of previous Olympic Games. In the Guidelines, the focus is given to the accessibility of venues and facilities, and attention is also paid to creating seamless connectivity in the accessible environment from the city to the venues. In addition, Beijing 2022 also prepared a series of technical guidance documents on the construction of accessible facilities at venues, and in September 2020, it published the Accessibility Guidelines for Olympic and Paralympic Winter Games Beijing 2022: An Illustrated Handbook.

All venues and facilities in the three zones in the Beijing 2022 Games have been constructed and delivered in accordance with the requirements of the above technical documents in terms of planning, design, construction, and operation.

In order to stage a Games that is "athlete-centred", the standards for the areas involved in the activities of athletes inside and outside the venues are appropriately improved. According to the physical characteristics and actual needs of athletes, automatic doors, accessible seats, accessible elevators, accessible bathrooms,

accessible showers, accessible ramps, tactile paving indicating the location of elevators, accessible changing rooms, low-height service desks, and accessible signage are provided and snow venues are also equipped with accessible wax cabins and gondola systems. Slight height differences should be eliminated and anti-slip safety measures should be added to ensure accessibility.

According to the Guidelines, the proportion of wheelchair seats for spectators in the venues for the Olympic Winter Games should be no less than 0.75% of the total seats in the venues, and the proportion of wheelchair seats for spectators in the venues for the Paralympic Winter Games should be no less than 1%. For the competition venues of the Paralympic Winter Games with wheelchair-using athletes, the wheelchair seats for spectators should be no less than 1.2%, and the wheelchair seats for spectators and companion seats should be set at a ratio of 1 : 1. No companion seats are required for wheelchair seats for athletes.

22. What contents have been added to the operational design of key venues for the Paralympic Winter Games?

A total of 28 venues were used during the Beijing 2022 Paralympic Winter Games, including 5 competition venues (National Aquatics Centre, National Indoor Stadium, National Alpine Skiing Centre, National Biathlon Centre, and Genting Snow Park) and 23 non-competition venues. They are located in the Beijing Zone, Yanqing Zone, and Zhangjiakou Zone. Except for Yanqing Medals Plaza for the Paralympic Winter Games, other venues continued to use the facilities that had served the Olympic Winter Games.

All venue drawings are marked with accessible facilities, such as accessible seats, accessible toilets, accessible elevators, accessible ramps, etc. In addition, for the 5 competition venues for the Paralympic Winter Games and 3 Paralympic Villages, drawings for the transition period are included in these drawings, which meet the special needs of the Paralympic Winter Games, such as the transition of the FOP and the changing rooms. Furthermore, the sizes of accessible facilities and the wheelchair flow are also specified in the drawings of the eight venues.

As all accessible facilities are covered in the venue drawings, no venue operation design is specially carried out for the Paralympic Winter Games, and the same set of design drawings for the Olympic Winter Games is shared.

北京赛区

Beijing
Zone

国家速滑馆-National Speed Skating Oval [NSS]
国家游泳中心-National Aquatics Centre [NAC]
国家体育馆-National Indoor Stadium [NIS]
首都体育馆-Capital Indoor Stadium [CTS]
首都花样滑冰训练馆-CTS Figure Skating Training Hall [CFT]
首体短道速滑训练馆-CTS Short Track Speed Skating Training Hall [CST]
五棵松体育中心-Wukesong Sports Centre [WKS]
五棵松冰球训练馆-WKS Ice Hockey Training Hall [WIT]
首钢滑雪大跳台-Big Air Shougang [BAS]
北京冬奥村/冬残奥村-Beijing Olympic/Paralympic Village [BVL]
主媒体中心-Main Media Centre [MMC]
北京颁奖广场-Beijing Medals Plaza [BMP]
奥林匹克大家庭酒店-Olympic Family Hotel [OFH]
北京奥林匹克公园公共区-Beijing Olympic Park [BOP]
北京冬奥组委总部-Beijing 2022 Headquarter [BHQ]
制服和注册中心-Uniform Distribution and Accreditation Centre [UAC]
运行指挥部调度中心-Beijing 2022 MOC Coordination Centre [MCC]

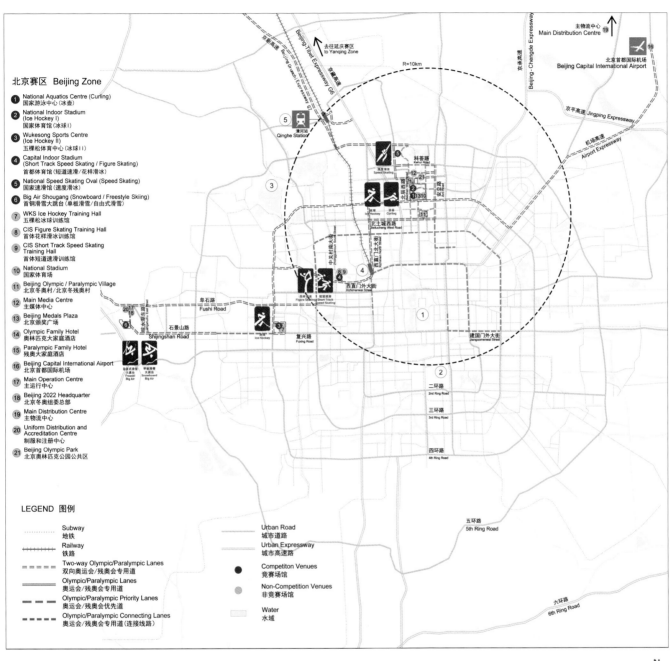

北京赛区场馆和基础设施布局图
Beijing Zone Venues and Infrastruction Layout

北京赛区位于北京中心城范围内，海拔约50m。北京赛区冬奥会共有25个场馆，包括6个竞赛场馆、3个训练场馆和16个非竞赛场馆（冬残奥会共有2个竞赛场馆和15个非竞赛场馆）。北京赛区共承担4个大项（冰壶、冰球、滑冰、滑雪）、7个分项（冰壶、冰球、短道速滑、花样滑冰、速度滑冰、单板滑雪、自由式滑雪）、37个小项的比赛。北京赛区的场馆主要分布在4个区域，分别是：北京奥林匹克公园、首都体育馆场馆群、五棵松体育中心和首钢/京能园区。

Beijing Zone is located in downtown Beijing, at an altitude of about 50m. It contains 25 venues, including 6 competition venues, 3 training venues, and 16 non-competition venues. It hosted 37 events in 7 disciplines (Curling, Ice Hockey, Short Track Speed Skating, Figure Skating, Speed Skating, Snowboard, and Freestyle Skiing) across 4 sports (Curling, Ice hockey, Skating, and Skiing).
Venues in this zone are categorised into 4 groups, namely the Beijing Olympic Park, the Capital Indoor Stadium venue cluster, Wukesong Sports Centre, and the Shougang/Jingneng Park.

场馆业主 提供
Provide by Venue Owner

国家速滑馆 [NSS]
National Speed Skating Oval

1. 场馆基本情况

国家速滑馆位于奥林匹克森林公园西侧，是北京2022年冬奥会的标志性新建场馆。国家速滑馆是一个关于"速度"的设计，将"冰"和"速度"相结合，形成"冰丝带"的概念，并与"鸟巢""水立方"交相辉映，成为冬夏两个奥运的地标场馆。国家速滑馆还集成了超大跨结构、自由曲面幕墙、环保节能型制冷系统等创新技术。

冬奥会期间，国家速滑馆承担速度滑冰项目的比赛和训练，产生14枚金牌，冬奥会后，将成为能够举办滑冰、冰球和冰壶等国际赛事及大众进行冰上活动的多功能场馆。

国家速滑馆总用地面积16.6万m²，总建筑面积12.6万m²。

2. FOP及相关区域

国家速滑馆采用1.2万m²的全冰面设计，使用二氧化碳跨临界直冷制冰技术。通过冰面分区控制，可满足速度滑冰、短道速滑、花样滑冰、冰壶、冰球等不同类型冰上运动的竞赛要求。

速度滑冰比赛赛道长400m，弯道内道边缘半径为26m，直道长度为110.43m。冰面海拔为43.6m。比赛赛道由内向外，包括5m宽热身道、4m宽内赛道和5m宽外赛道，赛道外侧设

1. Venue Overview

Located to the west of the Beijing Olympic Forest Park, the National Speed Skating Oval is a new landmark venue for the Beijing 2022 Olympic Winter Games. Around the theme of "speed", the design of the National Speed Skating Oval combines "ice" and "speed" and forms the concept of "Ice Ribbon".

The National Speed Skating Oval is a venue for speed skating competitions and training during the Olympic Winter Games Beijing 2022, with 14 gold medals won here. After the Games, the National Speed Skating Oval will become a multifunctional venue for hosting international Skating, Ice Hockey and Curling events as well as ice activities for the public.

The National Speed Skating Oval covers a total area of 166,000m² and has a total floor area of 126,000m².

2. FOP and Relevant Areas

The National Speed Skating Oval is designed with a 12,000m² full ice surface, with the CO_2 trans-critical refrigeration technology adopted. The venue can meet the competition requirements of different ice sports such as speed skating, short track speed skating, figure skating, curling, and ice hockey through ice surface zoning control.

The speed skating track inside the venue is 400m long, with an inner radius of 26m and straights of 110.43m long. The altitude of

0.8m宽防护垫。热身道内侧另设4m宽训练道。

3. 场馆前院及观众流线

国家速滑馆馆外中轴西侧和馆内观众厅区域为场馆前院区，为观众提供集散空间、观赛、售卖等服务。观众在赛时主要以地铁等公共交通，步行到达场馆外观众集散广场处安检、验票入馆，经过集散大厅进入看台观赛。

4. 场馆后院及注册人员流线

国家速滑馆馆外中轴东侧和馆内非观众厅区域为场馆后院区。

（1）运动员流线

运动员乘坐大巴，经奥林西路和速滑馆北路，通过车检进入场馆安保线内，经过东侧地下车道到达地下二层运动员大巴落客点，通过运动员入口进入更衣室，全程与其他客户群流线不交叉。

国家速滑馆赛时共设置了14套运动员更衣室，每套更衣室采用相似的大小及布局，包含更衣区、按摩室、卫生间、淋浴间等功能。运动员从更衣室出来后通过地下二层场心楼梯到达比赛场地（FOP）。

比赛结束后，通过场心楼梯回到地下二层，穿过混合采访区回到更衣室。

（2）技术官员流线

技术官员通过主馆地下二层东侧入口进入场馆，通过楼梯到达地下一层竞赛管理区。竞赛管理区共设置3间综合办公区，3间大会议室及多间办公、储藏室。

（3）奥林匹克大家庭成员流线

奥林匹克大家庭成员通过位于主馆东侧首层的大家庭入口进入场馆，经过电梯或扶梯到达二层大家庭区。大家庭区设有225m²开放的休息室，位于速滑馆幕墙空间下，充分体现"冰丝带"的美，另外还有108m²和122m²的两个独立休息室，可直接看见比赛大厅，也可以便捷到达看台。

国家速滑馆赛时还设置了国内贵宾休息室，位于二层西侧。

（4）媒体流线

媒体工作人员乘坐班车到达东北侧下沉庭院附近落客，通过首层媒体入口进入场馆、看台，到达媒体坐席和摄影位置。需要去地下一层媒体工作间和地下二层新闻发布厅的媒体工作人员，乘坐首层东北侧电梯可达。

转播工作人员到达场馆东南侧转播综合区附近落客，需进入场馆的工作人员从东南侧转播入口进入，经集散大厅后到达看台、评论员席、转播平台、观察员席、首层东北侧的评论员控制室、转播信息办公室等区域。需要去地下一层FOP缓冲区转播平台和地下二层混合区的工作人员，乘坐首层东北侧电梯可达。

拥有进入FOP区域权限的转播工作人员通过地下二层场心楼梯进入FOP。

5. 场馆坐席

国家速滑馆西侧为观众坐席，南北东为后院看台区。国家速滑馆坐席容量为11805个，包含95个无障碍坐席和95个无障碍陪同席。其中观众坐席为4615个（赛时为2892个）。注册坐席包括评论员坐席31个、观察员坐席59个、带桌媒体坐席182个、不带桌媒体坐席163个、运动员坐席208个、奥林匹克大家庭坐席332个。

the ice surface is 43.6m. From inside to outside, the track includes a 5m-wide warm-up lane, a 4m-wide inner lane, and a 5m-wide outer lane, with 0.8m-wide protective pads provided on the outer side of the track. A 4m-wide training lane is also set inside the warm-up lane.

3. Front of House and Spectator Flow

During the Games, spectators mainly take public transport, such as the subway, to reach the related station, then walk to the concourse area outside the venue, pass through security checks and ticket checking to enter the venue, and then pass through the concourse hall to reach the stand to watch competitions.

4. Back of House and Accreditation Flow

(1) Athlete Flow

During the Games, the National Speed Skating Oval provides a total of 14 athlete dressing rooms, with each of similar size and layout, including a dressing area, a massage room, a toilet, and a shower. After leaving their dressing rooms, athletes go to the FOP via the B2 central stairs.

(2) Technical Official Flow

Technical officials enter the venue via the east entrance on B2 of the main venue and then go to the B1 competition management area via the stairs. The competition management area has 3 comprehensive office areas, 3 large meeting rooms, and multiple offices and storage rooms.

(3) Olympic Family Flow

Olympic Family members enter the venue via the Olympic Family entrance on the first floor in the east of the main venue and go to the Olympic Family area on the second floor via the elevator or escalator. The Olympic Family area has a 225-square-metre open lounge under the venue's curtain wall space, which fully presents the beauty of the "Ice Ribbon", and also two separate lounges of 108m² and 122m² with direct views of the FOP and easy access to the stand.

(4) Media Flow

Media staff members take shuttle buses to get off near the sunken courtyard on the northeast side and then enter the venue or stand via the media entrance on the first floor to reach press tribunes and photo positions. Media staff who need to go to the B1 media workroom and B2 press conference room can take the elevator in the northeast of the first floor.

Broadcast staff members take vehicles to get off near the broadcast compound to the southeast of the venue. Those who need to enter the venue can enter from the southeast broadcaster entrance and then, via the concourse hall, go to the stand, commentary positions, broadcast platforms, observer seats, commentary control room in the northeast of the first floor, broadcast information office, etc.

5. Seating Area

The spectator seating area is in the west of the National Speed Skating Oval, and BOH seating areas are in the south, north, and east thereof. The seating capacity of the National Speed Skating Oval is 11,805, including 95 accessible seats and 95 companion seats. There are 4,615 (2,892 during the Games) spectator seats, and the accredited seats include 31 commentary positions, 59 observer seats, 182 tabled press tribune seats, 163 non-tabled press tribune seats, 208 spectator seats, and 332 Olympic Family seats.

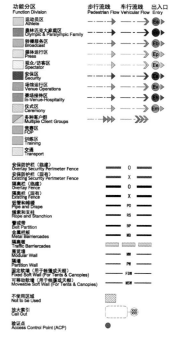

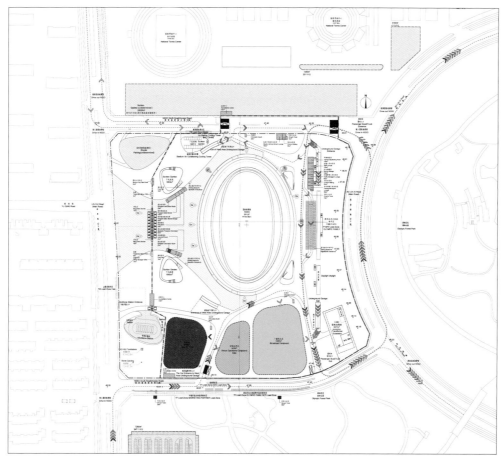

NSS 总平面图 OB1.2版
NSS Master Plan OB1.2

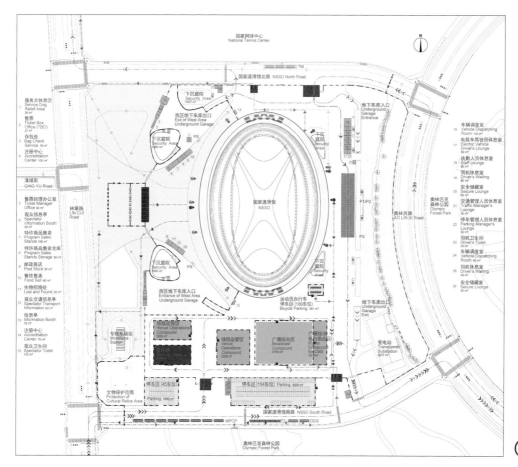

NSS 总平面图 OB2.1版
NSS Master Plan OB2.1

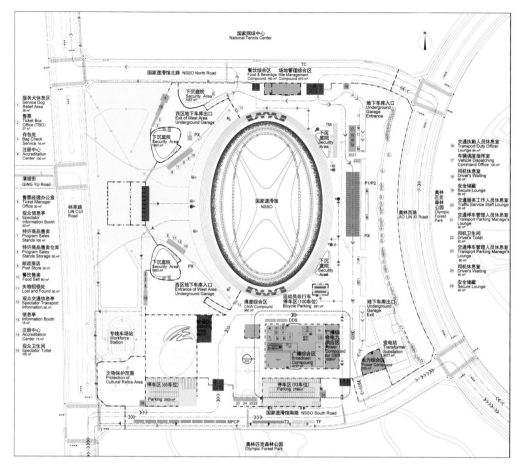

N
NSS 总平面图 OB3.0版
NSS Master Plan OB3.0

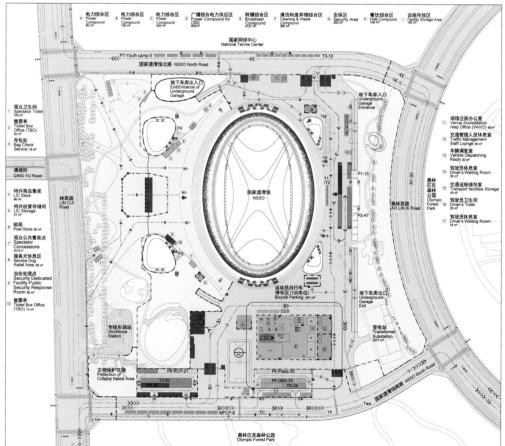

N
NSS 总平面图 OB4.0版
NSS Master Plan OB4.0

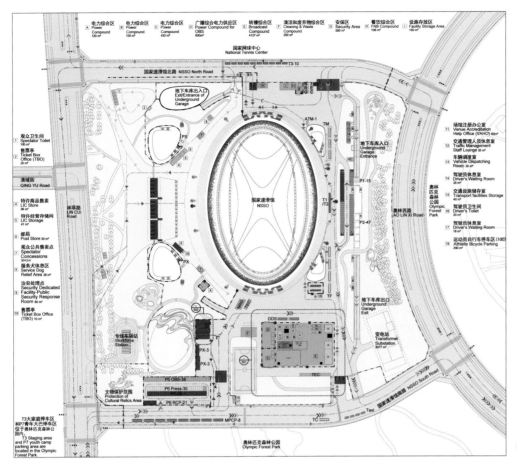

NSS 总平面图 OB5.0版
NSS Master Plan OB5.0

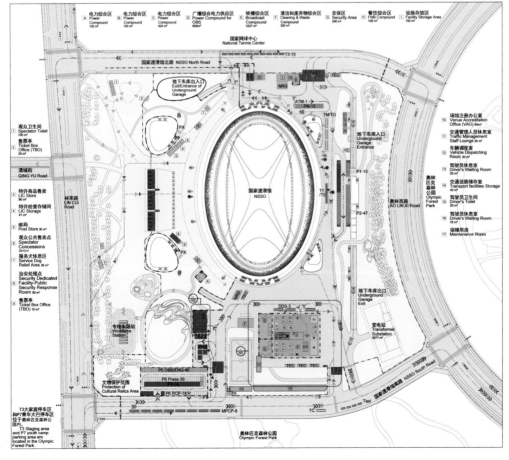

NSS 总平面图 OB6.0版
NSS Master Plan OB6.0

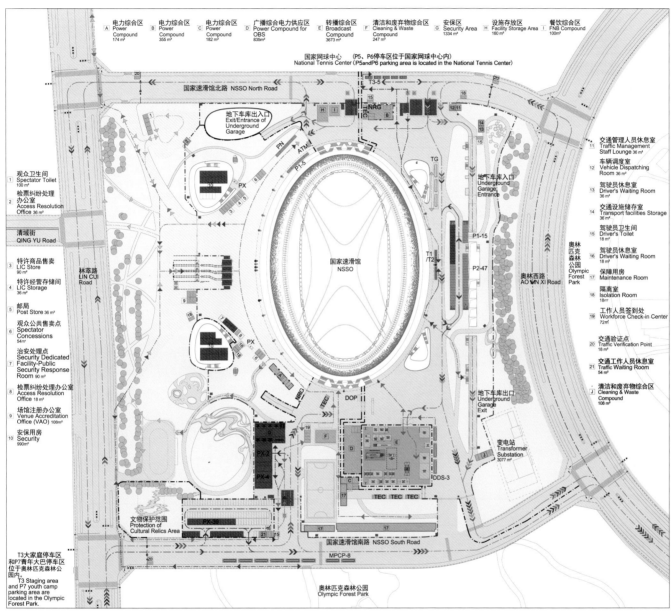

A 电力综合区 Power Compound 174 m²
B 电力综合区 Power Compound 355 m²
C 电力综合区 Power Compound 182 m²
D 广播综合电力供应区 Power Compound for OBS 835m²
E 转播综合区 Broadcast Compound 3673 m²
F 清洁和废弃物综合区 Cleaning & Waste Compound 247 m²
G 安保区 Security Area 1334 m²
H 设施存放区 Facility Storage Area 160 m²
I 餐饮综合区 FNB Compound 100m²

国家网球中心 （P5、P6停车区位于国家网球中心内）
National Tennis Center（P5andP6 parking area is located in the National Tennis Center）

国家速滑馆北路 NSSO North Road

地下车库出入口
Exit/Entrance of Underground Garage

清域街
QING YU Road

林萃路
LIN CUI Road

国家速滑馆
NSSO

奥林西路
AO LIN XI Road

奥林匹克森林公园
Olympic Forest Park

地下车库入口
Underground Garage Entrance

地下车库出口
Underground Garage Exit

变电站
Transformer Substation 3077 m²

国家速滑馆南路 NSSO South Road

文物保护范围
Protection of Cultural Relics Area

T3大家庭停车区和P7青年大巴停车区位于奥林匹克森林公园内。
T3 Staging area and P7 youth camp parking area are located in the Olympic Forest Park.

奥林匹克森林公园
Olympic Forest Park

1 观众卫生间 Spectator Toilet 100 m²
2 检票纠纷处理办公室 Access Resolution Office 36 m²
3 特许商品售卖 LIC Store 90 m²
4 特许经营储存间 LIC Storage 36 m²
5 邮局 Post Store 36 m²
6 观众公共售卖点 Spectator Concessions 54m²
7 治安处理点 Security Dedicated Facility-Public Security Response Room 90 m²
8 检票纠纷处理办公室 Access Resolution Office 18 m²
9 场馆注册办公室 Venue Accreditation Office (VAO) 108m²
10 安保用房 Security 990m²

11 交通管理人员休息室 Traffic Management Staff Lounge 36 m²
12 车辆调度室 Vehicle Dispatching Room 36 m²
13 驾驶员休息室 Driver's Waiting Room 36 m²
14 交通设施储存室 Transport facilities Storage 36 m²
15 驾驶员卫生间 Driver's Toilet 18 m²
16 驾驶员休息室 Driver's Waiting Room 18 m²
17 保障用房 Maintenance Room
18 隔离室 Isolation Room 18m²
19 工作人员签到处 Workforce Check-in Center 72m²
20 交通验证点 Traffic Verification Point 18 m²
21 交通工作人员休息室 Traffic Waiting Room 54 m²
J 清洁和废弃物综合区 Cleaning & Waste Compound 108 m²

NSS 总平面图 OB7.0版
NSS Master Plan OB7.0

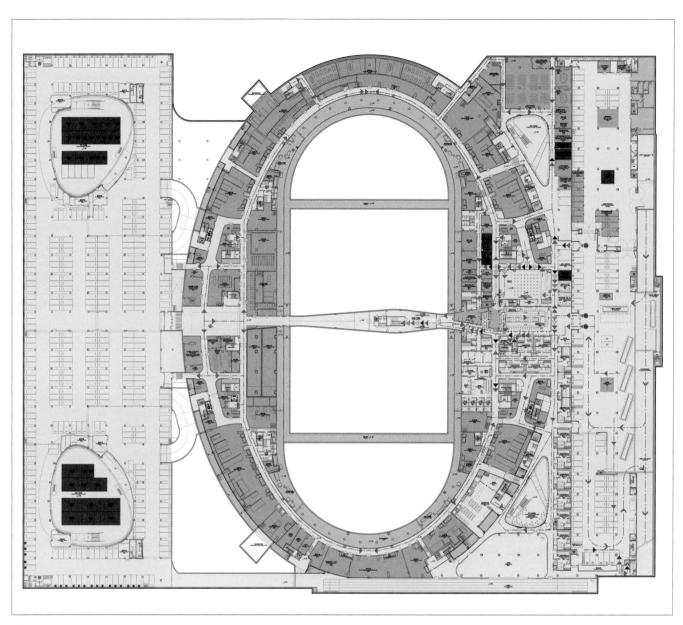

N

NSS 地下二层平面图 OB7.0版
NSS B2 Plan OB7.0

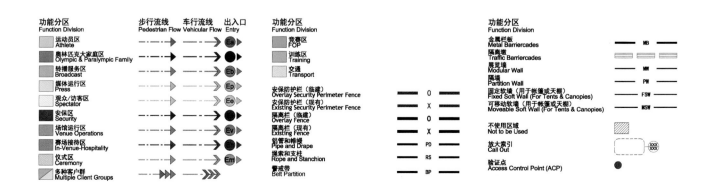

功能分区
Function Division

运动员区
Athlete

奥林匹克大家庭区
Olympic & Paralympic Family

转播服务区
Broadcast

媒体运行区
Press

观众/访客区
Spectator

安保区
Security

场馆运行区
Venue Operations

赛场接待区
In-Venue-Hospitality

仪式点
Ceremony

多种客户群
Multiple Client Groups

步行流线
Pedestrian Flow

车行流线
Vehicular Flow

出入口
Entry

Ea

Eb

Ep

Ee

Ev

Eih

Em

功能分区
Function Division

竞赛区
FOP

训练区
Training

交通
Transport

安保防护栏（临建）
Overlay Security Perimeter Fence

安保防护栏（现有）
Existing Security Perimeter Fence

隔离栏（临建）
Overlay Fence

隔离栏（现有）
Existing Fence

铝管和帷幕
Pipe and Drape

摸索和支柱
Rope and Stanchion

警戒带
Belt Partition

O

X

O

X

PD

RS

BP

功能分区
Function Division

金属栏板
Metal Barriercades

隔离墩
Traffic Barriercades

展览墙
Modular Wall

隔墙
Partition Wall

固定软墙（用于帐篷或天棚）
Fixed Soft Wall (For Tents & Canopies)

可移动软墙（用于帐篷或天棚）
Moveable Soft Wall (For Tents & Canopies)

不使用区域
Not to be Used

放大索引
Call Out

验证点
Access Control Point (ACP)

MB

MW

PW

FSW

MSW

XXX

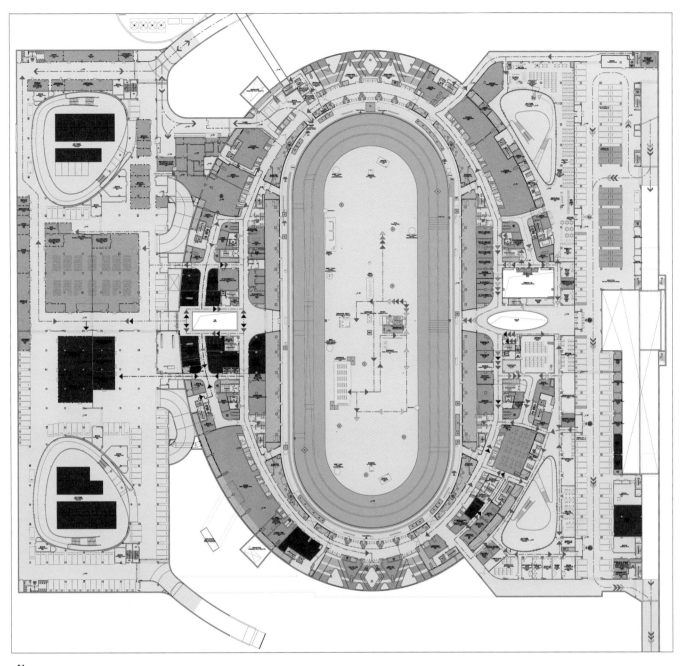

N

NSS 地下一层平面图 OB7.0版
NSS B1 Plan OB7.0

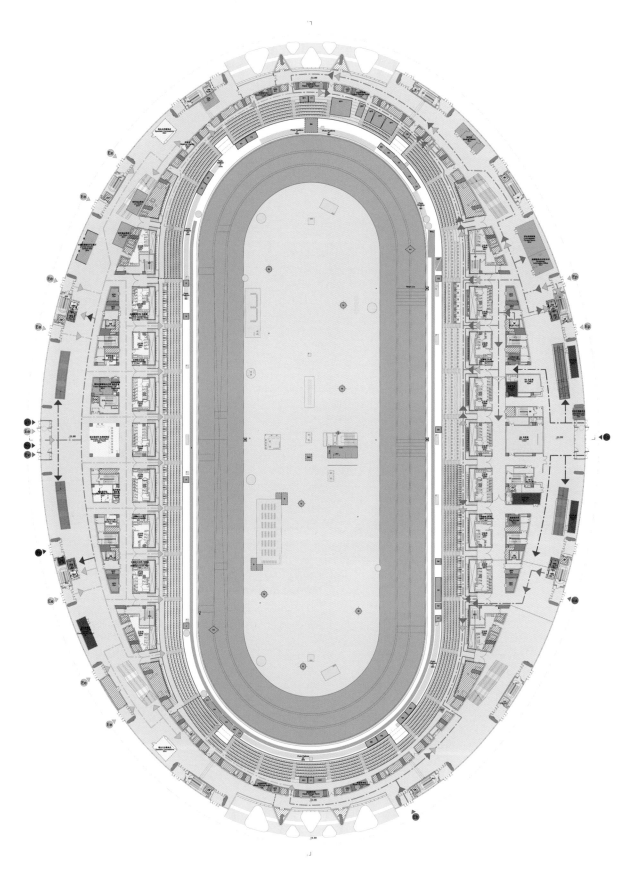

N
NSS 一层平面图 OB7.0版
NSS 1F Plan OB7.0

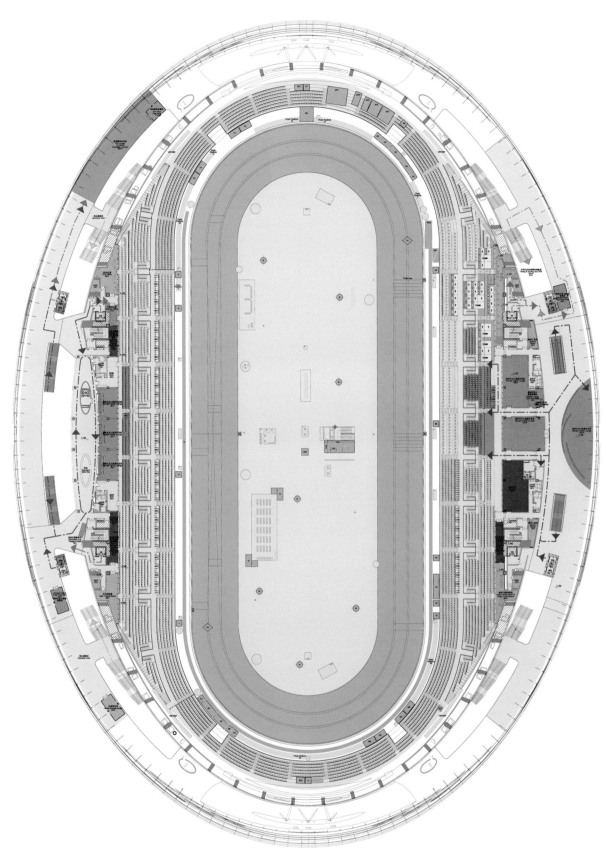

NSS 二层平面图 OB7.0版
NSS 2F Plan OB7.0

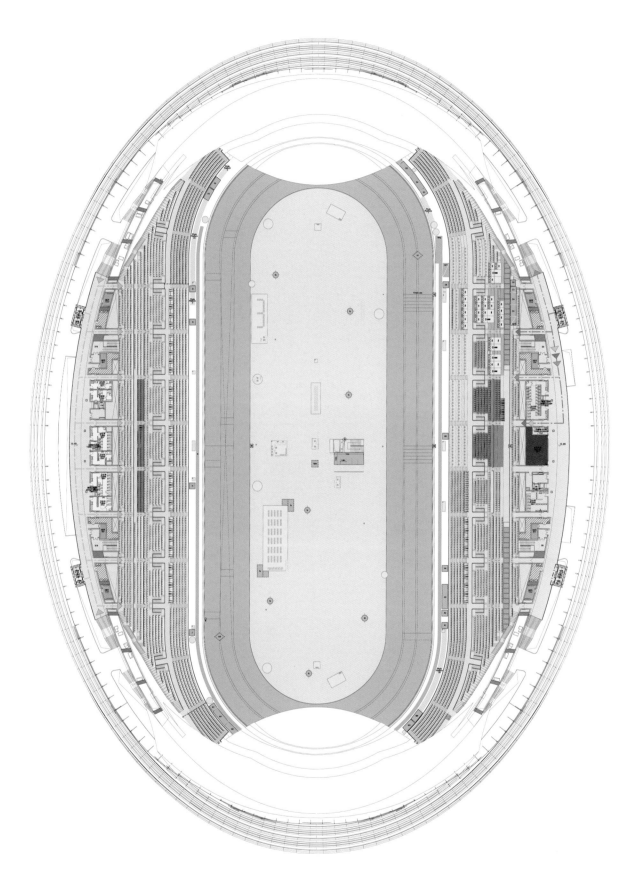

N
NSS 三层平面图 OB7.0版
NSS 3F Plan OB7.0

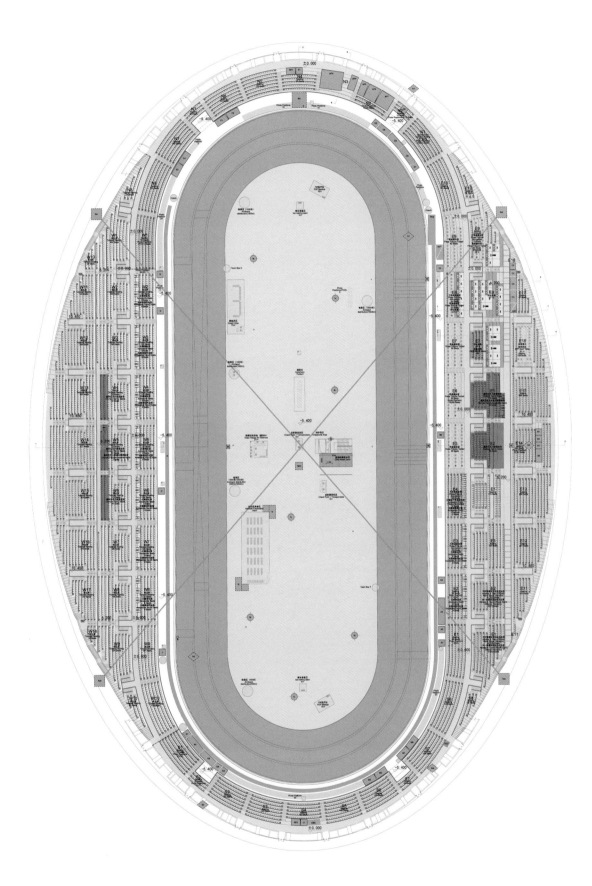

NSS 看台层平面图 OB7.0版
NSS Seat Bowl Plan OB7.0

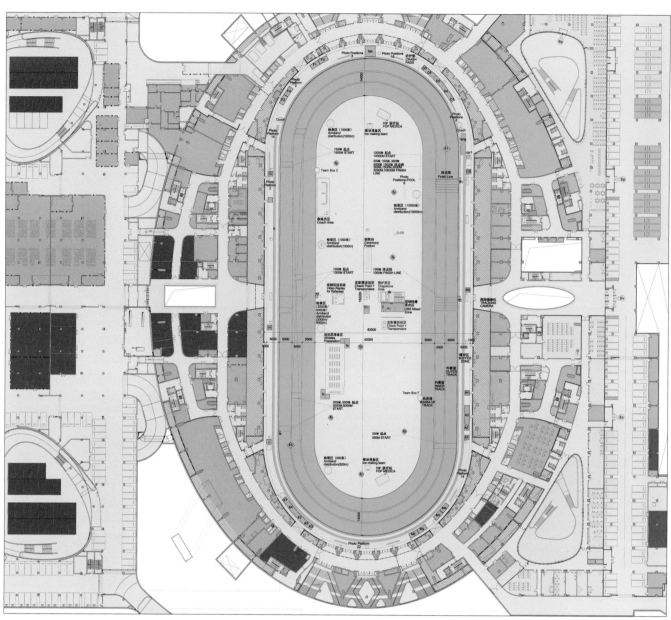

N
NSS FOP平面图 OB7.0版
NSS FOP Plan OB7.0

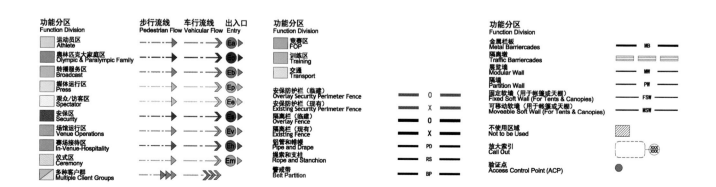

功能分区
Function Division

运动员区
Athlete

奥林匹克大家庭区
Olympic & Paralympic Family

转播服务区
Broadcast

媒体运行区
Press

观众/访客区
Spectator

安保区
Security

场馆运行区
Venue Operations

赛事接待区
In-Venue-Hospitality

仪式区
Ceremony

多种客户群
Multiple Client Groups

步行流线
Pedestrian Flow

车行流线
Vehicular Flow

出入口
Entry

Ea
Ep
Eb
Ep
Ee
Es
Ev
Eh
Em

功能分区
Function Division

竞赛区
FOP

训练区
Training

交通
Transport

安保防护栏（临建）
Overlay Security Perimeter Fence   O

安保防护栏（现有）
Existing Security Perimeter Fence   X

隔离栏（临建）
Overlay Fence   O

隔离栏（现有）
Existing Fence   X

铝管和帷幕
Pipe and Drape   PD

提索和支柱
Rope and Stanchion   RS

警戒带
Belt Partition   BP

功能分区
Function Division

金属栏板
Metal Barriercades   MB

隔离墩
Traffic Barriercades

展览墙
Modular Wall   MW

隔墙
Partition Wall   PW

固定软墙（用于帐篷或天棚）
Fixed Soft Wall (For Tents & Canopies)   FSW

可移动软墙（用于帐篷或天棚）
Moveable Soft Wall (For Tents & Canopies)   MSW

不使用区域
Not to be Used

放大索引
Call Out

验证点
Access Control Point (ACP)

082

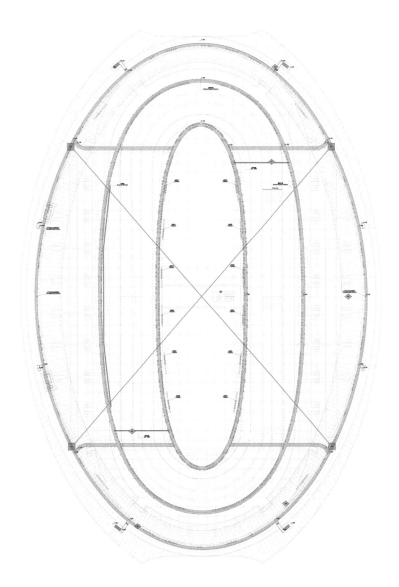

N NSS 马道平面图 OB7.0版
NSS Catwalk Plan OB7.0

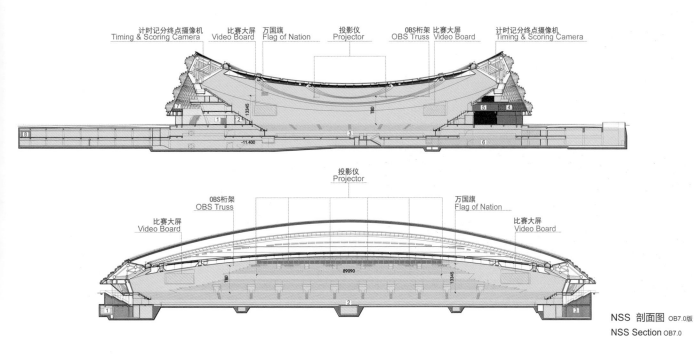

NSS 剖面图 OB7.0版
NSS Section OB7.0

国家游泳中心 [NAC]
National Aquatics Centre

1. 场馆基本情况

国家游泳中心位于北京奥林匹克公园中心区，在北京2008年夏奥会期间承担游泳、跳水、花样游泳和水球项目的比赛，是夏奥会的标志性场馆之一。国家游泳中心在北京冬奥会和冬残奥会期间承担冰壶和轮椅冰壶的比赛，分别产生3枚和1枚金牌。

国家游泳中心采用可逆的"水冰转换"设施来实现"水立方"到"冰立方"的功能转换，是目前世界上唯一的"水冰转换"双奥场馆。场馆总建筑面积约8万m²。

2. FOP及相关区域

FOP位于场馆地下一层比赛大厅，通过搭建可转换的钢架结构及可拆装的制冰系统，形成4条冰壶标准赛道，赛后制冰设备和冰层移除后，冰场即可还原为游泳池。赛道与周边区域高差0.6m，通过1/20的无障碍坡道连接。环绕赛道周边布置计时记分牌、教练员席、获奖运动员等候区、体育展示控制台、FOP医疗站、摄影位置等功能。

FOP北侧为运动员区，包含运动员更衣室、休息区、热身区、运动员医疗站及兴奋剂检查站等。FOP南侧为技术用房、

1. Venue Overview

Located in the central area of the Beijing Olympic Park, as one of the landmark venues of the Beijing 2008 Games, the National Aquatics Centre is the competition venue for Swimming, Diving, Synchronised Swimming and Water Polo events during the Beijing 2008 Games. It is also the competition venue for Curling events during the Beijing 2022 Olympic Winter Games, with 3 gold medals won here, and the competition venue for Wheelchair Curling competitions during the Beijing 2022 Paralympic Winter Games, with 1 gold medal won here.

The National Aquatics Centre realises the transformation from "Water Cube" to "Ice Cube" through the reversible "water ice conversion" and is currently the only venue for both the Summer and Winter Games in the world using such a method. The venue has a total floor area of about 80,000m².

2. FOP and Relevant Areas

The FOP is in the competition hall on B1 of the venue. A convertible steel frame structure and a removable ice-making system have been built to create 4 standard curling sheets. The ice rink can be restored to a swimming pool upon removing ice-making equipment and ice surface after the Games. Timing devices and scoreboards, coach

制冰设备用房及竞赛管理用房，其中竞赛管理用房包括世界壶联办公室、国际技术官员休息室、竞赛管理办公室、计时和统计办公区等。FOP东侧为媒体看台和运动员无障碍坡道，利用跳水池区域临时搭建而成，无障碍坡道总长120m，坡度1/20，运动员进入场馆后通过该坡道可便捷地到达运动员区。FOP西侧为媒体工作区，包括记者工作区、新闻发布厅、新闻运行工作区、转播信息办公室、评论员控制室等，利用原有游泳热身池临时搭建而成。

3. 场馆前院及观众流线

国家游泳中心南广场区域为场馆前院，观众从检票口进入南广场，从6号门进入场馆后，进入南侧观众坐席。在南侧大厅设有观众信息亭、特许经营商店、邮政商品售卖、邮政储存、失物招领处、观众售卖点、观众医疗站等设施。

4. 场馆后院及注册流线

国家游泳中心北广场和馆内非观众区域为场馆的后院区。

（1）运动员流线

运动员由奥运村乘坐大巴到达国家游泳中心，由场馆4号门进入场馆。通过楼梯或无障碍坡道进入地下一层运动员区域。根据参赛队伍数量，共设置了22套运动员更衣室，均为无障碍更衣室，并采用同样的大小及布局，包含更衣室、按摩室、卫生间、淋浴间等功能。其中10套集装箱更衣室，采用装配式的建造形式，另外12套利用原有永久房间改造。从更衣室可以便捷地到达比赛和热身区，比赛结束后，运动员在混合采访区接受采访后，返回运动员更衣室。

（2）技术官员流线

技术官员通过位于场馆后院的0号门进入场馆，由坡道直接进入到地下一层，到达办公区及休息室。

（3）奥林匹克大家庭成员流线

奥林匹克大家庭成员通过位于场馆后院的3号门进入场馆，然后乘坐专用电梯到达二层大家庭区域。大家庭区域设置了600m²的休息区及备餐间、大家庭看台及坐席区等，活动流线独立。

（4）媒体流线

转播及新闻媒体通过位于场馆后院的1号门进入场馆，可通过一层直接进入到媒体看台区域，也可以通过专用电梯和楼梯下到地下一层媒体工作区。媒体工作区1500m²，设有文字记者及摄影工作间、媒体休息区等用房。媒体工作区紧邻比赛场地、媒体混采区、媒体坐席及新闻发布厅，可在最短的时间内抵达各个点位。

（5）场馆室外综合区

室外综合区设置在场馆西侧，其中西北侧为闭环内区域，设置了闭环内停车场及转播综合区。西南侧为闭环外区域，设置了餐饮、物流、清废及电力综合区。

5. 场馆坐席

场馆坐席包括原有南北两侧固定坐席，以及东西两侧分别加建的临时媒体看台，坐席数3002个，包含58个无障碍坐席和58个无障碍陪同席。其中北侧看台中央设置奥林匹克大家庭坐席138个，包括14个无障碍坐席和无障碍陪同席；东北侧看台设置运动员坐席292个，包含12个无障碍坐席和无障碍陪同席；北侧看台、西北侧和东西两侧临时看台为转播与媒体席，其中转播坐席92个，媒体坐席230个；南侧看台设置观众坐席1296个。

benches, medallist waiting area, sport presentation console, FOP medial station, photo positions, etc. are arranged around the sheets. The athletes' compound is on the north side of the FOP, including the athlete dressing room, lounge, warm-up area, medical station, and doping control station. Technology rooms, ice-making equipment rooms, and competition management rooms are on the south side of the FOP. The competition management rooms include the WCF office, ITO lounge, competition management office, and timing and statistics office area. The press tribunes and athletes' accessible ramp are on the east side of the FOP. Temporarily built in the swimming pool area, the accessible ramp is 120m long with a slope of 1/20, via which athletes can conveniently reach the athletes' compound after entering the venue. The media work area is on the west side of the FOP.

3. Front of House and Spectator Flow

The South Square area of the National Aquatics Centre serves as the Front of House (FOH). Spectators enter the South Square from ticket check points, then enter the venue from Gate 6, and go to the spectator seating area in the south.

4. Back of House and Accreditation Flow

(1) Athlete Flow

Athletes take buses from the Olympic Village to the National Aquatics Centre and enter the venue from Gate 4. Then they enter the B1 athletes' compound via the stairs or accessible ramp. Depending on the number of the teams, a total of 22 athlete dressing rooms are provided, all of which are accessible ones of the same size and layout, each including a dressing area, a massage room, a toilet, and a shower. 10 are prefabricated container dressing rooms, and the other 12 are renovated from the original permanent rooms.

(2) Technical Official Flow

Technical officials enter the venue from Gate 0 in the BOH, then directly enter B1 from the ramp, and then go to their office area and lounge.

(3) Olympic Family Flow

Olympic Family members enter the venue from Gate 3 in the BOH and then take the dedicated elevator to the Olympic Family area on the second floor. The Olympic Family area has a 600-square-metre lounge and food preparation room as well as an Olympic Family stand and a seating area.

(4) Media Flow

Broadcast and media personnel enter the venue from Gate 1 in the BOH and can then directly enter the press tribunes on the first floor or take the dedicated elevator and stairs to the B1 media work area. With an area of 1,500m², the media work area has rooms such as press and photographer work rooms and media lounge.

5. Seating Area

The total capacity of the National Aquatics Centre is 3,002, including 58 accessible seats and 58 companion seats. In the north stand, there are 138 Olympic Family seats in the middle, including 14 accessible seats and companion seats; in the northeast stand, there are 292 athlete seats, including 12 accessible seats and companion seats; in the north stand, northwest temporary stand, and east and west temporary stands, there are broadcast and press tribune seats, including 92 broadcast seats and 230 press tribune seats; in the south stand, there are 1,296 spectator seats. seats.

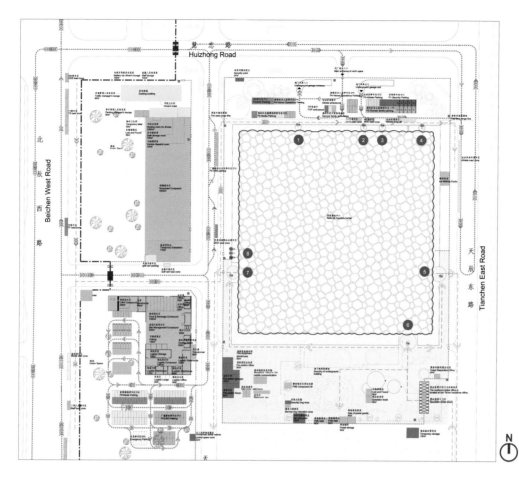

NAC 总平面图 OB1.2版
NAC Master Plan OB1.2

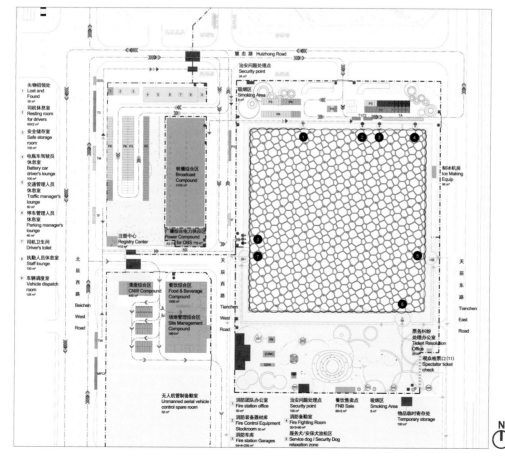

失物招领处
Lost and
Found
50 m²

司机休息室
Resting room
for drivers
60X2 m²

安全储存室
Safe storage
room
100 m²

电瓶车驾驶员
休息室
Battery car
driver's lounge
100 m²

交通管理人员
休息室
Traffic manager's
lounge
60 m²

停车管理人员
休息室
Parking
manager's
lounge
60 m²

司机卫生间
Driver's toilet

执勤人员休息室
Staff lounge
100 m²

车辆调度室
Vehicle dispatch
room
128 m²

无人机管制备勤室
Unmanned aerial vehicle
control spare room
32 m²

消防团队办公室
Fire station office
50 m²

消防装备材料库
Fire Control Equipment
Stockroom 50 m²

消防车库
Fire station Garages
64+256 m²

治安问题处理点
Security point
24 m²

消防备勤室
Fire Fighting Room
30×90 m²

服务犬/安保大放松区
Service dog / Security Dog
relaxation zone

餐饮售卖点
FNB Sale
60×2 m²

物品临时寄存处
Temporary storage
100 m²

吸烟区
Smoking Area
8 m²

NAC 总平面图 OB2.1版
NAC Master Plan OB2.1

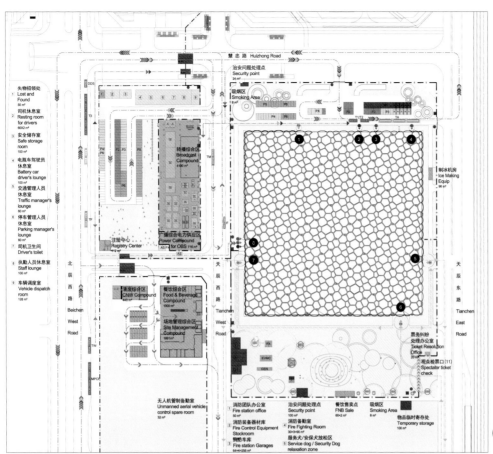

1 失物招领处 Lost and Found 50 m²
2 司机休息室 Resting room for drivers 60×2 m²
3 安全储存室 Safe storage room 100 m²
4 电瓶车驾驶员休息室 Battery car driver's lounge 100 m²
5 交通管理人员休息室 Traffic manager's lounge 60 m²
6 停车管理人员休息室 Parking manager's lounge 60 m²
7 司机卫生间 Driver's toilet
8 执勤人员休息室 Staff lounge 100 m²
9 车辆调度室 Vehicle dispatch room 126 m²

慧忠路 Huizhong Road
治安问题处理点 Security point 24 m²
吸烟区 Smoking Area
转播综合区 Broadcast Compound 4100 m²
制冰机房 Ice Making Equip 96 m²
广播综合电力供应区 Power Compound for OBS 716 m²
注册中心 Registry Center 412 m²
清废综合区 CNW Compound 440 m²
餐饮综合区 Food & Beverage Compound 1000 m²
场地管理综合区 Site Management Compound 1881 m²
北辰西路 Beichen West Road
天辰西路 Tianchen West Road
天辰东路 Tianchen East Road
票务纠纷处理办公室 Ticket Resolution Office 20 m²
观众检票口 (11) Spectator ticket check

无人机管制备勤室 Unmanned aerial vehicle control spare room 32 m²
消防团队办公室 Fire station office 50 m²
消防装备器材库 Fire Control Equipment Stockroom 30×3×92 m²
消防车库 Fire station Garages 64×4×256 m²
治安问题处理点 Security point 100 m²
消防备勤室 Fire Fighting Room 30×2 m²
服务犬/安保犬放松区 Service dog / Security Dog relaxation zone
餐饮售卖点 FNB Sale 60×2 m²
吸烟区 Smoking Area 8 m²
物品临时存存处 Temporary storage 100 m²

N
NAC 总平面图 OB3.0版
NAC Master Plan OB3.0

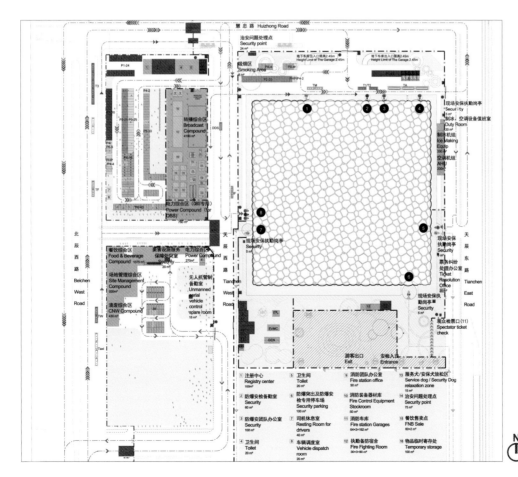

慧忠路 Huizhong Road
治安问题处理点 Security point 24 m²
吸烟区 Smoking Area
地下东南出入口限高2.45m Height Limit of The Garage 2.45m
地下东南出入口限高2.45m Height Limit of The Garage 2.45m
转播综合区 Broadcast Compound 4100 m²
现场安保执勤岗亭 Security 5 m²
制冰、空调设备值班室 Duty Room 20 m²
制冰机组 Ice Making Equip 200 m²
空调机组 AHU 200 m²
电力综合区（OBS专用）Power Compound (for OBS) 750 m²
现场安保执勤岗亭 Security 5 m²
餐饮综合区 Food & Beverage Compound 1075 m²
装备设施服务保障处突室 Security 20 m²
电力综合区 Power Compound 270 m²
场地管理综合区 Site Management Compound 920 m²
无人机管制备勤室 Unmanned aerial vehicle control spare room 15 m²
清废综合区 CNW Compound 430 m²
北辰西路 Beichen West Road
天辰西路 Tianchen West Road
天辰东路 Tianchen East Road
现场安保执勤岗亭 Security 5 m²
票务纠纷处理办公室 Ticket Resolution Office
现场安保执勤岗亭 Security 5 m²
观众检票口 (11) Spectator ticket check
游客出口 Exit
安检入口 Entrance

1 注册中心 Registry center 100m²
2 防爆安检备勤室 Security 60 m²
3 防爆安检团队办公室 Security 100 m²
4 卫生间 Toilet 20 m²
5 卫生间 Toilet 20 m²
6 防爆突出出及防爆安检专用停车场 Security parking 100 m²
7 司机休息室 Resting Room for drivers 100 m²
8 车辆调度室 Vehicle dispatch room 20 m²
9 消防团队办公室 Fire station office 50 m²
10 消防装备器材库 Fire Control Equipment Stockroom
11 消防车库 Fire station Garages 64×3×192 m²
12 执勤备防宿舍 Fire Fighting Room 30×3×90 m²
13 服务犬/安保犬放松区 Service dog / Security Dog relaxation zone 15 m²
14 治安问题处理点 Security point 75 m²
15 餐饮售卖点 FNB Sale 60×2 m²
16 物品临时客存处 Temporary storage 100 m²

N
NAC 总平面图 OB4.0版
NAC Master Plan OB4.0

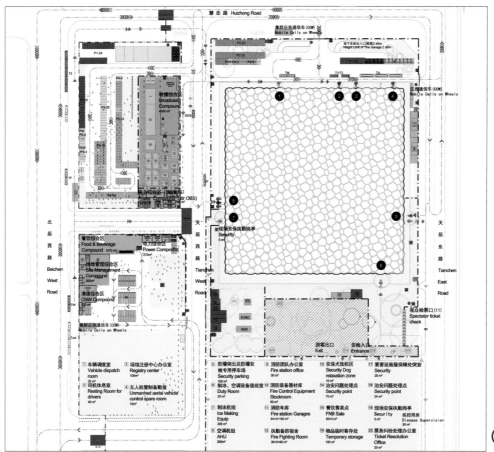

NAC 总平面图 OB5.0版
NAC Master Plan OB5.0

① 车辆调度室 Vehicle dispatch room 20 ㎡	③ 场馆注册中心办公室 Registry center 100㎡	⑥ 防爆突出及防爆安 检专用停车场 Security parking 100 ㎡	⑩ 消防团队办公室 Fire station office 50 ㎡	⑰ 安保犬放松区 Security Dog relaxation zone 15 ㎡	⑳ 要客设施保障处突室 Security 20 ㎡
② 司机休息室 Resting Room for drivers 40 ㎡	④ 无人机管制备勤室 Unmanned aerial vehicle control spare room 15㎡	⑦ 制冰、空调设备值班室 Duty Room 20 ㎡	⑪ 消防装备器材库 Fire Control Equipment Stockroom 50 ㎡	⑱ 治安问题处理点 Security point 75 ㎡	治安问题处理点 Security point 24 ㎡
		⑧ 制冰机组 Ice Making Equip 200㎡	⑫ 消防车库 Fire station Garages 64×3=192 ㎡	⑲ 餐饮售卖点 FNB Sale 60×2 ㎡	现场安保执勤岗房 Security 5 ㎡ 疾控用房 Disease Supervision
		⑨ 空调机组 AHU 200㎡	扈勤备防宿舍 Fire Fighting Room 30×3=90 ㎡	物品临时寄存处 Temporary storage 100 ㎡	票务纠纷处理办公室 Ticket Resolution Office 20 ㎡

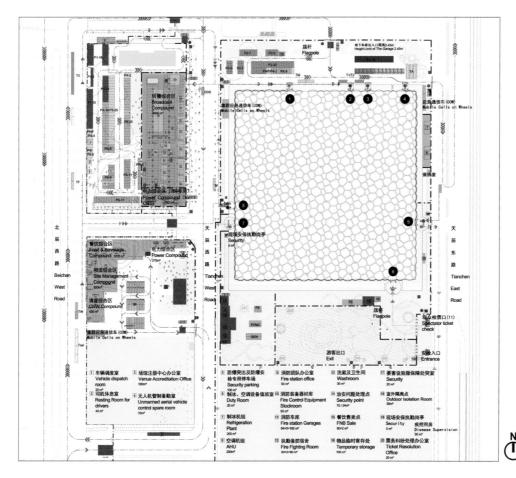

NAC 总平面图 OB6.0版
NAC Master Plan OB6.0

① 车辆调度室 Vehicle dispatch room 20 ㎡	③ 场馆注册中心办公室 Venue Accreditation Office 100㎡	⑥ 防爆突出及防爆安 检专用停车场 Security parking 100 ㎡	⑩ 消防团队办公室 Fire station office 50 ㎡	⑰ 洗漱及卫生间 Washroom 30 ㎡	⑳ 要客设施服保障处突室 Security
② 司机休息室 Resting Room for drivers 40 ㎡	④ 无人机管制备勤室 Unmanned aerial vehicle control spare room 15㎡	⑦ 制冰、空调设备值班室 Duty Room 20 ㎡	⑪ 消防装备器材库 Fire Control Equipment Stockroom 50 ㎡	⑱ 治安问题处理点 Security point 75 / 24㎡	室外隔离点 Outdoor Isolation Room 30㎡
		⑧ 制冰机组 Refrigeration Plant 200 ㎡	⑫ 消防车库 Fire station Garages 64×3=192 ㎡	⑲ 餐饮售卖点 FNB Sale 60×2 ㎡	现场安保执勤岗房 Security 5 ㎡ 疾控用房 Disease Supervision
		⑨ 空调机组 AHU 200㎡	扈勤备防宿舍 Fire Fighting Room 30×3=90 ㎡	物品临时寄存处 Temporary storage 100 ㎡	票务纠纷处理办公室 Ticket Resolution Office 20 ㎡

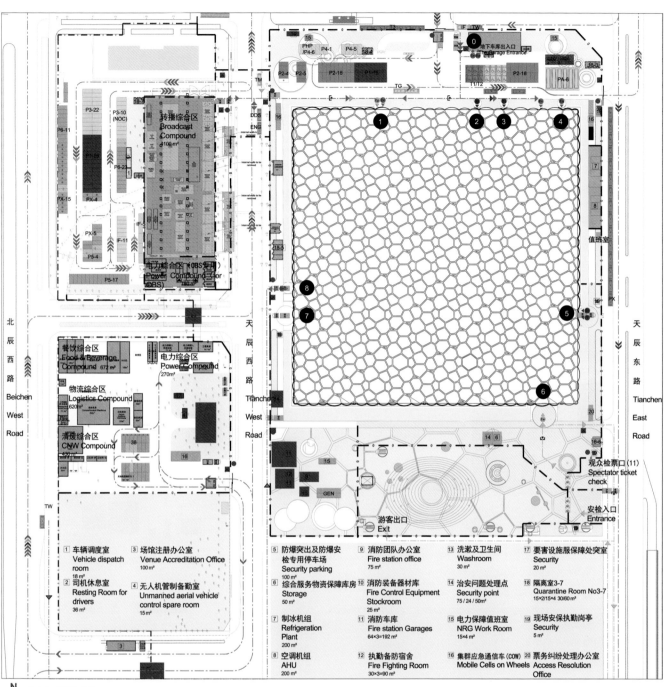

NⒸ NAC 总平面图 OB7.0版
NAC Master Plan OB7.0

①	车辆调度室 Vehicle dispatch room 18 m²	③	场馆注册办公室 Venue Accreditation Office 100 m²	⑤	防爆突出及防爆安 检专用停车场 Security parking 100 m²	⑨	消防团队办公室 Fire station office 75 m²	⑬	洗漱及卫生间 Washroom 30 m²	⑰	要害设施服务保障处突室 Security 20 m²
②	司机休息室 Resting Room for drivers 36 m²	④	无人机管制备勤室 Unmanned aerial vehicle control spare room 15 m²	⑥	综合服务物资保障库房 Storage 50 m²	⑩	消防装备器材库 Fire Control Equipment Stockroom 25 m²	⑭	治安问题处理点 Security point 75 / 24 / 50m²	⑱	隔离室3-7 Quarantine Room No3-7 15×2/15×4 30/60 m²
				⑦	制冰机组 Refrigeration Plant 200 m²	⑪	消防车库 Fire station Garages 64×3=192 m²	⑮	电力保障值班室 NRG Work Room 15×4 m²	⑲	现场安保执勤岗亭 Security 5 m²
				⑧	空调机组 AHU 200 m²	⑫	执勤备勤宿舍 Fire Fighting Room 30×3=90 m²	⑯	集群应急通信车 (COW) Mobile Cells on Wheels	⑳	票务纠纷处理办公室 Access Resolution Office

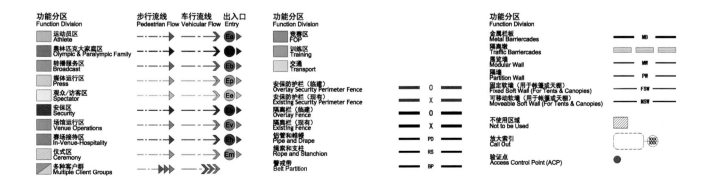

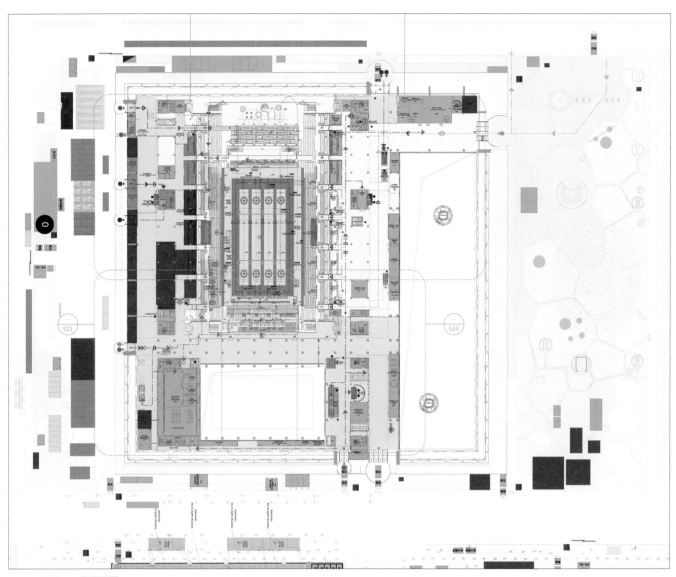

N ⊕ NAC 一层平面图 OB7.0版
NAC 1F Plan OB7.0

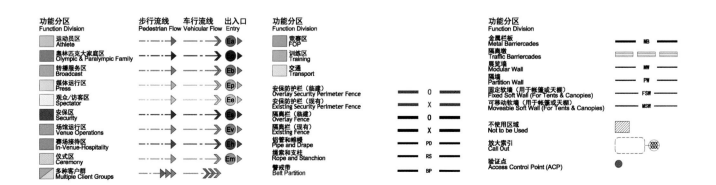

功能分区
Function Division

- 运动员区
  Athlete
- 奥林匹克大家庭区
  Olympic & Paralympic Family
- 转播服务区
  Broadcast
- 媒体运行区
  Press
- 观众/访客区
  Spectator
- 安保区
  Security
- 场馆运行区
  Venue Operations
- 赛场接待区
  In-Venue-Hospitality
- 仪式区
  Ceremony
- 多种客户群
  Multiple Client Groups

步行流线
Pedestrian Flow

车行流线
Vehicular Flow

出入口
Entry

- Ea
- Eb
- Ep
- Ee
- Eb
- Ev
- Eh
- Em

功能分区
Function Division

- 竞赛区
  FOP
- 训练区
  Training
- 交通
  Transport

安保防护栏（临建）
Overlay Security Perimeter Fence

安保防护栏（现有）
Existing Security Perimeter Fence

隔离栏（临建）
Overlay Fence

隔离栏（现有）
Existing Fence

铝管和帷幕
Pipe and Drape

缆索和支柱
Rope and Stanchion

警戒带
Belt Partition

- 0
- X
- 0
- X
- PD
- RS
- BP

功能分区
Function Division

金属栏板
Metal Barriercades

隔离墩
Traffic Barriercades

展览墙
Modular Wall

隔墙
Partition Wall

固定软墙（用于帐篷或天棚）
Fixed Soft Wall (For Tents & Canopies)

可移动软墙（用于帐篷或天棚）
Moveable Soft Wall (For Tents & Canopies)

不使用区域
Not to be Used

放大索引
Call Out

验证点
Access Control Point (ACP)

- MB
- MW
- PW
- FSW
- MSW

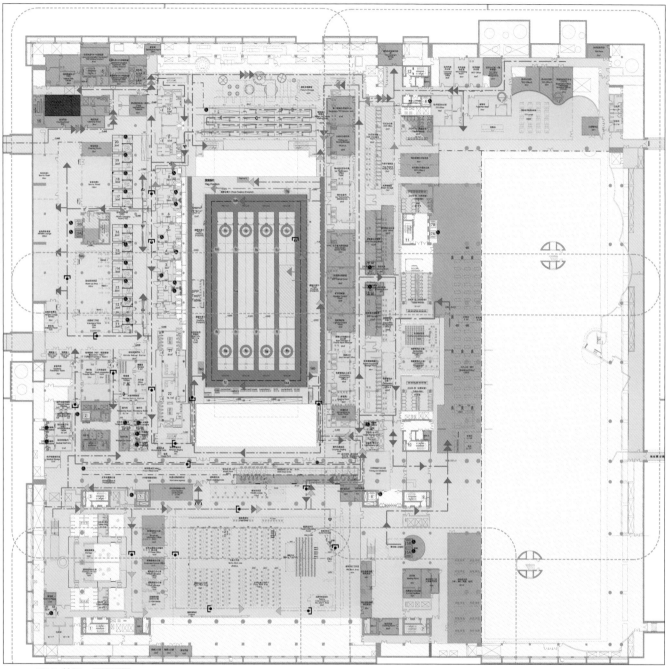

N NAC 地下一层平面图 OB7.0版
NAC B1 Plan OB7.0

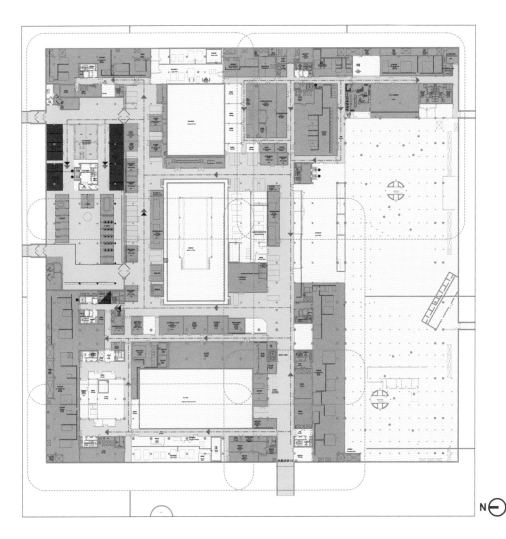

NAC 地下二层平面图 OB7.0版
NAC B2 Plan OB7.0

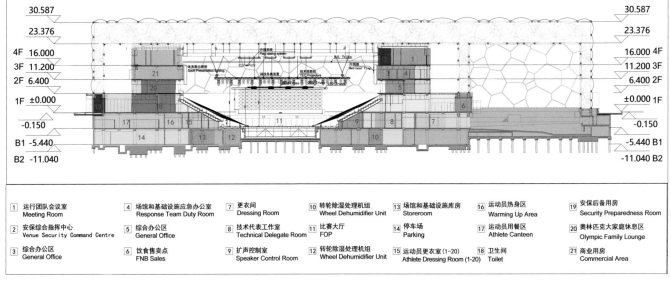

1	运行团队会议室 Meeting Room	4	场馆和基础设施应急办公室 Response Team Duty Room	7	更衣间 Dressing Room	10	转轮除湿处理机组 Wheel Dehumidifier Unit	13	场馆和基础设施库房 Storeroom	16	运动员热身区 Warming Up Area	19	安保后备用房 Security Preparedness Room
2	安保综合指挥中心 Venue Security Command Centre	5	综合办公区 General Office	8	技术代表工作室 Technical Delegate Room	11	比赛大厅 FOP	14	停车场 Parking	17	运动员用餐区 Athlete Canteen	20	奥林匹克大家庭休息区 Olympic Family Lounge
3	综合办公区 General Office	6	饮食售卖点 FNB Sales	9	扩声控制室 Speaker Control Room	12	转轮除湿处理机组 Wheel Dehumidifier Unit	15	运动员更衣室（1-20） Athlete Dressing Room (1-20)	18	卫生间 Toilet	21	商业用房 Commercial Area

NAC 剖面图 OB7.0版
NAC Section OB7.0

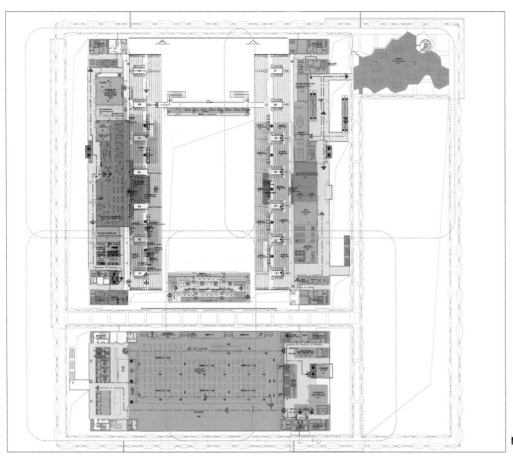

NAC 二层平面图 OB7.0版
NAC 2F Plan OB7.0

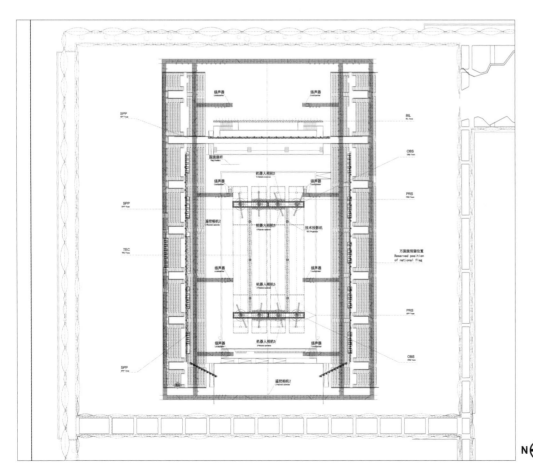

NAC 马道平面图 OB7.0版
NAC Catwalk Plan OB7.0

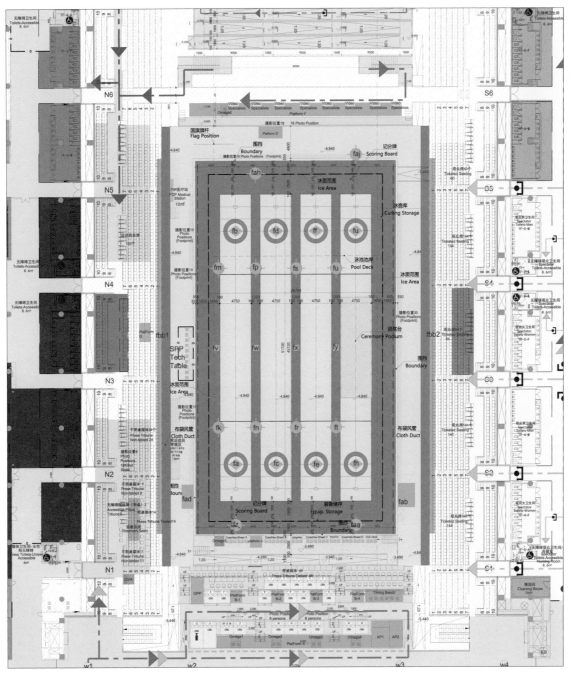

NAC FOP平面图 OB7.0版
NAC FOP Plan OB7.0

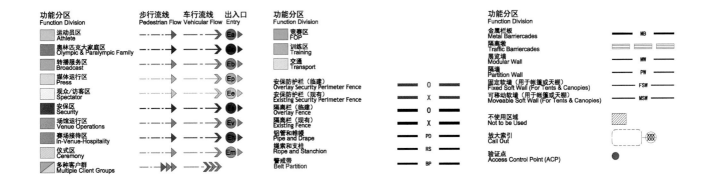

北京冬奥组委 提供
Provide by BOCOG

摄影 刘兴华
Photo by Liu Xinghua

国家体育馆 [NIS]
National Indoor Stadium

1. 场馆基本情况

　　国家体育馆位于北京奥林匹克公园中心区，在北京2008年夏奥会期间承担体操、手球、排球等项目的比赛，场馆总建筑面积约10万m²。

　　国家体育馆在北京2022年冬奥会期间承担男子冰球项目的比赛和决赛、女子冰球项目的部分比赛；在冬残奥会期间承担残奥冰球项目的全部比赛，分别产生各1枚金牌。场馆屋顶起伏变化，犹如乘风破浪的风帆，昵称"冰之帆"。

2. FOP相关区域

　　根据冬奥会和冬残奥会比赛要求，国家体育馆改建了1块竞赛冰面，新建了1块训练冰面。

　　竞赛冰面FOP区在原有楼板上增加了制冰环管及构造做法层，整体垫高了0.6m。场地周边采用1：12的无障碍坡道进行过渡。为满足冬奥会赛时及赛后的使用要求，共设置30m×60m和26m×60m两种不同尺寸的冰面及板墙预埋件，可在两种冰场尺寸中快速转换。

　　紧邻FOP区域东侧设置了4套运动员赛时更衣室，运动员可以从更衣室通过1：16.7的无障碍坡道进入FOP区。浇冰车室及赛事管理用房设置在FOP南侧，浇冰车进入FOP流线短捷。

1. Venue Overview

Located in the central area of the Beijing Olympic Park, the National Indoor Stadium is the competition venue for Gymnastics, Handball and Volleyball events during the Beijing 2008 Summer Olympics, with a total floor area of about 100,000m².

The National Indoor Stadium is the venue for all competitions including the final of Ice Hockey Men's tournament and some competitions of Ice Hockey women tournament during the Beijing 2022 Olympic Winter Games, with one gold medal won here, and the venue for all competitions of Para Ice Hockey during the Beijing 2022 Paralympic Winter Games, with one gold medal won here. With the roof flowing like a sail that braves the wind and the waves, the venue is thus nicknamed "Sail of Ice".

2. FOP and Relevant Areas

According to the competition requirements of the Beijing 2022 Olympic and Paralympic Winter Games, one ice rink for competitions has been renovated and one ice rink for trainings has been newly constructed in the National Indoor Stadium.

Refrigeration annular pipes and constructed layers have been added to the original slabs in the FOP, to increase the height by 0.6m. A 1:12 accessible ramp is used around the FOP for transition. To meet Games-time and post-Games use requirements, two different sizes

媒体工作区设置于FOP西侧，媒体混合采访区位于FOP北侧。

3. 场馆前院及观众流线

国家体育馆东侧、南侧的广场和观众厅区域为场馆前院区，面向观众开放。赛时观众从场馆东门平层进入主馆二层观众厅及观众看台观看比赛，比赛结束后通过场馆南门离开。

4. 场馆后院及注册流线

国家体育馆西侧下沉区和馆内非观众厅区域为场馆后院区。

（1）运动员流线

运动员由冬奥村乘坐大巴到达地下一层西北角，进入运动员更衣室。根据参赛队伍数量，冬奥会在竞赛冰面和训练冰面之间，设置了14套运动员更衣室，运动员可以便捷到达比赛和训练场地。

更衣室采用临时集装箱体拼装搭建的方式，可快速建设，赛事结束后可迅速复原并将集装箱回收再利用。每套更衣室采用同样的大小及布局，包含更衣区、按摩室、教练室、卫生间、淋浴间等功能。

比赛期间，运动员由运动员更衣室出发，沿专用通道抵达比赛场地附近的4套运动员赛时更衣室。赛时更衣室采用"两用两备"的模式，第1场比赛时，即将进行第2场比赛的两支球队可以进入赛时更衣室备赛。比赛结束后，运动员在混合采访区接受采访后，返回运动员更衣室。

运动员区域在冬奥会期间即充分考虑无障碍设计，所有卫生间、坡道、扶手等无障碍设施都一次建设到位，冬残奥会前可以迅速转换。

（2）技术官员流线

技术官员通过位于主馆西南角的技术官员入口进入场馆，可快速到达办公区及更衣室。在紧邻FOP上场通道的位置设置2间ITO更衣室及1间NTO休息室。

（3）奥林匹克大家庭成员流线

奥林匹克大家庭成员通过主馆西侧的大家庭入口进入场馆，场馆内设有250m²的大家庭休息室及配套空间。大家庭成员流线独立设置。

（4）媒体流线

转播及新闻媒体通过位于主馆西侧的媒体入口直接进入媒体工作区，工作区内设置有文字记者及摄影工作间、媒体休息区等功能用房。媒体工作区紧邻比赛场地、媒体混采区、媒体坐席及新闻发布厅，可以在最短的时间内抵达各个点位。主要媒体工作间均采用"功能柱"的布线方式，从固定在房间顶部的"功能柱"上将强弱电线缆拉到房间的任意位置，保证使用的灵活性和便利性。

（5）场馆室外综合区

赛时场馆室外综合区包含转播综合区、餐饮综合区、清废综合区及注册办公室。

5. 场馆坐席

国家体育馆总的坐席容量为18881个。赛时西侧坐席为注册坐席，包含奥林匹克大家庭坐席、评论员席、观察员席、带桌媒体席、不带桌媒体席、观赛运动员坐席，坐席数量共计1483个。各类注册人群均设置了无障碍坐席。

本次冬奥会观众坐席位于二层东侧，共计1300个，其中包含30个观众无障碍席位及30个陪同席位。

of ice rinks, 30m × 60m and 26m × 60m, and board embedded parts are provided, to quickly switch between ice rinks of two sizes.

3. Front of House and Spectator Flow

The squares on the east and south sides of the National Indoor Stadium and the spectator hall area constitute the Front of House (FOH) open to spectators. During the Games, spectators enter from the venue's east gate level to the main venue's second-floor spectator hall and spectator stand to watch competitions, and after competitions, they leave from the venue's south gate.

4. Back of House and Accreditation Flow

(1) Athlete Flow

Athletes take shuttle buses from the Olympic Village to the northwest corner of B1 and then go to athlete dressing rooms. Depending on the number of the teams, there are 14 athlete dressing rooms between the competition ice rink and training ice rink during the Games, from which athletes can conveniently reach the competition and training fields.

Dressing rooms are converted from prefabricated containers and can be quickly built and promptly restored, recycled and reused after the Games. Each dressing room is of the same size and layout, including a dressing area, a massage room, a coach room, a toilet, and a shower.

During competition periods, athletes depart from athlete dressing rooms and walk along the dedicated passage to get to the 4 athlete dressing rooms near the FOP. The dressing rooms adopt the "two-in-use, two-on-standby" mode, namely, during the first competition, the two teams for the second competition can enter the said rooms to prepare. After competitions, athletes go to the mixed zone to be interviewed and then return to athlete dressing rooms.

(2) Technical Official Flow

Via the technical official entrance in the southwest corner of the main venue, technical officials can enter the venue to quickly reach their office areas and dressing rooms. Two ITO dressing rooms and one NTO lounge are set next to the passage to access the FOP.

(3) Olympic Family Flow

Olympic Family members enter the venue from the Olympic Family entrance in the west of the main venue. There is a 250-square-metre Olympic Family lounge and supporting space inside the venue. The Olympic Family flow is set independently.

(4) Media Flow

Broadcast and media personnel directly enter the media work area from the media entrance in the west of the main venue. The work area has press and photographer work rooms, a media lounge, and other functional rooms. The media work area is next to the FOP, mixed zone, press tribunes, and press conference room, allowing access to all points within the shortest time.

5. Seating Area

The total seating capacity of the National Indoor Stadium is 18,881. During the Games, accredited seats are on the west side and include Olympic Family seats, commentary positions, observer seats, tabled and non-tabled press tribune seats, and spectating athlete seats, with a total of 1,483. Accessible seats are provided for various accredited persons.

During the Games, there are a total of 1,300 spectator seats in the east of the second floor, including 30 accessible seats and 30 companion seats.

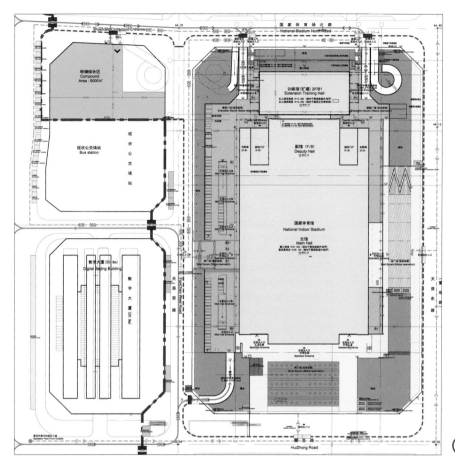

NIS 总平面图 OB1.2版
NIS Master Plan OB1.2

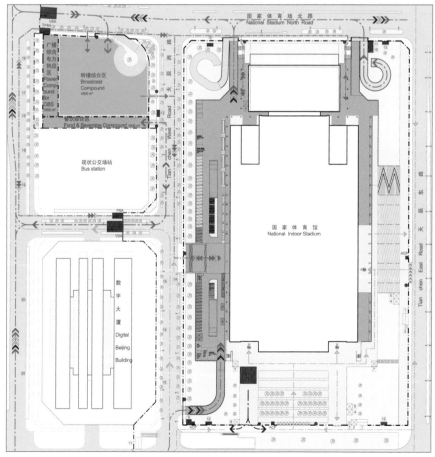

NIS 总平面图 OB2.1版
NIS Master Plan OB2.1

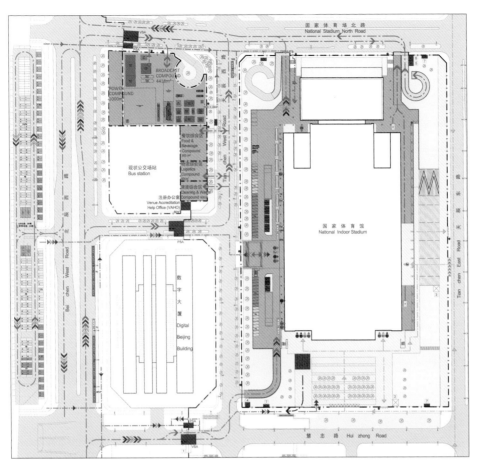

NIS 总平面图 OB3.0版
NIS Master Plan OB3.0

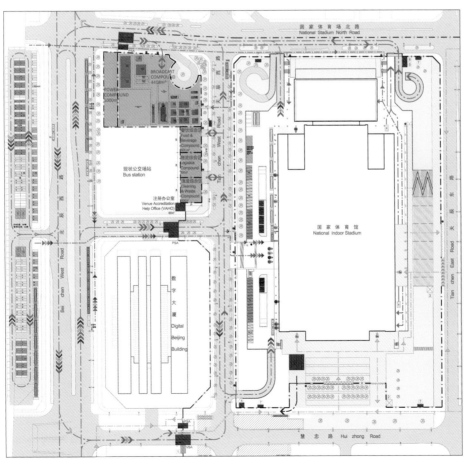

NIS 总平面图 OB4.0版
NIS Master Plan OB4.0

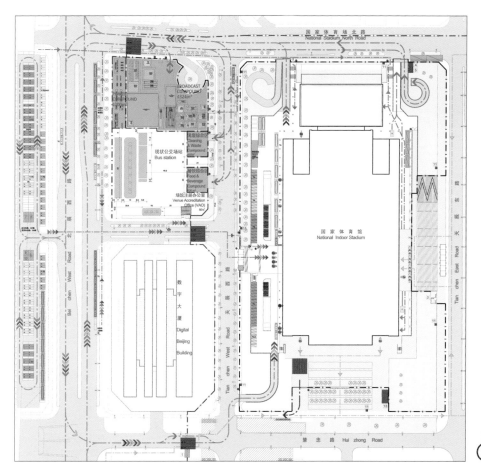

NIS 总平面图 OB5.0版
NIS Master Plan OB5.0

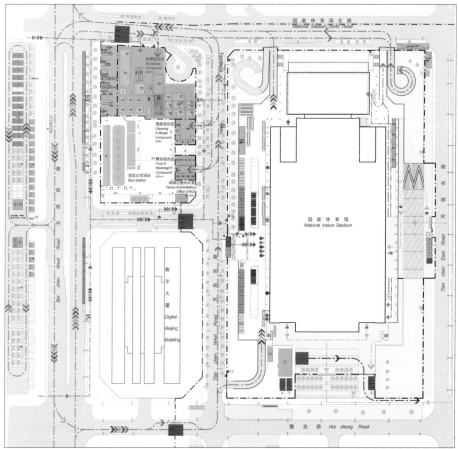

NIS 总平面图 OB6.1版
NIS Master Plan OB6.1

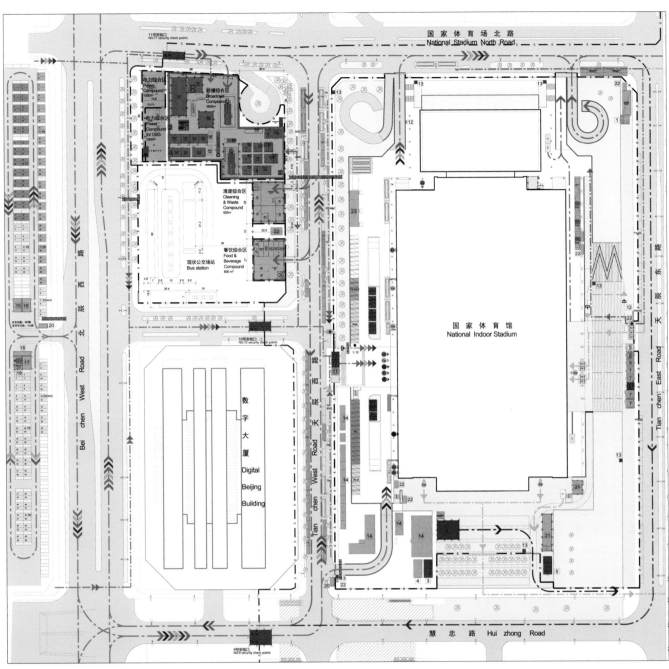

NIS 总平面图 OB7.0版
NIS Master Plan OB7.0

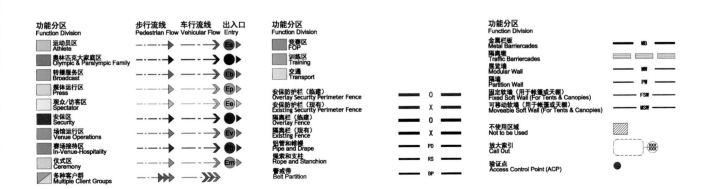

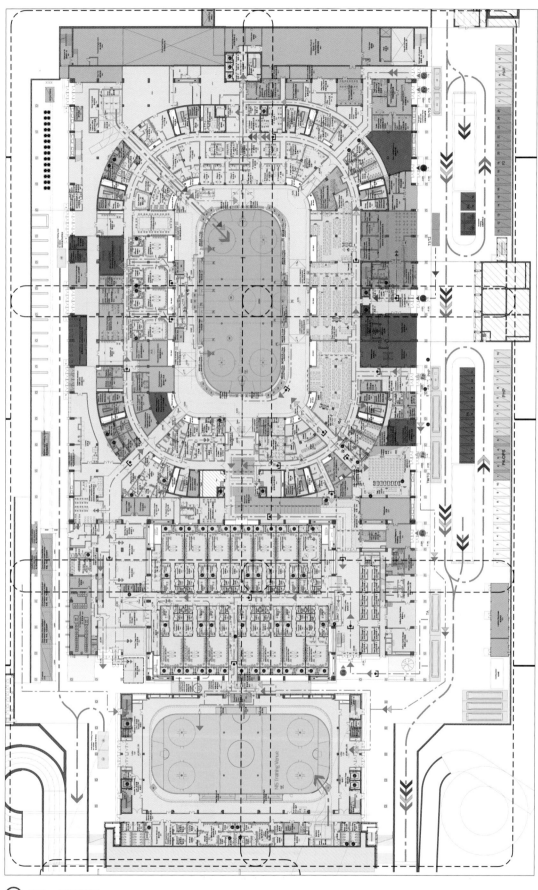

NIS 一层平面图 OB7.0版
N NIS 1F Plan OB7.0

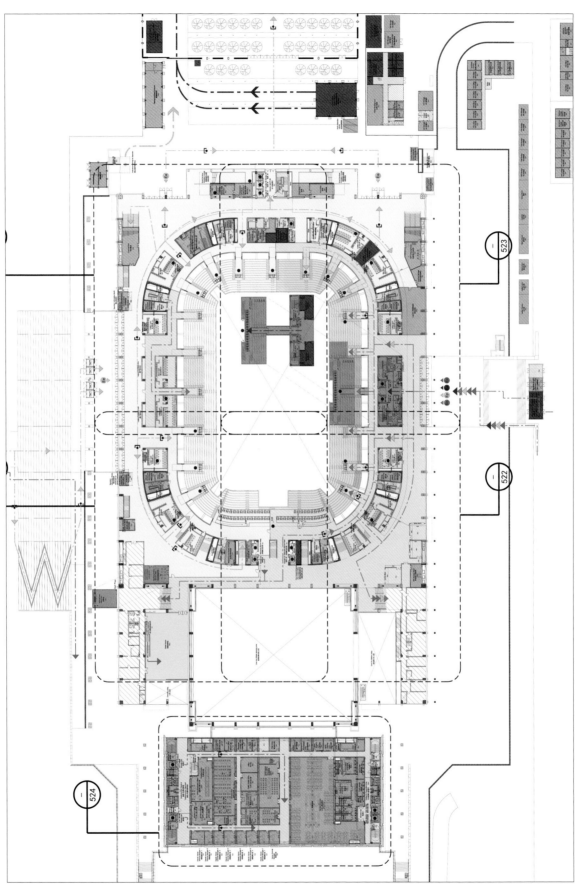

NIS 二层平面图 OB7.0版
NIS 2F Plan OB7.0

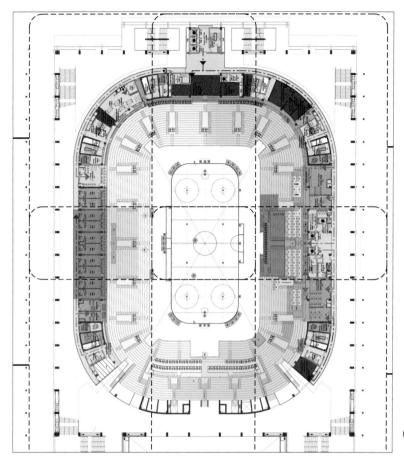

NIS 三层平面图 OB7.0版
NIS 3F Plan OB7.0

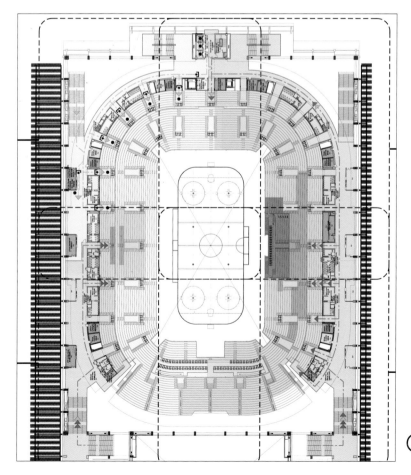
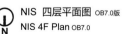

NIS 四层平面图 OB7.0版
NIS 4F Plan OB7.0

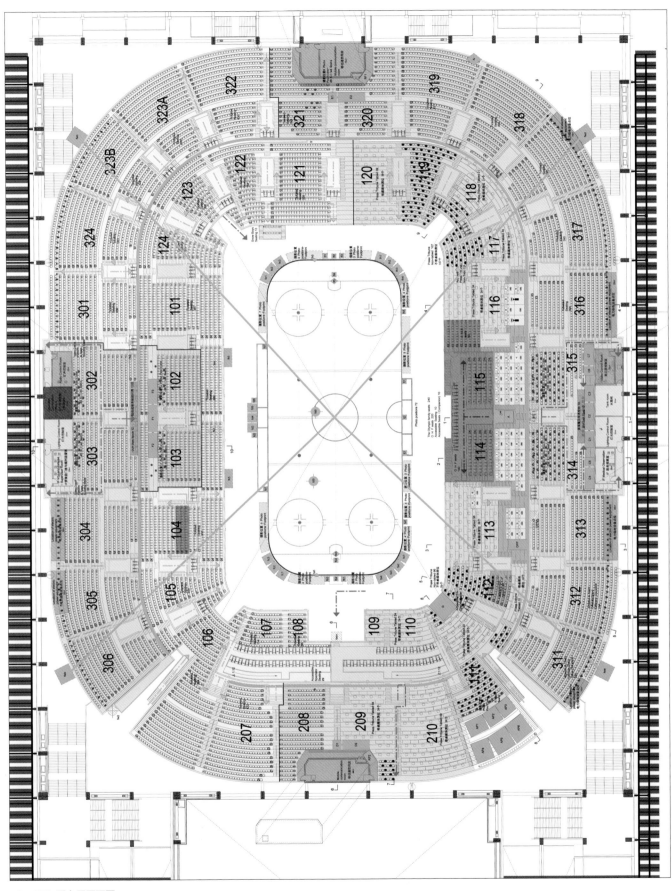

NIS 看台层平面图 OB7.0版
NIS Seat Bowl Plan OB7.0

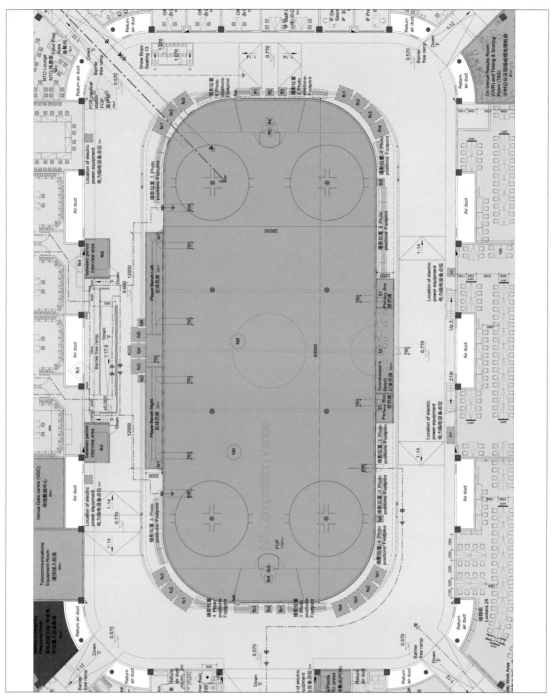

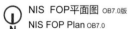

NIS FOP平面图 OB7.0版
NIS FOP Plan OB7.0

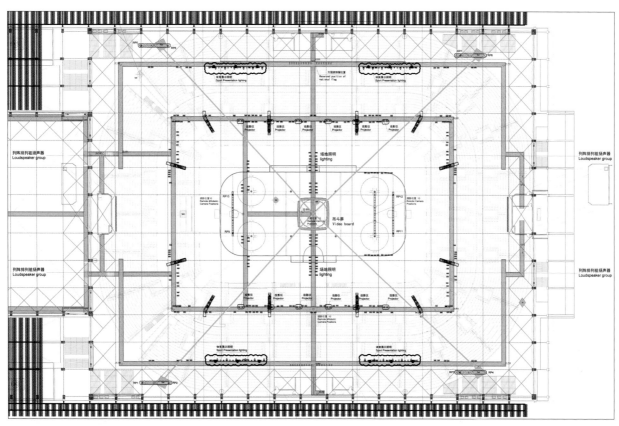

NIS 马道平面图 OB7.0版
NIS Catwalk Plan OB7.0

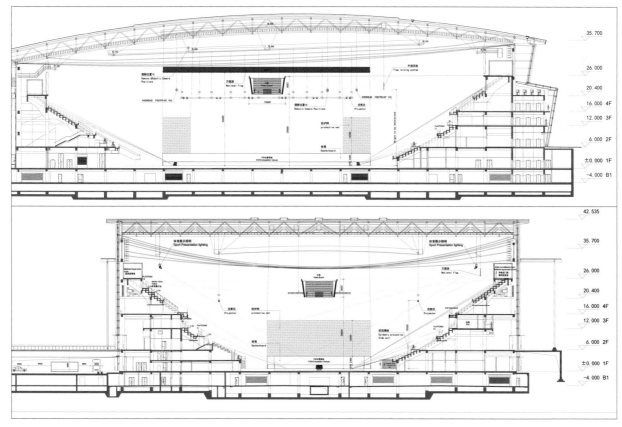

NIS 剖面图 OB7.0版
NIS Section OB7.0

摄影 杨超英
Photo by Yang Chaoying

摄影 杨超英
Photo by Yang Chaoying

摄影 王绍强
Photo by Wang Shaoqiang

摄影 杨超英
Photo by Yang Chaoying

111

首都体育馆 [CTS]
Capital Indoor Stadium

1. 场馆基本情况

首都体育馆位于北京动物园西侧，是中国最早兴建的大型室内体育馆，其室内冰场是中国第一块室内人工冰场。首都体育馆在北京2008年夏奥会期间承担排球项目的比赛，在北京2022年冬奥会期间承担花样滑冰和短道速滑的比赛，产生14枚金牌。

花样滑冰和短道速滑两项赛事有着不同的冰面温度和硬度要求，首都体育馆采用新型环保的二氧化碳跨临界直冷制冰技术，可以在两小时内实现两种比赛冰面的转换。同时在冰场屋顶布置了巨型投影屏幕，可以通过影像技术为冰场投射出"最美的冰"。场馆总建筑面积约4.5万m²。

2. FOP相关区域

根据北京2022年冬奥会要求，首都体育馆对原有冰面进行了改造。竞赛冰面FOP区整体更新了制冰环管及构造做法层。

FOP区域南侧设置了运动员入口，花样滑冰和短道速滑两个项目分设了各自入口，运动员可以从更衣室通过运动员等候区进入FOP区。浇冰车室及赛事管理用房设置在FOP东侧，浇冰车可方便快捷进入FOP区。混合采访区及媒体工作区设置于FOP西侧。FOP北侧设置裁判台，两个项目裁判台尺寸不同，在赛事期间可进行转换。

1. Venue Overview

Located to the west of the Beijing Zoo, the Capital Indoor Stadium is the first large indoor stadium built in China, and its indoor ice rink is the first artificial indoor ice rink in China. The Capital Indoor Stadium is the competition venue for Volleyball competitions during the Beijing 2008 Olympic Games and for Figure Skating and Short Track Speed Skating competitions during the Beijing 2022 Olympic Winter Games, with 14 gold medals won here.

Figure Skating and Short Track Speed Skating have different requirements for ice surface temperature and hardness. With the new eco-friendly CO_2 trans-critical refrigeration technology, the Capital Indoor Stadium can realise ice surface conversion for the two disciplines within two hours. The venue has a total floor area of about 45,000m².

2. FOP and Relevant Areas

According to the requirements of the Beijing 2022 Olympic and Paralympic Winter Games, the original ice surface of the Capital Indoor Stadium has been renovated. Refrigeration annular pipes and constructed layers have been updated for the FOP.

Athlete entrances are set on the south side of the FOP separately for Figure Skating and Short Track Speed Skating. Athletes can go from athlete dressing rooms to the FOP via the athlete waiting area.

花样滑冰项目在FOP区域西侧设置了团队坐席,在西南侧设置了候分室及等分席。短道速滑项目在FOP区域西北及东南侧设置了弯道管理员区,北侧设置了发令台、教练员席位、教练指挥区、器材师区等区域。

3. 场馆前院及观众流线

首都体育馆南侧的广场和馆内观众区为场馆前院区,面向观众开放。赛时观众从南门进入首都体育馆,进入二层观众厅、三层休息厅及观众看台观看比赛,比赛结束后通过场馆南门离开。

4. 场馆后院及注册流线

首都体育馆除南院区南广场及馆内观众厅区域外,皆为场馆后院区。

（1）运动员流线

运动员由冬奥村乘坐大巴到达首都体育馆东门,进入东门后可直接到达花样滑冰训练馆。如果前往短道速滑训练馆则不需要下车,继续乘坐大巴车到下一站短道速滑训练馆东门下车。

进入首都体育馆东门后沿东环廊及南环廊,经过磨刀室、按摩室、兴奋剂检查站等房间到达运动员更衣室。

比赛期间,运动员由运动员更衣室出发,通过运动员等候区抵达比赛场地。等候区西侧门供花样滑冰项目使用,东侧门供短道速滑项目使用。运动员更衣室西侧为2间运动员休息室。

（2）技术官员流线

技术官员通过比赛馆东北角的技术官员入口进入场馆,可快速到达办公区及休息室。FOP北侧专门设置了技术官员的上场通道。

（3）奥林匹克大家庭成员流线

奥林匹克大家庭成员通过比赛馆北侧的大家庭入口进入场馆,场馆内设有377m²的大家庭休息室及配套空间。大家庭成员流线独立设置,可直达大家庭坐席区,同时设置无障碍升降梯及无障碍卫生间,方便残障大家庭成员观赛。

（4）媒体流线

转播及新闻媒体通过位于比赛馆西北侧的媒体落客区落客,比赛馆西北侧设置400m²的临时记者工作区。临时记者工作区采用临时篷房搭建方式。媒体人员从比赛馆西北门进入媒体工作区,工作区内设置有文字记者及摄影工作间、媒体休息区等功能用房。媒体工作区紧邻比赛场地、媒体混采区、媒体坐席及新闻发布厅,可以在最短的时间内抵达各个点位。在比赛馆西门还设有1条室外媒体快速通道,可让记者绕过混采区直接到达新闻发布厅。

（5）场馆室外综合区

赛时场馆外围设置了室外综合区域,包含转播综合区、电力综合区、清废综合区及注册办公室。

5. 场馆坐席

首都体育馆总坐席容量为13273个。赛时东、西、北侧坐席为注册坐席,包含奥林匹克大家庭坐席、评论员席、观察员席、带桌媒体席、不带桌媒体席、运动员坐席,花样滑冰项目注册坐席数量共计1557个,短道速滑项目注册坐席数量共计1516个。媒体和大家庭设置了无障碍坐席。

本次冬奥会观众坐席位于二层南侧,共计1711个,其中包含8个观众无障碍席位及8个陪同席位。

The ice resurfacing machine room and Games management room are on the east side of the FOP, and ice resurfacing machines can conveniently enter the FOP. The mixed zone and media work area are on the west side of the FOP. The judge stand is on the north side of the FOP, which is of different size for the 2 disciplines, and can be converted during the Games.

For Figure Skating, team seats are set on the west side of the FOP, and a score waiting room and a kiss & cry area are set on the southwest side. For Short Track Speed Skating, track steward areas are set on the northwest and southeast sides of the FOP, and the starter's stand, coach seats, coaching area, and equipment engineer area are set on the north side.

3. Front of House and Spectator Flow

The square on the south side of the Capital Indoor Stadium and the spectator area inside constitute the Front of House (FOH) open to spectators. During the Games, spectators enter the Capital Indoor Stadium from the south gate, then go to the second-floor spectator hall and third-floor lounge and spectator stand to watch competitions.

4. Back of House and Accreditation Flow

(1) Athlete Flow

During competitions, athletes depart from athlete dressing rooms and reach the FOP via the athlete waiting area, with the west door in the waiting area for figure skating athletes to use and the east door for short track speed skating athletes to use. There are two athlete lounges to the west of athlete dressing rooms.

(2) Technical Official Flow

Via the technical official entrance in the northeast corner of the competition venue, technical officials enter the venue to quickly reach their office areas and lounges.

(3) Olympic Family Flow

Olympic Family members enter the venue from the Olympic Family entrance in the north of the competition venue. There is a 377m² Olympic Family lounge and supporting space inside the venue. The Olympic Family flow is independent with direct access to the Olympic Family seating area, and accessible lifts and toilets are provided to facilitate Paralympic Family members to watch competitions.

(4) Media Flow

Broadcast and media personnel get off in the media drop-off zone on the northwest side of the competition venue, where there is a 400-square-metre temporary press work area set up in a temporary tent. Media personnel enter the media work area from the northwest gate of the competition venue. The work area has journalist and photographer work rooms, a media lounge, and other functional rooms.

5. Seating Area

The total seating capacity of the Capital Indoor Stadium is 13,273. During the Games, accredited seats are on the east, west and north sides and include Olympic Family seats, commentary positions, observer seats, tabled and non-tabled press tribune seats, and athlete seats, with a total of 1,557 for the Figure Skating discipline or 1,516 for the Short Track Speed Skating discipline. Accessible seats are provided for the media and Olympic Family.

During the Games, there are a total of 1,711 spectator seats on the second floor in the south, including 8 accessible spectator seats and 8 companion seats.

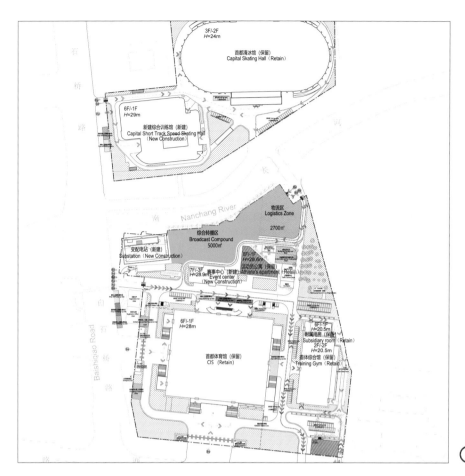

CTS 总平面图 OB1.2版
CTS Master Plan OB1.2

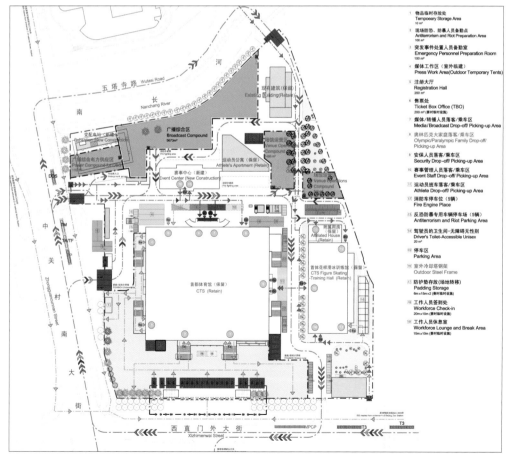

1. 物品临时存放处
   Tempoeary Storage Area
   10 m²
2. 现场防恐、防暴人员备勤点
   Antiterrorism and Riot Preparation Area
   100 m²
3. 突发事件处置人员备勤室
   Emergency Personnel Preparation Room
   100 m²
4. 媒体工作区（室外临建）
   Press Work Area(Outdoor Temporary Tents)
5. 注册大厅
   Registration Hall
   200 m²
6. 售票处
   Ticket Box Office (TBO)
   200 m²（赛时临时设施）
7. 媒体/转播人员落客/乘车区
   Media/Broadcast Drop-off/ Picking-up Area
8. 奥林匹克大家庭落客/乘车区
   Olympic/Paralympic Family Drop-off/
   Picking-up Area
9. 安保人员落客/乘车区
   Security Drop-off/ Picking-up Area
10. 赛事管理人员落客/乘车区
    Event Staff Drop-off/ Picking-up Area
11. 运动员班车落客/乘车区
    Athlete Drop-off/ Picking-up Area
12. 消防车停车位（5辆）
    Fire Engine Place
13. 反恐防暴专用车辆停车场（5辆）
    Antiterrorism and Riot Parking Area
14. 驾驶员的卫生间-无障碍无性别
    Driver's Toilet-Accessible Unisex
    20 m²
15. 停车区
    Parking Area
16. 室外冷却塔钢架
    Outdoor Steel Frame
17. 防护垫存放（场地转移）
    Padding Storage
    6m×15m×2（赛时临时设施）
18. 工作人员签到处
    Workforce Check-in
    20m×10m（赛时临时设施）
19. 工作人员休息室
    Workforce Lounge and Break Area
    15m×10m（赛时临时设施）

CTS 总平面图 OB2.1版
CTS Master Plan OB2.1

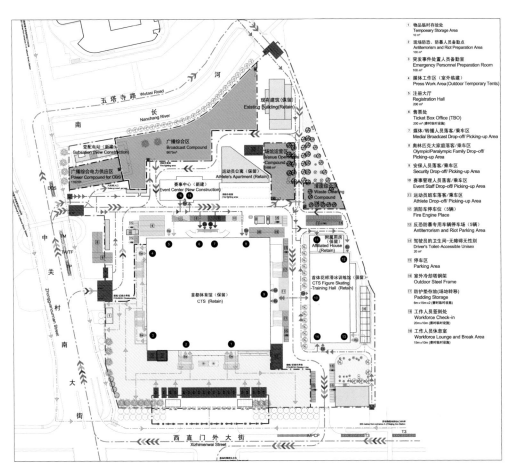

1 物品临时存放处
Tempoeary Storage Area
10 m²

2 现场防恐、防暴人员备勤点
Antiterrorism and Riot Preparation Area
100 m²

3 突发事件处置人员备勤室
Emergency Personnel Preparation Room
100 m²

4 媒体工作区（室外临建）
Press Work Area (Outdoor Temporary Tents)

5 注册大厅
Registration Hall
200 m²

6 售票处
Ticket Box Office (TBO)
200 m²（赛时临时设置）

7 媒体/转播人员落客/乘车区
Media/ Broadcast Drop-off/ Picking-up Area

8 奥林匹克大家庭落客/乘车区
Olympic/Paralympic Family Drop-off/
Picking-up Area

9 安保人员落客/乘车区
Security Drop-off/ Picking-up Area

10 赛事管理人员落客/乘车区
Event Staff Drop-off/ Picking-up Area

11 运动员班车落客/乘车区
Athlete Drop-off/ Picking-up Area

12 消防车停车位（5辆）
Fire Engine Place

13 反恐防暴专用车辆停车场（5辆）
Antiterrorism and Riot Parking Area

14 驾驶员的卫生间-无障碍无性别
Driver's Toilet-Accessible Unisex
20 m²

15 停车区
Parking Area

16 室外冷却塔钢架
Outdoor Steel Frame

17 防护垫存放(场地转移)
Padding Storage
6m×15m×2（赛时临时设置）

18 工作人员签到处
Workforce Check-in
20m×10m（赛时临时设置）

19 工作人员休息室
Workforce Lounge and Break Area
15m×10m（赛时临时设置）

CTS 总平面图 OB3.0版
CTS Master Plan OB3.0

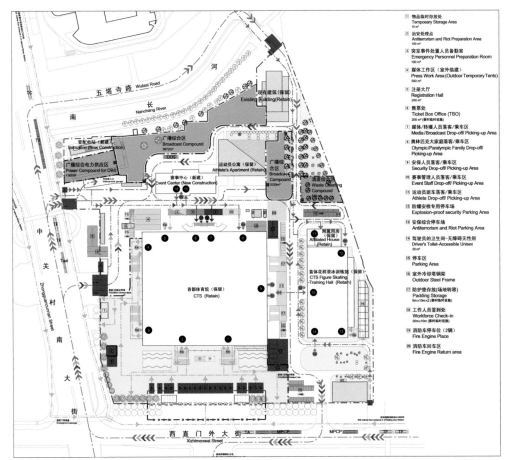

1 物品临时存放处
Tempoeary Storage Area
10 m²

2 治安处理点
Antiterrorism and Riot Preparation Area
100 m²

3 突发事件处置人员备勤室
Emergency Personnel Preparation Room
100 m²

4 媒体工作区（室外临建）
Press Work Area (Outdoor Temporary Tents)
500 m²

5 注册大厅
Registration Hall
200 m²

6 售票处
Ticket Box Office (TBO)
200 m²（赛时临时设置）

7 媒体/转播人员落客/乘车区
Media/Broadcast Drop-off/ Picking-up Area

8 奥林匹克大家庭落客/乘车区
Olympic/Paralympic Family Drop-off/
Picking-up Area

9 安保人员落客/乘车区
Security Drop-off/ Picking-up Area

10 赛事管理人员落客/乘车区
Event Staff Drop-off/ Picking-up Area

11 运动员班车落客/乘车区
Athlete Drop-off/ Picking-up Area

12 防爆安检专用停车场
Explosion-proof security Parking Area

13 安保综合停车场
Antiterrorism and Riot Parking Area

14 驾驶员的卫生间-无障碍无性别
Driver's Toilet-Accessible Unisex
20 m²

15 停车区
Parking Area

16 室外冷却塔钢架
Outdoor Steel Frame

17 防护垫存放(场地转移)
Padding Storage
6m×15m×2（赛时临时设置）

18 工作人员签到处
Workforce Check-in
20m×10m（赛时临时设置）

19 消防车停车位（2辆）
Fire Engine Place

20 消防车回车区
Fire Engine Return area

CTS 总平面图 OB4.0版
CIS Master Plan OB4.0

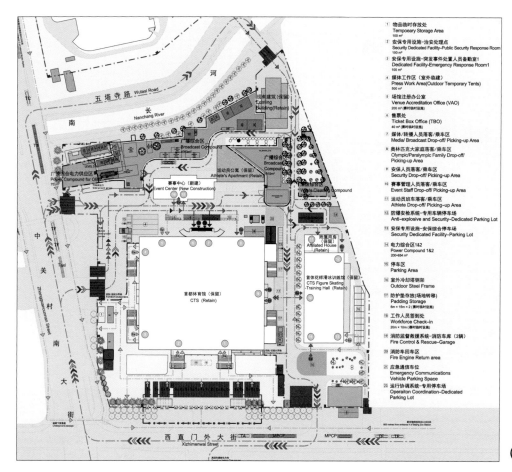

1 物品临时存放处
　Tempoeary Storage Area
　100 m²
2 安保专用设施-治安处理点
　Security Dedicated Facility-Public Security Response Room
　100 m²
3 安保专用设施-突发事件处置人员备勤室1
　Dedicated Facility-Emergency Response Room1
　100 m²
4 媒体工作区（室外临建）
　Press Work Area(Outdoor Temporary Tents)
　500 m²
5 场馆注册办公室
　Venue Accreditation Office (VAO)
　200 m²（赛时临时设施）
6 售票处
　Ticket Box Office (TBO)
　40 m²（赛时临时设施）
7 媒体/转播人员落客/乘车区
　Media/ Broadcast Drop-off/ Picking-up Area
8 奥林匹克大家庭落客/乘车区
　Olympic/Paralympic Family Drop-off/
　Picking-up Area
9 安保人员落客/乘车区
　Security Drop-off/ Picking-up Area
10 赛事管理人员落客/乘车区
　Event Staff Drop-off/ Picking-up Area
11 运动员班车落客/乘车区
　Athlete Drop-off/ Picking-up Area
12 防爆安检系统-专用车辆停车场
　Anti-explosive and Security-Dedicated Parking Lot
13 安保专用设施-安保综合停车场
　Security Dedicated Facility-Parking Lot
14 电力综合区1&2
　Power Compound 1&2
　200+654 m²
15 停车区
　Parking Area
16 室外冷却塔钢架
　Outdoor Steel Frame
17 防护垫存放（场地转移）
　Padding Storage
　6m × 15m × 2（赛时临时设施）
18 工作人员签到处
　Workforce Check-in
　20m × 10m（赛时临时设施）
19 消防监督救援系统-消防车库（2辆）
　Fire Control & Rescue-Garage
20 消防车回车区
　Fire Engine Return area
21 应急通信车位
　Emergency Communications
　Vehicle Parking Space
22 运行协调系统-专用停车场
　Operaiton Coordination-Dedicated
　Parking Lot

N
CTS 总平面图 OB5.0版
CTS Master Plan OB5.0

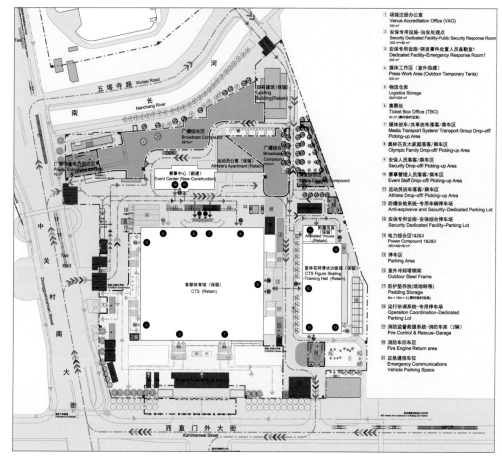

1 场馆注册办公室
　Venue Accreditation Office (VAO)
　100 m²
2 安保专用设施-治安处理点
　Security Dedicated Facility-Public Security Response Room
　200 m²+90 m²
3 安保专用设施-突发事件处置人员备勤室1
　Dedicated Facility-Emergency Response Room1
　200 m²
4 媒体工作区（室外临建）
　Press Work Area (Outdoor Temporary Tents)
　500 m²
5 物流仓库
　Logistics Storage
　32×7=224 m²
6 售票处
　Ticket Box Office (TBO)
　40 m²（赛时临时设施）
7 媒体班车/共享班车落客/乘车区
　Media Transport System/ Transport Group Drop-off/
　Picking-up Area
8 奥林匹克大家庭落客/乘车区
　Olympic Family Drop-off/ Picking-up Area
9 安保人员落客/乘车区
　Security Drop-off/ Picking-up Area
10 赛事管理人员落客/乘车区
　Event Staff Drop-off/ Picking-up Area
11 运动员班车落客/乘车区
　Athlete Drop-off/ Picking-up Area
12 防爆安检系统-专用车辆停车场
　Anti-explosive and Security-Dedicated Parking Lot
13 安保专用设施-安保综合停车场
　Security Dedicated Facility-Parking Lot
14 电力综合区1&2&3
　Power Compound 1&2&3
　200+400+50 m²
15 停车区
　Parking Area
16 室外冷却塔钢架
　Outdoor Steel Frame
17 防护垫存放（场地转移）
　Padding Storage
　6m × 15m × 2（赛时临时设施）
18 运行协调系统-专用停车场
　Operaiton Coordination-Dedicated
　Parking Lot
19 消防监督救援系统-消防车库（2辆）
　Fire Control & Rescue-Garage
20 消防车回车区
　Fire Engine Return area
21 应急通信车位
　Emergency Communications
　Vehicle Parking Space

N
CTS 总平面图 OB6.0版
CTS Master Plan OB6.0

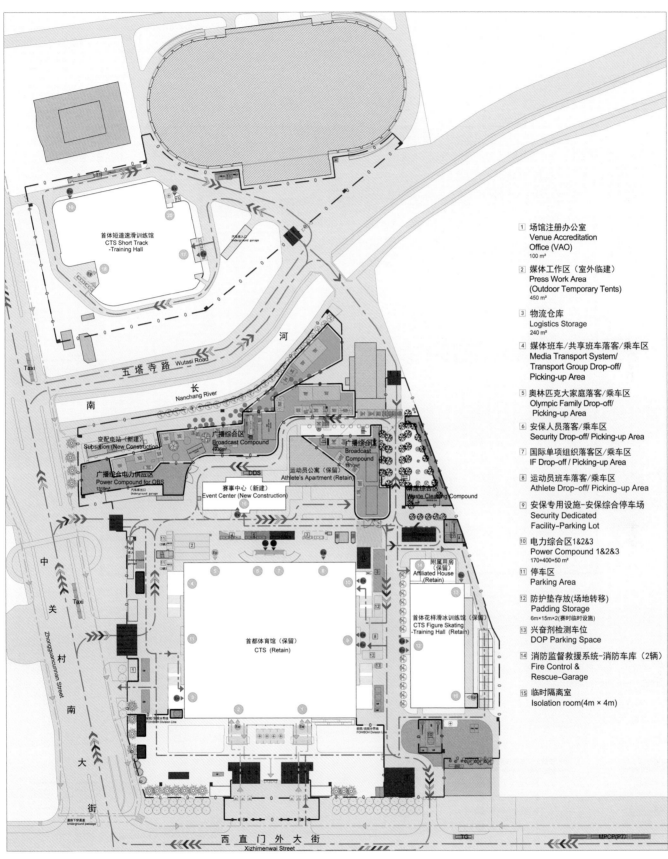

①	场馆注册办公室 Venue Accreditation Office (VAO) 100 m²
②	媒体工作区（室外临建） Press Work Area (Outdoor Temporary Tents) 450 m²
③	物流仓库 Logistics Storage 240 m²
④	媒体班车/共享班车落客/乘车区 Media Transport System/ Transport Group Drop-off/ Picking-up Area
⑤	奥林匹克大家庭落客/乘车区 Olympic Family Drop-off/ Picking-up Area
⑥	安保人员落客/乘车区 Security Drop-off/ Picking-up Area
⑦	国际单项组织落客区/乘车区 IF Drop-off / Picking-up Area
⑧	运动员班车落客/乘车区 Athlete Drop-off/ Picking-up Area
⑨	安保专用设施-安保综合停车场 Security Dedicated Facility–Parking Lot
⑩	电力综合区1&2&3 Power Compound 1&2&3 170+400+50 m²
⑪	停车区 Parking Area
⑫	防护垫存放(场地转移) Padding Storage 6m×15m×2(赛时临时设施)
⑬	兴奋剂检测车位 DOP Parking Space
⑭	消防监督救援系统-消防车库（2辆） Fire Control & Rescue–Garage
⑮	临时隔离室 Isolation room(4m × 4m)

CTS 总平面图 OB7.0版
CTS Master Plan OB7.0

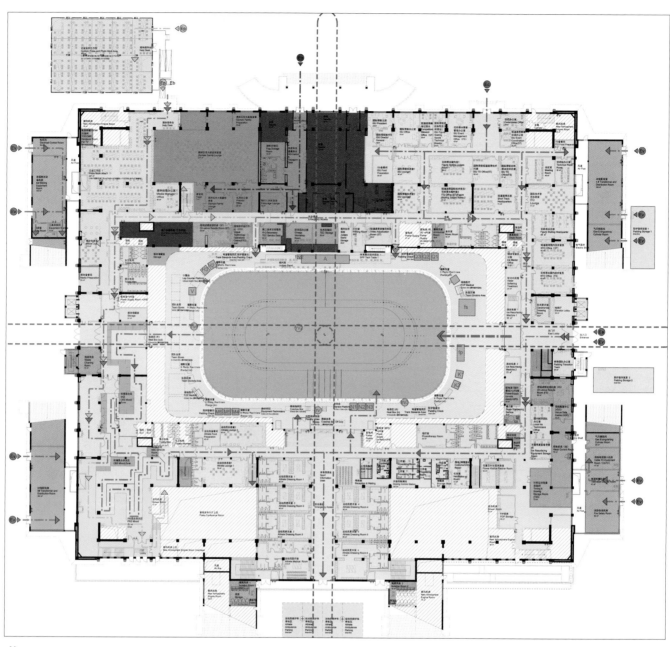

N

CTS 一层平面图—短道速滑 OB7.0版
CTS 1F Plan - Short Track OB7.0

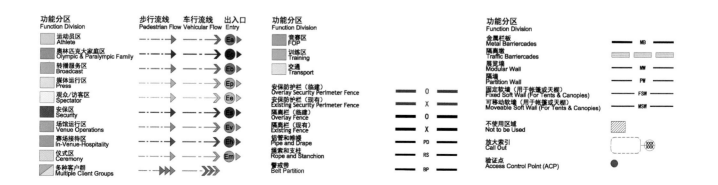

功能分区
Function Division

运动员区
Athlete

奥林匹克大家庭区
Olympic & Paralympic Family

转播服务区
Broadcast

媒体运行区
Press

观众/访客区
Spectator

安保区
Security

场馆运行区
Venue Operations

赛事接待区
In-Venue-Hospitality

仪式区
Ceremony

多种客户群
Multiple Client Groups

步行流线
Pedestrian Flow

车行流线
Vehicular Flow

出入口
Entry

Ea

Eb

Ep

Ee

Es

Ev

Eh

Em

功能分区
Function Division

竞赛区
FOP

训练区
Training

交通
Transport

安保防护栏（临建）
Overlay Security Perimeter Fence

安保防护栏（现有）
Existing Security Perimeter Fence

隔离栏（临建）
Overlay Fence

隔离栏（现有）
Existing Fence

铝管和帷幔
Pipe and Drape

绳索和支柱
Rope and Stanchion

警戒带
Belt Partition

O

X

O

X

PD

RS

BP

功能分区
Function Division

金属栏板
Metal Barriercades

隔离墩
Traffic Barriercades

展览墙
Modular Wall

隔墙
Partition Wall

固定软墙（用于帐篷或天棚）
Fixed Soft Wall (For Tents & Canopies)

可移动软墙（用于帐篷或天棚）
Moveable Soft Wall (For Tents & Canopies)

不使用区域
Not to be Used

放大索引
Call Out

验证点
Access Control Point (ACP)

MB

MW

PW

FSW

MSW

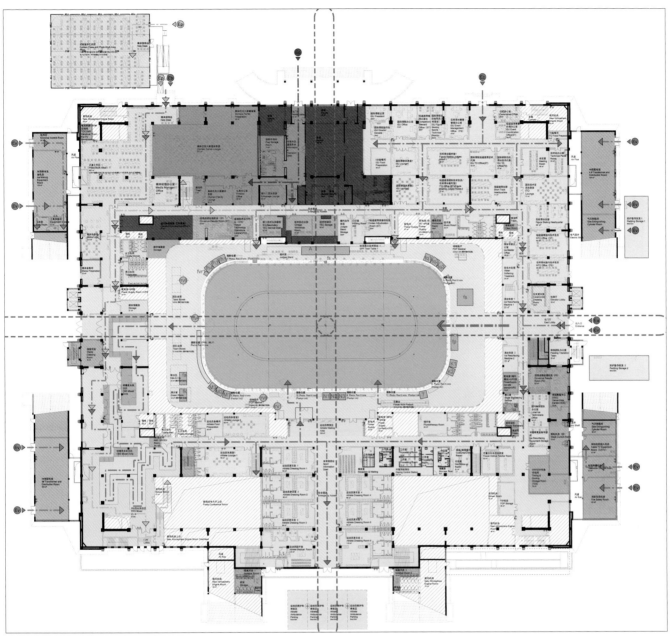

N

CTS 一层平面图—花样滑冰 OB7.0版
CTS 1F Plan — Figure Skating OB7.0

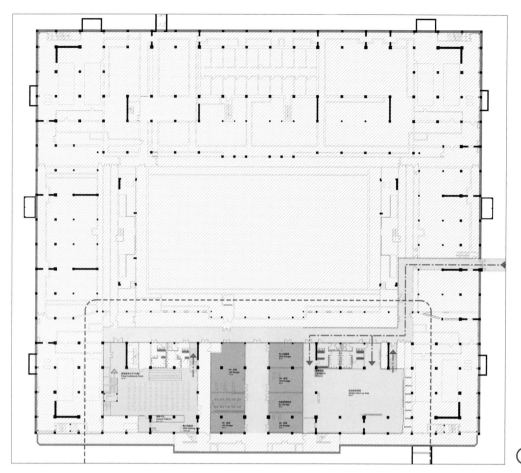

CTS 地下一层平面图 OB7.0版
CTS B1 Plan OB7.0

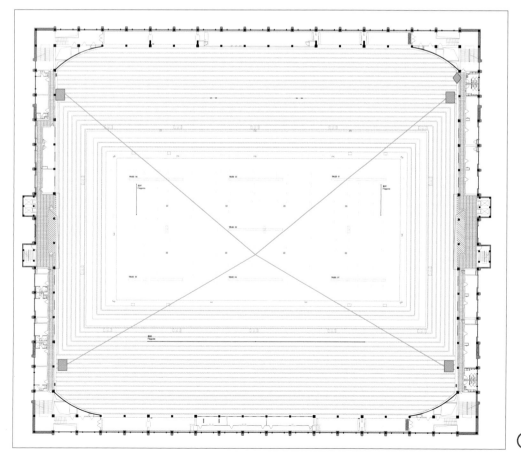

CTS 马道平面图 OB7.0版
CTS Catwalk Plan OB7.0

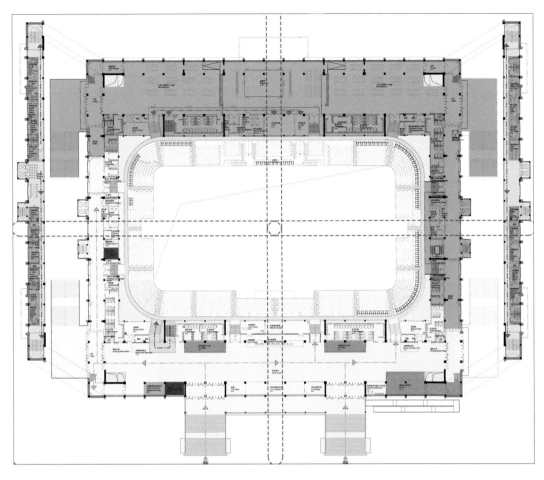

CTS 二层平面图 OB7.0版
CTS 2F Plan OB7.0

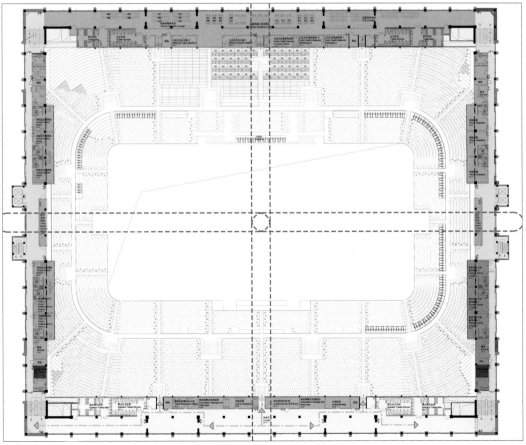

CTS 三层平面图 OB7.0版
CTS 3F Plan OB7.0

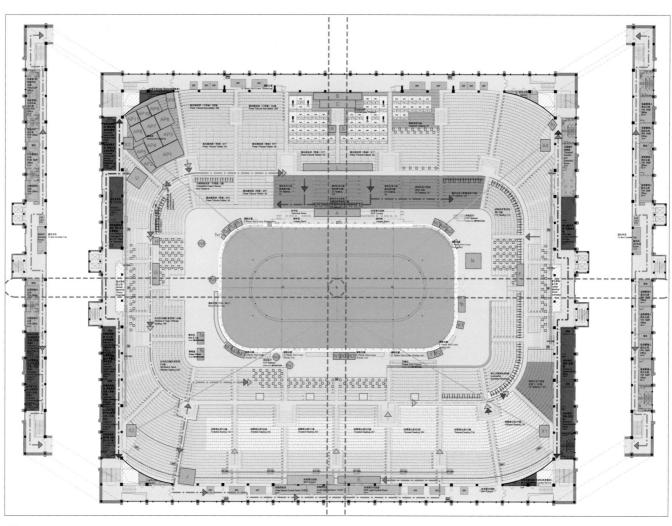

CTS 看台层平面图—花样滑冰 OB7.0版
CTS Seat Bowl Plan — Figure Skating OB7.0

功能分区 Function Division	步行流线 Pedestrian Flow	车行流线 Vehicular Flow	出入口 Entry
运动员区 Athlete			Ea
奥林匹克大家庭区 Olympic & Paralympic Family			Eo
转播服务区 Broadcast			Eb
媒体运行区 Press			Ep
观众/访客区 Spectator			Ee
安保区 Security			Es
场馆运行区 Venue Operations			Ev
赛场接待区 In-Venue-Hospitality			Eh
仪式区 Ceremony			Em
多种客户群 Multiple Client Groups			

功能分区 Function Division	
竞赛区 FOP	
训练区 Training	
交通 Transport	
安保防护栏（临建）Overlay Security Perimeter Fence	O
安保防护栏（现有）Existing Security Perimeter Fence	X
隔离栏（临建）Overlay Fence	O
隔离栏（现有）Existing Fence	X
铝管和帷幔 Pipe and Drape	PD
揽管和支柱 Rope and Stanchion	RS
警戒带 Belt Partition	BP

功能分区 Function Division	
金属栏板 Metal Barriercades	MB
隔离墩 Traffic Barriercades	
展览墙 Modular Wall	MW
隔墙 Partition Wall	PW
固定软墙（用于帐篷或天棚）Fixed Soft Wall (For Tents & Canopies)	FSW
可移动软墙（用于帐篷或天棚）Moveable Soft Wall (For Tents & Canopies)	MSW
不使用区域 Not to be Used	
放大索引 Call Out	XXX
验证点 Access Control Point (ACP)	●

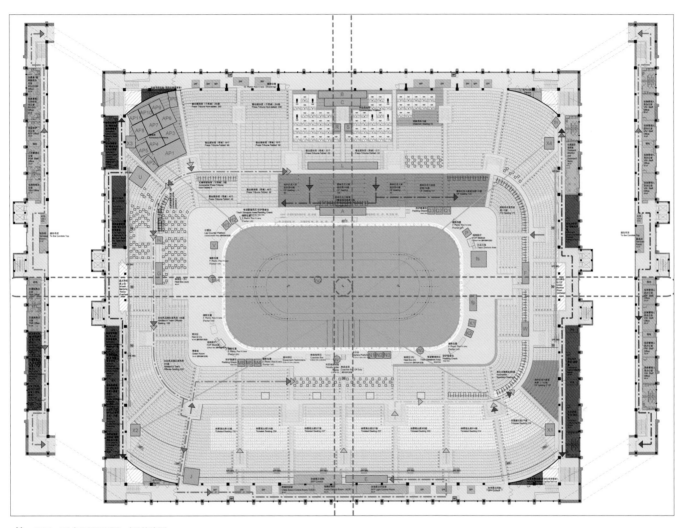

N CTS 看台层平面图—短道速滑 OB7.0版
CTS Seat Bowl Plan — Short Track OB7.0

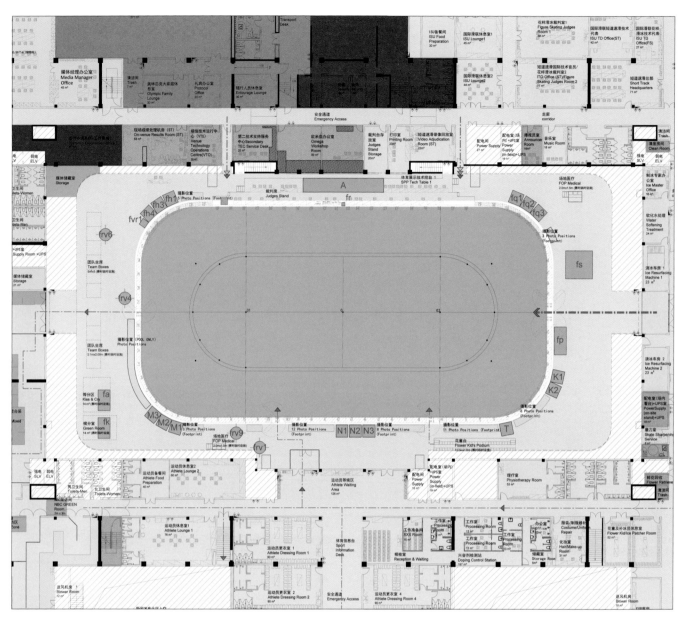

N
CTS FOP平面图—花样滑冰 OB7.0版
CTS FOP Plan — Figure Skating OB7.0

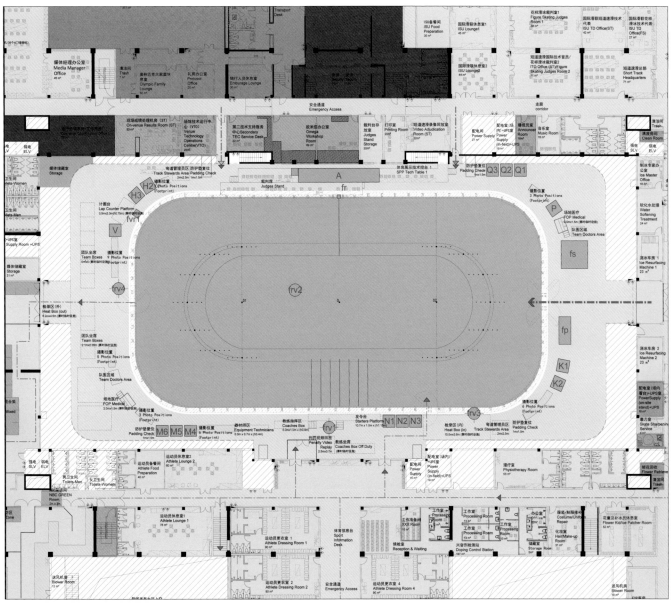

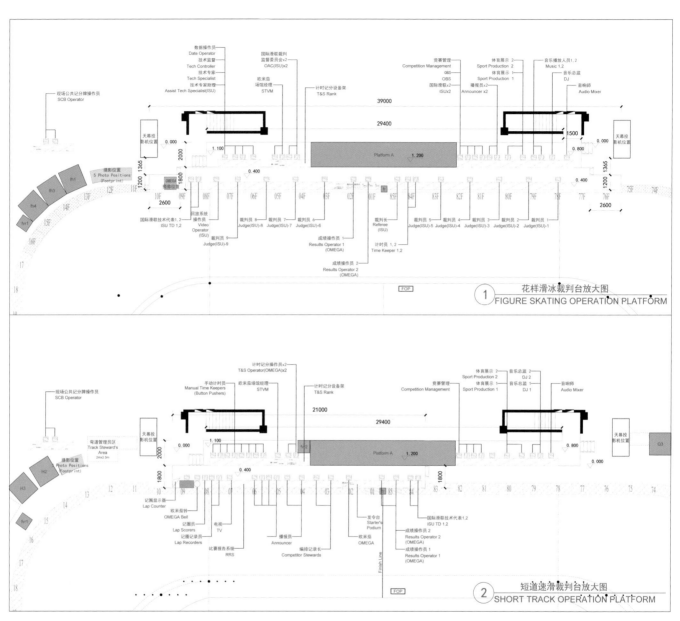

① 花样滑冰裁判台放大图
FIGURE SKATING OPERATION PLATFORM

② 短道速滑裁判台放大图
SHORT TRACK OPERATION PLATFORM

CTS 裁判台平面图 OB7.0版
CTS Judges Stand Plan OB7.0

功能分区 Function Division	步行流线 Pedestrian Flow	车行流线 Vehicular Flow	出入口 Entry
运动员区 Athlete			Ea ▶
奥林匹克大家庭区 Olympic & Paralympic Family			Eo ▶
转播服务区 Broadcast			Eb ▶
媒体运行区 Press			Ep ▶
观众/访客区 Spectator			Ee ▶
安保区 Security			Es ▶
场馆运行区 Venue Operations			Ev ▶
赛ища接待区 In-Venue-Hospitality			Eh ▶
仪式区 Ceremony			Em ▶
多种客户群 Multiple Client Groups	▶▶▶	▶▶	

功能分区 Function Division	
竞赛区 FOP	
训练区 Training	
交通 Transport	
安保防护栏（临建）Overlay Security Perimeter Fence	O
安保防护栏（现有）Existing Security Perimeter Fence	X
隔离栏（临建）Overlay Fence	O
隔离栏（现有）Existing Fence	X
铝管和帷幕 Pipe and Drape	PD
提索和帷柱 Rope and Stanchion	RS
警戒带 Belt Partition	BP

功能分区 Function Division	
金属栏板 Metal Barriercades	MB
隔离墩 Traffic Barriercades	
展览墙 Modular Wall	MW
隔墙 Partition Wall	PW
固定软墙（用于帐篷或天棚）Fixed Soft Wall (For Tents & Canopies)	FSW
可移动软墙（用于帐篷或天棚）Moveable Soft Wall (For Tents & Canopies)	MSW
不使用区域 Not to be Used	
放大索引 Call Out	XXX
验证点 Access Control Point (ACP)	●

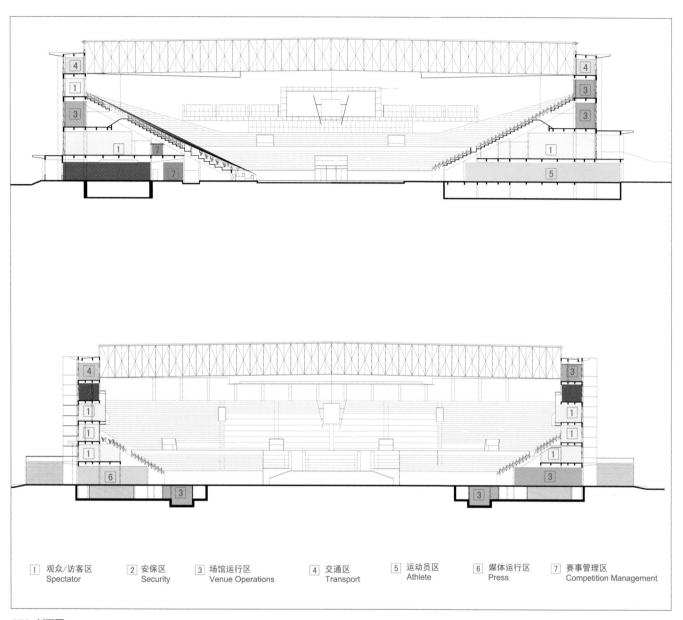

| 1 | 观众/访客区 Spectator | 2 | 安保区 Security | 3 | 场馆运行区 Venue Operations | 4 | 交通区 Transport | 5 | 运动员区 Athlete | 6 | 媒体运行区 Press | 7 | 赛事管理区 Competition Management |

CTS 剖面图 OB7.0版
CTS Section OB7.0

首都花样滑冰训练馆 [CFT]

CTS Figure Skating Training Hall

首体花样滑冰训练馆位于首都体育馆东侧，在冬奥会期间作为花样滑冰项目的训练之用。花样滑冰训练馆共3层，有1块标准冰面，场馆建筑面积约1.37万m²，活动座位数约100席。

标准冰面位于地下一层，西侧设置了2套运动员更衣室，并有地下通道直接连通竞赛馆地下一层。训练冰面南侧为媒体看台区、媒体混合区，冰面东侧也设置少量媒体看台。训练冰面北侧为浇冰车房，浇冰车可以方便快捷地进入冰面。

运动员由冬奥村乘坐大巴到达首都体育馆东门，进入东门后可直接到达首体花样滑冰训练馆，并进入场馆地下一层训练冰面进行训练。

转播及新闻媒体通过位于训练馆东南角的媒体出入口进入，经过楼梯到达地下一层媒体看台区域。工作完毕后沿原路线离开场馆。

Located to the east of the Capital Indoor Stadium, the CTS Figure Skating Training Hall is used for Figure Skating training during the Games. The CTS Figure Skating Training Hall has a total of three floors, a standard ice rink. It has floor area of about 13,700m², and about 100 movable seats.

The standard ice rink is on B1, with two athlete dressing rooms on the west side and an underground passage connecting directly to the B1 of the competition venue. Press tribunes and a mixed zone are on the south side of the training ice rink, and a few press tribune seats are also set on the east side of the ice rink. The ice resurfacing machine room is on the north side of the training ice rink, and ice resurfacing machines can conveniently enter the ice rink.

Athletes take shuttle buses from the Olympic Village to the east gate of the Capital Indoor Stadium and after entering the east gate, they can directly reach the CTS Figure Skating Training Hall and enter the training ice surface on B1 of the venue.

Broadcast and media personnel enter from the media entrance in the southeast corner of the training hall and go to the press tribunes on B1 via the stairs. They leave the venue along the same route after finishing their work.

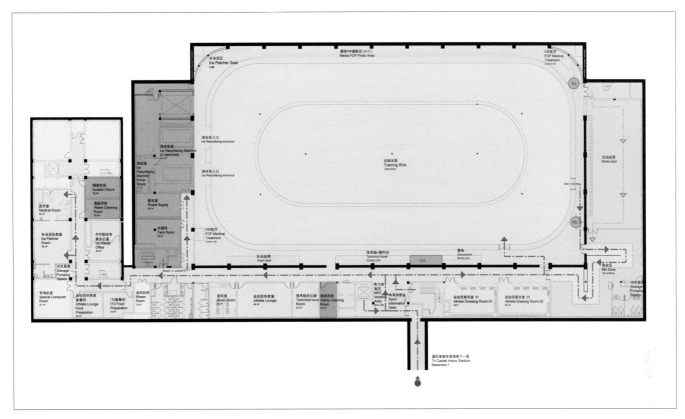

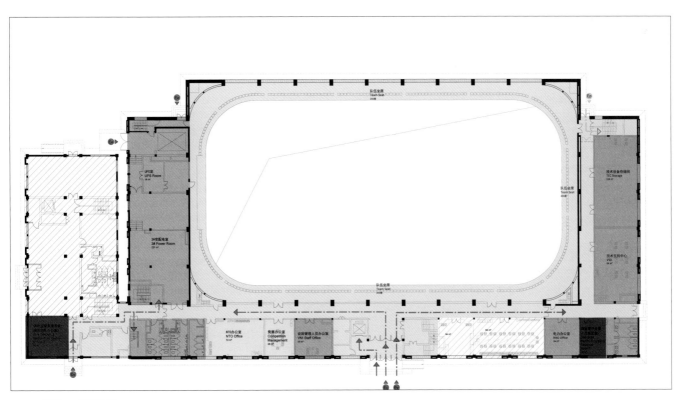

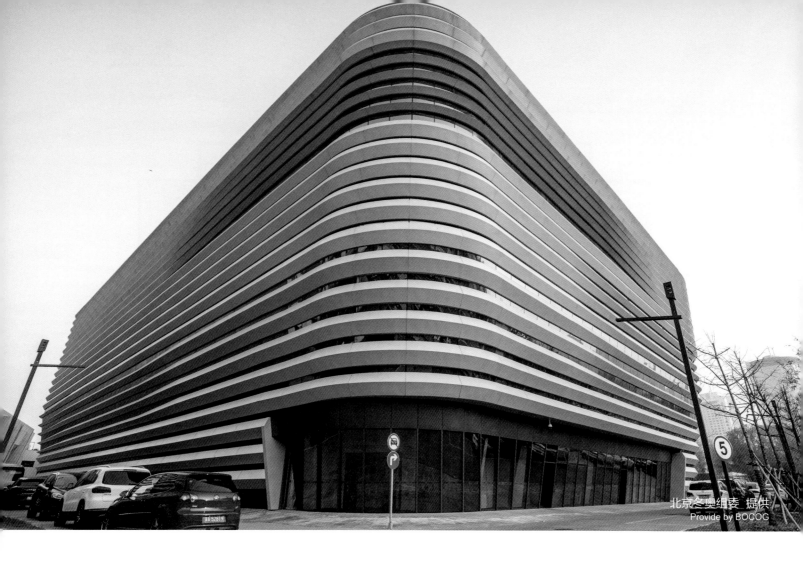

首体短道速滑训练馆 [CST]

CTS Short Track Speed Skating Training Hall

首体短道速滑训练馆位于首都体育馆北侧，在北京2022年冬奥会期间作为短道速滑项目的训练之用，赛后可根据需要转换成为各种冰上运动赛场，也可成为全民健身的场所。

首体短道速滑训练馆是新建场馆，采用多层立体设计，分层包含2块标准冰场、2块陆上训练场地，以及科研、医疗、康复用房、运动员宿舍和餐厅等配套功能。2块冰场均采用二氧化碳跨临界直接制冷系统，环保、节能，冬奥会期间使用其中的1块作为短道速滑训练使用。场馆总建筑面积约3.3万m²，设置400个临时坐席。

冬奥会期间使用地下1层及地上4层部分区域。运动员、技术官员、媒体及场馆运行人员由一层通过各自的出入口进入场馆。场馆三层设有3套运动员更衣室，包含更衣区、卫生间及淋浴间。运动员休息室临近更衣室，运动员热身区毗邻训练冰面。训练结束后，运动员可在混合采访区接受采访。

媒体人员通过一层西侧入口进入场馆，去往新闻混合区及看台席。其他人员按照防疫分区规定，分别由西北门和东北门进入场馆。

Located to the north of the Capital Indoor Stadium, the CTS Short Track Speed Skating Training Hall is used for Short Track Speed Skating training during the Beijing 2022 Olympic Winter Games and can turn into a venue for various ice sports or a place for fitness activities for the public after the Games.

The CTS Short Track Speed Skating Training Hall is a newly built venue in multi-tiered design, including 2 standard ice rinks, 2 dryland training sites, and supporting facilities such as rooms for scientific research, medical services and rehabilitation, athlete dormitories, and dining halls. Both ice rinks use an eco-friendly energy-saving CO_2 trans-critical refrigeration system, with one of them used for short track speed skating training during the Games. The venue has a total floor area of about 33,000m² and 400 temporary seats.

B1 and part of the four above-ground floors of the venue are used during the Games. Athletes, technical officials, media and venue operation personnel enter the venue from their respective entrances on the first floor. There are 3 athlete dressing rooms on the third floor of the venue, with each including a changing area, a toilet, and a shower. The athlete lounge is adjacent to the dressing rooms, and the athlete warm-up area is adjacent to the ice rink for training. After training, athletes can go to the mixed zone to be interviewed.

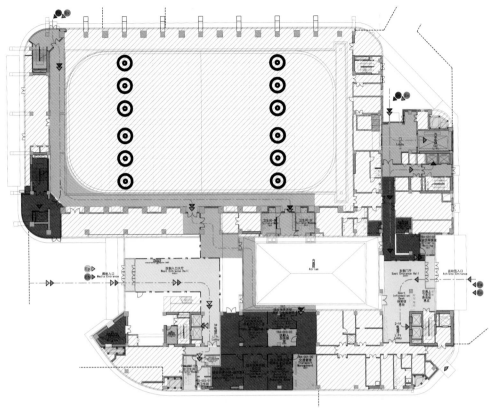

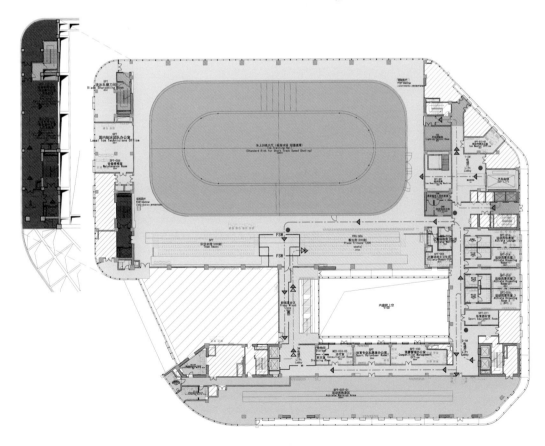

五棵松体育中心 [WKS]

Wukesong Sports Centre

1. 场馆基本情况

五棵松体育中心位于北京五棵松华熙商业区，建筑面积约6.3万m²，在北京2008年夏季奥运会期间承担篮球项目的比赛，在北京2022年冬奥会期间承担女子冰球部分比赛、决赛以及部分男子冰球小组赛，产生1枚金牌。

五棵松体育中心是国内第一座专业篮球馆，并在建设之初就预装了制冰系统和制冷管道，可在6小时内进行冰球模式和篮球模式的"冰篮转换"。

2. FOP及相关区域

根据北京冬奥会要求，在30m×60m的冰面尺寸基础上，增加了26m×60m的冰面模式，两种尺寸可方便转换。制冷系统沿用原有管道，制冷剂更换为更加环保的R449A。

浇冰车用房设置在FOP东北角，赛事管理用房位于FOP东侧，运动员更衣室位于FOP南侧，媒体运行区位于FOP西北角，各相关业务领域注册人员均可便捷到达比赛场地。

3. 场馆前院及观众流线

五棵松体育中心南广场、西侧疏散通道和馆内首层观众大

1. Venue Overview

Located in Beijing Wukesong Bloomage LIVE, with a floor area of about 63,000m², the Wukesong Sports Centre is the competition venue for basketball events during the Beijing 2008 Olympic Games and for some competitions including the final of Ice Hockey Women's tournament and some preliminary round competitions of Ice Hockey Men's tournament during the Beijing 2022 Olympic Winter Games, with one gold medal won here.

As the first professional basketball court in China, the Wukesong Sports Centre has been pre-installed an ice-making system and refrigeration piping at the beginning of construction and can realise conversion from a basketball court into an ice rink within six hours.

2. FOP and Relevant Areas

According to the requirements of the Beijing 2022 Olympic and Paralympic Winter Games, a 26m×60m ice rink mode has been added in addition to the 30m×60m ice rink mode, to conveniently switch between the two sizes. The refrigeration system continues to use the original piping, with the refrigerant changed to the eco-friendlier R449A.

厅、观众看台区域为场馆前院区，赛时面向观众开放。观众于南广场安检后，从场馆南门平层进入首层观众大厅及观众看台，观赛结束后通过场馆南门及西门疏散离开。

4. 场馆后院及注册流线

五棵松体育中心场馆后院区包括场馆北侧广场、东侧广场、下沉环廊以及馆内非观众厅区域。注册人员主要入口集中布置在下沉环廊及首层北侧。

（1）运动员流线

根据参赛队伍数量，五棵松体育中心及五棵松冰球训练馆共设置了10套运动员更衣室及2套赛时更衣室，其中，主馆设置4套运动员更衣室及2套赛时更衣室，训练馆设置6套运动员更衣室。赛时主馆与训练馆之间设置临时通道，运动员可快速往返于两馆之间。

运动员乘坐大巴到达五棵松体育中心下沉环廊西南角的落客区，经由南侧运动员入口进入FOP层运动员更衣室区。赛时更衣室靠近FOP入口，运动员从赛时更衣室出发后通过场地西南角、东南角的运动员通道进入FOP。比赛结束后，由西南角运动员通道离开场地，进入混合采访区，接受采访后返回其更衣室。

（2）技术官员流线

场馆内设置2间ITO更衣室及1间NTO休息室。ITO更衣室位于FOP层北侧，紧邻比赛场地入口，技术官员于下沉环廊东侧下车后通过专用入口进入场馆，快速到达紧靠入口处的ITO休息区及热身区，经由内部通道到达ITO更衣室。NTO休息室位于场馆东南角附属建筑二层，可通过室外楼梯直达。

（3）奥林匹克大家庭流线

奥林匹克大家庭区集中位于场馆北部区域，流线独立。大家庭成员于下沉环廊北侧落客位下车，由FOP层北侧大家庭入口进入其接待区，再通过专用电梯到达FOP夹层的休息室，然后经专用通道直达大家庭看台。

（4）媒体流线

转播服务及媒体运行人员由西侧的媒体入口直接进入位于场馆FOP层西北部媒体工作区。工作区内设有文字记者工作间、摄影记者工作间、媒体休息区等用房，紧邻FOP、混合采访区、媒体坐席及新闻发布厅，流线便捷。新闻混合区与新闻发布厅共用同一空间，于不同时段分别使用，比赛后可快速转换其功能。赛时媒体人员通过场馆西北角电梯及楼梯到达首层看台注册坐席区。

（5）场馆室外综合区

转播综合区位于场地西北角，物流综合区、清废综合区位于场地北侧，餐饮综合区设置于下沉环廊。

5. 场馆坐席

五棵松体育中心场馆容量为14614席。冬奥会赛时注册坐席集中在看台区域北部，包含奥林匹克大家庭坐席318个、奥林匹克大家庭无障碍坐席及陪同席各3个，评论员席40个、观察员席40个、播报席4个、摄像平台23个，同竞赛项目运动员及随队官员坐席68个、不同竞赛项目运动员及随队官员坐席100个、带桌媒体席158个、不带桌媒体席45个、含无障碍不带桌媒体席2个、看台摄影位置76个、无障碍摄影位置2个。球探席、视频教练席、数据统计席及IF坐席位于首层看台南侧。

观众坐席集中位于首层看台东、西两侧及包厢层，共计3127个。结合新冠肺炎疫情防疫政策，赛时观众坐席共计1200个，其中包含6个无障碍坐席及6个无障碍陪同席。

3. Front of House and Spectator Flow

The south square and west evacuation route of and the first-floor spectator hall and spectator stand area inside the Wukesong Sports Centre constitute the Front of House (FOH) open to spectators during the Games. After passing security checks in the south square, spectators enter from the venue's south gate to the first-floor spectator hall and spectator stand area, and after competitions, they leave from the venue's south gate and west gate.

4. Back of House and Accreditation Flow

(1) Athlete Flow

Depending on the number of the teams, the Wukesong Sports Centre and WKS Ice Hockey Training Hall have a total of 10 athlete dressing rooms and two competition-day dressing rooms, with 4 athlete dressing rooms and 2 competition-day dressing rooms set in the main venue and 6 athlete dressing rooms set in the training hall. A temporary passage is set between the main venue and the training hall during the Games for athletes to travel quickly between the two venues. Athletes take buses to the drop-off zone in the southwest corner of the sunken circular corridor of the Wukesong Sports Centre and then go to the athlete dressing room area on the FOP level from the athlete entrance in the south. Competition-day dressing rooms are near the FOP entrance.

(2) Technical Official Flow

Two ITO dressing rooms and one NTO lounge are set inside the venue. ITO dressing rooms are in the north of the FOP level and next to the FOP entrance. After getting off on the east side of the sunken circular corridor, technical officials enter the venue from their dedicated entrance, then quickly reach the ITO lounge and warm-up area next to the entrance, and go to the ITO dressing rooms via an internal passage.

(3) Olympic Family Flow

The Olympic Family area is in the northern part of the venue, with an independent flow. The Olympic Family members get off the bus at the drop-off site in the north of the sunken corridor, enter the Olympic Family reception area from the Olympic Family entrance on the north of the FOP level, arrive at the lounge of the FOP mezzanine via the dedicated elevator, and then reach the Olympic Family stand via the dedicated passageway.

(4) Media Flow

The broadcast and media personnel directly enter the media work area on the northwest of the FOP level of the venue via the media entrance in the west. The media work area includes journalist work room, photographer work room, media lounge, and other rooms, which is adjacent to the FOP, mixed zone, press tribunes, and press conference room, with a convenient flow.

5. Seating Area

The venue capacity of Wukesong Sports Centre is 14,614. The Games-time accredited seating is in the north of the stand area, including 318 Olympic Family seats, 3 Olympic Family accessible seats, and 3 companion seats; 40 commentary positions, 40 observer seats, 4 announce positions, 23 camera platforms; 68 seats for same discipline athletes and team officials, 100 seats for different discipline athletes and team officials; 158 tabled press tribune seats, 45 non-tabled press tribune seats, including 2 accessible non-tabled press tribune seats, 76 stand camera positions, and 2 accessible camera positions.

The spectator seats are in the east and west of 1F seating area and the balcony level, with a total number of 3,127. Based on the COVID-19 countermeasures, there are 1,200 spectator seats, including 6 accessible seats and 6 companion seats.

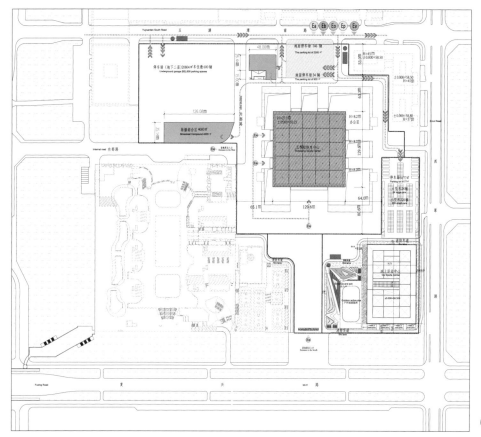

WKS 总平面图 OB1.2版
WKS Master Plan OB1.2

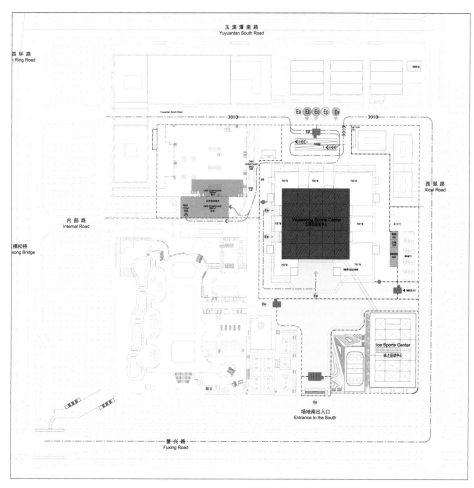

WKS 总平面图 OB2.1版
WKS Master Plan OB2.1

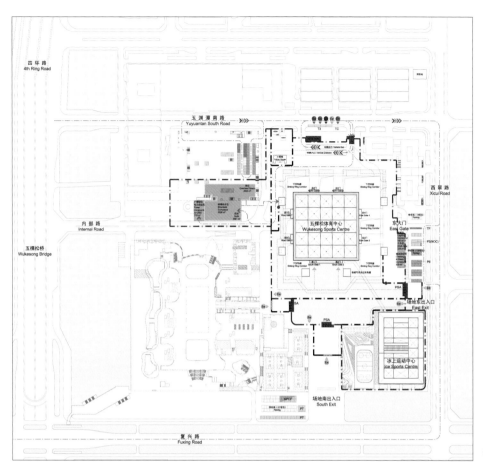

WKS 总平面图 OB3.0版
WKS Master Plan OB3.0

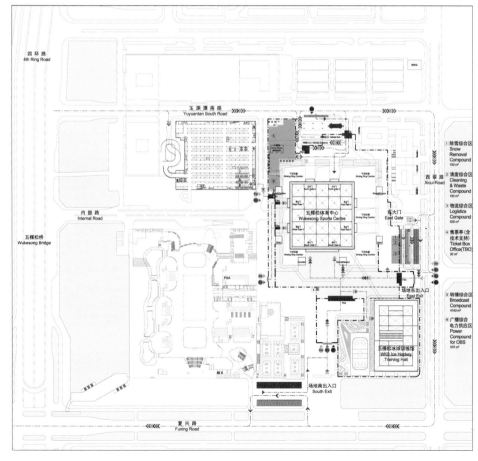

WKS 总平面图 OB4.0版
WKS Master Plan OB4.0

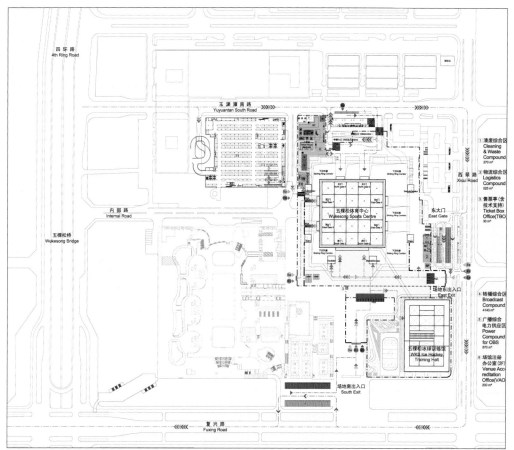

①	清废综合区 Cleaning & Waste Compound	270 m²
②	物流综合区 Logistics Compound	525 m²
③	售票亭(含技术支持) Ticket Box Office(TBO)	30 m²
④	转播综合区 Broadcast Compound	4143 m²
⑤	广播综合电力供应区 Power Compound for OBS	570 m²
⑥	场馆注册办公室(2F) Venue Accreditation Office(VAO)	200 m²

WKS 总平面图 OB5.0版
WKS Master Plan OB5.0

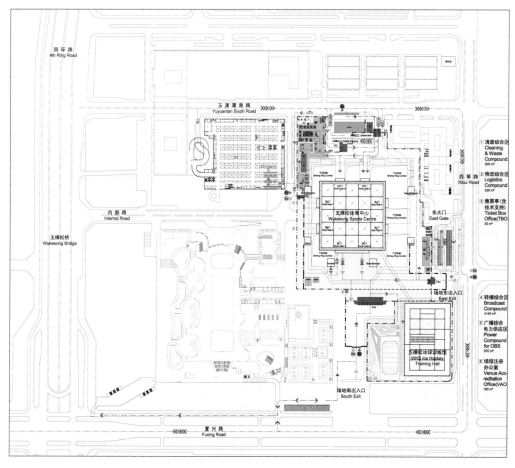

①	清废综合区 Cleaning & Waste Compound	300 m²
②	物流综合区 Logistics Compound	525 m²
③	售票亭(含技术支持) Ticket Box Office(TBO)	30 m²
④	转播综合区 Broadcast Compound	4143 m²
⑤	广播综合电力供应区 Power Compound for OBS	570 m²
⑥	场馆注册办公室 Venue Accreditation Office(VAO)	180 m²

WKS 总平面图 OB6.0版
WKS Master Plan OB6.0

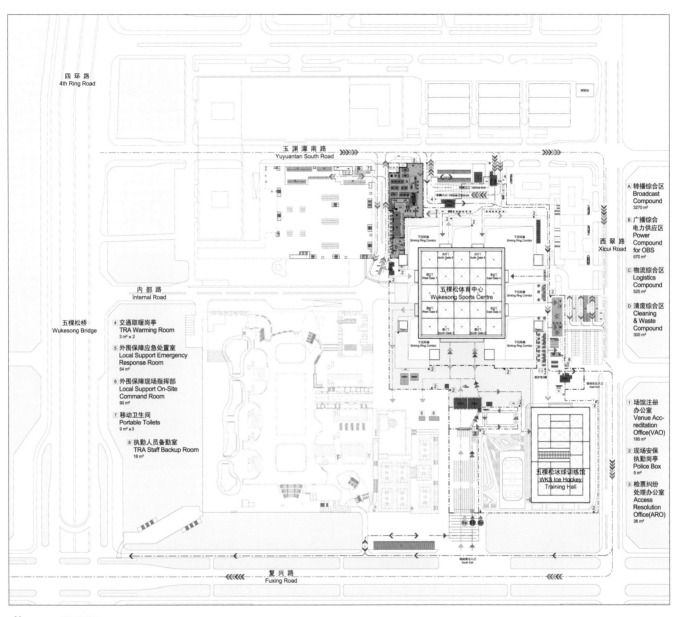

A 转播综合区
Broadcast
Compound
3270 m²

B 广播综合
电力供应区
Power
Compound
for OBS
570 m²

C 物流综合区
Logistics
Compound
525 m²

D 清废综合区
Cleaning
& Waste
Compound
300 m²

1 场馆注册
办公室
Venue Acc-
reditation
Office(VAO)
180 m²

2 现场安保
执勤岗亭
Police Box
5 m²

3 检票纠纷
处理办公室
Access
Resolution
Office(ARO)
36 m²

4 交通取暖岗亭
TRA Warming Room
3 m² × 2

5 外围保障应急处置室
Local Support Emergency
Response Room
54 m²

6 外围保障现场指挥部
Local Support On-Site
Command Room
90 m²

7 移动卫生间
Portable Toilets
9 m² ×3

8 执勤人员备勤室
TRA Staff Backup Room
18 m²

四 环 路
4th Ring Road

玉 渊 潭 南 路
Yuyuantan South Road

内 部 路
Internal Road

五棵松桥
Wukesong Bridge

复 兴 路
Fuxing Road

西翠路
Xicui Road

五棵松体育中心
Wukesong Sports Centre

五棵松冰球训练馆
WKS Ice Hockey
Training Hall

WKS 总平面图 OB7.0版
WKS Master Plan OB7.0

139

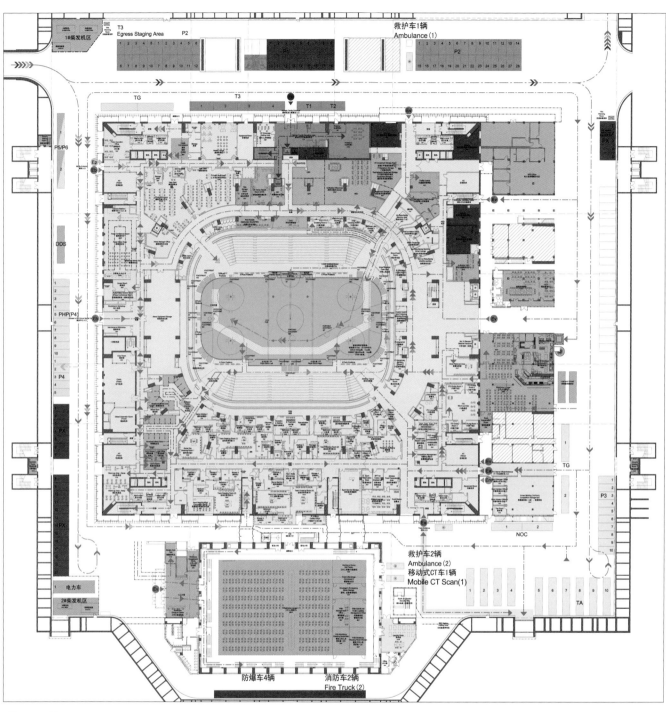

WKS 地下一层平面图 OB7.0版
WKS B1 Plan OB7.0

功能分区 Function Division	步行流线 Pedestrian Flow	车行流线 Vehicular Flow	出入口 Entry	功能分区 Function Division	功能分区 Function Division	
运动员区 Athlete			Ea	竞赛区 FOP	金属栏板 Metal Barriercades	MB
奥林匹克大家庭区 Olympic & Paralympic Family				训练区 Training	隔离墩 Traffic Barriercades	
转播服务区 Broadcast			Eb	交通 Transport	展览墙 Modular Wall	MW
媒体运行区 Press			Ep		隔墙 Partition Wall	PW
观众/访客区 Spectator			Ee	安保防护栏（临建） Overlay Security Perimeter Fence	固定软墙（用于帐篷或天棚） Fixed Soft Wall (For Tents & Canopies)	FSW
安保区 Security				安保防护栏（现有） Existing Security Perimeter Fence	可移动软墙（用于帐篷或天棚） Moveable Soft Wall (For Tents & Canopies)	MSW
场馆运行区 Venue Operations			Ev	隔离栏（临建） Overlay Fence		
赛场接待区 In-Venue-Hospitality			Eh	隔离栏（现有） Existing Fence	不使用区域 Not to be Used	
仪式区 Ceremony			Em	铝管和帷幔 Pipe and Drape	放大索引 Call Out	
多种客户群 Multiple Client Groups				揽索和帷柱 Rope and Stanchion	验证点 Access Control Point (ACP)	
				警戒带 Belt Partition		

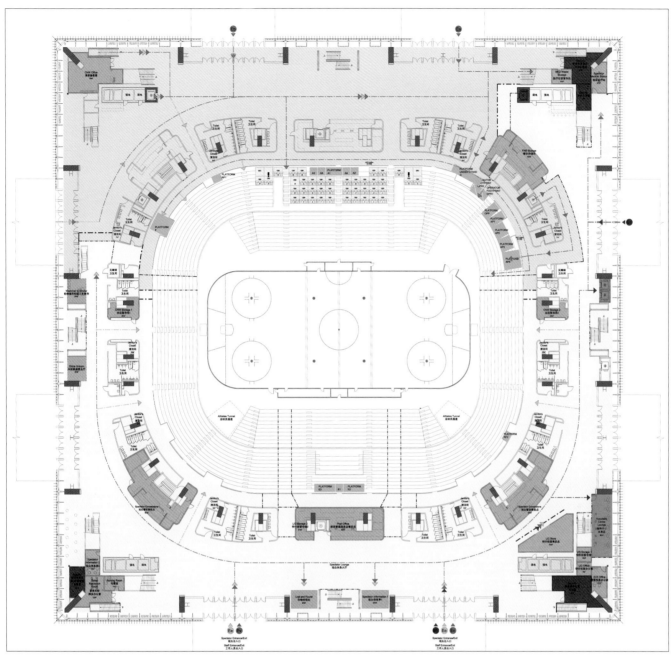

N WKS 一层平面图 OB7.0版
WKS 1F Plan OB7.0

141

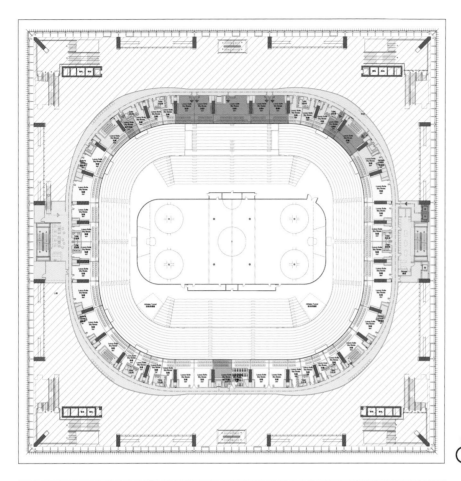

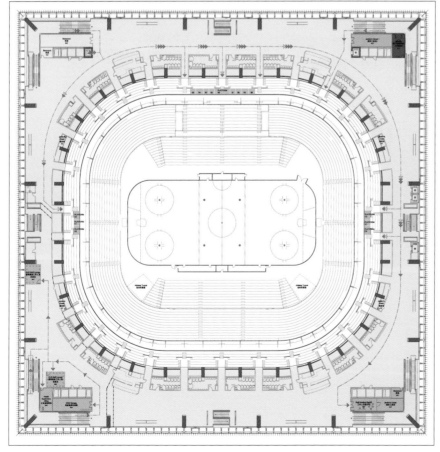

WKS 二层平面图 OB7.0版
WKS 2F Plan OB7.0

WKS 三层平面图 OB7.0版
WKS 3F Plan OB7.0

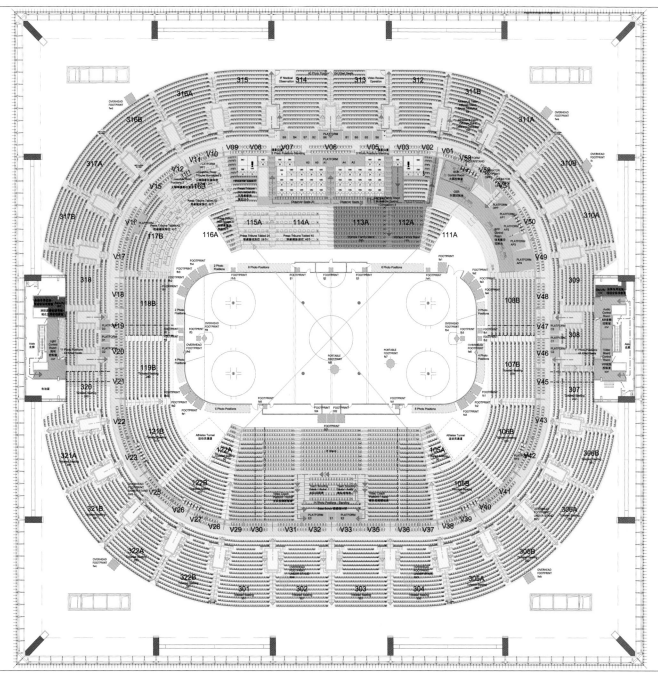

WKS 看台层平面图 OB7.0版
WKS Seat Bowl Plan OB7.0

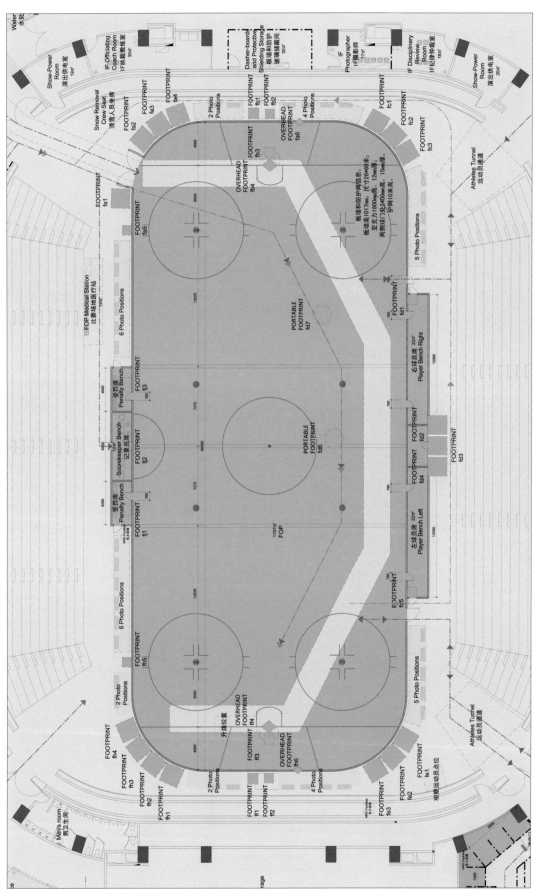

WKS FOP平面图 OB7.0版
WKS FOP Plan OB7.0

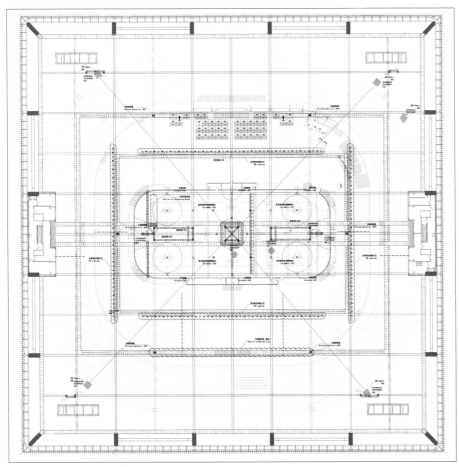

N

WKS 马道平面图 OB7.0版
WKS Catwalk Plan OB7.0

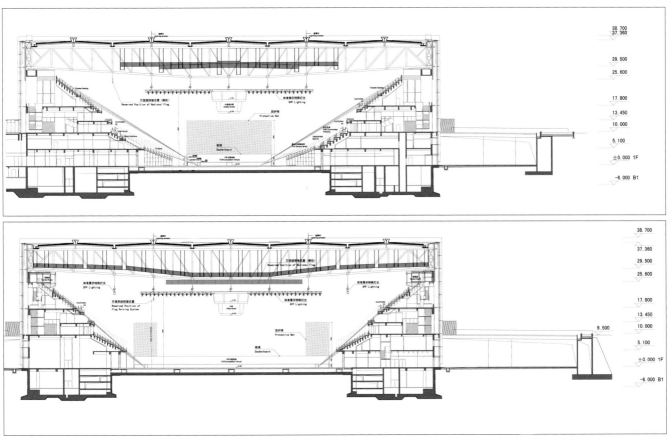

WKS 剖面图 OB7.0版
WKS Section OB7.0

场馆业主 提供
Provide by Venue Owner

五棵松冰球训练馆 [WIT]

WKS Ice Hockey Training Hall

　　五棵松冰球训练馆位于五棵松体育中心的东南侧，冬奥会期间承担女子冰球项目的训练。训练馆以一片片飘落的"冰菱花"飞舞聚合成冰雪纹理的形象，昵称"冰菱花"。场馆总建筑面积约4万m²。

　　冬奥会期间训练馆使用的是地下二层、地下一层及首层部分区域。训练馆设置了6套运动员更衣室，运动员通过地下4m宽的运动员专用通道与五棵松体育中心相连。媒体人员、安保及场馆运行人员由训练馆一层西侧入口进入场馆抵达各自区域。

　　训练馆共有2块标准冰面，北侧冰面在赛时供运动员训练使用，为满足赛时及赛后的使用要求，设置30m×60m和26m×60m两种不同尺寸的冰面及板墙预埋件，可在两种冰场尺寸中快速转换。

Located in the southeast of Wukesong Sports Centre, the WKS Ice Hockey Training Hall is the venue for the training in Women's Ice Hockey events during the Olympic Winter Games Beijing 2022. The external curtain wall of the training hall features a pattern of flying ice crystals, hence nicknamed "Ice Crystal". The venue has a total floor area of about 40,000m².

During the Games, some areas of B2, B1, and F1 of the training hall are used. The training hall has 6 sets of athletes' dressing rooms and athletes enter Wukesong Sports Centre via the 4m wide underground dedicated passage. The media personnel, security, and venue operation personnel enter the venue and reach respective areas from the west entrance of F1 of the training hall.

The training hall provides 2 standard ice rinks. The north ice surface is used for athlete training during the Games. To meet the Games-time and post-Games use requirements, 2 different sizes of ice rinks, 30m×60m and 26m×60m and wall inserts are provided, which ensures a quick switch between the two sizes of ice rinks.

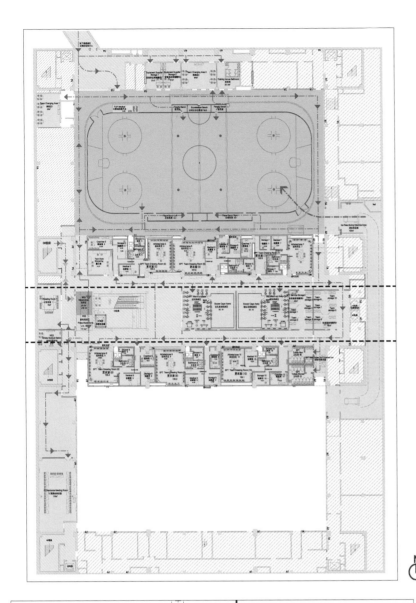

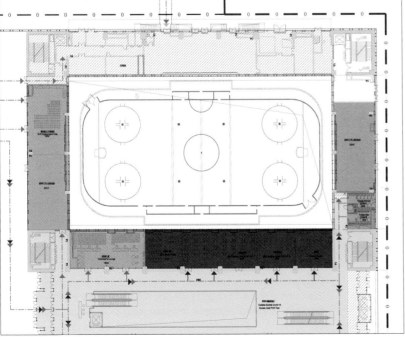

北京冬奥组委 提供
Provide by BOCOG

首钢滑雪大跳台 [BAS]

Big Air Shougang

首钢滑雪大跳台位于北京市石景山区首钢园区内,是世界上第一个永久保留的滑雪大跳台场地,在北京2022年冬奥会期间承担单板滑雪大跳台及自由式滑雪大跳台2项比赛,共产生4枚金牌。

首钢滑雪大跳台坐落于首钢工业遗址园区内,连同北京冬奥组委总部办公区等项目的建设,带动了整个首钢园区的复兴和发展。大跳台赛道两侧的防风网,其建筑造型融入了敦煌壁画中"飞天"的元素,所以首钢滑雪大跳台又昵称"雪飞天"。

大跳台以4座标志性冷却塔为背景,形成独特的冬奥会景观,赛后将作为北京冬季奥林匹克公园的一部分面向市民开放。

1. 场馆基本情况

场馆赛时安保封闭线范围北至群明湖北路,东至群明湖大街,南至制氧厂南,直至西侧的厂区西围墙,占地面积为32.1hm²(含群明湖)。场馆安保封闭线长度约2.5km,前院区占地面积1.5万m²,后院区占地面积7.79万m²。

2. FOP及相关区域

首钢滑雪大跳台位于群明湖西南,冷却塔南侧20m,根据

Located in the Shougang Park, Shijingshan District, Beijing, Big Air Shougang is the world's first permanently reserved big air venue. Big Air Shougang is the competition venue for Snowboard and Freeski Big Air events, during the Olympic Winter Games Beijing 2022, with four gold medals won here.

Situated in the Shougang Park, Big Air Shougang drives the revitalisation and development of the entire Shougang Park together with such projects as building the Beijing 2022 Headquarters in the park. The architectural style of wind fences at both sides of the course is integrated with the element of "Flying Apsaras" of Dunhuang Mural, so Big Air Shougang is also nicknamed "Snow Flying Ribbon".

1. Venue Overview

The Front of House (FOH) area covers a land area of 15,000m² and the Back of House (BOH) area covers an area of 77,900m².

2. FOP and Relevant Areas

Big Air Shougang is located to the southwest of Qunming Lake, 20m to the south of cooling towers. According to the wind direction, sunlight, and the principle of minimising occupation to Qunming Lake, Big Air Shougang has an angle of 10° south of east, the

风向、日照及最少占用群明湖原则，大跳台角度为东偏南10°，出发区高度47.5m，结束区沉入水面4m，垂直落差51.5m，总高度60.5m。赛道结构总长度160m，宽度10～30m。裁判塔高度22.6m。跳台钢结构设计还预留了未来竞赛剖面变化的可能性。

3. 前院区及观众流线

赛时观众由群明湖南路引导至安检通道，进入前院区集散广场后步行约120m可抵达观众席。场馆容量坐席5761个，其中永久坐席4059个，临时坐席1702个，无障碍及陪同席30个。位于前院区的制氧主厂房改造项目在赛时承担了观众服务功能，在首层提供观众售卖、医疗、邮局、特许商品经营等服务，二层为志愿者服务、场馆接待功能，三层及局部四层为安保用房，赛后改造为办公楼。原冷却泵站改造为前院区安检楼，首层架空，赛时作为观众安检通道，原有顶部的冷却塔则保留外壳放入新的冷却设备，为该区域提供配套支撑。

4. 场馆后院及注册流线

后院区安检入口分布在场馆南北两侧，南侧为注册人群人检入口，位于观众人检口西侧，群明湖北大街分别设置3个注册人群人车同检入口。位于冷却塔东侧的新建五星级酒店，是赛时主要的后院区用房，包含场馆管理、场馆和基础设施、交通及安保等业务领域办公，以及工作人员餐厅、厨房等功能，赛后归还酒店运营管理。

（1）运动员流线

运动员由奥运村乘坐大巴到达首钢滑雪大跳台，首先进入运动员跳台出发区底部的运动员区，在此完成热身检录、打蜡、乘坐斜行电梯到达出发区，经过混合采访区搭乘接驳车返回出发区，或通过运动员通道到达媒体中心。该区域设置了热身篷、14个打蜡房、运动员休息室、运动员医疗站、兴奋剂检查站、领队会议室等临时设施。

（2）技术官员流线

技术官员通过位于安保区北侧安检口进入场馆，可快速到达位于FOP下方的办公区及休息室。

（3）奥林匹克大家庭成员流线

奥林匹克大家庭成员通过位于安保区北侧的安检口进入场馆，区域内设置有180m²奥林匹克大家庭休息室及配套用房。奥林匹克大家庭成员可乘坐专车到达停车区、休息区及奥林匹克大家庭看台休息区，活动流线独立。

（4）媒体流线

转播及新闻媒体通过位于安保区北侧的安检口直接进入场馆媒体中心。工作区内设置有文字记者及摄影工作间、媒体休息区等功能用房，并可通过媒体专用流线到达混采区及媒体坐席区。

5. 场馆坐席

根据新冠肺炎疫情防控需要，赛时场馆最终观众坐席1215个，注册坐席包含：评论员席15个，媒体播报席4个（位于评论员席厢房屋顶），观察员席20个，不带桌媒体席30个，摄影位置86个，运动员站席53个（位于结束区北侧），大家庭坐席138个（位于大家庭休息室顶部室外），国内贵宾坐席53个（位于观众席区域大家庭休息室外）。

start area is 47.5m in height, the finish area is 4m below the water surface, with a vertical fall of 51.5m and a total height of 60.5m, and the course structure is 160m long and 10-30m wide. The judge tower is 22.6m tall. Further competition profile changes have also been taken into consideration in the steel structure design of Big Air Shougang.

3. Front of House and Spectator Flow

During the Games, spectators are guided from Qunminghu South Road to the security check passage, enter the concourse of the Front of House, and walk for about 120m to the spectator seats.

4. Back of House and Accreditation Flow

The security check entrances of the Back of House are distributed in the south and north of the venue, and the south one is the pedestrian screening entrance for accredited groups, located on the west side of the spectator pedestrian screening entrance. Qunming Lake North Avenue is set with 3 screening entrances for pedestrians and vehicles for accredited groups. The new five-star hotel located in the east of the cooling tower is the Back of House area during the Games.

(1) Athlete Flow

Athletes arrive at Big Air Shougang by bus from the Olympic Village and enter the athletes' compound at the bottom of the start area. Here, the athletes warm up, go to the call area, and wax their skis, then take the ramp elevator to the start area, return to the start area via the mixed zone by the shuttle bus, or arrive at the Media Centre via the athletes' passageway. This area is provided with warm-up tents, 14 wax cabins, the athlete lounge, athlete medical station, doping control station, team supervisor meeting room, and other temporary facilities.

(2) Technical Official Flow

Technical officials enter the venue from the screening area on the north side of the security area and can quickly arrive at the office area and the lounge under FOP.

(3) Olympic Family Flow

The Olympic Family members enter the venue through the screening area on the north side of the security area and this area is provided with a 180-square-metre Olympic Family lounge and supporting rooms.

(4) Media Flow

The broadcasting and media personnel directly enter the Venue Media Centre through the screening area on the north side of the security area. The office area is provided with press journalist and photographer workrooms, media lounge, and other functional rooms. They can reach the mixed zone and the press tribunes through the dedicated media flow.

5. Seating Area

According to the COVID-19 prevention and control requirements, there are 1,215 Game-time spectator seats in the venue, the accredited seating includes 15 commentary positions, 4 announce positions (located on the roof of the commentary position room), 20 observer seats, 30 non-tabled press tribune seats, 86 photo camera positions, 53 athlete standing positions (located on the north side of the finish area), 138 Olympic Family seats (outdoor, above the Olympic Family lounge), and 53 domestic dignitary seats (located outside the Olympic Family lounge in the spectator seat area).

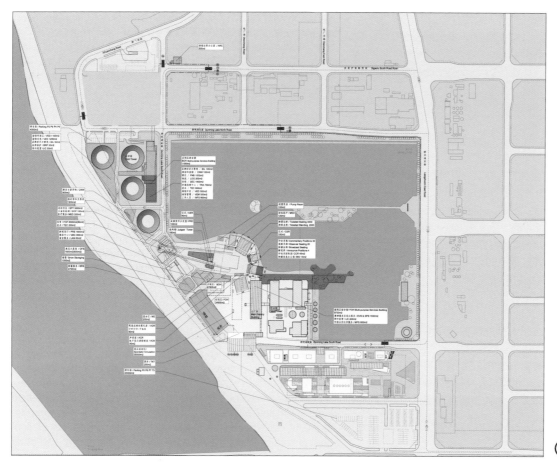

BAS 总平面图 OB1.2版
BAS Master Plan OB1.2

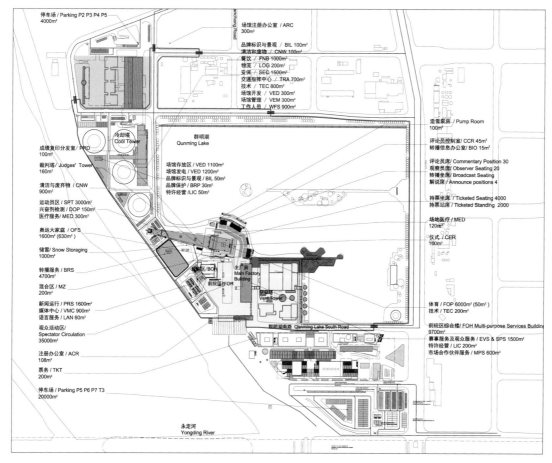

BAS 总平面图 OB2.1版
BAS Master Plan OB2.1

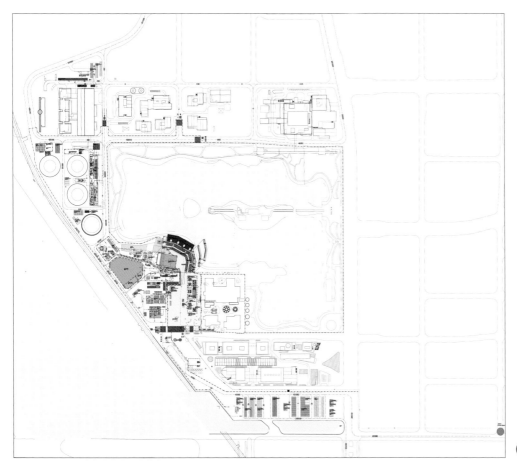

N BAS 总平面图 OB3.0版
BAS Master Plan OB3.0

N BAS 总平面图 OB4.0版
BAS Master Plan OB4.0

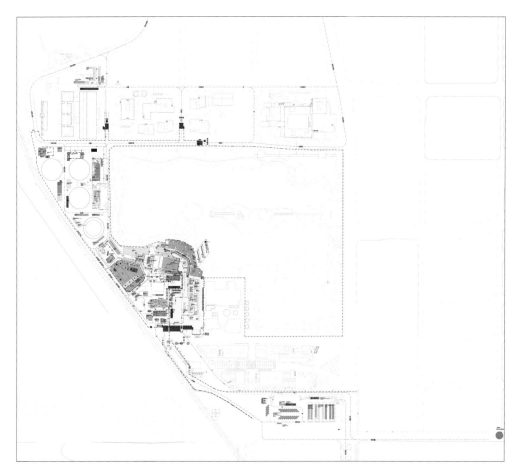

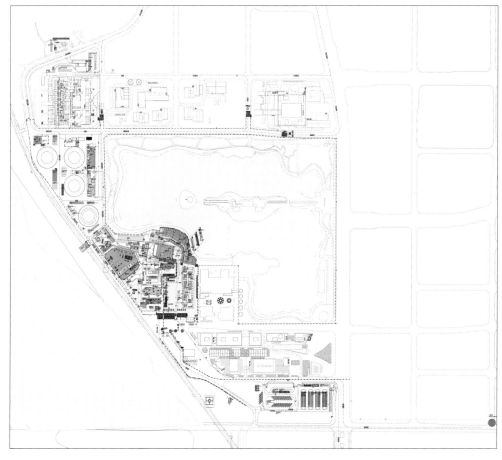

N

BAS 总平面图 OB6.0版
BAS Master Plan OB6.0

N

BAS 总平面图 OB7.0版
BAS Master Plan OB7.0

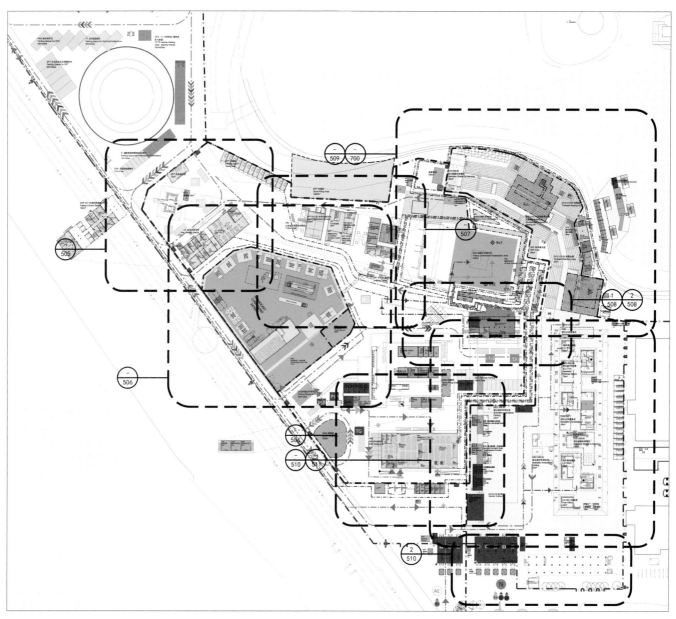

BAS 放大平面图一 OB7.0版
BAS Enlarged Plan 1 OB7.0

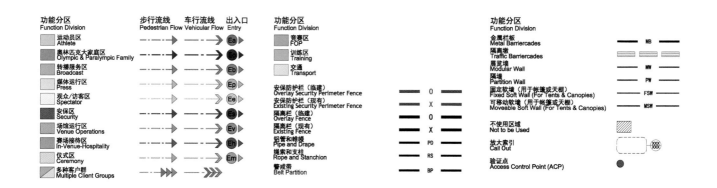

功能分区 Function Division	步行流线 Pedestrian Flow	车行流线 Vehicular Flow	出入口 Entry	功能分区 Function Division	功能分区 Function Division
运动员区 Athlete			Ea	竞赛区 FOP	金属栏板 Metal Barriercades — MB
奥林匹克大家庭区 Olympic & Paralympic Family			Eg	训练区 Training	隔离墩 Traffic Barriercades
转播服务区 Broadcast			Eb	交通 Transport	展览墙 Modular Wall — MW
媒体运行区 Press			Ep		隔墙 Partition Wall — PW
观众/访客区 Spectator			Ee	安保防护栏（临建）Overlay Security Perimeter Fence — O	固定软墙（用于帐篷或天棚）Fixed Soft Wall (For Tents & Canopies) — FSW
安保区 Security			Es	安保防护栏（现有）Existing Security Perimeter Fence — X	可移动软墙（用于帐篷或天棚）Moveable Soft Wall (For Tents & Canopies) — MSW
场馆运行区 Venue Operations			Ev	隔离栏（临建）Overlay Fence — O	
赛场接待区 In-Venue-Hospitality			Eh	隔离栏（现有）Existing Fence — X	不使用区域 Not to be Used
仪式区 Ceremony			Em	铝管和帷幔 Pipe and Drape — PD	放大索引 Call Out
多种客户群 Multiple Client Groups				绳索和支柱 Rope and Stanchion — RS	验证点 Access Control Point (ACP)
				警戒带 Belt Partition — BP	

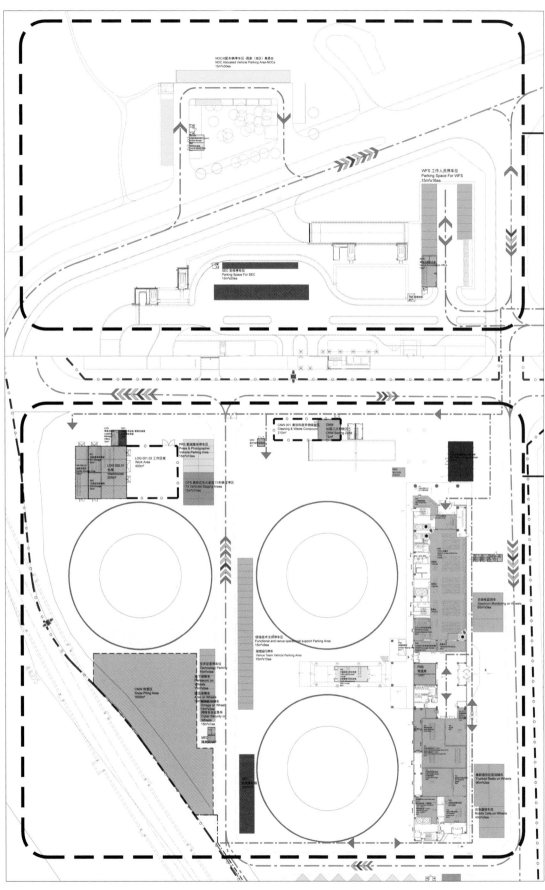

BAS 放大平面图二 OB7.0版
BAS Enlarged Plan 2 OB7.0

N BAS FOP平面图一 OB7.0版
BAS FOP Plan 1 OB7.0

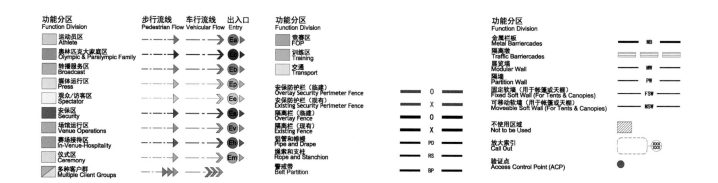

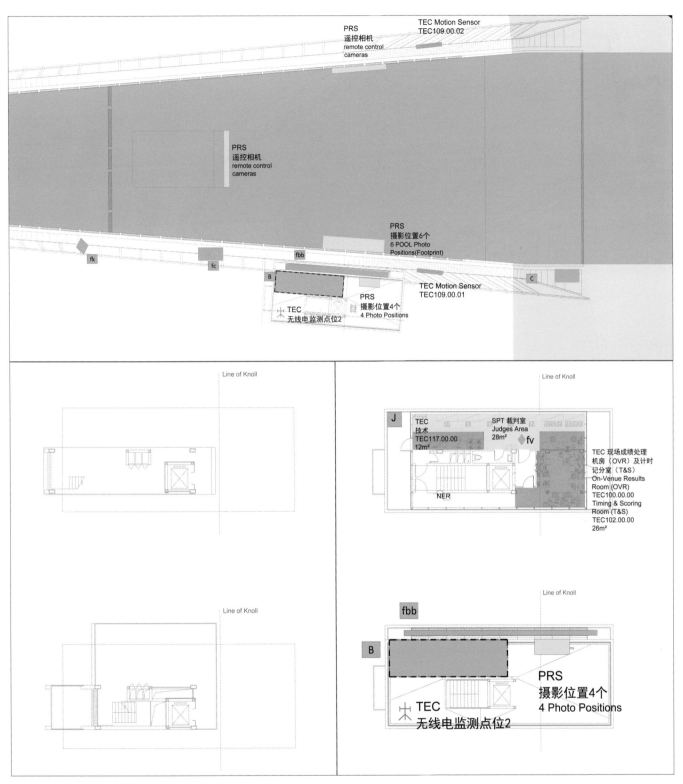

BAS FOP 平面图二 OB7.0版
BAS FOP Plan 2 OB7.0

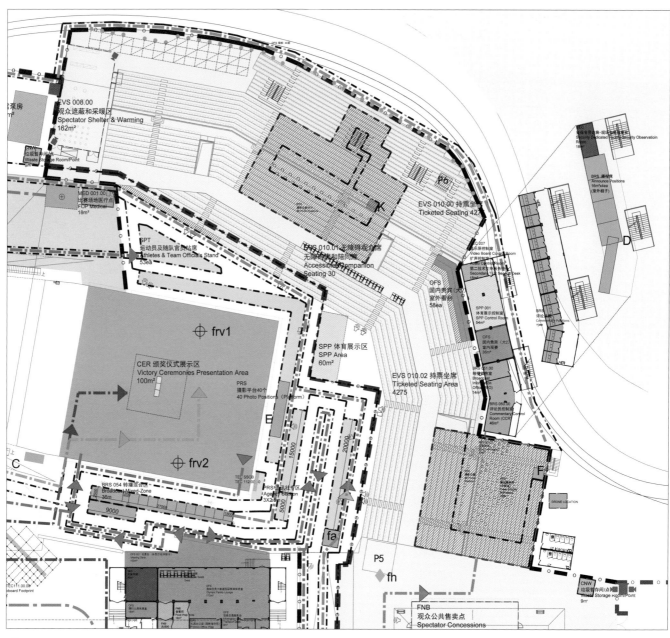

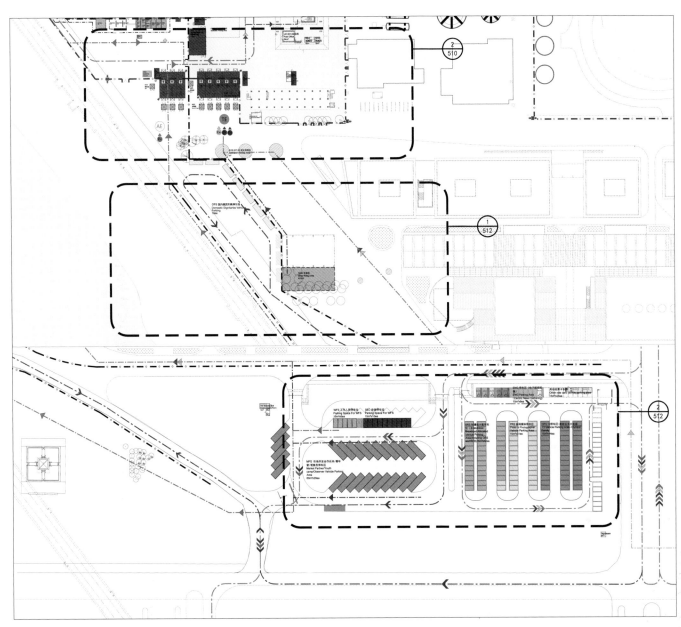

摄影 赵曾辉
Photo by Zhao Zenghui

摄影 桂琳
Photo by Gui Lin

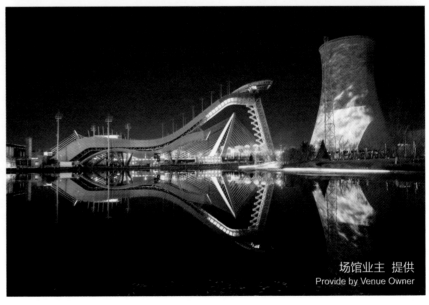

场馆业主 提供
Provide by Venue Owner

摄影 赵曾辉
Photo by Zhao Zenghui

北京冬奥村/冬残奥村 [BVL]
Beijing Olympic/Paralympic Village

1. 场馆基本情况

　　北京冬奥村/冬残奥村位于北京奥林匹克公园东南侧，赛时为运动员及随队官员提供居住、生活、娱乐和休闲等功能的场所。

　　北京冬奥村/冬残奥村由居住区、运行区和广场区组成。居住区位于冬奥村北侧，设计概念源自中国传统的院落形制，以清代冰嬉图构成院落的景观核心；运行区位于冬奥村西侧，由既有工业厂房改造而成，包含代表团接待中心、访客中心、媒体中心、安保中心等功能空间，厂房改造过程中保留现状树木形成景观中庭等休闲空间；广场区位于冬奥村中心区域，利用现状城市商业空间，为运动员设立生活、娱乐等配套服务功能空间。居住区总建筑面积约为33万m²，在冬奥会期间提供2338个床位，在冬残奥会期间提供1040个床位。

2. 场馆分区及注册流线

　　（1）运动员流线

　　运动员首次抵达时，由机场乘坐大巴到达北京冬奥村/冬残奥村接待中心门前，落客后进入接待中心进行安检、注册、验证，穿过接待中心到达运行区与居住区的验证点，验证后进入居住区。

　　赛时期间，运动员通过居住区与交通场站间的验证点进入交通场站区域，根据站牌位置乘坐开往不同场馆的班车，由场

1. Venue Overview

The Beijing Olympic/Paralympic Village is composed of the Residential Zone, the Operational Zone, and the Plaza. The Residential Zone is located in the north of the Village and the layout draws inspiration from traditional quadrangle courtyards, and the centre of the courtyard is decorated by a pattern similar to the famous Qing Dynasty painting portraying the scene of people enjoying outdoor activities on ice. The Operational Zone is located in the west of the Village, which is renovated from an existing plant, including such functional spaces as the Team Processing Centre, Guest Pass Centre, Media Centre, and Security Centre, and existing trees are retained to form a landscaped atrium and other leisure spaces. The Plaza is located in the central area of the Village, where existing urban commercial space is used to provide functional spaces of supporting services such as living and entertainment. The Residential Zone has a total floor area of about 330,000m², providing 2,338 beds during the Beijing 2022 Olympic Winter Games and 1,040 beds during the Beijing 2022 Paralympic Winter Games.

2. Venue Zoning and Accreditation Flow
(1) Athlete Flow
When athletes arrive for the first time, they take the bus from the airport to the front of the Team Processing Centre at the

馆回村时，统一在交通场站落客区落客，进行验证、安检后进入居住区。居住区与广场区之间设有2处验证点，其位置均为观赏居住区的最佳角度。赛时在入口前分别设置会徽和吉祥物的景观设施，作为运动员的拍照打卡地点。

（2）访客流线

访客乘车到达访客中心前停车场落客后，首先可以看到改造时为保留现状树木所做的入口，建筑与树木的融合，体现了北京冬奥村/冬残奥村"绿色、简约"的理念。进入访客中心后进行验证、安检、换卡的步骤后，穿过访客中心到达室外平台，室外平台高于旗帜广场区域1.5m，在此可以观赏到居住区公寓楼群、旗帜广场与奥林匹克休战壁画，平台上设有由吉祥物组成的景观设施。

有居住区权限的访客可通过验证点进入居住区，无居住区权限的访客仅可到达广场区及运行区。级别较高的访客可通过同时位于平台上的礼宾中心入口进入村长会客区，礼宾中心以《千里江山图》及《沁园春·雪》诗词作为墙壁装饰，展现了中国文化特色。

（3）媒体流线

转播及新闻媒体通过访客中心进入，进行验证、安检、换卡后，进入西侧通道媒体中心区域，首先进入文字记者及摄影工作间，空间高大、采光充足，再通过西侧连廊依次经过媒体见面区、采访间、媒体休息区等功能用房，这些功能房间为旧厂房改造而成，整条流线给人新旧交替的工业氛围感。媒体中心与访客中心之间的中庭区域及访客中心东侧平台区域作为媒体混采区及转播机位所在区域。中庭内保留了场地内原有的高大乔木，配合木质地板，营造了一种闲适的氛围。转播机位所在的区域为冬奥村内景观角度最好的区域。

（4）其他注册人员流线

其他注册人员主要分为两条流线。工作人员乘坐班车于北京冬奥村东北角落客，然后进行验证、安检，进入安保线，居住区工作人员通过就近的验证点进入居住区，非居住区工作人员沿居住区外侧流线进入广场区及运行区。合同商人员乘坐班车于北京冬奥村东南角落客，落客后进行验证、安检，进入安保线。其他场馆注册人员流线均设置在场馆东侧，最大限度地避免了与运动员流线的交叉。

3. 场馆内车辆流线

场馆内车辆主要分为运动员乘坐车辆、访客及媒体乘坐车辆、NOC车辆和后勤保障车辆。运动员车辆由西侧大门驶入后经验证进入交通场站区域，车辆由北辰路与奥体中路交叉口的场站出口驶出。访客及媒体车辆由北辰路与北土城东路交叉口附近入口进入访客中心停车场，落客后由同一出入口驶出。NOC车辆由奥园西路入口进入NOC停车场，并由附近出口驶出。后勤车辆由奥园路车辆入口驶入，祥园路车辆出口驶出。

4. 注册分区及防疫分区

北京冬奥村/冬残奥村根据防疫需要划分为闭环内区域及闭环外区域，两区域独立运行管理。闭环内区域主要包含居住、广场区、部分运行区（接待中心、访客中心、媒体中心、安保中心、交通指挥中心）。闭环外主要包含设备机房区及闭环外工作人员的办公区域。闭环内外在安保中心附近设置交接区，如遇特殊情况需传递物品或文件，则需在此处进行消杀后传递。

Beijing Olympic/Paralympic Village, get off the bus and enter the Team Processing Centre for security check, accreditation, and validation, go through the Team Processing Centre and arrive at the Accreditation Check Point (ACP) of the Operational Zone and the Residential Zone to verify before entering the Residential Zone.

During the Games, athletes enter the transport mall area through the ACP between the Residential Zone and the transport mall, take the shuttle bus to different venues, get off in the transport mall drop-off area when returning to the Village, and enter the Residential Zone after accreditation and security check. There are two ACPs between the Residential Zone and the Plaza, both located at positions with the best angle to view the Residential Zone. During the Games, emblems and mascots are set respectively at the entrance as look items, offering athletes a place to photograph.

(2) Guest Flow

After getting off in the parking lot in front of the Guest Pass Centre, the guests will firstly see the entrance made for retaining existing trees, and the integration of buildings and trees embodies the concept of "Green and Simple" of the Beijing Olympic/Paralympic Village. After entering the Guest Pass Centre, the guests go through the steps of accreditation check, security check, and card change, and pass the Guest Pass Centre to reach the outdoor platform. The outdoor platform is 1.5m higher than the flag mall area, where they can view the apartment buildings of the Residential Zone, flag mall, and Olympic Truce Mural. On the platform there are look elements featuring mascots.

(3) Media Flow

The broadcast and media personnel enter the Guest Pass Centre for accreditation check, security check, and card exchange, enter the Media Centre area of the west passageway, firstly enter the press journalist and photographer workrooms with large space and sufficient lighting, and then the west corridor, followed by functional rooms such as the media meeting room, the interview room, and the media lounge, and these functional rooms are renovated from the old plant. The whole flow presents an industrial atmosphere combining the new and the old. The atrium area between the Media Centre and the Guest Pass Centre and the east platform area of Guest Pass Centre are the areas where the mixed zone and the broadcasting position are located. In the atrium, the original tall trees in the venue are retained and create a comfortable atmosphere with wood flooring. The area where the broadcasting position is located owns the best view angle in the Village.

3. Vehicle Flow in the Venue

The vehicles in the venue are mainly composed of vehicles for athletes, vehicles for guests and media personnel, NOC vehicles, and logistics vehicles. Vehicles for athletes enter the transport mall area through the west gate and exit from the transport mall exit at the intersection of Beichen Road and Aoti Middle Road. Vehicles for guests and media personnel enter the Guest Pass Centre parking lot from the entrance near the intersection of Beichen Road and Beitucheng East Road, and exit from the same entrance/exit after drop-off. NOC vehicles enter the NOC parking lot at the entrance at Aoyuan West Road and exit from a nearby exit. Logistics vehicles enter from the vehicle entrance at Aoyuan Road and exit from the vehicle exit at Xiangyuan Road.

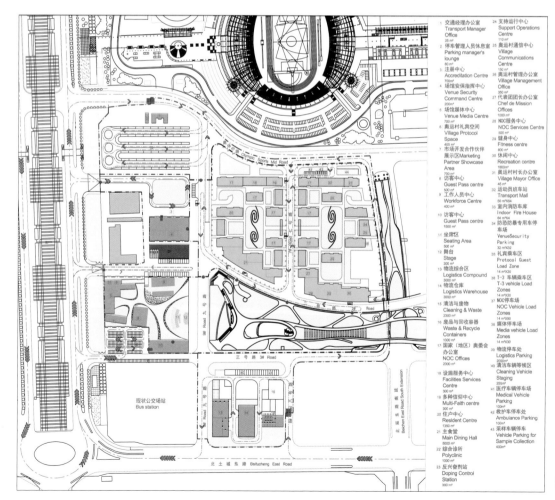

BVL 总平面图 OB1.2版
BVL Master Plan OB1.2

1	交通经理办公室 Transport Manager Office 25 m²	24	支持运行中心 Support Operations Centre 110 m²
2	停车管理人员休息室 Parking manager's lounge 60 m²	25	奥运村通信中心 Village Communications Centre 150 m²
3	注册中心 Accreditation Centre 700 m²	26	奥运村管理办公室 Village Management Office 350 m²
4	场馆安保指挥中心 Venue Security Command Centre 200 m²	27	代表团团长办公室 Chef de Mission Offices
5	场馆媒体中心 Venue Media Centre 700 m²	28	NOC服务中心 NOC Services Centre 500 m²
6	奥运村礼宾空间 Village Protocol Space 400 m²	29	健身中心 Fitness centre 800 m²
7	市场开发合作伙伴展示区 Marketing Partner Showcase Area 700 m²	30	休闲中心 Recreation centre 1800 m²
8	访客中心 Guest Pass centre 500 m²	41	奥运村村长办公室 Village Mayor Office 45 m²
9	工作人员中心 Workforce Centre 400 m²	32	运动员班车站 Transport Mall 50 m²X64
10	访客中心 Guest Pass centre 1500 m²	33	室内消防车库 Indoor Fire House 64 m²X4
11	坐席区 Seating Area 500 m²	34	防恐防暴专用车停车场 VenueSecurity Parking 32 m²X32
12	舞台 Stage 200 m²	35	礼宾乘车区 Protocol Guest Load Zone 14 m²X30
13	物流综合区 Logistics Compound 3000 m²	36	T-3 车辆乘车区 T-3 vehicle Load Zones 14 m²X30
14	物流仓库 Logistics Warehouse 3000 m²	37	NOC停车场 NOC Vehicle Load Zones 14 m²X30
15	清洁与废物 Cleaning & Waste 2300 m²	38	媒体停车场 Media vehicle Load Zones 14 m²X30
16	废品与回收容器 Waste & Recycle Containers 1000 m²	39	物流停车处 Logistics Parking 2000m²
17	国家(地区)奥委会办公室 NOC Offices 2000 m²	40	清洁车辆等候区 Cleaning Vehicle Staging 250m²
18	设施服务中心 Facilities Services Centre 300 m²	41	医疗车辆停车场 Medical Vehicle Parking 100m²
19	多种信仰中心 Multi-Faith centre 300 m²	42	救护车停车处 Ambulance Parking 400m²
20	住户中心 Resident Centre 1350 m²	43	采样车辆停车 Vehicle Parking for Sample Collection 400m²
21	主食堂 Main Dining Hall 5000 m²		
22	综合诊所 Polyclinic 1000 m²		
23	反兴奋剂站 Doping Control Station 300 m²		

BVL 总平面图 OB2.1版
BVL Master Plan OB2.1

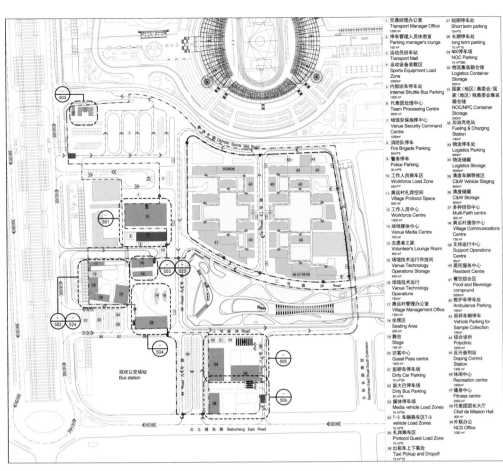

1	交通经理办公室 Transport Manager Office 1200 m²	27	短期停车处 Short term parking
2	停车管理人员休息室 Parking manager's lounge 100 m²	28	长期停车处 long term parking 15 m²*15
3	运动员班车站 Transport Mall	29	NOC停车场 NOC Parking 15 m²*280
4	运动设备装载区 Sports Equipment Load Zone 2000m²	30	物流集装箱仓储 Logistics Container Storage 200m²
5	内部班车停车处 Internal Shuttle Bus Parking 1200 m²	31	国家(地区)奥委会/国 家(地区)残奥委会集装 箱仓储 NOC/NPC Container Storage 200m²
6	代表团处理中心 Team Processing Centre 3600 m²		
7	场馆安保指挥中心 Venue Security Command Centre 1000m²	32	加油充电站 Fueling & Charging Station 200m²
8	消防队停车 Fire Brigade Parking 500m²*5	33	物流停车处 Logistics Parking 600m²
9	警务停车 Police Parking 30 m²*6	34	物流储藏 Logistics Storage 3500m²
10	工作人员乘车区 Workforce Load Zone 50m²*7	35	清废车辆等候区 C&W Vehicle Staging 600m²
11	奥运村礼宾空间 Village Protocol Space 600 m²	36	清废储藏 C&W Storage 800m²
12	工作人员中心 Workforce Centre 1300 m²	37	多种信仰中心 Multi-Faith centre 300 m²
13	场馆媒体中心 Venue Media Centre 700 m²	38	奥运村通信中心 Village Communications Centre 130 m²
14	志愿者之家 Volunteer's Lounge Room 450 m²	39	支持运行中心 Support Operations Centre 85m²
15	场馆技术运行存放间 Venue Technology Operations Storage 540 m²	40	居民服务中心 Resident Centre 300 m²
16	场馆技术运行 Venue Technology Operations 750m²	41	餐饮综合区 Food and Beverage compound 6000m²
17	奥运村管理办公室 Village Management Office 1350 m²	42	救护车停车处 Ambulance Parking 100m²
18	坐席区 Seating Area 200 m²	43	采样车辆停车 Vehicle Parking for Sample Collection 100m²
19	舞台 Stage 100 m²	44	综合诊所 Polyclinic 2200 m²
20	访客中心 Guest Pass centre 1500 m²	45	反兴奋剂站 Doping Control Station 1300 m²
21	脏轿车停车场 Dirty Car Parking 15 m²*90	46	休闲中心 Recreation centre 1000 m²
22	脏大巴停车场 Dirty Bus Parking 50 m²*9	47	健身中心 Fitness centre 2200 m²
23	媒体停车场 Media vehicle Load Zones 15 m²*24	48	代表团团长大厅 Chef de Mission Hall 300 m²
24	T-3 车辆乘车T-3 vehicle Load Zones 15 m²*2	49	外联办公 NCS Office 1000 m²
25	礼宾乘车区 Protocol Guest Load Zone 15 m²*6		
26	出租车上下客处 Taxi Pickup and Dropoff 15 m²*18		

BVL 总平面图 OB3.0版
BVL Master Plan OB3.0

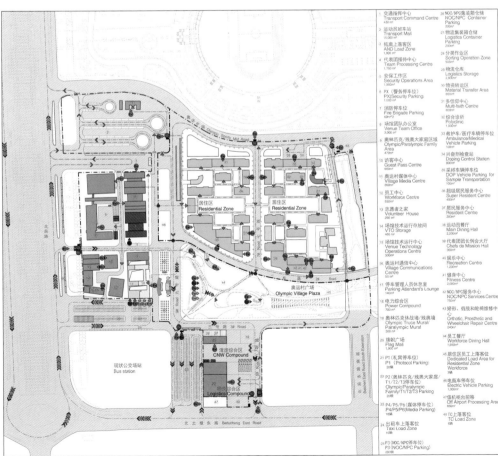

1	交通指挥中心 Transport Command Centre 432 m²	26	NOC/NPC集装箱仓储 NOC/NPC Container Parking 200m²
2	运动员班车站 Transport Mall 15,000 m²	27	物流集装箱仓储 Logistics Container Parking 200m²
3	抵离上落客区 AND Load Zone 1,000 m²	28	分类作业区 Sorting Operation Zone 500m²
4	代表团接待中心 Team Processing Centre 1,750 m²	29	物流仓库 Logistics Storage 3500m²
5	安保工作区 Security Operations Area 1,000m²	30	物流转运区 Material Transfer Area 930m²
6	PX (警务停车位) PX(Security Parking) 1,000 m²	31	多信仰中心 Multi-faith Centre 150m²
7	消防停车位 Fire Brigade Parking 60m²*2	32	综合诊所 Polyclinic 1,000m²
8	场馆团队办公室 Venue Team Office 3,000 m²	33	救护车/医疗车辆停车位 Ambulance/Medical Vehicle Parking 200m²
9	奥林匹克/残奥大家庭区域 Olympic/Paralympic Family Area 470m²	34	兴奋剂检查站 Doping Control Station 1000m²
10	访客中心 Guest Pass Centre 500m²	35	采样车辆停车位 DOP Vehicle Parking for Sample Transportation 100m²
11	奥运媒体中心 Village Media Centre 360m²	36	超级居民服务中心 Super Resident Centre 450m²
12	员工中心 Workforce Centre 520m²	37	居民服务中心 Resident Centre 300m²
13	志愿者之家 Volunteer House	38	运动员餐厅 Main Dining Hall 2,200m²
14	场馆技术运行存放间 VTO Storage 465 m²	39	代表团团长例会大厅 Chefs de Mission Hall 300 m²
15	场馆技术运行中心 Venue Technology Operations Centre 300m²	40	娱乐中心 Recreation Centre 1,200m²
16	奥运村通信中心 Village Communications Centre 50 m²	41	健身中心 Fitness Centre 2,000m²
17	停车管理人员休息室 Parking Attendant's Lounge 140m²	42	NOC/NPC服务中心 NOC/NPC Services Centre 750m²
18	电力综合区 Power Compound 700 m²	43	矫形、假肢和轮椅维修中 心 Orthotic, Prosthetic and Wheelchair Repair Centre 240m²
19	奥林匹克休战墙/残奥墙 Olympic Truce Mural/ Paralympic Mural		
20	旗帜广场 Flag Mall 1,900 m²	44	员工餐厅 Workforce Dining Hall 500m²
21	P1 (礼宾停车位) P1 (Protocol Parking) 20辆	45	居住区员工上落客位 Dedicated Load Area for Residential Zone Workforce 3辆
22	P2 (奥林匹克/残奥大家庭/ T1/T2/T3停车位) Olympic/Paralympic Family/T1/T2/T3 Parking 20辆	46	电瓶车停车位 Electric Vehicle Parking 20辆
23	P4/P5/P6 (媒体停车位) P4/P5/P6 (Media Parking) 20辆	47	值机柜台前移 Off Airport Processing Area 10辆
24	出租车上落客位 Taxi Load Zone 10辆	48	TC上落客位 TC Load Zone 6辆
25	P3 (NOC/NPC停车位) P3 (NOC/NPC Parking)		

BVL 总平面图 OB4.0版
BVL Master Plan OB4.0

167

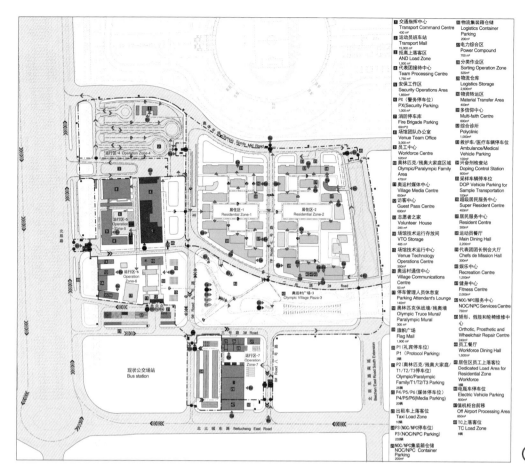

N
BVL 总平面图 OB5.0版
BVL Master Plan OB5.0

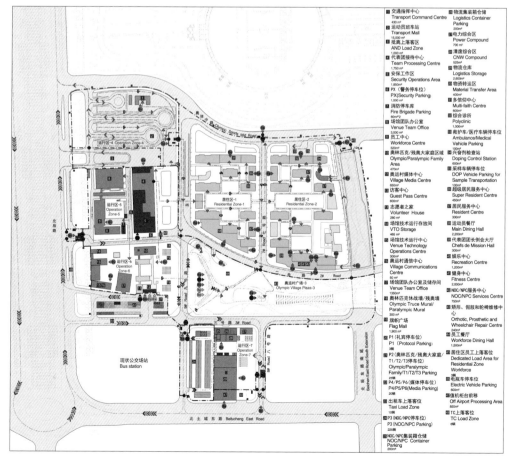

N
BVL 总平面图 OB6.0版
BVL Master Plan OB6.0

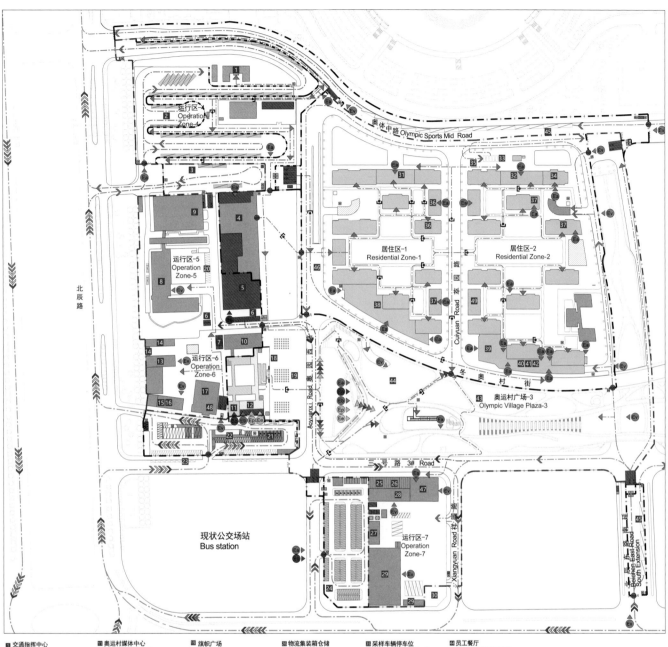

运行区 Operation Zone-4

奥体中路 Olympic Sports Mid Road

北辰路

运行区-5 Operation Zone-5

居住区-1 Residential Zone-1

居住区-2 Residential Zone-2

翠园路 Cuiyuan Road

运行区-6 Operation Zone-6

冬奥村街 Olympic Village Plaza-3

奥运村广场-3 Olympic Village Plaza-3

Aoyunxi Road 奥运西路

号路 3# Road

现状公交场站 Bus station

运行区-7 Operation Zone-7

Xiangyuan Road 祥园路

北辰东路南延 Beichen East Road South Extension

1 交通指挥中心 Transport Command Centre 430m²	**13** 奥运村媒体中心 Village Media Centre 650m²	**19** 旗帜广场 Flag Mall 112根	**30** 物流集装箱仓储 Logistics Container Parking 200m²	**39** 采样车辆停车位 DOP Vehicle Parking for Sample Transportation 100m²
2 运动员班车站 Transport Mall 15,000 m²	**14** 访客中心 Guest Pass Centre 600m²	**20** P1（礼宾停车位） P1 (Protocol Parking) 10辆	**31** 电力综合区 Power Compound 700 m²	**40** 超级居民服务区 Super Resident Centre 450m²
3 抵离上落客区 AND Load Zone 1,000 m²	**15** 场馆技术运行存放间 VTO Storage 465 m²	**21** P2（奥林匹克/残奥大家庭/T1/T2/T3停车位） Olympic/Paralympic Family/T1/T2/T3 Parking 25辆	**32** 清废综合区 CNW Compound 525m²	**41** 居民服务中心 Resident Centre 300m²
4 代表团接待中心 Team Processing Centre 1,750 m²	**16** 志愿者之家 Volunteer House 280 m²	**22** P4/P5/P6（媒体停车位） P4/P5/P6(Media Parking) 20辆	**33** 物流仓库 Logistics Storage 2,600m²	**42** 运动员餐厅 Main Dining Hall 2,200m²
5 安保工作区 Security Operations Area 1,850m²	**17** 场馆技术运行中心 Venue Technology Operations Centre 300m²	**23** 出租车上落客区 Taxi Load Zone 10辆	**34** 物资转运区 Material Transfer Area 400m²	**43** 代表团团长例会大厅 Chefs de Mission Hall 300m²
6 PX（警务停车位） PX(Security Parking) 1,000 m²	**18** 奥运村通信中心 Village Communications Centre 50 m²	**24** P3（NOC/NPC停车位） P3 (NOC/NPC Parking) 170辆	**35** 多信仰中心 Multi-faith Centre 600m²	**44** 娱乐中心 Recreation Centre 1,200m²
7 消防停车库 Fire Brigade Parking 60m²×2		防疫团队/服务商/储存间 Epidemic Prevention Team / Cervice Provider / Storage 1350m²	**25** NOC/NPC集装箱仓库 NOC/NPC Container Parking 200m²	**36** 综合诊所 Polyclinic 1,000m²	**45** 健身中心 Fitness Centre 2,000m²
8 场馆团队办公室 Venue Team Office 3,000 m²		奥林匹克休战墙/残奥墙 Olympic Truce Mural/ Paralympic Mural 300 m²		**37** 救护车/医疗车辆停车位 Ambulance/Medical Vehicle Parking 100m²	**46** NOC/NPC服务中心 NOC/NPC Services Centre 750m²
9 运行团队大会议室 Venue Team Meeting Room 520m²				**38** 兴奋剂检查站 Doping Control Station 600m²	**47** 矫形、假肢和轮椅维修中心 Orthotic, Prosthetic and Wheelchair Repair Centre 240m²
10 奥林匹克/残奥大家庭区域 Olympic/Paralympic Family Area 470m²					

48 员工餐厅 Workforce Dining Hall 1,500m²		
49 员工上落客位 Dedicated Load Area for Workforce 15辆		
电瓶车停车位 Electric Vehicle Parking 600m²		
值机柜台前移 Off Airport Processing Area 850m²		
运行区核酸检测点 Nucleic Acid Testing Area 220m²		
居住区核酸检测点 Nucleic Acid Testing Area 150m²		

BVL 总平面图 OB7.0版
BVL Master Plan OB7.0

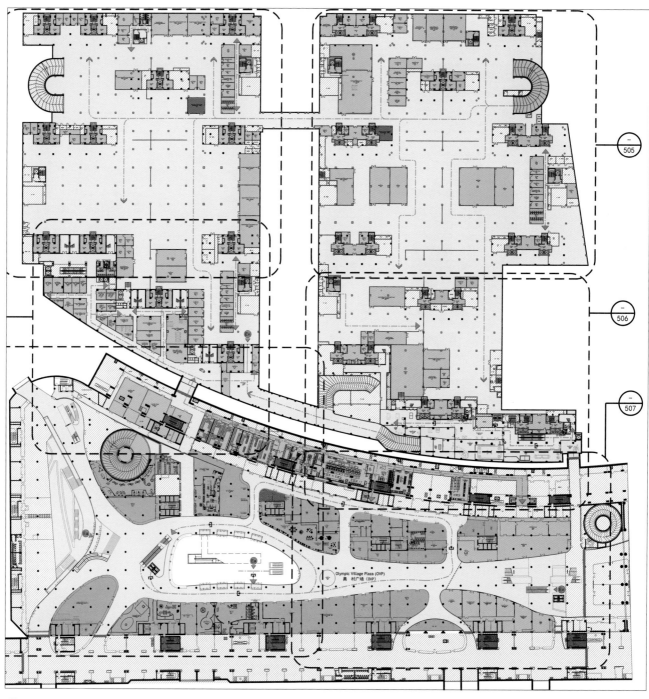

N
BVL 地下二层平面图 OB7.0版
BVL B2 Plan OB7.0

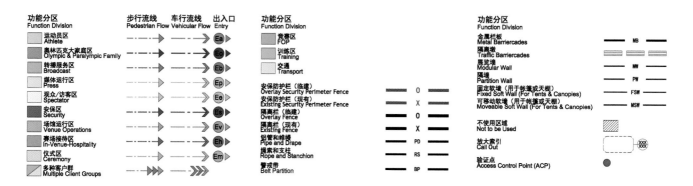

功能分区 Function Division		步行流线 Pedestrian Flow	车行流线 Vehicular Flow	出入口 Entry	功能分区 Function Division		功能分区 Function Division	
	运动员区 Athlete			Ea		竞赛区 FOP		金属栏板 Metal Barriercades
	奥林匹克大家庭区 Olympic & Paralympic Family			Eo		训练区 Training		隔离墩 Traffic Barriercades
	转播服务区 Broadcast			Eb		交通 Transport		展览墙 Modular Wall
	媒体运行区 Press			Ep				隔墙 Partition Wall
	观众/访客区 Spectator			Ee	安保防护栏（临建） Overlay Security Perimeter Fence			固定软墙（用于帐篷或天棚） Fixed Soft Wall (For Tents & Canopies)
	安保区 Security			Es	安保防护栏（现有） Existing Security Perimeter Fence			可移动软墙（用于帐篷或天棚） Moveable Soft Wall (For Tents & Canopies)
	场馆运行区 Venue Operations			Ev	隔离栏（临建） Overlay Fence			
	赛场接待区 In-Venue-Hospitality			Eh	隔离栏（现有） Existing Fence			不使用区域 Not to be Used
	仪式区 Ceremony			Em	铝管和帷幕 Pipe and Drape			放大索引 Call Out
	多种客户群 Multiple Client Groups				绳索和支柱 Rope and Stanchion			验证点 Access Control Point (ACP)
					警戒带 Belt Partition			

O	MB
X	
O	MW
X	PW
PD	FSW
RS	MSW
BP	

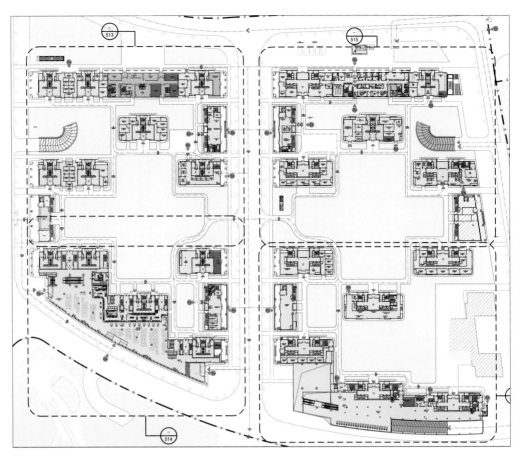

N

BVL 居住区一层平面图 OB7.0版
BVL Residential Zone 1F Plan OB7.0

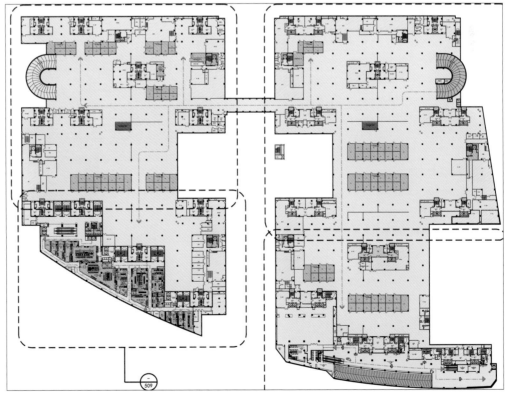

N

BVL 居住区地下一层平面图 OB7.0版
BVL Residential Zone B1 Plan OB7.0

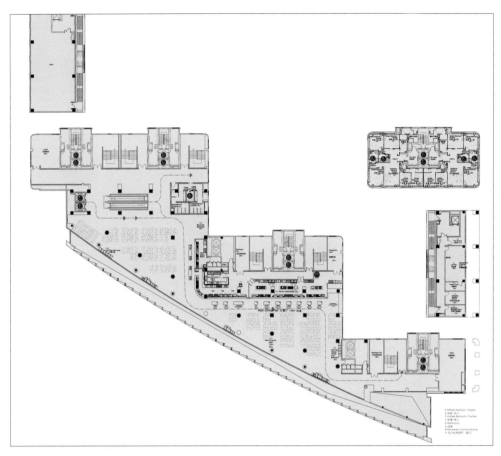

N BVL 居住区放大一层平面图 OB7.0版
BVL Residential Zone Enlarged 1F Plan OB7.0

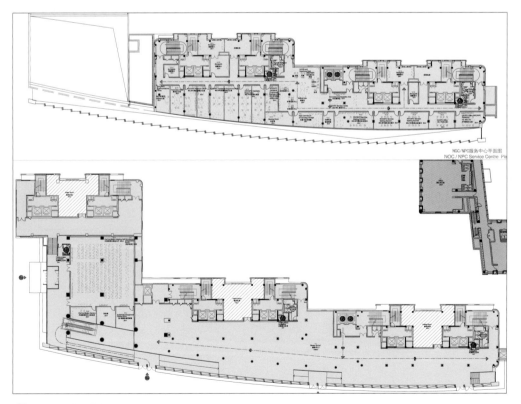

N BVL 居住区放大二层平面图一 OB7.0版
BVL Residential Zone Enlarged 2F Plan 1 OB7.0

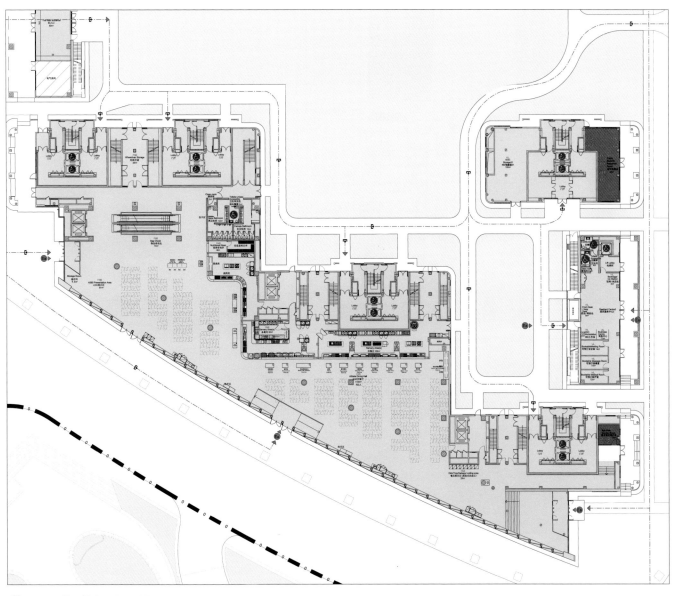

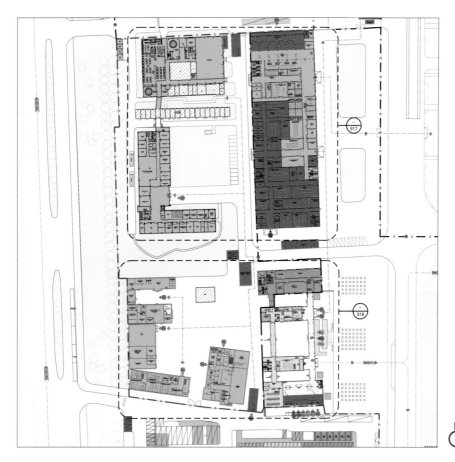

N
BVL 运行区一层平面图一 OB7.0版
BVL Operation Zone 1F Plan 1 OB7.0

N
BVL 运行区一层平面图二 OB7.0版
BVL Operation Zone 1F Plan 2 OB7.0

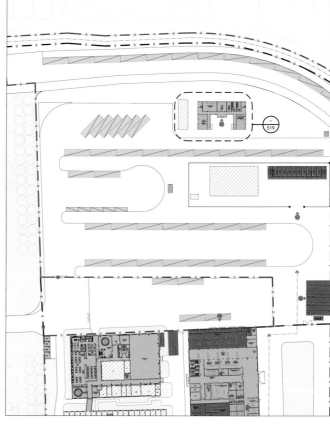

N
BVL 运行区一层平面图三 OB7.0版
BVL Operation Zone 1F Plan 3 OB7.0

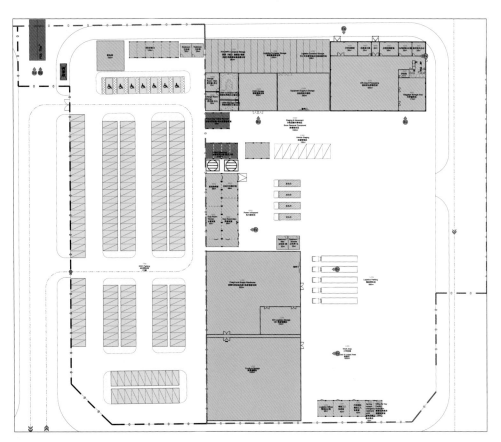

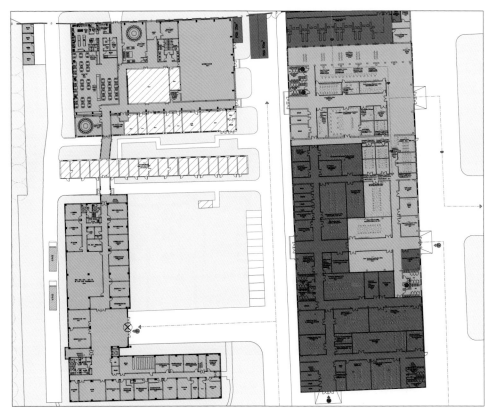

BVL 运行区放大一层平面图一 OB7.0版
BVL Operation Zone 1F Enlarged Plan 1 OB7.0

BVL 运行区放大一层平面图二 OB7.0版
BVL Operation Zone 1F Enlarged Plan 2 OB7.0

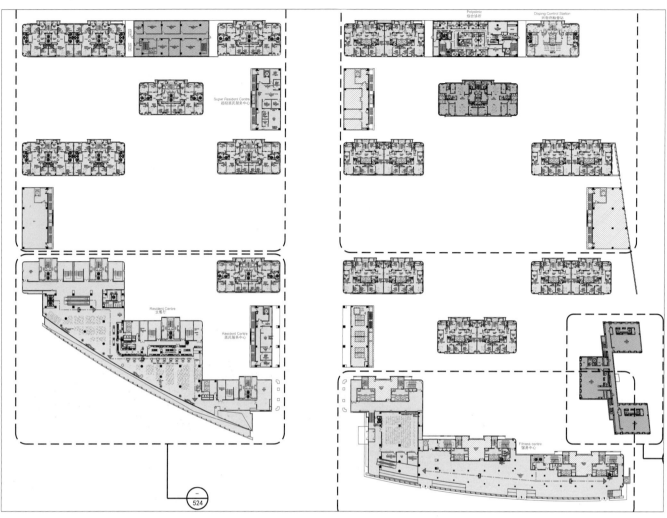

N
BVL 居住区二层平面图 OB7.0版
BVL Residential Zone 2F Plan OB7.0

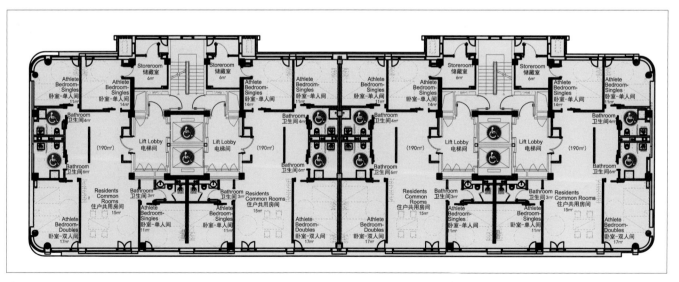

N
BVL 居住区标准层平面图 OB7.0版
BVL Residential Zone Standard Floor Plan OB7.0

北京冬奥组委　提供
Provide by BOCOG

摄影 李亮
Photo by Li Liang

主媒体中心[MMC]

Main Media Centre

1. 场馆基本情况

　　主媒体中心位于奥林匹克公园中心区西北侧国家会议中心二期项目内，是北京2022年冬奥会和冬残奥会北京赛区规模最大的新建场馆。主媒体中心包含国际广播中心（IBC）和主新闻中心（MPC）两个非竞赛内容。国际广播中心是OBS和持权转播商在赛时进行转播工作的核心区域，包含各个转播商演播室、转播商办公区域以及核心技术机房等；主新闻中心是文字与摄影媒体的赛时工作大本营，包含新闻发布厅、各个新闻大社办公区、媒体租用办公区等。这是奥运史上首次将国际广播中心和主新闻中心两项非竞赛内容整合到一起，组成主媒体中心。

　　主媒体中心以"鲲鹏展翅"作为建筑造型的设计理念，出挑深远的屋檐形成一条优美曲线，同时外幕墙的群鸟型开窗"飞鸟如斯"与之呼应。"迥临飞鸟上，高出世尘间"，巨大的体量却展现出简洁、轻盈、灵动的态势。场馆总建筑面积约42万m²，其中12万m²的区域在赛时开放，为一万两千余名注册媒体和转播商提供24小时支持和服务保障。

2. 场馆前院及注册流线

　　主媒体中心东广场和天辰东路为场馆前院区。天辰东路设有TG班车场站，天辰东路以东区域为媒体采访区。注册及访客服务中心位于大屯路及天辰东路路口处，完成注册后由天辰东

The Main Media Centre (MMC) is located in the China National Convention Centre Phase II in the northwest of the central area of the Beijing Olympic Park and is the largest new venue in the Beijing Zone of the Beijing 2022 Olympic and Paralympic Winter Games.

The MMC includes the International Broadcast Centre (IBC) and the Main Press Centre (MPC) which perform non-competition functions. The IBC is the core area for OBS and rights-holding broadcasters to carry out broadcasting during the Games, including broadcaster studios, the office area of broadcasters, the core technical computer room, etc. The MPC is the Games-time headquarters for the written and photographic press, including the press conference room, the offices of news agencies, the offices for media, etc.

The Beijing 2022 Olympic and Paralympic Winter Games is the first in the Olympic history to integrate the IBC and the MPC into the MMC.

The gross floor area of the venue is about 420,000m², of which 120,000m² is opened during the Games, providing 24h support to over 12,000 accredited media and broadcasters.

The Broadcasters enter the MMC from the main entrance of the East Square, and there are 12 work areas of rights-holding broadcasters on 1F and 2F of the MMC. After passing through the broadcaster work areas on 1F, the broadcasters can enter the satellite farm and the dedicated logistics work area located on the west side of Tianchen West Road and the north side of Datun North Road from

路南安检口进入东广场。注册媒体和转播商、奥运大家庭成员等通过主出入口进入场馆。运动员通过主媒体中心南侧通道和入口进入新闻发布厅。

（1）转播流线

转播商由东广场主入口进入主媒体中心，主媒体中心1F层和2F层共设置12个持权转播商工作区。穿过1F层转播商工作区后，转播商可以从主媒体中心西侧出入口的专用通道进入位于天辰西路西侧和大屯北路北侧的卫星场站与专用物流工作区。

（2）媒体流线

媒体可由东广场主入口进入主媒体中心，来到1F或2F层的4个新闻发布厅，或乘扶梯进入2F层南侧和B2层的媒体工作区，也可以直接由东广场室外扶梯和楼梯进入B2层下沉广场，由下沉广场进入媒体工作区。

（3）场馆运行人员流线

运行人员可从东广场主入口进入主媒体中心，或从主媒体中心南侧专用入口进入南配楼，乘坐电梯到达位于2FM1～3FM2层的场馆运行工作区。

（4）运动员流线

参加新闻发布的运动员乘坐大巴到达东广场运动员专用落客区，进入东广场后从南侧专用通道进入南侧出入口，再由此直接进入新闻发布厅。

（5）奥林匹克大家庭成员流线

奥林匹克大家庭成员乘车通过东广场专用落客区进入东广场，可由东广场主入口进入主媒体中心，也可从南侧专用通道通过南侧出入口进入新闻发布厅。

3. 场馆后院及运行流线

主媒体中心西侧为场馆后院区，主要为运行保障区域，设有电力综合区、专用调车场、OBS卫星场站、物流综合区、消防综合区等。

the dedicated passageway of the west entrance/exit of the MMC.

The media personnel can enter the MMC from the main entrance of the East Square, go to the 4 press conference rooms on 1F or 2F, or take the escalator to enter the Media Work Area on the south side of 2F and B2. They can also enter the sunken square on B2 directly from the outdoor escalator and staircase of the East Square, and enter the Media Work Area from the sunken square.

The operation workforce can enter the MMC from the main entrance of the East Square, or enter the south annex building from the south dedicated entrance of the MMC, and take the elevator to the Venue Operation Area on 2FM1–3FM2.

Athletes participating in the press conference take a bus to the dedicated drop-off area for athletes at the East Square, enter the south entrance/exit through the south dedicated passageway after entering the East Square, and directly enter the press conference room through the south entrance/exit.

The Olympic Family members take a bus to the dedicated drop-off area in the East Square, enter the East Square, enter the MMC from the main entrance/exit of the East Square, or enter the press conference room from the south entrance/exit via the south dedicated passageway.

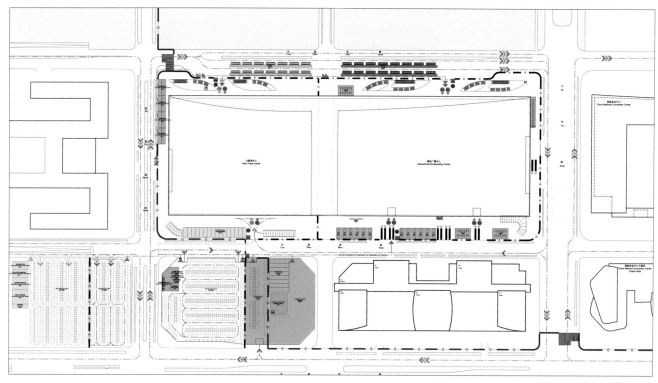

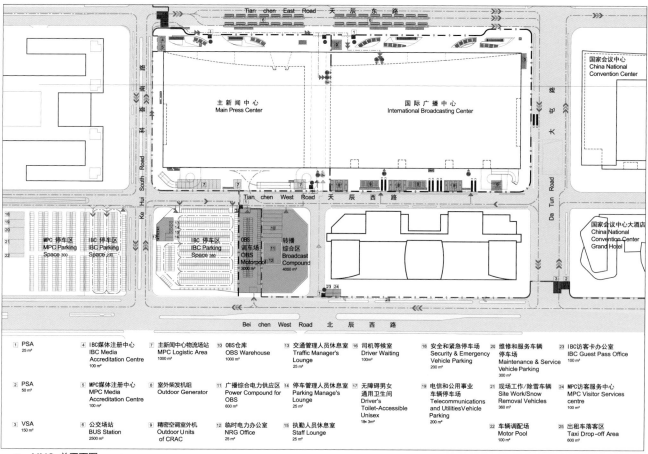

MMC 总平面图 OB2.1版
MMC Master Plan OB2.1

1 PSA 25 m²	4 IBC媒体注册中心 IBC Media Accreditation Centre	7 主新闻中心物流场站 MPC Logistic Area 1000 m²	10 OBS仓库 OBS Warehouse 1000 m²	13 交通管理人员休息室 Traffic Manager's Lounge	16 司机等候室 Driver Waiting 100m²	18 安全和紧急停车场 Security & Emergency Vehicle Parking 200 m²	23 IBC访客卡办公室 IBC Guest Pass Office 100 m²
2 PSA 50 m²	5 MPC媒体注册中心 MPC Media Accreditation Centre 100 m²	8 室外柴发机组 Outdoor Generator	11 广播综合电力供应区 Power Compound for OBS 600 m²	14 停车管理人员休息室 Parking Manage's Lounge 25 m²	17 无障碍男女 通用卫生间 Driver's Toilet-Accessible Unisex 19x 3m²	19 电信和公用事业 车辆停车场 Telecommunications and Utilities Vehicle Parking 200 m² 20 维修和服务车辆 停车场 Maintenance & Service Vehicle Parking 300 m²	24 MPC访客服务中心 MPC Visitor Services centre
3 VSA 150 m²	6 公交场站 BUS Station 2500 m²	9 精密空调室外机 Outdoor Units of CRAC	12 临时电力办公室 NRG Office 25 m²	15 执勤人员休息室 Staff Lounge 25 m²		21 现场工作/除雪车辆 Site Work/Snow Removal Vehicles 360 m² 22 车辆调配场 Motor Pool 100 m²	25 出租车落客区 Taxi Drop-off Area 600 m²

MMC 总平面图 OB3.0版
MMC Master Plan OB3.0

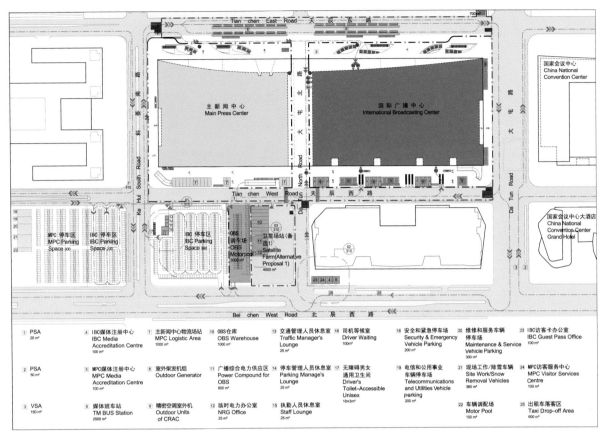

#	中文 / English		#	中文 / English		#	中文 / English
1	PSA 25㎡		10	OBS仓库 OBS Warehouse		19	电信和公用事业车辆停车场 Telecommunications and Utilities Vehicle parking 200㎡
2	PSA 50㎡		11	广播综合电力供应区 Power Compound for OBS 600㎡		20	维修和服务车辆停车场 Maintenance & Service Vehicle Parking 300㎡
3	VSA 150㎡		12	临时电力办公室 NRG Office 25㎡		21	现场工作/除雪车辆 Site Work/Snow Removal Vehicles 360㎡
4	IBC媒体注册中心 IBC Media Accreditation Centre 100㎡		13	交通管理人员休息室 Traffic Manager's Lounge 25㎡		22	车辆调配场 Motor Pool 100㎡
5	MPC媒体注册中心 MPC Media Accreditation Centre 100㎡		14	停车管理人员休息室 Parking Manage's Lounge 25㎡		23	IBC访客卡办公室 IBC Guest Pass Office
6	媒体班车站 TM BUS Station 2500㎡		15	执勤人员休息室 Staff Lounge 25㎡		24	MPC访客服务中心 MPC Visitor Services Centre 100㎡
7	主新闻中心物流站 MPC Logistic Area 1000㎡		16	司机等候室 Driver Waiting 100㎡		25	出租车落客区 Taxi Drop-off Area 600㎡
8	室外柴发机组 Outdoor Generator		17	无障碍男女通用卫生间 Driver's Toilet-Accessible Unisex 18×3㎡			
9	精密空调室外机 Outdoor Units of CRAC		18	安全和紧急停车场 Security & Emergency Vehicle Parking 200㎡			

N

MMC 总平面图 OB4.0版
MMC Master Plan OB4.0

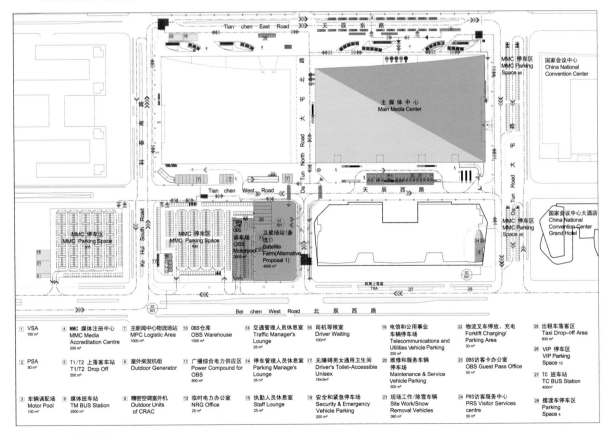

#	中文 / English		#	中文 / English		#	中文 / English
1	VSA 150㎡		10	OBS仓库 OBS Warehouse 1000㎡		19	电信和公用事业车辆停车场 Telecommunications and Utilities Vehicle Parking 200㎡
2	PSA 50㎡		11	广播综合电力供应区 Power Compound for OBS 600㎡		20	维修和服务车辆停车场 Maintenance & Service Vehicle Parking 300㎡
3	车辆调配场 Motor Pool 100㎡		12	临时电力办公室 NRG Office 25㎡		21	现场工作/除雪车辆 Site Work/Snow Removal Vehicles 360㎡
4	MMC媒体注册中心 MMC Media Accreditation Centre 200㎡		13	交通管理人员休息室 Traffic Manager's Lounge 25㎡		22	物流叉车停放、充电 Forklift Charging/Parking Area 30㎡
5	T1/T2 上落客车站 T1/T2 Drop Off		14	停车管理人员休息室 Parking Manage's Lounge 25㎡		23	OBS访客卡办公室 OBS Guest Pass Office 50㎡
6	媒体班车站 TM BUS Station 2500㎡		15	执勤人员休息室 Staff Lounge 25㎡		24	PRS访客服务中心 PRS Visitor Services centre 50㎡
7	主新闻中心物流站 MPC Logistic Area 1000㎡		16	司机等候室 Driver Waiting 100㎡		25	出租车落客区 Taxi Drop-off Area 600㎡
8	室外柴发机组 Outdoor Generator		17	无障碍男女通用卫生间 Driver's Toilet-Accessible Unisex		26	VIP 停车区 VIP Parking Space 10
9	精密空调室外机 Outdoor Units of CRAC		18	安全和紧急停车场 Security & Emergency Vehicle Parking 200㎡		27	TC班车站 TC BUS Station 400㎡
						28	摆渡车停车区 Parking Space 4

N

MMC 总平面图 OB5.0版
MMC Master Plan OB5.0

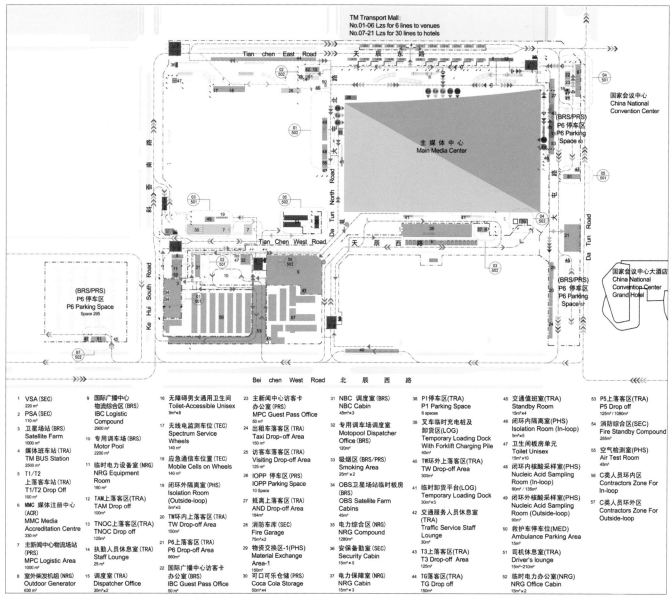

TM Transport Mall:
No.01-06 Lzs for 6 lines to venues
No.07-21 Lzs for 30 lines to hotels

1	VSA (SEC) 220 m²
2	PSA (SEC) 110 m²
3	卫星场站 (BRS) Satellite Farm 1000 m²
4	媒体班车站 (TRA) TM BUS Station 2500 m²
5	T1/T2 上落客区 (TRA) T1/T2 Drop Off 100 m²
6	MMC 媒体注册中心 (ACR) MMC Media Accreditation Centre 330 m²
7	主新闻中心物流场站 (PRS) MPC Logistic Area 1000 m²
8	室外柴发机组 (NRG) Outdoor Generator 630 m²

9	国际广播中心物流综合区 (BRS) IBC Logistic Compound 2900 m²
10	专用调车场 (BRS) Motor Pool 2200 m²
11	临时电力设备室 (NRG) NRG Equipment Room 180 m²
12	TAM上落客区 (TRA) TAM Drop off 100m²
13	TNOC上落客区 (TRA) TNOC Drop off 25 m²
14	执勤人员休息室 (TRA) Staff Lounge 25 m²
15	调度室 (TRA) Dispatcher Office 15m²×2

16	无障碍男女通用卫生间 Toilet-Accessible Unisex 9m²×8
17	无线电监测车位 (TEC) Spectrum Service Wheels 140 m²
18	应急通信车位置 (TEC) Mobile Cells on Wheels 140 m²
19	闭环外隔离室 (PHS) Isolation Room (Outside-loop) 5m²×5
20	TW环内上落客区 (TRA) TW Drop-off Area 150m²
21	P6上落客区 (TRA) P6 Drop-off Area 660m²
22	国际广播中心访客卡办公室 (BRS) IBC Guest Pass Office 50 m²

23	主新闻中心访客卡办公室 (PRS) MPC Guest Pass Office 50 m²
24	出租车落客区 (TRA) Taxi Drop-off Area 150 m²
25	访客车落客区 (TRA) Visiting Drop-off Area 125 m²
26	IOPP 停车区 (PRS) IOPP Parking Space 10 Space
27	抵离上落客区 (TRA) AND Drop-off Area 184m²
28	消防车库 (SEC) Fire Garage 75m²×2
29	物资交换区-1(PHS) Material Exchange Area-1 150m²
30	可口可乐仓储 (PRS) Coca Cola Storage 50m²×4

31	NBC 调度室 (BRS) NBC Cabin 45m²×3
32	专用调车场调度室 (TRA) Motopool Dispatcher Office (BRS) 120m²
33	吸烟区 (BRS/PRS) Smoking Area 25m²×2
34	OBS卫星场站临时板房 (BRS) OBS Satellite Farm Cabins 45m²
35	电力综合区 (NRG) NRG Compound
36	安保备勤室 (SEC) Security Cabin
37	电力保障室 (NRG) NRG Cabin 15m²×3

38	P1停车区 (TRA) P1 Parking Space 6 spaces
39	叉车临时充电桩及卸货区(LOG) Temporary Loading Dock With Forklift Charging Pile 40m²
40	TW环外上落客区 (TRA) TW Drop-off Area 300m²
41	临时卸货平台(LOG) Temporary Loading Dock 30m²×3
42	交通服务人员休息室 (TRA) Traffic Service Staff Lounge 30m²
43	T3上落客区 (TRA) T3 Drop-off Area 125m²
44	TG落客区 (TRA) TG Drop off 150m²

45	交通值班室 (TRA) Standby Room 15m²×4
46	闭环内隔离室 (PHS) Isolation Room (In-loop) 5m²×5
47	卫生间板房 (PHS) Toilet Unisex 15m²×10
48	闭环内核酸采样室 (PHS) Nucleic Acid Sampling Room (In-loop) 90m² / 135m²
49	闭环外核酸采样室 (PHS) Nucleic Acid Sampling Room (Outside-loop) 90m²
50	救护车停车位 (MED) Ambulance Parking Area 15m²
51	司机休息室 (TRA) Driver's lounge 15m²-210m²
52	临时电力办公室 (NRG) NRG Office Cabin 15m²×2

53	P5上落客区 (TRA) P5 Drop off 125m² / 1080m²
54	消防综合区 (SEC) Fire Standby Compound 255m²
55	空气检测室 (PHS) Air Test Room 45m²
56	C类人员环内区 Contractors Zone For In-loop
57	C类人员环外区 Contractors Zone For Outside-loop

MMC 总平面图 OB7.0版
MMC Master Plan OB7.0

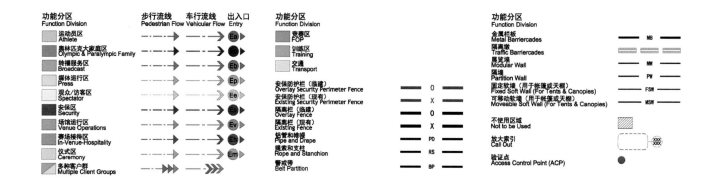

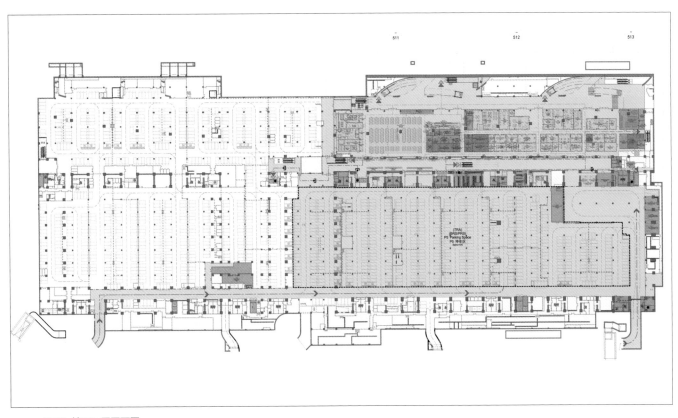

N MMC 地下二层平面图 OB7.0版
MMC B2 Plan OB7.0

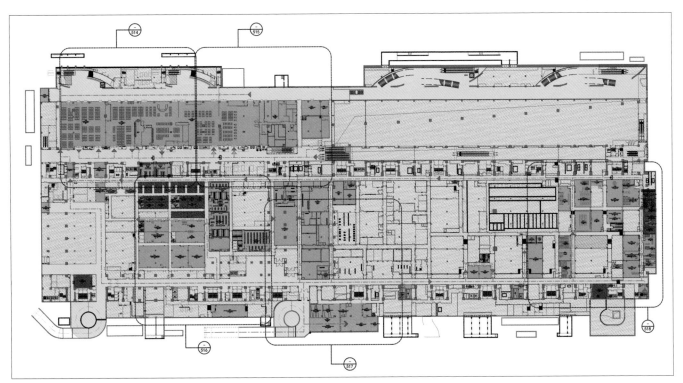

N MMC 地下一层平面图 OB7.0版
MMC B1 Plan OB7.0

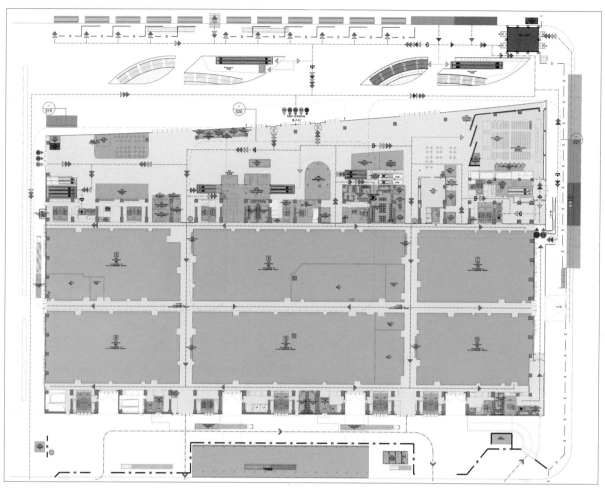

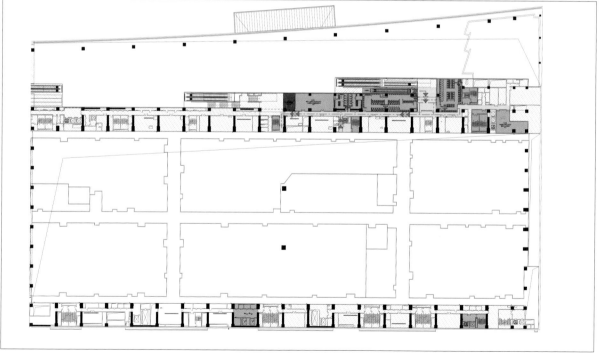

MMC 一层平面图 OB7.0版
MMC 1F Plan OB7.0

MMC 一层夹层平面图 OB7.0版
MMC 1F Mezzanine Plan OB7.0

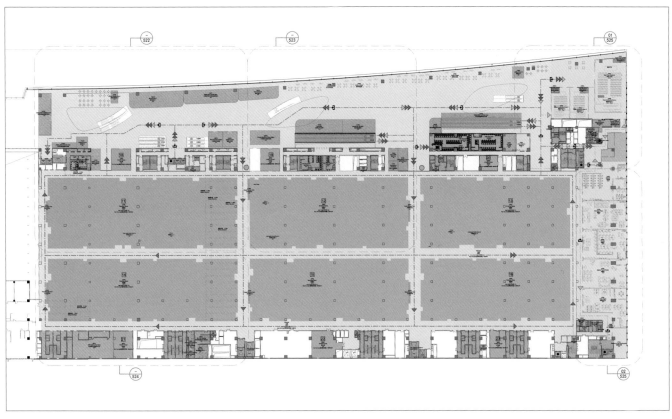

N MMC 二层平面图 OB7.0版
MMC 2F Plan OB7.0

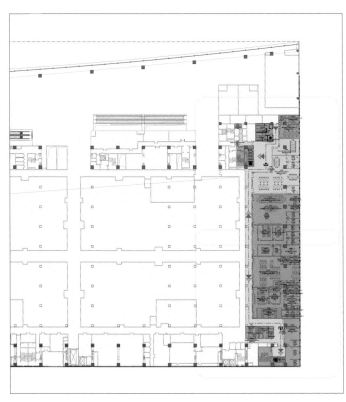

N MMC 二层夹层平面图 OB7.0版
MMC 2F Mezzanine Plan OB7.0

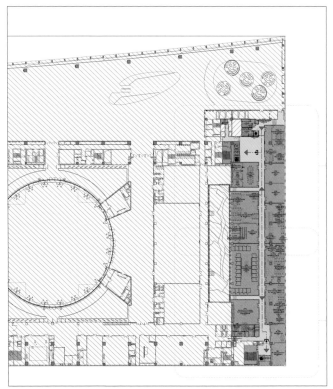

N MMC 三层平面图 OB7.0版
MMC 3F Plan OB7.0

北京冬奥组委　提供
Provide by. BOCOG

摄影 赵曾辉
Photo by Zhao Zenghui

北京颁奖广场 [BMP]

Beijing Medals Plaza

1. 场馆基本情况

北京颁奖广场位于北京奥林匹克公园内，在国家体育场和国家游泳中心之间，是完全由临时设施搭建而成的场馆。冬奥会期间，北京颁奖广场连续12天、为31个项目的获奖运动员颁发奖牌，并通过一系列演出活动展示中国文化、烘托现场气氛，为获奖运动员打造难忘的高光时刻。

北京颁奖广场主要分为五大区域，包括舞台区、后台制作区、转播媒体区、奥林匹克大家庭区域和观众区，其中舞台区是颁奖广场的核心，主舞台以水立方为背景，正对鸟巢中轴线。场馆占地面积约1.8万m²。

2. 重点区域

根据冬奥会要求，北京颁奖广场新建了临时舞台，舞台充分运用"雪屋"的视觉元素进行延伸设计，屋顶呈现雪花造型，结合冰立方背景，形成冰雪交相辉映的冬奥元素呈现。基座尺寸为南北向长41m、东西向长23m，舞台穹顶建筑宽32.6m，舞台基座高度1.2m，舞台总高16m，台口宽度约22.4m、高约10m，台口两侧设4.5m×8m大屏幕，舞台深度19m。舞台北侧和西侧设置无障碍坡道。

1. Venue Overview

The Beijing Medals Plaza is divided into 5 areas, including the Stage Area, the Backstage Production Area, the Broadcast Media Area, the Olympic Family Area, and the Spectator Area. The Stage Area is the core of the Medals Plaza. The main stage is set against the central axis of the Bird's Nest, with the Water Cube as the background. The venue covers an area of about 18,000m².

2. Key Areas

The pedestal is 41m long in the north-south direction and 23m long in the east-west direction. This stage features a 32.6m wide dome, a 1.2m tall pedestal, a total height of 16m, a proscenium width of about 22.4m, an entrance height of about 10m, 4.5m×8m screens at both sides of the proscenium, and a stage depth of 19m. Accessible ramps are set up on the north and west sides of the stage.

3. Front of House and Spectator Flow

The two control towers are in the north and south of the Beijing Medals Plaza, and the square area on the east side of the control towers is the Front of House area of the venue, which is open to spectators, where many spectator service facilities are provided. On regular competition days, spectators enter the venue from the east ticket check point and leave the Plaza along the original route after the ceremony.

围绕舞台布置其他功能区。舞台北侧布置运动员候场区，舞台东北侧布置奥林匹克大家庭区域，舞台南侧布置混合采访区和演员候场区，舞台东侧布置滑轨摄像机、摇臂摄像机、摄像摄影平台和控制塔。

3. 场馆前院及观众流线

北京颁奖广场南北两个控制塔东侧广场区域为场馆前院区，面向观众开放，前院区设置了多个观众服务设施。常规比赛日，观众从东侧票检口进入场馆，观礼结束后沿原路离开颁奖广场。

4. 场馆后院及注册流线

北京颁奖广场除南北两个控制塔东侧广场区域外，均为场馆后院区。后院区内设置了候场室、兴奋剂检查站、医疗站、演员候场区、混合采访区、南北控制塔、电力综合区等多处服务保障设施。

（1）获奖运动员流线

获奖运动员和观礼运动员从冬奥村乘坐大巴到达天辰东路，在指定区域落客，获奖运动员进入运动员候场室；观礼运动员从运动员候场室东侧进入运动员观礼站席区。

颁奖仪式开始前，获奖运动员由运动员候场室出发，在礼仪人员引导下沿专用通道从舞台后台到达舞台南侧上台口。颁奖仪式结束后，运动员在混合采访区接受采访后，返回运动员候场室。

临近运动员候场室布置兴奋剂检查站和运动员医疗站，方便获奖运动员快速到达。

（2）奥林匹克大家庭成员流线

奥林匹克大家庭成员通过位于场馆西侧的大家庭入口进入场馆，场馆内为闭环内外大家庭人员分别设置了两个大家庭休息室及配套空间。闭环内大家庭休息室（包括颁奖嘉宾）位于运动员候场室东侧，闭环外大家庭休息室位于南侧控制塔二层。大家庭成员流线独立设置。

（3）媒体流线

转播及新闻媒体通过位于场馆西南侧的媒体入口直接进入媒体工作区。工作区内设置有评论员控制室、转播信息办公室、新闻运行办公室等功能用房。转播及新闻媒体工作区紧邻舞台、混合采访区、摄像摄影平台和各类摄影机位，可以在最短的时间内抵达各个点位。

（4）场馆室外综合区

赛时北京颁奖广场后院区内设置了电力综合区，为舞台提供不间断稳定的电力保障；其他综合区域结合周边场馆配合保障，清废和物流依托北京奥林匹克公园公共区保障，场馆内仅设置少量功能用房；转播依托国家体育场保障。

5. 场馆站席

北京颁奖广场设置了两个观众站席区。控制塔西侧到舞台前的广场区域为闭环内观众站席区，包括运动员站席区、奥运大家庭站席区、媒体站席区和观众（闭环内）站席区，各区域设置了独立的通道和出入口，避免流线交叉，区域之间均设置了隔离栏保障各人群间的防疫距离；控制塔东侧广场区域为闭环外观众站席区，为保障该区域观众观礼体验，在两个控制塔东侧设置了两面大屏幕，实时播放颁奖画面。

4. Back of House and Accreditation Flow

The Back of House area of the Beijing Medals Plaza includes all areas except for the square area on the east side of the two control towers. The Back of House area is provided with many service support facilities such as the green room, doping control station, medical station, performers' waiting area, mixed zone, south and north control towers, and energy compound.

(1) Medallist Flow

Medallists and spectating athletes take buses from the Olympic/Paralympic Village to Tianchen East Road and get off in the designated area, and medallists enter the athletes' green room; spectating athletes enter the athletes' standing area from the east side of the athletes' green room.

Before the victory ceremony starts, the medallists start from the athletes' green room and reach the stage proscenium on the south side of the stage from the backstage along the dedicated passageway guided by the victory ceremony personnel. After the victory ceremony, the medallists go to the mixed zone for interviews and return to the athletes' green room.

(2) Olympic Family Flow

The Olympic Family members enter the venue through the Olympic Family entrance on the west side of the venue. Two Olympic Family lounges and supporting spaces are set up in the venue for the Olympic Family members inside and outside the closed loop. The Olympic Family lounge inside the closed loop (including medal presenters) is located on the east side of the athletes' green room, and the Olympic Family lounge outside the closed loop is located on L2 of the south control tower. The Olympic Family flow is independent from flows of other stakeholders.

(3) Media Flow

The broadcast and media personnel directly enter the media work area through the media entrance on the southwest side of the venue. The work area is arranged with such functional rooms as the commentary control room, broadcast information office, and press operations office. The broadcast and media work area is adjacent to the stage, mixed zone, camera platform, and various camera positions, and each spot can be reached in the shortest time.

5. Standing Area

The Beijing Medals Plaza provides two standing areas for spectators. The square area from the west side of the control tower to the front of the stage is the standing area for spectators inside the closed loop, including the standing area for athletes, the standing area for the Olympic Family, the standing area for media, and the standing area for spectators (inside the closed loop). Independent passageways and entrances/exits are set up in each area to avoid crossing of flows, and isolation fences are set up between the areas for different groups to ensure COVID-19 prevention and control. The square area on the east side of the control tower is the standing area for spectators outside the closed loop. In order to ensure that spectators in this area enjoy the ceremony, two large screens are set up on the east side of the two control towers.

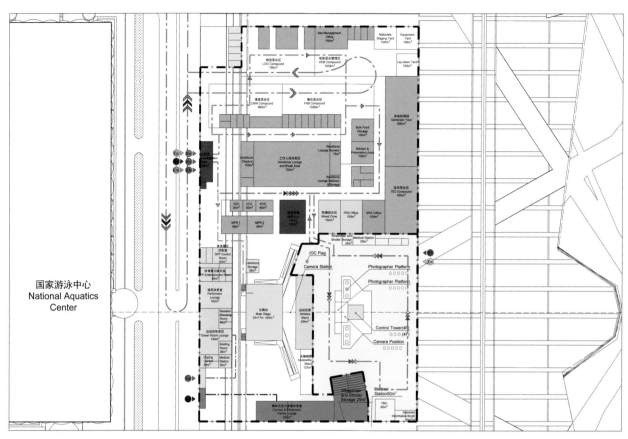

N BMP 总平面图 OB2.1版
BMP Master Plan OB2.1

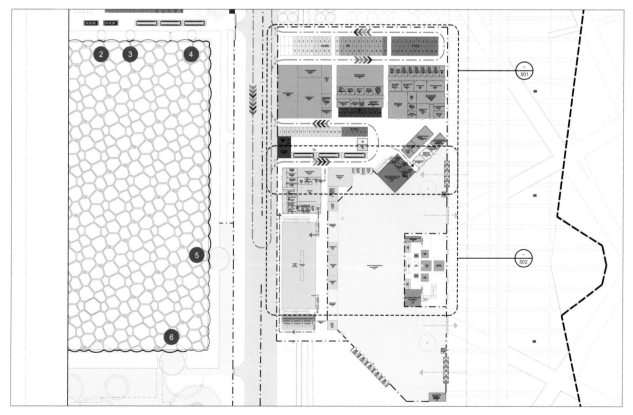

N BMP 总平面图 OB3.0版
BMP Master Plan OB3.0

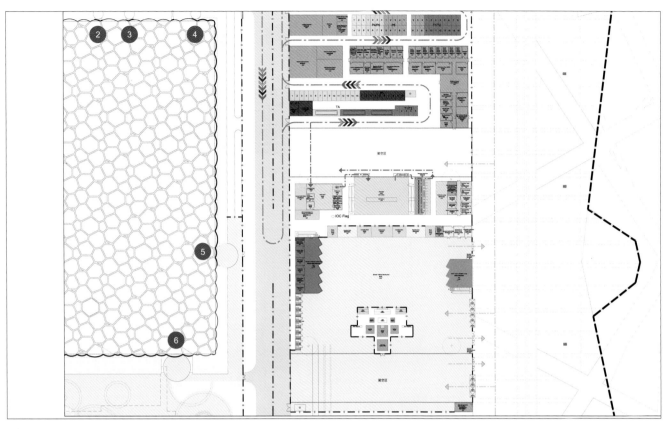

N
BMP 总平面图 OB3.1版
BMP Master Plan OB3.1

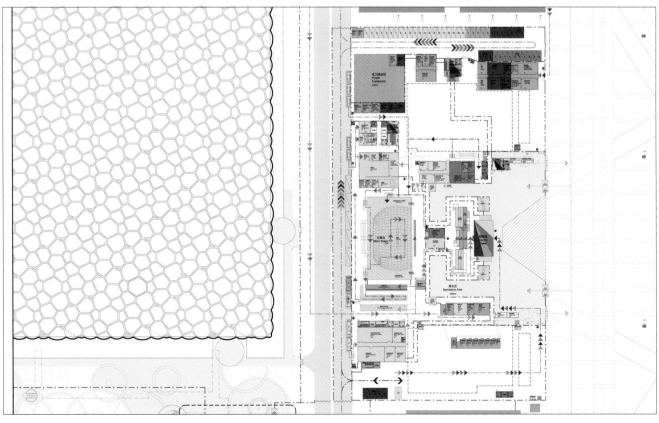

N
BMP 总平面图 OB6.0版
BMP Master Plan OB6.0

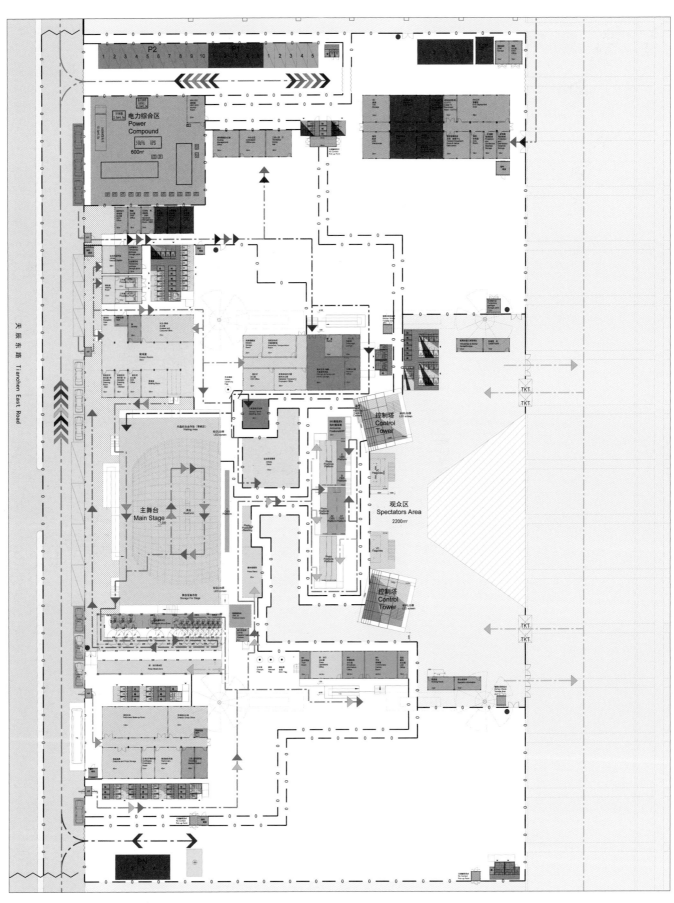

北京赛区 / Beijing Zone

BMP 总平面图 OB7.0版
BMP Master Plan OB7.0

摄影 赵曾辉
Photo by Zhao Zenghui

摄影 刘兴华
Photo by Liu Xinghua

奥林匹克大家庭酒店 [OFH]

Olympic Family Hotel

　　奥林匹克大家庭酒店位于北京奥林匹克公园周边，包含国家会议中心一期C区、北辰洲际酒店、北辰五洲皇冠国际酒店、五洲大酒店等设施，在北京2022年冬奥会期间为奥林匹克大家庭成员提供住宿、餐饮等服务，也是赛前国际奥林匹克委员会全体会议的所在地。

　　北京2022年冬残奥会期间，国家会议中心一期C区和北辰洲际酒店继续作为残奥大家庭酒店提供服务。

The Olympic Family Hotels, located near the Beijing Olympic Park, include facilities such as Zone C of China National Convention Centre Phase I, InterContinental Beijing Beichen, V-Continent Beijing Parkview Wuzhou Hotel, and Beijing Continental Grand Hotel. During the Beijing 2022 Olympic Winter Games, they offer accommodation and food and beverage services for the Olympic Family members. They are also the site of the IOC Session before the Games.

During the Beijing 2022 Paralympic Winter Games, Zone C of China National Convention Centre Phase I and InterContinental Beijing Beichen continue to serve as the Paralympic Family hotels.

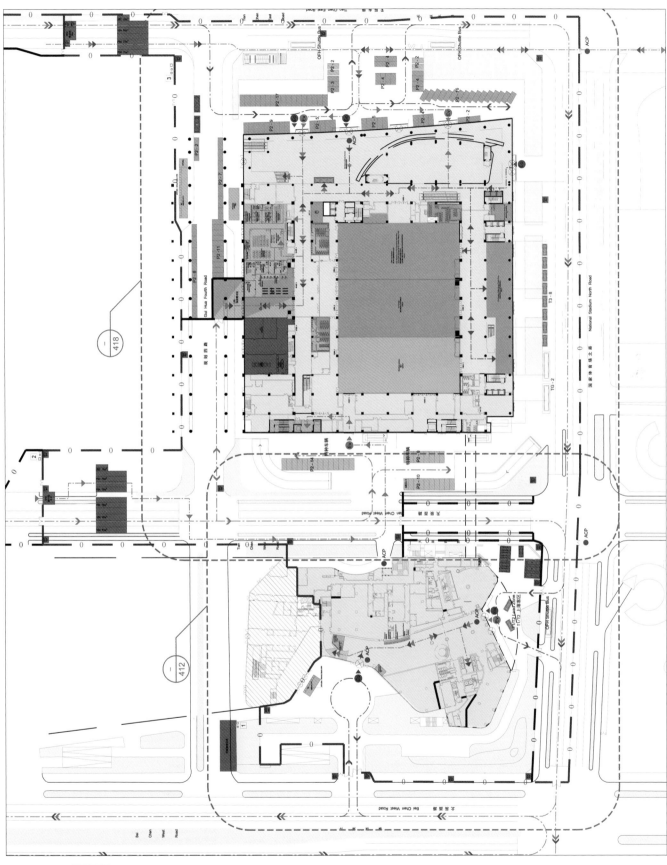

N

OFH 一层平面图 OB7.0版
OFH 1F Plan OB7.0

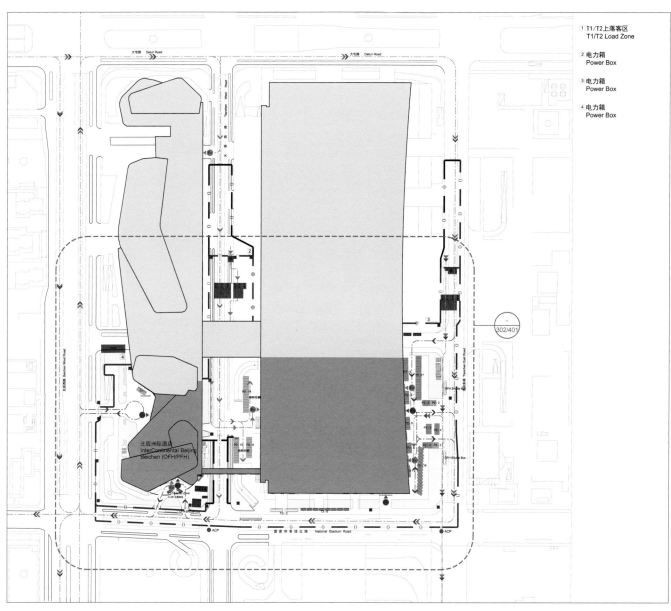

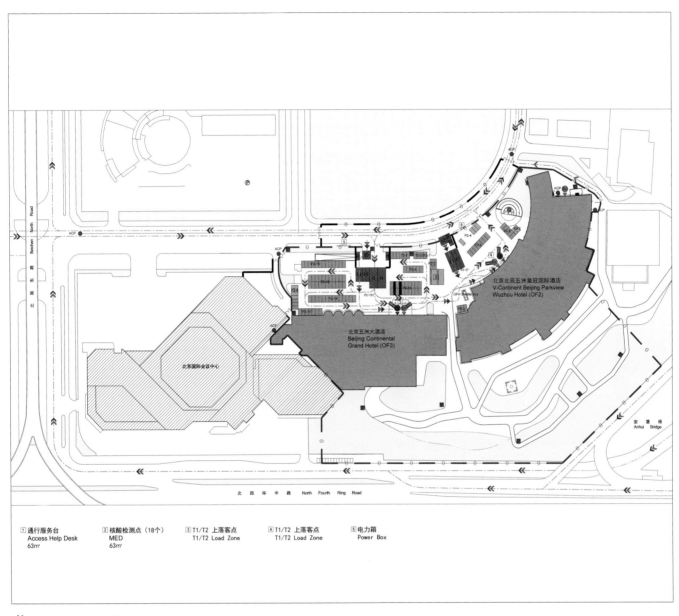

N
OF2/OF3 一层平面图 OB7.0版
OF2/OF3 1F Plan OB7.0

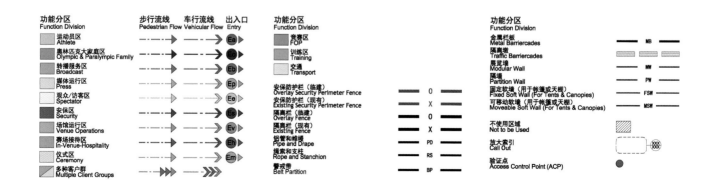

功能分区 Function Division	步行流线 Pedestrian Flow	车行流线 Vehicular Flow	出入口 Entry
运动员区 Athlete			Ea
奥林匹克大家庭区 Olympic & Paralympic Family			Ef
转播服务区 Broadcast			Eb
媒体运行区 Press			Ep
观众/访客区 Spectator			Ee
安保区 Security			Es
场馆运行区 Venue Operations			Ev
赛场接待区 In-Venue-Hospitality			Eh
仪式区 Ceremony			Em
多种客户群 Multiple Client Groups			

功能分区 Function Division		
竞赛区 FOP		
训练区 Training		
交通 Transport		
安保防护栏（临建） Overlay Security Perimeter Fence		0
安保防护栏（现有） Existing Security Perimeter Fence		X
隔离栏（临建） Overlay Fence		0
隔离栏（现有） Existing Fence		X
铝管和帷幔 Pipe and Drape		PD
绳索和立柱 Rope and Stanchion		RS
警带 Belt Partition		BP

功能分区 Function Division	
金属栏板 Metal Barriercades	MB
隔离墩 Traffic Barriercades	
展览墙 Modular Wall	MW
隔墙 Partition Wall	PW
固定软墙（用于帐篷或天棚） Fixed Soft Wall (For Tents & Canopies)	FSW
可移动软墙（用于帐篷或天棚） Moveable Soft Wall (For Tents & Canopies)	MSW
不使用区域 Not to be Used	
放大索引 Call Out	XXX
验证点 Access Control Point (ACP)	●

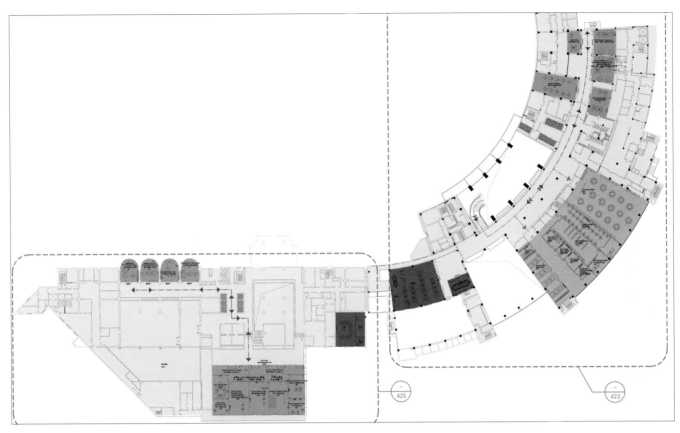

N

OF2/OF3 二层平面图 OB7.0版
OF2/OF3 2F Plan OB7.0

北京冬奥组委 提供
Provide by BOCOG

北京奥林匹克公园公共区 [BOP]
Beijing Olympic Park

北京奥林匹克公园公共区位于北京奥林匹克公园，是北京2008年夏奥会的重要遗产。北京2022年冬奥会期间，公共区安保封闭线范围和2008年夏奥会相比大幅度减小，总占地约1.1km²。公共区封闭线内包含国家游泳中心、国家体育馆两个竞赛场馆和国家体育场、北京颁奖广场两个非竞赛场馆。另外，主媒体中心的电视演播厅也设在公共区内。公共区赛时临时设施建筑面积约4.1万m²，其中约2.1万m²利用现状空间进行建设。

赛时，公共区的中轴大道西侧以及天辰东路部分区域为场馆前院区，面向观众开放，前院区设置了观众服务设施和服务志愿者部署区。开闭幕式日，观众沿着中轴大道南侧从12号安检口进入公共区；常规比赛日，观众沿中轴大道北侧从5号安检口进入公共区。

赛时公共区的天辰西路、湖景西路和湖景东路沿线为场馆后院区，设置了两个清废综合区、两个工作人员餐厅以及物流综合区等。

The Beijing Olympic Park is an important legacy of the Beijing 2008 Olympic Games. During the Beijing 2022 Olympic Winter Games, the scope of the secure perimeter in the Park is significantly reduced compared with that of the Beijing 2008 Olympic Games, covering a total area of about 1.1km². Within the secure perimeter there are 2 competition venues, the National Aquatics Centre and the National Indoor Stadium, and 2 non-competition venues, the National Stadium and the Beijing Medals Plaza. In addition, the TV Studio of the MMC is also set in the Park. The floor area of Games-time temporary facilities is about 41,000m², of which about 21,000m² are constructed using the existing space.

During the Games, the west side of Central Axis Avenue and part of Tianchen East Road in the Park constitute the Front of House area of the venue, which is open to the spectators, and the Front of House area is equipped with spectator service facilities and volunteer deployment area. On the days of opening and closing ceremonies, spectators enter the Park from the Screening Area No. 12 along the south side of the Central Axis Avenue. On the regular competition days, spectators enter the Park from the Screening Area No. 5 along the north side of Central Axis Avenue.

During the Games, Tianchen West Road, Hujing West Road, and Hujing East Road in the Park are the Back of House area of the venue, with two cleaning and waste compounds, two workforce dining halls, a logistics compound, etc.

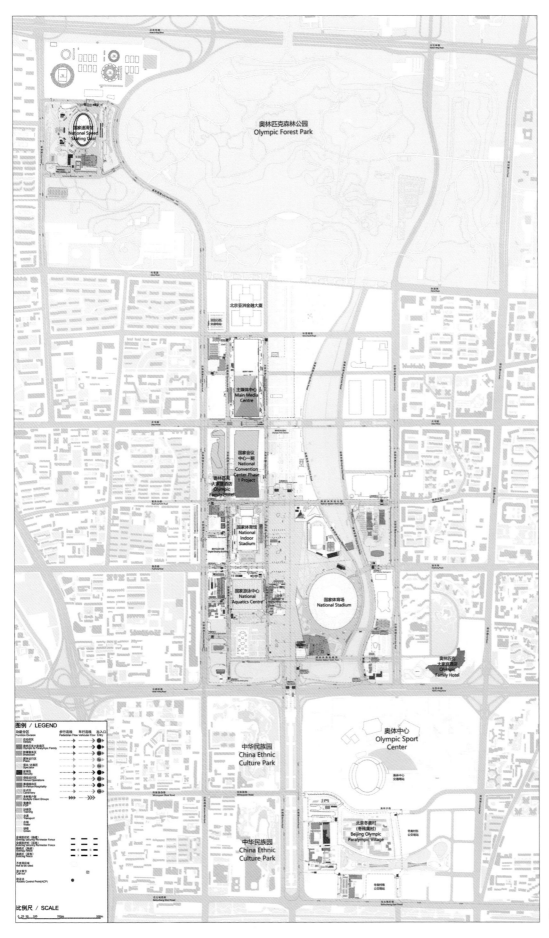

BOP 区域场馆布局图
BOP Area Venue Layout

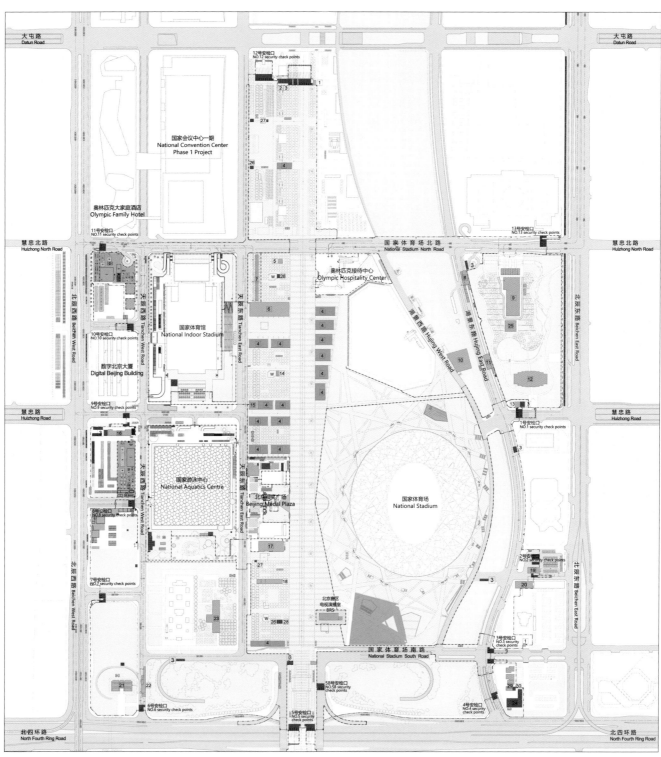

BOP公共区总平面图 OB6.0版
BOP Common Domain Master Plan OB6.0

1	售票房 (TBO) Ticket Box Office (TBO)	4	安保人员备勤室 Security Personnel Room	7	现状公共卫生间 Current Public Toilet	11	综合仓储区 Comprehensive Storage Area	14	运行协调系统–工作用房 Operaiton Coordination –Office 20m²	17	牡丹餐厅 Peony Dining Room 3150m²
2	赛事服务点位 EVS Point	5	突发事件处置人员备勤室 Emergency Response Room 54m²	8	治安处理点 Public Security Response Room 54m²	12	医疗站 Medical Station 75m²	15	外事警察会谈室 Foreign Affairs Police Meeting Room 54m²	18	清废/技术/公共卫生 综合办公楼 CNW & TEC & PHDS Comprehensive Office Building 1830m²
3	防爆安检团队休息室 Anti-explosive and Security Personnel Room 105m²	6	消防车库 Fire Garage 150m²	9	电力保障团队办公室 NRG Office	13	赛事服务工作部署区/设备 存放和分配室/赛事服务管理 办公室 Event Services Deployment Area/Equipment Storage & Distribution Room/Event Services Management Office 600m²	16	西侧办公楼 West Office Building 730m²	19	清废综合区（南侧） Cleaning & Waste Compound (South) 554m²
				10	现场安保观察室 Security Observatioin Room						

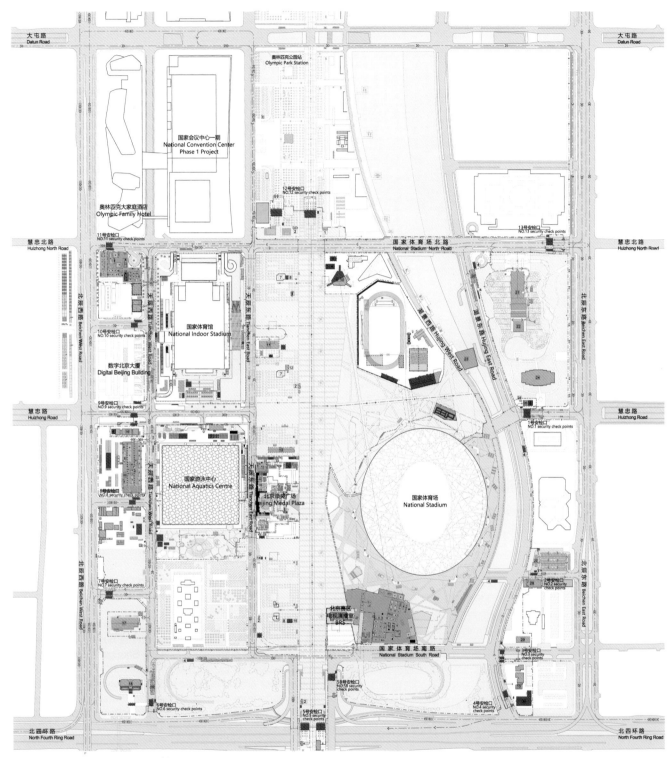

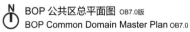

BOP 公共区总平面图 OB7.0版
BOP Common Domain Master Plan OB7.0

20 清废综合区（北侧） Cleaning & Waste Compound(North) 730m²	**26** 工作人员签到处/ 工作人员储藏间 Workforce Check-in point/ Workforce Storage 125m²	**32** 超级商店 Superstore 3000m²
23 交通办公区 TRA Office 234m²	**28** 集中办公楼 Office Building 2000m²	**33** 邮票售卖点 Stamp Sales Office 440m²
21 如意餐厅 Ruyi Dining Room 6150m²	**24** 工作人员物资储藏室 Workforce Material Storage 1000m²	**29** 电瓶车调度中心 Battery Car Dispatching Center	**34** 观众餐厅 Spectator Restaurant 1500m²
22 志愿者之家 Volunteer's Lounge Room 1150m²	**25** 驾驶员休息室 Driver's Lounge 18m²	**27** 场馆注册办公室/ 综合办公室 Venue Accreditation Office/ Comprehensive Office 162m²	**30** 安保指挥部 Security Command 1850m²	**31** 合作伙伴现场展示 Marketing Partner Showcasing Area

北京冬奥组委总部 [BHQ]

Beijing 2022 Headquarter

　　北京冬奥组委总部位于北京石景山区首钢园区内，是北京冬奥会第一个建成并投入使用的非竞赛场馆。2016年6月，第一批冬奥组委工作人员约180人入驻筒仓，场馆赛前正式运行。场馆筹办期间最多可容纳办公人员约1500人。

　　北京冬奥组委总部办公区的建筑空间，均是利用首钢园区原有料仓、筒仓、转运站、联合泵站等一系列的工业厂房改造而成。办公区内的绿化树木采用了首钢园区原有的植物种类，室外地面铺装大量采用了建筑垃圾回收后重新制作而成的透水地砖，整个区域践行了绿色可持续的环保理念。冬奥会前，北京冬奥组委总部已成为由工业遗产改造为现代化办公区的典范工程，并带动了首钢园区停产10年后的全面复兴与发展。

　　在冬奥会筹办的6年时间里，北京冬奥组委总部作为北京2022年冬奥会和冬残奥会组织委员会的办公机构，承担着保障所有部门正常运转的功能。赛时，北京冬奥组委总部又是重要的非竞赛场馆，内部还包含了运行指挥部调度中心、冬奥交通指挥中心等非竞赛场馆和相关保障设施。

Located in Shougang Park, Shijingshan District, the Beijing 2022 Headquarter is the first non-competition venue built and put into use for the Beijing 2022 Games.

The building spaces of the Beijing 2022 Headquarter are transformed from a series of factory remains such as the bunker, silos, transfer stations, and united pump stations in the Shougang Park. The trees in the office area are the original plant species in Shougang Park, and the outdoor ground is paved with a large number of permeable floor tiles made from recycled construction waste. The concept of green and sustainable environmental protection is practiced in the whole area. Before the Beijing 2022 Olympic and Paralympic Winter Games, the Beijing 2022 Headquarter had become a model project for the renovation of the industrial site into a modern office area and had driven the overall revitalisation and development of the Shougang Park after 10 years of shutdown.

Before the games, Beijing 2022 Headquarter was used as the office of the Beijing Organising Committee for the 2022 Olympic and Paralympic Winter Games, ensuring the normal operation of all departments. During the Games, the Beijing 2022 Headquarter was also an important non-competition venue. It also includes non-competition venues such as the MOC Coordination Centre, the Olympic Transport Command Centre, and related supporting facilities.

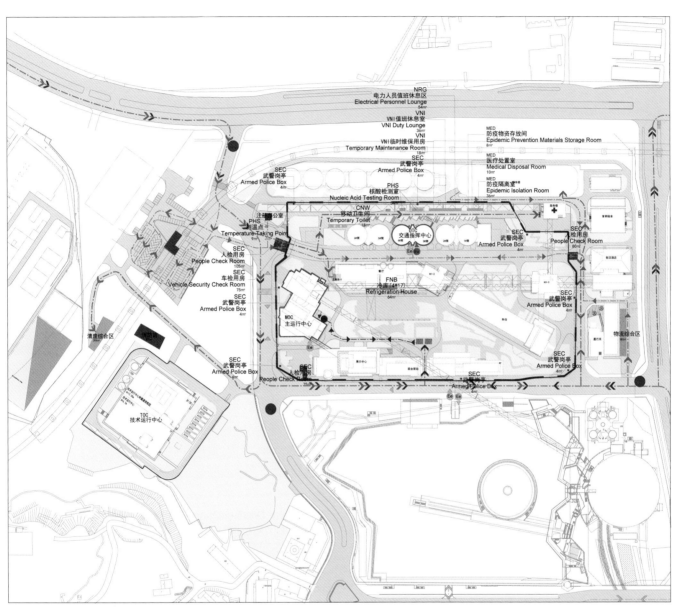

BHQ 总平面图 OB7.0版
BHQ Master Plan OB7.0

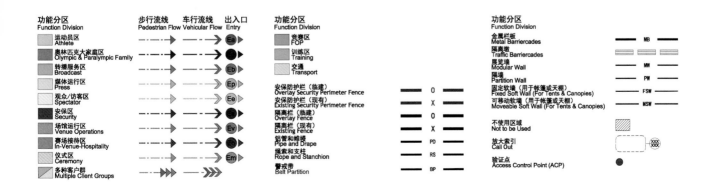

制服和注册中心
Uniform Distribution and Accreditation Centre

场馆业主 提供
Provide by Venue Owner

制服和注册中心 [UAC]
Uniform Distribution and Accreditation Centre

制服和注册中心位于京能集团石景山热电厂院内，由原有余热泵房和物资库房改造而成，赛时的主要功能是为北京赛区的冬奥会和冬残奥会工作人员、志愿者办理证件注册和制服发放业务，具有人员流量大、投入运行早、运行时间长、仓储物流要求高等特点。场馆建筑共2层，总建筑面积约1.14万m²。

场馆周边由外向内分为交通控制区、场馆区和安保封闭区三个范围，分区域执行相应通行政策和管理措施。由石景山热电厂门前到石景山火车站物流入口区域，为交通控制区；石景山热电厂院内为场馆区；场馆区内设置了安保封闭区。车辆安检口设于西侧安保封闭线，人员安检口设于东侧安保封闭线。

场馆北侧为场馆前院区，需制证或领取制服的人员通过东侧人检口进入前院，通过建筑北侧走廊便捷地到达制服区或注册区办理业务。场馆南侧为后院区，是场馆运行管理、场馆工作人员使用的区域。

The Uniform Distribution and Accreditation Centre, located in the Shijingshan Thermal Power Plant of Beijing Energy Holding Co., Ltd., is renovated from the original waste heat pump room and material warehouse. As for main functions during the Games, it was mainly used for accreditation and uniform distribution for the workforce and volunteers of the Beijing 2022 Olympic and Paralympic Winter Games in the Beijing Zone. It features a large personnel flow, early operation, long operation time, and high requirements of warehousing and logistics. The venue has two levels, with a total floor area of about 11,400m².

The surrounding of the venue is divided into 3 zones, namely, the traffic control zone, the venue zone, and the enclosed zone from the outside to the inside, and corresponding access policies and management measures are implemented for each zone. The area from the front of Shijingshan Thermal Power Plant to the logistics entrance of Shijingshan Railway Station is the traffic control zone; the courtyard of Shijingshan Thermal Power Plant is the venue zone; the enclosed zone is set in the venue zone. The vehicle screening area is located within the secure perimeter on the west side and the pedestrian screening area is located within the secure perimeter on the east side.

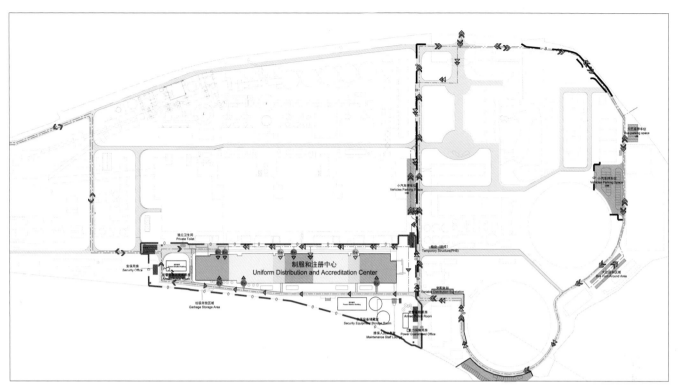

N UAC 总平面图 OB7.0版
UAC Master Plan OB7.0

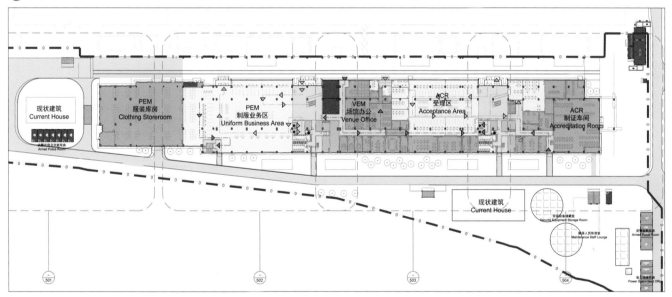

N UAC 一层平面图 OB7.0版
UAC 1F Plan OB7.0

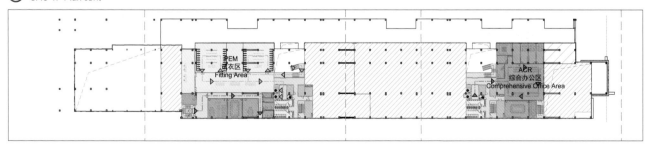

N UAC 二层平面图 OB7.0版
UAC 2F Plan OB7.0

运行指挥部调度中心 [MCC]

Beijing 2022 MOC Coordination Centre

运行指挥部调度中心位于首钢园区北京冬奥组委总部办公区院内，是北京2022年冬奥会和冬残奥会的赛事核心决策机构，是赛时的指挥与调度中心。主运行中心利用北京冬奥组委现有会议楼改造而成，一层主要为主运行大厅，二层主要为会议室等，总建筑面积约3600m²。

运行指挥部调度中心位于北京冬奥组委总部场馆安保封闭线内，赛时场馆运行团队工作人员通过冬奥组委总部东西两侧统一的安检口进入办公区，再通过会议楼北侧和东侧入口进入场馆内部。

场馆赛时分前院区和后院区。一楼主运行大厅和二楼会议室等工作区域为后院区，只有场馆运行工作人员可以进入。主运行大厅的南侧留有参观走廊通道和参观广场区，为前院区，外来参观人员可通过参观广场南侧的人检口，到达主运行中心参观走廊，参观完毕后由场馆专用西侧单向出口离开，全程不进入场馆其他区域。

Located in the office area of the Beijing 2022 Headquarters in Shougang Park, the MOC Coordination Centre is the core decision-making body of the Olympic and Paralympic Winter Games Beijing 2022 and the Games-time command and dispatch centre. The MOC Coordination Centre is renovated from the existing conference building of the Beijing 2022. 1F is the Main Operation Hall and conference rooms are mainly on 2F. The MCC has a total floor area of about 3,600m².

The MOC Coordination Centre is located within the secure perimeter of the Beijing 2022 Headquarters. During the Games, the workforce of the Venue Operations Team enters the office area through the screening areas on both east and west sides of the headquarters, access the MOC Coordination Centre through the north and east entrances to the Conference Building.

The venue is divided into a Front of House area and a Back of House area during the Games. The work areas such as the Main Operation Hall on 1F and the conference rooms on 2F are the Back of House area, which are accessible only to the venue operation workforce. The corridor and square area for visitors on the south side of the Main Operation Hall are the Front of House area. Visitors can reach the corridor through the pedestrian screening area on the south side of the square, and leave through the one-way exit on the west side of the venue, without accessing other areas of the venue.

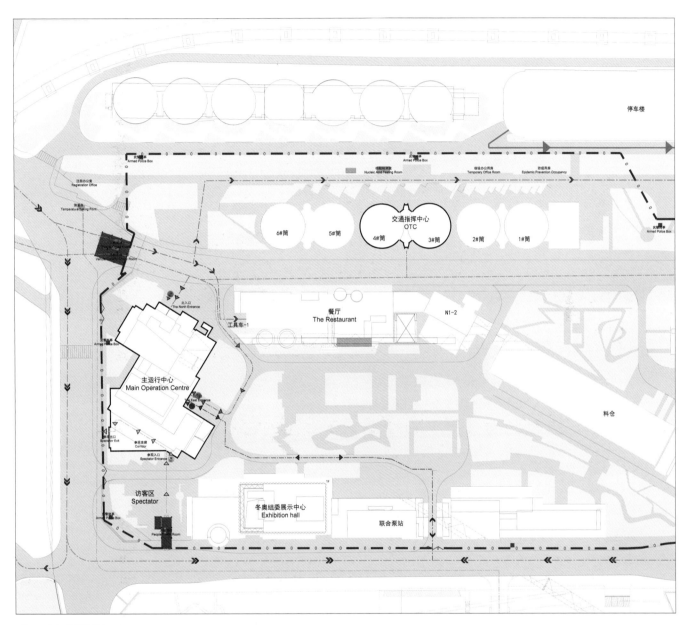

停车楼

武警岗亭
Armed Police Box

注册办公室
Registration Office

测温点
Temperature Taking Point

核酸检测点
Nucleic Acid Testing Room

临时办公用房
Temporary Office Room

防疫用房
Epidemic Prevention Occupancy

武警岗亭
Armed Police Box

武警岗亭
Armed Police Box

车辆消杀点
Vehicle Disinfect Room

交通指挥中心
OTC

6#筒   5#筒   4#筒   3#筒   2#筒   1#筒

北入口
The North Entrance

工具车-1

餐厅
The Restaurant

N1-2

武警岗亭
Armed Police Box

主运行中心
Main Operation Centre

东入口
The East Entrance

料仓

参观出口
Spectator Exit

参观走廊
Corridor

参观入口
Spectator Entrance

访客区
Spectator

1F

冬奥组委展示中心
Exhibition hall

联合泵站

武警岗亭
Armed Police Box

测温点
People's Test Room

N

MCC 总平面图 OB7.0版
MCC Master Plan OB7.0

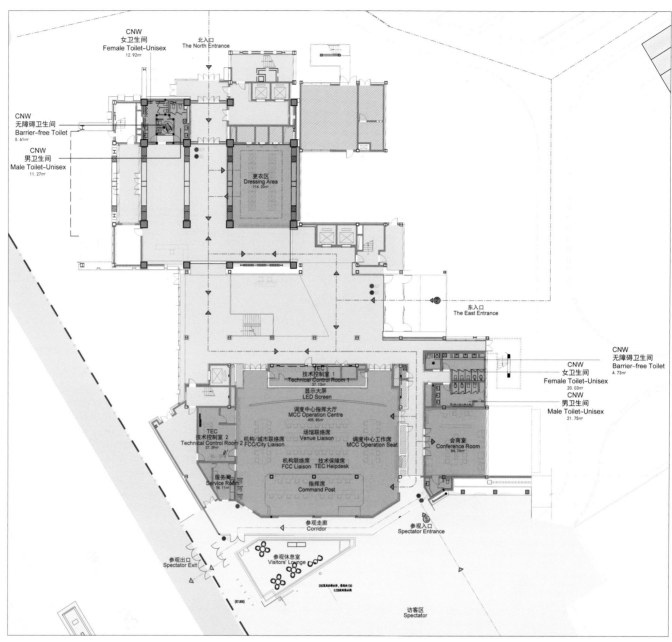

CNW
女卫生间
Female Toilet-Unisex
12.92㎡

北入口
The North Entrance

CNW
无障碍卫生间
Barrier-free Toilet
5.61㎡

CNW
男卫生间
Male Toilet-Unisex
11.27㎡

更衣区
Dressing Area
114.20㎡

东入口
The East Entrance

CNW
无障碍卫生间
Barrier-free Toilet
4.73㎡

CNW
女卫生间
Female Toilet-Unisex
20.03㎡

CNW
男卫生间
Male Toilet-Unisex
21.75㎡

TEC
技术控制室 1
Technical Control Room 1
37.13㎡

显示大屏
LED Screen

调度中心指挥大厅
MCC Operation Centre
405.85㎡

TEC
技术控制室 2
Technical Control Room 2
37.39㎡

机构/城市联络席
FCC/City Liaison

场馆联络席
Venue Liaison

调度中心工作席
MCC Operation Seat

会商室
Conference Room
84.74㎡

机构联络席
FCC Liaison

技术保障席
TEC Helpdesk

服务间
Service Room
18.11㎡

指挥席
Command Post

参观走廊
Corridor

参观入口
Spectator Entrance

参观出口
Spectator Exit

参观休息室
Visitors' Lounge

访客区
Spectator

N MCC 一层平面图 OB7.0版
MCC 1F Plan OB7.0

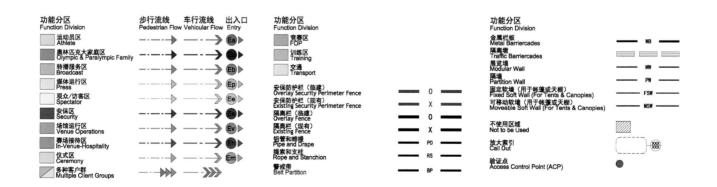

功能分区 Function Division	步行流线 Pedestrian Flow	车行流线 Vehicular Flow	出入口 Entry
运动员区 Athlete			Ea
奥林匹克大家庭区 Olympic & Paralympic Family			
转播服务区 Broadcast			Eb
媒体运行区 Press			Ep
观众/访客区 Spectator			Ee
安保区 Security			Es
场馆运行区 Venue Operations			Ev
赛场接待区 In-Venue-Hospitality			Eh
仪式区 Ceremony			Em
多种客户群 Multiple Client Groups			

功能分区 Function Division	
竞赛区 FOP	
训练区 Training	
交通 Transport	
安保防护栏（临建） Overlay Security Perimeter Fence	O
安保防护栏（现有） Existing Security Perimeter Fence	X
隔离栏（临建） Overlay Fence	O
隔离栏（现有） Existing Fence	X
铝管和帷幔 Pipe and Drape	PD
绳索和支柱 Rope and Stanchion	RS
警戒带 Belt Partition	BP

功能分区 Function Division	
金属栏板 Metal Barriercades	MB
隔离墩 Traffic Barriercades	
展览墙 Modular Wall	MW
隔墙 Partition Wall	PW
固定软墙（用于帐篷或天棚） Fixed Soft Wall (For Tents & Canopies)	FSW
可移动软墙（用于帐篷或天棚） Moveable Soft Wall (For Tents & Canopies)	MSW
不使用区域 Not to be Used	
放大索引 Call Out	XXX
验证点 Access Control Point (ACP)	●

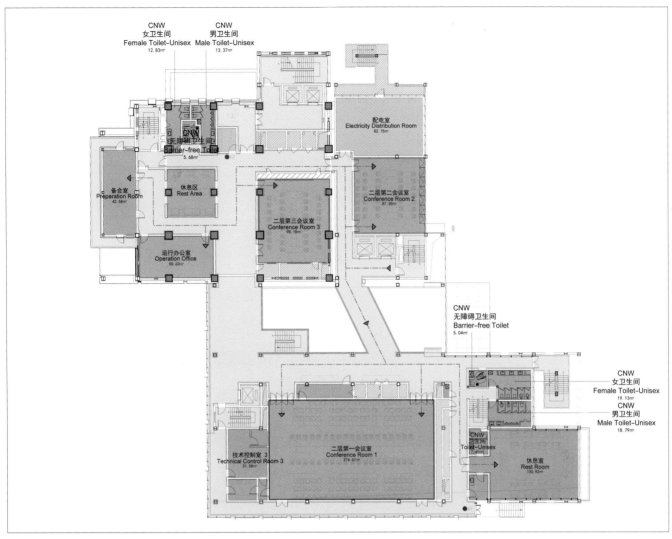

CNW
女卫生间
Female Toilet-Unisex
12. 83㎡

CNW
男卫生间
Male Toilet-Unisex
13. 37㎡

CNW
无障碍卫生间
Barrier-free Toilet
5. 68㎡

配电室
Electricity Distribution Room
82. 75㎡

备会室
Preparation Room
42. 58㎡

休息区
Rest Area

二层第三会议室
Conference Room 3
98. 18㎡

二层第二会议室
Conference Room 2
87. 30㎡

运行办公室
Operation Office
50. 63㎡

CNW
无障碍卫生间
Barrier-free Toilet
5. 04㎡

CNW
女卫生间
Female Toilet-Unisex
19. 13㎡

CNW
男卫生间
Male Toilet-Unisex
18. 79㎡

CNW
卫生间
Toilet-Unisex
7. 41㎡

技术控制室 3
Technical Control Room 3
31. 58㎡

二层第一会议室
Conference Room 1
274. 61㎡

休息室
Rest Room
100. 92㎡

MCC 二层平面图 OB7.0版
MCC 2F Plan OB7.0

摄影 桂琳
Photo by Gui Lin

延庆赛区

Yanqing Zone

国家高山滑雪中心-Yanqing National Alpine Skiing Centre [YAS]

国家雪车雪橇中心-Yanqing National Sliding Centre [YSC]

延庆冬奥村/冬残奥村-Yanqing Olympic/Paralympic Village [YVL]

延庆赛区核心区公共区-Yanqing Zone Core Public Area

阪泉综合服务中心-Yanqing Banquan Service Centre [YBS]

延庆制服和注册分中心-Yanqing Uniform Distribution and Accreditation Centre [YUA]

延庆残奥颁奖广场-Yanqing Paralympic Medals Plaza [YMP]

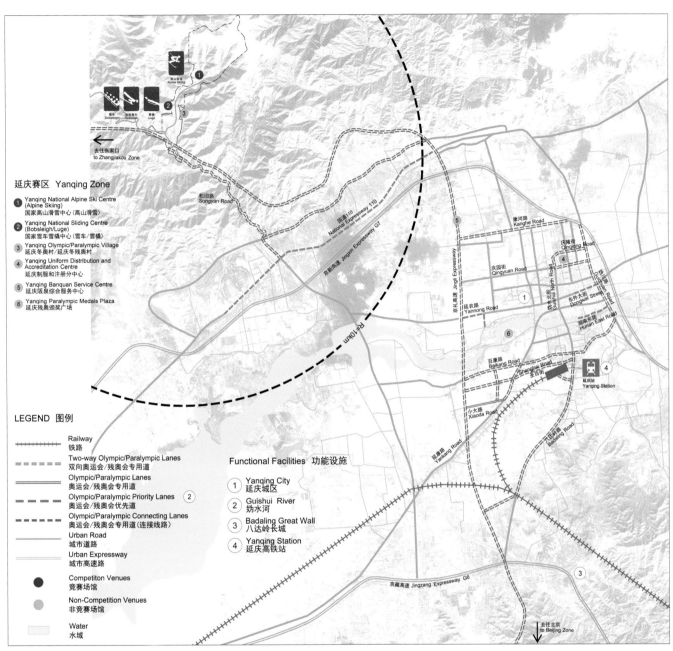

延庆赛区 Yanqing Zone

1 Yanqing National Alpine Ski Centre
(Alpine Skiing)
国家高山滑雪中心 (高山滑雪)

2 Yanqing National Sliding Centre
(Bobsleigh/Luge)
国家雪车雪橇中心 (雪车/雪橇)

3 Yanqing Olympic/Paralympic Village
延庆冬奥村/延庆冬残奥村

4 Yanqing Uniform Distribution and
Accreditation Centre
延庆制服和注册分中心

5 Yanqing Banquan Service Centre
延庆阪泉综合服务中心

6 Yanqing Paralympic Medals Plaza
延庆残奥颁奖广场

LEGEND 图例

Railway 铁路	
Two-way Olympic/Paralympic Lanes 双向奥运会/残奥会专用道	
Olympic/Paralympic Lanes 奥运会/残奥会专用道	
Olympic/Paralympic Priority Lanes 奥运会/残奥会优先道	2
Olympic/Paralympic Connecting Lanes 奥运会/残奥会专用道(连接线路)	
Urban Road 城市道路	
Urban Expressway 城市高速路	
Competiton Venues 竞赛场馆	
Non-Competition Venues 非竞赛场馆	
Water 水域	

Functional Facilities 功能设施

1 Yanqing City
延庆城区

2 Guishui River
妫水河

3 Badaling Great Wall
八达岭长城

4 Yanqing Station
延庆高铁站

延庆赛区场馆和基础设施布局图
Yanqing Zone Venues and Infrastructure Layout

延庆赛区位于北京赛区的西北方向，冬奥会共有5个场馆，其中竞赛场馆2个、非竞赛场馆3个（冬残奥会共有竞赛场馆1个、非竞赛场馆4个），核心区位于小海坨山区域。延庆赛区承担3个大项（高山滑雪、雪车、雪橇）、4个分项（高山滑雪、雪车、钢架雪车、雪橇）、21个小项的比赛。

延庆赛区残奥颁奖广场和延庆制服和注册分中心位于延庆城区内。阪泉综合服务中心位于京礼高速上。

Situated in the northwest of Beijing Zone, Yanqing Zone contains 5 venues, including 2 competition venues and 3 non-competition venues. The core area is located in the Xiaohaituo Mountain. A total of 21 events in 4 disciplines (Alpine Skiing, Bobsleigh, Skeleton, and Luge) across 3 sports (Alpine Skiing, Bobsleigh, Luge) are held in the zone.

Yanqing Paralympic Medals Plaza and Yanqing Uniform Distribution and Accreditation Centre are situated in the urban area of Yanqing. Yanqing Banquan Service Centre sits on the Beijing-Chongli Expressway.

国家高山滑雪中心 [YAS]
Yanqing National Alpine Skiing Centre

1. 场馆基本情况

国家高山滑雪中心位于延庆赛区核心区，冬奥会期间承担男女滑降、回转、大回转、超级大回转、全能和混合团体的比赛，产生11块金牌。冬残奥会期间承担男女视障、站姿、坐姿的滑降、超级大回转、大回转、回转的比赛，产生30块金牌。

国家高山滑雪中心总用地面积432.4hm²，包含山顶出发区、中间平台、竞技结束区、竞速结束区集散广场、索道等建筑及设施，总建筑面积约6.3万m²，其中永久建筑约4.3万m²，临时建筑约2万m²。场馆布局像一只振翅欲飞的"燕子"，昵称"雪飞燕"。

2. FOP相关区域

国家高山滑雪中心设有竞速和竞技2块比赛场地、3条竞赛雪道、4条训练雪道及其他联系雪道和技术雪道，雪道总长度约25km。竞速赛道又称"岩石道"，含9个赛段和4个跳点，垂直落差约890m；竞技赛道又称"冰河道"，含7个赛段，垂直落差约440m；团体赛道又称"彩虹道"，含3个赛段。

国家高山滑雪中心共设5条吊厢式索道（A1、A2、B1、B2、C）、4条吊椅式索道（D、E、F、G）和2条拖牵索道（H1、H2），全长约10.3km。其中，A、B索道单向运量可达每小时3200人，吊厢有座椅加热、定位系统和无线广播等装置。

1. Venue Overview

Located within the core area of the Yanqing Zone, the Yanqing National Alpine Skiing Centre is the competition venue for Alpine Skiing Men's and Women's Downhill, Slalom, Giant Slalom, Super-G, Alpine Combined and mixed team events during the Beijing 2022 Olympic Winter Games, with 11 gold medals won here, and the competition venue for Para Alpine Skiing Men's and Women's Downhill, Super-G, Giant Slalom and Slalom events (visually impaired, downhill, standing) during the Beijing 2022 Paralympic Winter Games, with 30 gold medals won here.

The National Alpine Skiing Centre covers an area of 432.4 hectares, including the mountaintop start area, middle platform, technical finish area, concourse, and ropeway, and has a total floor area of about 63,000m², including 43,000m² of permanent buildings and about 20,000m² of overlays. The venue is nicknamed the "Snow Swallow" owing to its contour like a swallow poised to fly.

2. FOP and Relevant Areas

The Yanqing National Alpine Skiing Centre has 3 competition courses, 4 training courses, and other connection courses and technology courses, with an overall length of courses of about 25km. Also known as "The Rock" course, the speed course includes nine sections and four take-off points, with a vertical drop of about 900m;

3. 场馆前院及观众流线

国家高山滑雪中心集散广场一层、竞速结束区五层环外区域、竞技结束区三层环外区域、竞速及竞技看台观众区为场馆前院区，面向观众开放。赛时观众在阪泉综合服务中心完成安检和验票后，乘坐TS班车进入场馆集散广场一层或竞技结束区三层TS班车上落客区，通过室外楼梯到达观众看台。

4. 场馆后院及注册流线

国家高山滑雪中心非观众区域为场馆后院区。

（1）运动员流线

运动员从延庆村或打蜡房出发，乘坐索道或TA班车进入运动员休息室。运动员休息室共有6个，分别位于山顶出发区、拖牵索道上站、G索道上站、集散广场四层、G索道下站、D索道下站。每个休息室都紧邻索道及雪道，方便到达。

竞速项目比赛时，运动员从集散四层休息室更换雪板等装备后，乘坐B+C缆车或F+H缆车到达山顶出发区或T-bar上站休息室准备比赛；竞技项目比赛时，运动员从G索道或D索道下站休息室更换雪板等装备后，乘坐G缆车到达上站休息室准备比赛。比赛结束后，运动员通过离场门进入混合采访区接受采访后，返回运动员休息区。

（2）技术官员流线

技术官员通过TF或TG班车到达延庆赛区核心区换乘A缆车进入场馆。紧邻竞速和竞技结束区FOP雪道边设置IF休息室和办公室。

（3）奥林匹克大家庭成员流线

奥林匹克大家庭成员在阪泉综合服务中心或海陀收费站通过安检和验证进入赛区，乘坐T1/T2/T3-bus交通到达竞速结束区FOP桥头上落客区或竞技结束区三层上落客区后步行进入大家庭休息室。

（4）媒体流线

媒体人员在阪泉综合服务中心安检及验证后，乘坐TG班车到达延庆赛区核心区换乘A缆车进入场馆，也可乘坐TW班车直接到达场馆竞速结束区FOP桥头上落客区或竞技结束区三层上落客区后步行进入场馆。

竞速及竞技结束区分别设置场馆媒体中心、媒体混合采访区、摄影位置、媒体席位，赛道周边设置"媒体+"摄影点位，供摄影记者拍摄精彩画面。

竞速赛道周边设置24个转播平台；竞技赛道周边设置19个转播平台，包含一组飞猫摄像机；在团体赛道周边设置9个转播平台。转播工作人员乘坐TM、DDS班车或ENG小车进入场馆后，经由缆车和滑雪到达相应转播点位。

5. 场馆坐席

国家高山滑雪中心分为竞速和竞技两个结束区临时看台，含看台站席、雪面站席及坐席。

竞速结束区临时看台容量为2400席，含1116个看台站席、1204个看台坐席、40个无障碍坐席和40个陪同席。其中观众可用坐席为796个。注册坐席包括运动员席20个、观察员席40个、文字媒体30个、摄影媒体席30个、大家庭席216个。

竞技结束区临时看台容量为1900席，包含366个看台站席、418个雪面站席、1078个看台坐席、19个无障碍坐席和19个陪同席。其中观众可用坐席为518个。注册坐席包括运动员席20个、观察员席40个、文字媒体30个、摄影媒体席30个。

also known as "The Glacier" course, the technical course includes 7 sections, with a vertical drop of about 420m; also known as "The Rainbow" course, the team course includes three sections.

The National Alpine Skiing Centre has a total of 5 gondola ropeways, 4 chairlift ropeways, and 2 T-bar ropeways, which have an overall length of about 10.3km. Ropeway A/B has can carry up to 3,200 people per hour in one direction, and the gondolas are equipped with seat heating, positioning system and radio broadcasting devices.

3. Front of House and Spectator Flow

The first floor of the concourse, the area outside the loop on the fifth floor of the speed finish area, the area outside the loop on the third floor of the technical finish area, and spectator areas at the speed and technical finish areas are the Front of House (FOH) of the National Alpine Skiing Centre and open to the spectators. During the Games, after passing through security checks and ticket checking in the Banquan Service Centre, spectators take TS shuttle buses to the first floor of the concourse or the TS shuttle bus pick-up and drop-off zone on the third floor of the technical finish area and then go to the spectator stand via the outdoor stairs.

4. Back of House and Accreditation Flow

(1) Athlete Flow

Athletes depart from the Yanqing Olympic Village or wax cabins and take cable cars or TA shuttle buses to athlete lounges. There are a total of six athlete lounges located in the mountaintop start area, T-bar upper station, Cableway G upper station, concourse fourth floor, Cableway G lower station, and Cableway D lower station, respectively. Each lounge is next to a cableway and course for the convenience of the athletes.

(2) Technical Official Flow

Technical officials take TF or TG shuttle buses to the core area of the Yanqing Zone and then transfer to Gondola A to the venue. IF lounges and offices are provided next to speed and technical finish areas near the FOP.

(3) Olympic Family Flow

Olympic Family members enter the competition zone after passing through security and accreditation checks in the Banquan Service Centre or Haituo Tollgate, take T1/T2/T3 buses to the FOP bridgehead pick-up and drop-off zone of the speed finish area or the third-floor pick-up and drop-off zone of the technical finish area, and then walk to the Olympic Family lounge.

(4) Media Flow

After passing through security and accreditation checks in the Banquan Service Centre, media personnel take TG shuttle buses to the core area of the Yanqing Zone and transfer to Gondola A to enter the venue, or they can take TW shuttle buses directly to the FOP bridgehead pick-up and drop-off zone of the speed finish area or the third-floor pick-up and drop-off zone of the technical finish area and then walk to the venue.

5. Seating Area

The National Alpine Skiing Centre has temporary stands in the speed finish area and technical finish area, including standing positions in the stand and snow standing positions and seats.

The capacity of the temporary stand in the speed finish area is 2,400, in the technical finish area of the National Alpine Skiing Centre is 1,900.

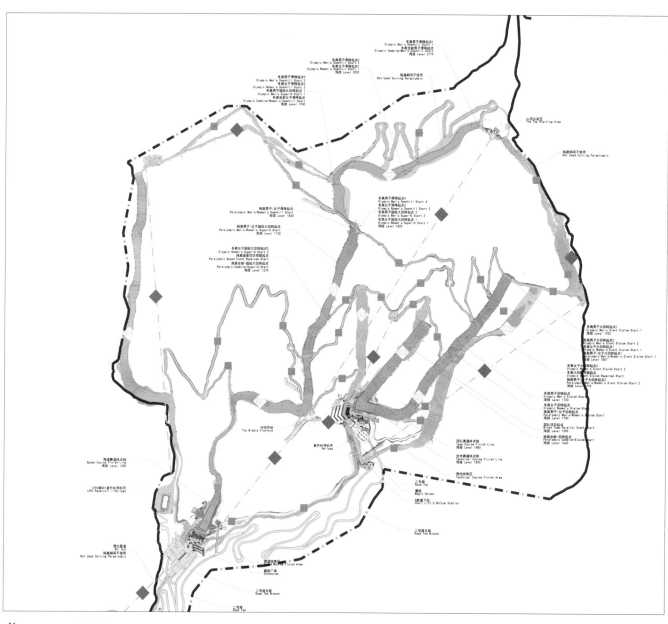

冬奥男子滑降起点1
冬奥全能男子滑降起点
Olympic Men's Downhill Start 1
Olympic Combine-Men's Downhill Start
海拔 Level 2179

残奥期间不使用
Not Used Durning Paralympic

山顶出发区
The Top Starting Area

冬奥男子滑降起点3
Olympic Men's Downhill Start 3
冬奥女子滑降起点2
Olympic Women's Downhill Start 2
冬奥男子超级大回转起点2
Olympic Men's Super-G Start 2
冬奥全能女子滑降起点1
Olympic Combine-Women's Downhill Start 1
海拔 Level 1930

残奥期间不使用
Not Used Durning Paralympic

冬奥男子滑降起点4
Olympic Men's Downhill Start 4
冬奥女子滑降起点3
Olympic Women's Downhill Start 3
冬奥男子超级大回转起点1
Olympic Men's Super-G Start 1
海拔 Level 1825

残奥男子/女子滑降起点
Paralympic Men's/Women's Downhill Start
海拔 Level 1830

残奥男子/女子超级大回转起点
Paralympic Men's/Women's Super-G Start
海拔 Level 1735

冬奥女子超级大回转起点2
Olympic Women's Super-G Start 2
残奥速度项目预留起点
Paralympic Speed Event Reserved Start
残奥全能-超级大回转起点
Paralympic Combine-Super-G Start
海拔 Level 1675

冬奥男子大回转起点1
Olympic Men's Giant Slalom Start 1
海拔 Level 1920

冬奥男子大回转起点2
Olympic Men's Giant Slalom Start 2
冬奥女子大回转起点1
Olympic Women's Giant Slalom Start 1
残奥男子/女子大回转起点1
Paralympic Men's/Women's Giant Slalom Start 1
海拔 Level 1857

冬奥女子大回转起点2
Olympic Women's Giant Slalom Start 2
残奥大回转预留起点
Paralympic Giant Slalom Reserved Start
海拔 Level 1775

冬奥男子回转起点
Olympic Men's Slalom Start
冬奥女子回转起点
Olympic Women's Slalom Start
残奥男子/女子回转起点
Paralympic Men's/Women's Slalom Start
海拔 Level 1700

团队赛道起点
Team Parallel Event Start
残奥全能-回转起点
Paralympic Combine-Slalom Start
海拔 Level 1660

团队赛道终点线
Team Course Finish Line
技术赛道终点线
Technical Course Finish Line
海拔 Level 1500

技术赛道终点区
Technical Course Finish Area

二号路
Road Two
吊椅下站
Chair Lift G Bottom Station

二号路支路
Road Two Branch

中间平台
The Middle Platform

直升机停机坪
Helipad

速度赛道终点线
Speed Course Finish Line
海拔 Level 1386

1290蓄水池+直升机停机坪
1290 Reservoir + Helipad

竞速赛道终点区
Speed Course Finish Area
残奥期间不使用
Not Used Durning Paralympic

集散广场
Concourse

出口车道
Exit
残奥期间不使用
Not Used Durning Paralympic

二号路支路
Road Two Branch

二号路
Road Two

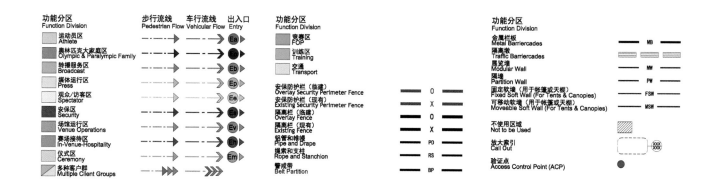

功能分区 Function Division		步行流线 Pedestrian Flow	车行流线 Vehicular Flow	出入口 Entry	功能分区 Function Division		功能分区 Function Division	
运动员区 Athlete				Ea ▶	竞赛区 FOP		金属栏板 Metal Barriercades	MB
奥林匹克大家庭区 Olympic & Paralympic Family				● ▶	训练区 Training		隔离栅 Traffic Barriercades	
转播服务区 Broadcast				Eb ▶	交通 Transport		展览墙 Modular Wall	MW
媒体运行区 Press				Ep ▶			隔墙 Partition Wall	PW
观众/访客区 Spectator				Ee ▶	安保防护栏（临建） Overlay Security Perimeter Fence	O	固定软墙（用于帐篷或天棚） Fixed Soft Wall (For Tents & Canopies)	FSW
安保区 Security				Es ▶	安保防护栏（现有） Existing Security Perimeter Fence	X	可移动软墙（用于帐篷或天棚） Moveable Soft Wall (For Tents & Canopies)	MSW
场馆运行区 Venue Operations				Ev ▶	隔离栏（临建） Overlay Fence	O	不使用区域 Not to be Used	
赛场接待区 In-Venue-Hospitality				Eh ▶	隔离栏（现有） Existing Fence	X	放大索引 Call Out	
仪式区 Ceremony				Em ▶	铝管和帷幔 Pipe and Drape	PD		
多种客户群 Multiple Client Groups					揽索和支柱 Rope and Stanchion	RS	验证点 Access Control Point (ACP)	●
					警戒带 Belt Partition	BP		

216

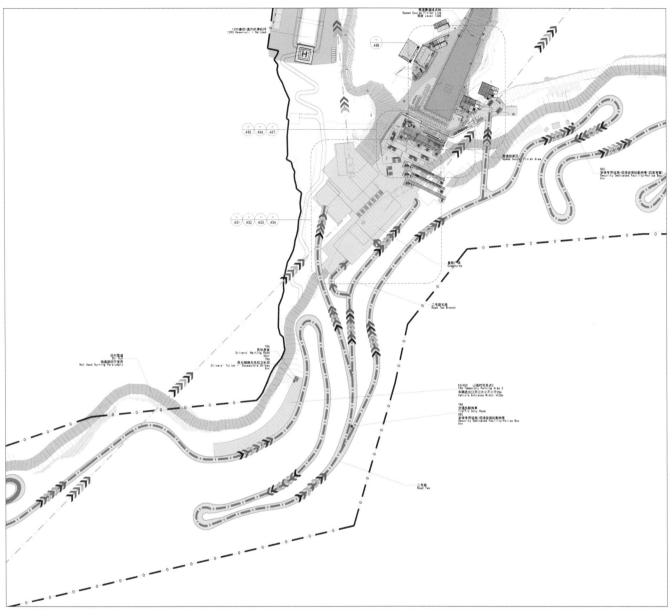

N

YAS 竞速结束区放大平面图 OB7.0版
YAS Speed Courses Finish Area Enlarged Plan OB7.0

217

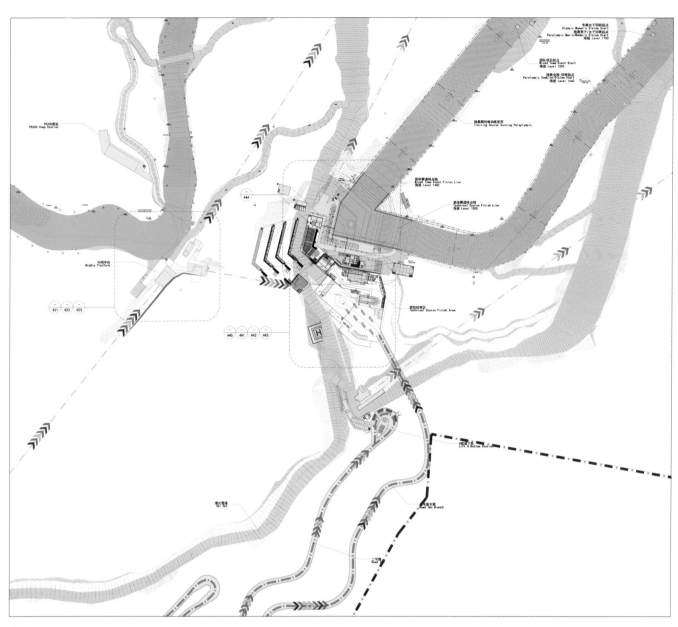

N YAS 竞技结束区放大平面图 OB7.0版
YAS Technical Course Finish Area Enlarged Plan OB7.0

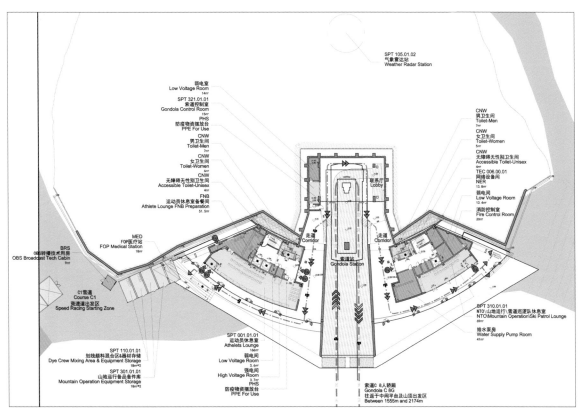

弱电室
Low Voltage Room
14㎡

SPT 321.01.01
索道控制室
Gondola Control Room
15㎡

PHS
防疫物资摆放台
PPE For Use

CNW
男卫生间
Toilet-Men
7㎡

CNW
女卫生间
Toilet-Women
7㎡

CNW
无障碍无性别卫生间
Accessible Toilet-Unisex
4㎡

FNB
运动员休息室备餐间
Athlete Lounge FNB Preparation
51.5㎡

MED
FOP医疗站
FOP Medical Station
18㎡

BRS
OBS转播技术用房
OBS Broadcast Tech Cabin
9㎡

C1雪道
Course C1
竞速道出发区
Speed Racing Starting Zone

SPT 110.01.01
划线颜料混合区&器材存储
Dye Crew Mixing Area & Equipment Storage
18㎡*2

SPT 301.01.01
山地运行备品备件库
Mountain Operation Equipment Storage
18㎡*2

SPT 001.01.01
运动员休息室
Athlelts Lounge
166㎡

弱电间
Low Voltage Room
3.6㎡

强电间
High Voltage Room
3.7㎡

PHS
防疫物资摆放台
PPE For Use

SPT 105.01.02
气象雷达站
Weather Radar Station

联系厅
Lobby

走道
Corridor

走道
Corridor

索道站
Gondola Station

CNW
男卫生间
Toilet-Men
7㎡

CNW
女卫生间
Toilet-Women
5㎡

CNW
无障碍无性别卫生间
Accessible Toilet-Unisex
4㎡

TEC 006.00.01
网络设备间
NER
13.㎡

弱电间
Low Voltage Room
13.4㎡

消防控制室
Fire Control Room
20㎡

SPT 310.01.01
NTO\山地运行\雪道巡逻队休息室
NTO\Mountain Operation\Ski Patrol Lounge
69㎡

给水泵房
Water Supply Pump Room
41㎡

索道C 8人轿厢
Gondola C 8G
往返于中间平台及山顶出发区
Between 1555m and 2174m

N
YAS 山顶出发区一层平面图 OB7.0版
YAS Top Start Area 1F Plan OB7.0

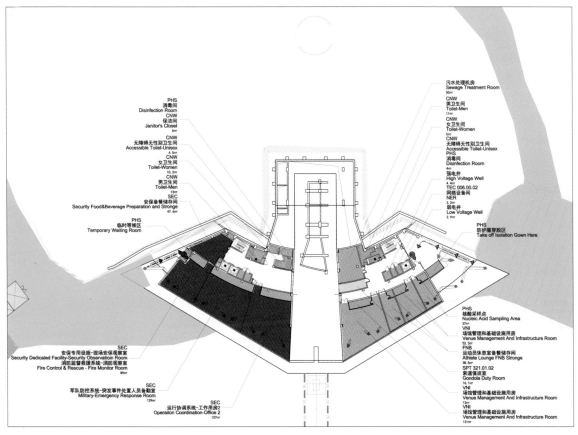

PHS
消毒间
Disinfection Room

CNW
保洁间
Janitor's Closet
5㎡

CNW
无障碍无性别卫生间
Accessible Toilet-Unisex
4.5㎡

CNW
女卫生间
Toilet-Women
10.2㎡

CNW
男卫生间
Toilet-Men
13㎡

SEC
安保备餐储存间
Security Food&Beverage Preparation and Stronge
47.4㎡

PHS
临时等候区
Temporary Waiting Room

SEC
安保专用设施-现场安保观察室
Security Dedicated Facility-Security Observatoin Room
消防监督救援系统-消防观察室
Fire Control & Rescue - Fire Monitor Room
89㎡

SEC
军队防控系统-突发事件处置人员备勤室
Military-Emergency Response Room
129㎡

SEC
运行协调系统-工作用房2
Operaiton Coordination-Office 2
157㎡

污水处理机房
Sewage Treatment Room
50㎡

CNW
男卫生间
Toilet-Men
11㎡

CNW
女卫生间
Toilet-Women
5㎡

CNW
无障碍无性别卫生间
Accessible Toilet-Unisex
PHS
消毒间
Disinfection Room
4㎡

强电井
High Voltage Well
4.4㎡

TEC 006.00.02
网络设备间
NER
3.2㎡

弱电井
Low Voltage Well
2.9㎡

PHS
防护服穿脱区
Take off Isolation Gown Here

PHS
核酸采样点
Nucleic Acid Sampling Area
37㎡

VNI
场馆管理和基础设施用房
Venue Management And Infrastructure Room
52.3㎡

FNB
运动员休息室备餐储存间
Athlete Lounge FNB Stronge
36.5㎡

SPT 321.01.02
索道值班室
Gondola Duty Room
14.1㎡

VNI
场馆管理和基础设施用房
Venue Management And Infrastructure Room
12㎡

VNI
场馆管理和基础设施用房
Venue Management And Infrastructure Room
131㎡

N
YAS 山顶出发区二层平面图 OB7.0版
YAS Top Start Area 2F Plan OB7.0

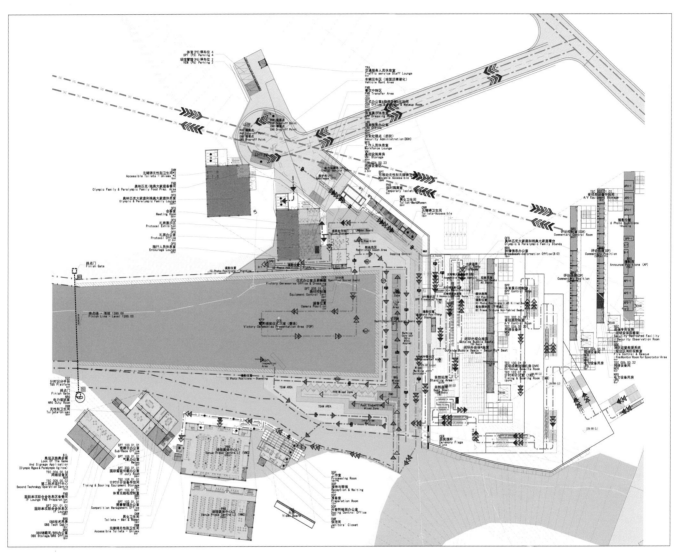

YAS 竞速结束区看台及比赛场地平面图 OB7.0版
YAS Speed Courses Finish Area Stand and FOP Plan OB7.0

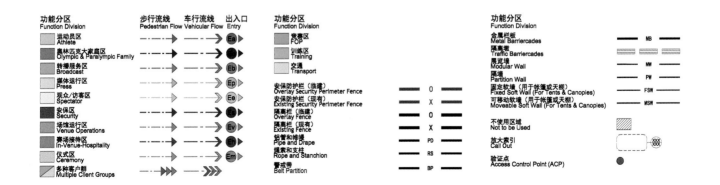

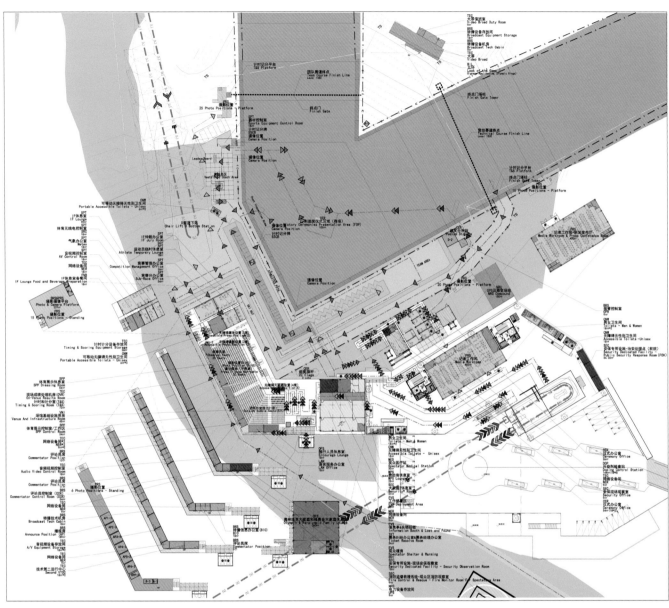

N
YAS 竞技结束区看台及比赛场地平面图 OB7.0版
YAS Technical Finish Area Stand and FOP Plan OB7.0

摄影 刘玉民
Photo by Liu Yumin

北京冬奥组委 提供
Provide by BOCOG

北京冬奥组委 提供
Provide by BOCOG

中建院 提供
Provide by CADG

国家雪车雪橇中心 [YSC]

Yanqing National Sliding Centre

1. 场馆基本情况

国家雪车雪橇中心位于延庆赛区核心区，小海坨山南侧山脊之上，在北京冬奥会期间承担雪车、钢架雪车、雪橇项目的比赛，产生10枚金牌。场馆采用全赛道屋面遮阳系统，中国式传统木架屋顶体系借鉴了中国南方传统的风雨长廊的设计理念。从空中鸟瞰，赛道犹如在山中游走的巨龙，俊朗灵逸，故昵称"雪游龙"。

国家雪车雪橇中心以支撑赛道并容纳制冷主管的U型槽为基础，以赛道为核心，沿赛道布置出发区、结束区、运营区、后勤综合区等建筑，并通过保护赛道的坡屋面将这些建筑串联起来，场馆建筑面积5.25万m²（不含赛道）。该赛道是国际雪车联合会和国际雪橇联合会共同认证的世界第17条、亚洲第3条、国内第一条雪车雪橇赛道。

2. FOP及相关区域区

国家雪车雪橇中心赛道全长1975m，垂直落差121m，赛道为长线型空间双曲面板壳结构，共由16个角度、倾斜度都不同的弯道组成，其中第11个弯道为独具特色的360°螺旋弯道。赛道设置3个出发区，共6个出发口，其中螺旋弯北侧的出发口是为赛后游客体验服务设置的。除此之外，赛道还设置了1个最低点收车区和4个不同结束位置的收车区，以满足运动员的不同需求。

1. Venue Overview

Located within the core area of the Yanqing Zone, on the southern ridge of Xiaohaituo Mountain, the Yanqing National Sliding Centre is the competition venue for Bobsleigh, Skeleton and Luge events during the Olympic Winter Games Beijing 2022, with 10 gold medals won here. The venue uses a full-track roof shading system, with a traditional Chinese timber-frame roof system that uses the design philosophy of wind-and-rain corridor bridges in villages in South China. From an aerial view, the track looks like an agile and elegant giant dragon wandering through the mountains and is thus nicknamed the "Snow Dragon".

The Yanqing National Sliding Centre takes the U-groove that supports the track and contains the main refrigeration tube as the foundation, with the track as the core to arrange the start area, finish area, operations area, logistics compound, etc., along it, which are connected by a slope roof to protect the track. The venue has a floor area of 52,500m² (excluding the track). The track is the world's 17th, Asia's 3rd and China's 1st sliding track jointly homologated by the IBSF and FIL.

2. FOP and Relevant Areas

The Yanqing National Sliding Centre has a track of 1,975m long, with a vertical drop of 121m. The track has a long linear shell structure with double-curved plates and consists of 16 curves with different angles and slopes, of which the 11th curve is a unique 360° spiral

3. 场馆前院及观众流线

观众主广场与观众主看台为场馆前院区。赛时观众乘车抵达位于一号路旁的上落客区，在此落客后步行沿五号路、塘坝进入观众隧道抵达观众主广场。观众可在此通过赛道和大屏欣赏比赛，也可沿隧道进入观众休息区取暖休息。

4. 场馆后院及注册流线

国家雪车雪橇中心出发区、结束区、运营区、后勤综合区、转播综合区等区域均为场馆后院区，在此区域进行场馆运行与赛事管理等工作。场馆共设有4个后院入口。

（1）运动员流线

运动员由延庆冬奥村乘坐大巴来到国家雪车雪橇中心，首先前往团队集装箱停放区提取装备，携带装备乘车前往出发区1、出发区2的更衣室。运动员在此可短暂休整，在餐饮区自行选择饮食，在热身区热身后前往出发点参加比赛。比赛结束后，运动员在混合采访区接受采访，并可前往看台观看其余比赛。

（2）技术官员流线

技术官员通过场馆南端入口乘车进入场馆，可快速到达其办公区域。出发区1、出发区2均设置了NTO工作区。

（3）奥运大家庭成员流线

奥运大家庭休息室位于结束区。大家庭成员通过电力综合区旁的入口乘车进入场馆，绕制冷机房由三号路抵达位于结束区东侧的大家庭落客区，乘坐电梯进入大家庭休息室与大家庭看台区。大家庭成员流线独立设置。

（4）媒体流线

转播与新闻媒体注册人员由转播综合区入口进入场馆，转播部分人员在此下车进入转播综合区工作，其余人员乘车沿三号路抵达工作区域。场馆媒体中心位于结束区。新闻媒体人员乘车沿三号路抵达摄影点位，并可以沿伴随路根据工作需要自由活动。

（5）场馆室外综合区

场馆南端设置综合区，转播综合区主要为OBS服务，电力综合区为转播综合区提供电力保障服务。

5. 注册坐席

国家雪车雪橇中心场馆观众区集中在赛道14、15、16弯道的观众主广场和观众主看台处，场馆总容量为7500个，赛时开放观众席150个。

场馆共设置4处注册坐席区，出发区1设置本项目运动员站席10席、奥林匹克大家庭站席10席；出发区2设置本项目运动员站席10席；结束区西侧坐席共计230席，包含为非本项目运动员观赛席40个、观察员席25个、文字媒体席20个、摄影媒体席20个；结束区东侧坐席为奥林匹克大家庭坐席24个。各类注册人群均设置了无障碍坐席。

curve. The track has three start areas and six start openings, with the start opening on the north side of the spiral curve is provided for tourists' experience activities after the Games. Furthermore, there is 1 lowest-point retrieval area and 4 retrieval areas in different finish positions to facilitate athletes' different needs.

3. Front of House and Spectator Flow

The main spectator plaza and main spectator stand constitute the Front of House (FOH). During the Games, spectators take vehicles to arrive in the pick-up and drop-off zone by No.1 Road, then get off, and walk along No.5 Road and the small reservoir to the main spectator plaza via the spectator tunnel. In the plaza, spectators can watch competitions that take place on the track directly or via the big screen and can also enter the spectator lounge via the tunnel to get warm and take a break.

4. Back of House and Accreditation Flow

(1) Athlete Flow

After taking buses from the Yanqing Olympic Village to the National Sliding Centre, athletes first go to pick up their equipment in the team container area and then take vehicles with their equipment to the dressing rooms in start area 1 and start area 2. Athletes can then rest briefly, choose food in the food and beverage area, and go to the start area to compete after warming up in the warm-up area. After competitions, athletes go to the mixed zone to be interviewed and can then go to the stand to watch the remaining competitions.

(2) Technical Official Flow

Via the south entrance of the venue, technical officials take vehicles to the venue to quickly reach their office areas. NTO work areas are set in start area 1 and start area 2.

(3) Olympic Family Flow

The Olympic Family lounge is in the finish area. Olympic Family members take vehicles to the venue via the entrance next to the energy compound, then go to the Olympic Family drop-off zone on the east side of the finish area via No.3 Road after bypassing the refrigeration room, and then take the elevator to the Olympic Family lounge and Olympic Family stand area.

(4) Media Flow

Accredited broadcast and media personnel enter the venue via the broadcast compound entrance, and then broadcast personnel get off to enter the broadcast compound, while other personnel take vehicles to their work areas along No.3 Road. The Venue Media Centre is in the finish area.

5. Seating Area

The spectator area of the National Sliding Centre mainly consists of the main spectator plaza and main spectator stand at Curves 14, 15 and 16. The venue has a total capacity of 7,500 seats, with 150 spectator seats open during the Games.

The venue has four accredited seating areas, with 10 standing positions for athletes of the same discipline and 10 standing positions for Olympic Family in start area 1, 10 standing positions for athletes of the same discipline in start area 2, a total of 230 seats on the west side of the finish area, including 40 for athletes of different disciplines, 25 for observers, 20 for press journalists, and 20 for photographers, and 24 Olympic Family seats on the east side of the finish area. Accessible seats are provided for various accredited persons.

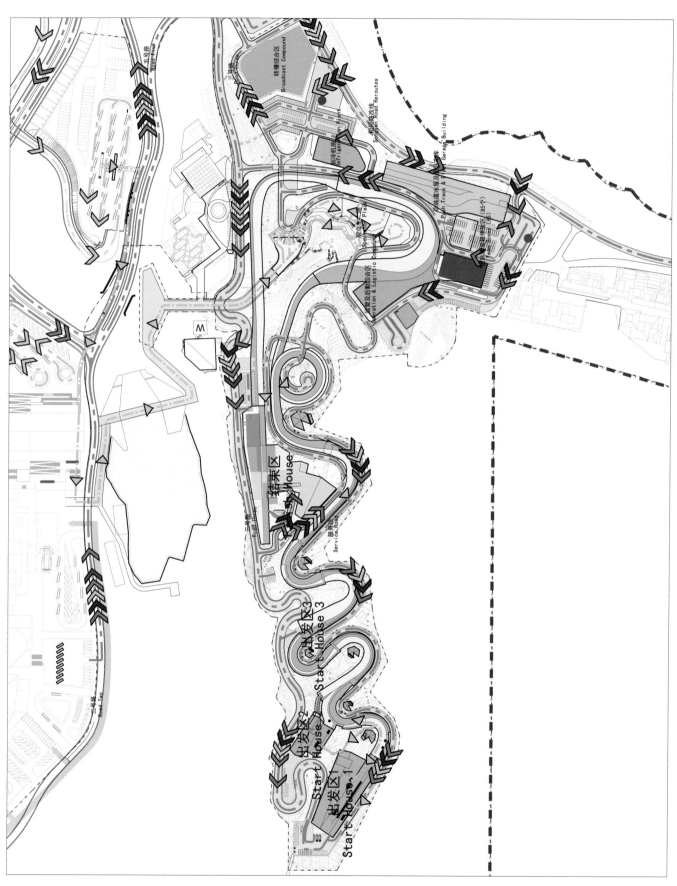

YSC 总平面图 OB2.1版
YSC Master Plan OB2.1

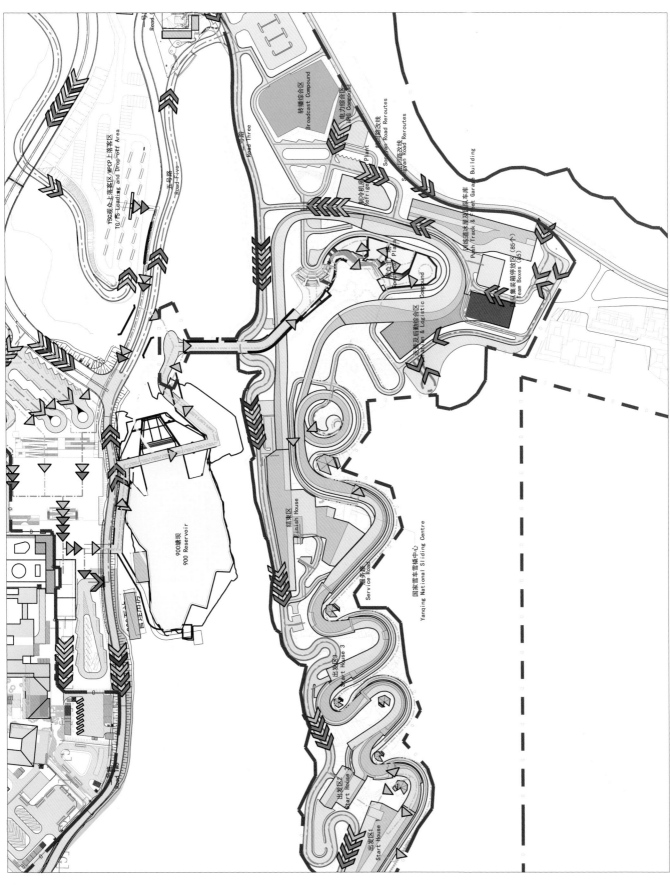

YSC 总平面图 OB4.0版
YSC Master Plan OB4.0

227

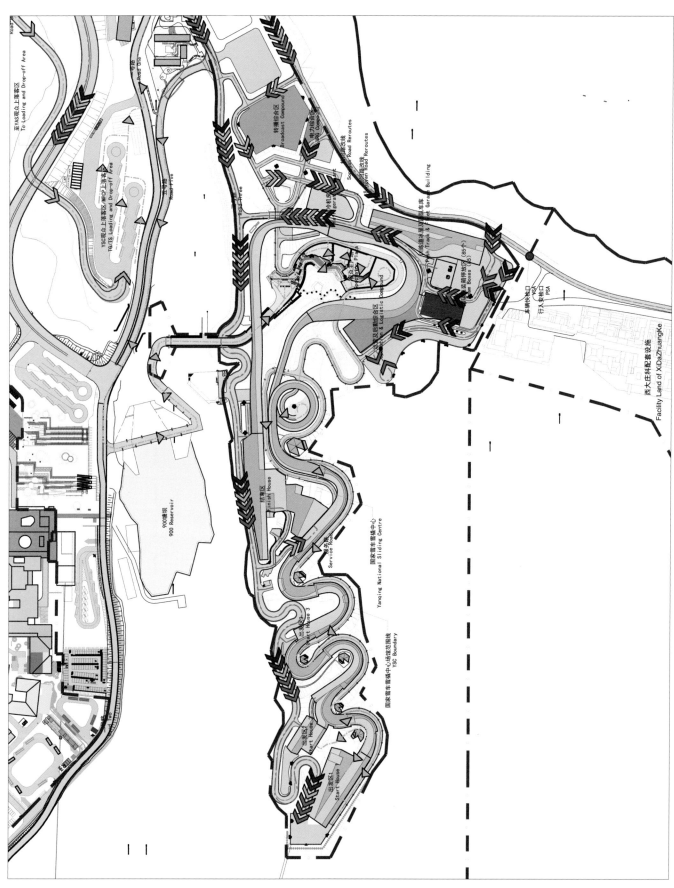

至YAS观众上落客区
To Loading and Drop-off Area

YSC观众上落客区/MPCP上落客区
To TS Loading and Drop-off Area

二号路
Road Two

立号路
Road Five

900塘坝
900 Reservoir

立号路
Road Three

Road One

转播综合区
Broadcast Compound

电力综合区
IPG Compound

各路改线
South Road Reroutes
各路改线
Xiyan Road Reroutes

冷机房
gerat

出发区3
Start House 3

结束房
Finish House

服务路
Service Road

出发区2
Start House

出发区1
Start House

赛车及出发区域停车库
Finish Track & Start Garage Building

赛道冰屋及结束区车库
Finish Track & Start Garage Building

运及物流综合区
Run & Logistic Compound

车辆停放区（85个）
Tram Boxes（85）

车辆快地口 VSR
行人安地口 PSA

国家雪车雪橇中心
Yanqing National Sliding Centre

国家雪车雪橇中心场馆范围线
YSC Boundary

西大庄科配套设施
Facility Land of XIDaZhuangKe

⊕
N

YSC 总平面图 OB6.0版
YSC Master Plan OB6.0

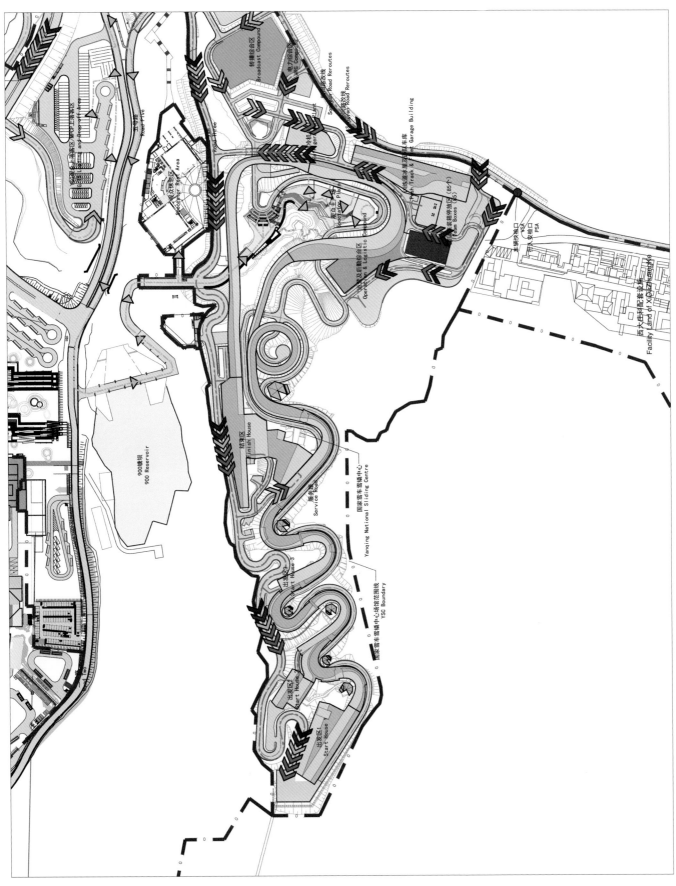

YSC 总平面图 OB7.0版
YSC Master Plan OB7.0

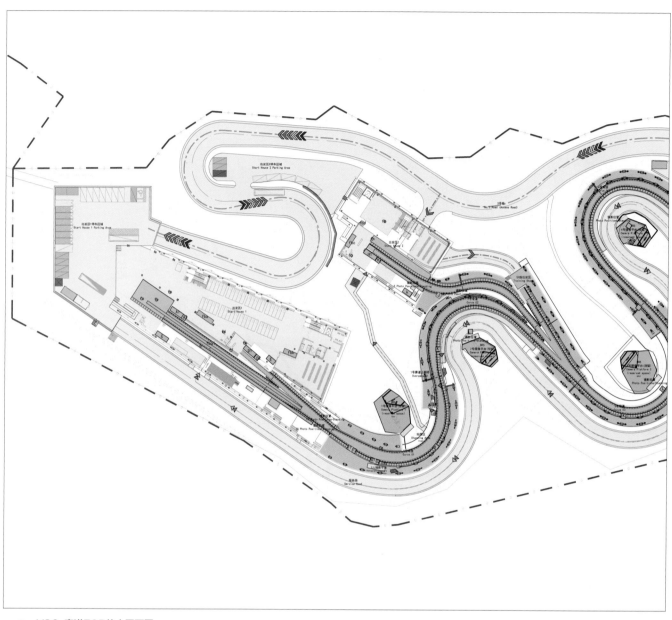

N ⊕ YSC 赛道FOP放大平面图一 OB 7.0版
YSC Track FOP Enlarged Plan 1 OB7.0

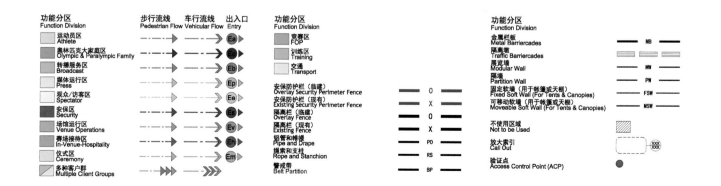

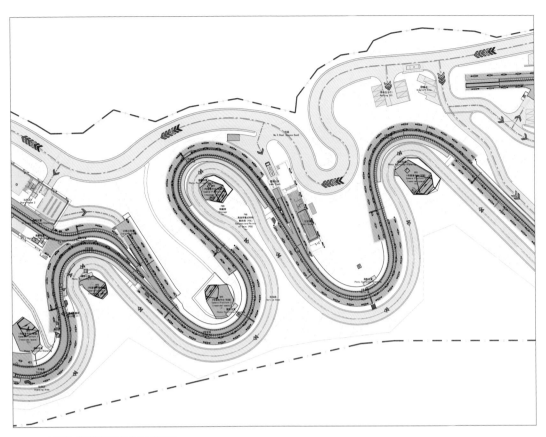

YSC 赛道FOP放大平面图二 OB 7.0版
YSC Track FOP Enlarged Plan 2 OB7.0

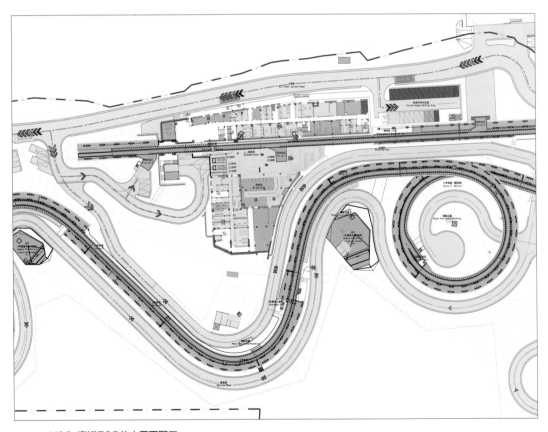

YSC 赛道FOP放大平面图三 OB 7.0版
YSC Track FOP Enlarged Plan 3 OB7.0

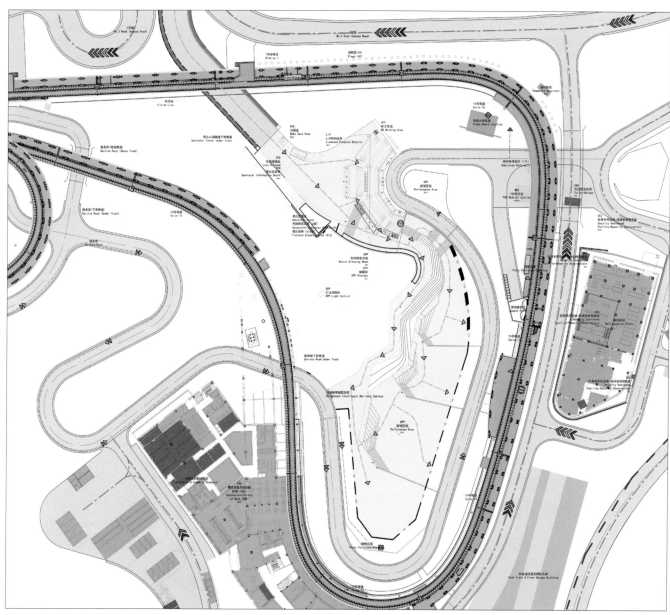

YSC 赛道FOP放大平面图四 OB7.0版
YSC Track FOP Enlarged Plan 4 OB7.0

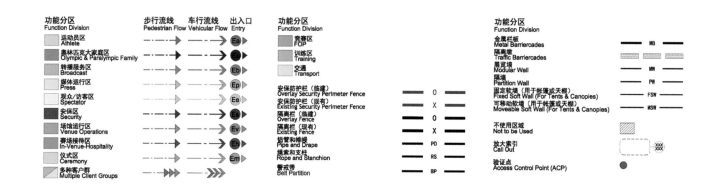

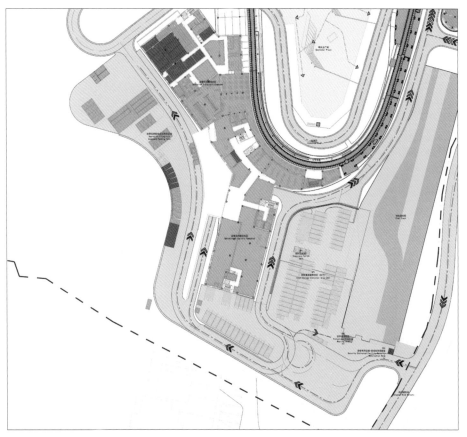

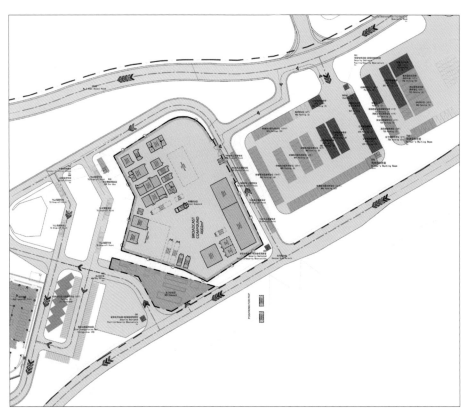

YSC 赛道FOP放大平面图五 OB7.0版
YSC Track FOP Enlarged Plan 5 OB7.0

YSC 赛道FOP放大平面图六 OB7.0版
YSC Track FOP Enlarged Plan 6 OB7.0

延庆冬奥村/冬残奥村 [YVL]

Yanqing Olympic/Paralympic Village

1. 场馆概况

延庆冬奥村/冬残奥村位于延庆赛区核心区，占地面积13.8万m²，总建筑面积约11.8万m²，毗邻国家雪车雪橇中心，运动员在30min内就可以到达赛区内的任意一个场馆任意一个赛道。

延庆冬奥村/冬残奥村依山而建，南北高差约46m，东西高差最大约30m，采用低层、高密度的"山村"式建筑布局，半开放式建筑庭院依山而建，既展现北京四合院的文化特色，又不破山型、不夺山景，体现出北方民居的建筑特色。

延庆冬奥村/冬残奥村以组团形式散落在山林间，共有6个居住组团和2个公共组团，居住组团主要为居住功能，共有570套公寓、839个房间，冬奥时提供1551个床位，冬残奥时提供683个床位。公共组团主要为综合服务功能，为运动员提供比赛装备保养、餐饮、休闲等综合服务。冬奥村还专门设计建造了地下暖廊。通过暖廊，运动员、教练员无需再穿厚重的外套就可以前往各个组团。

延庆冬奥村/冬残奥村的运行从1月23日预开村至3月16日冬残奥会闭村，全时运行53天。运行期间需提供住宿、餐饮、健身、娱乐、洗衣、美发等21项服务内容。

2. 安保封闭线

延庆赛区核心区是一个场馆群，国家高山滑雪中心、国家雪车雪橇中心和延庆冬奥村/冬残奥村外共享大安保封闭线，人

1. Venue Overview

Located in the core area of the Yanqing Zone, the Yanqing Olympic/Paralympic Village covers an area of 104,000m², has a total floor area of about 108,000m², and is adjacent to the National Sliding Centre. Athletes can reach any course/track of any venue in the competition zone within 30 min.

The Yanqing Olympic/Paralympic Village has clusters scattered among the mountains and forests. There are a total of 6 residential clusters and 2 public clusters. Residential clusters are mainly for residence, with a total of 570 apartments, 839 rooms, and 1,551 beds during the Olympic Winter Games or 683 beds during the Paralympic Winter Games. Public clusters are mainly for comprehensive services such as sport equipment maintenance, food and beverage, and leisure service to athletes. There is also a specially designed underground warm corridor in the Yanqing Olympic/Paralympic Village, via which athletes and coaches can go to each cluster without having to wear heavy coats.

2. Secure Perimeter

The core area of the Yanqing Zone is a venue cluster in which the National Alpine Skiing Centre, National Sliding Centre, and Yanqing Olympic/Paralympic Village share a greater secure perimeter. A remote security check policy is adopted for pedestrians and vehicles to enter the cluster, with the main security check areas being the Banquan Service Area and Yanqing Railway Station. No further security check facilities are set in the Yanqing Olympic/

车进入场馆群采取远端安检政策，主要安检区域为阪泉服务区和延庆火车站。延庆冬奥村/冬残奥村不再设安检设施，进入奥运村不做二次安检，在延庆村周边的封闭线上，设置了车辆验证点VPC和人员验证点ACP。

3. 交通流线

延庆冬奥村/冬残奥村设置3个交通场站，场站均设置无障碍落客位，其设置比例不小于3%（冬残奥标准）。国家奥委会（NOC）停车场共有253辆小车停车位，其中7辆无障碍车位；运动员大巴停车场共有4个中巴下客车位和4个大巴落客位，其中2个无障碍落客位；媒体访客停车场共有3辆中巴车落客位，其中1个无障碍落客位；延庆冬奥村/冬残奥村设置了一条完整的步行道连接各个组团，其中无障碍人群使用的人行步道均满足无障碍通行需求。

根据延庆村的地形特点和空间布局，村内设置了3条居民进村通道（运动员班车场站验证口通道，媒体、来访人员验证口通道，缆车站、回村雪道验证口通道）和2条工作人员进村通道（六组团工作人员从NOC停车场南侧验证口通道；其他组团工作人员从6号路验证口通道）。在村内的每个居住组团及公共组团分别设置了居民和工作人员进出流线及出入口。

运动员可采用电瓶车换乘到达每个居住组团地下车库，再通过无障碍电梯到达各层。

4. 运行功能布局

冬奥村整体功能布局分为运行区、广场区和居住区。

运行区包括欢迎中心、访客中心、设施服务中心、安保中心、技术支持、后厨服务、员工餐厅、垃圾中转、交通场站、物流广场、冬奥村管理办公、冬奥村通信中心、安保后勤等功能。

广场区包括媒体中心，商业服务、奥运大家庭等功能。

居住区包括运动员客房、NOC办公、主餐厅、休闲餐厅、综合诊所、娱乐健身中心、奥委会服务中心、多信仰中心等功能。

5. 冬残奥会转换阶段

冬奥会结束之后，场馆功能需要向冬残奥会转换。冬残奥会的规模比冬奥会小，居住区只开放1~2组团，需要的资源和基础设施也更少，但为实现高效顺利过渡，冬奥会运行设计阶段同时了考虑冬残奥会场馆通用设施，合理设置防疫和安保等临时设施，在转换期不再新增建设任务。

6. 赛后使用阶段

延庆冬奥村赛后为休闲度假酒店，因此在运行设计中尽可能做到物尽其用、减少永久建筑拆改工作，特殊赛时需求尽可能使用临时建筑，便于赛后尽快拆除、开放营业。

Paralympic Village, which means that no secondary security checks are required for entering the Village. Vehicle Permit Check (VPC) and Accreditation Check Point (ACP) are arranged on the secure perimeter of the Yanqing Olympic/Paralympic Village.

3. Transport Flow

The Yanqing Olympic/Paralympic Village has three transport malls that are provided with accessible drop-off points, accounting for not less than 3% of the total (Paralympic standard). The NOC parking area has parking spaces for 253 passenger cars, including 7 accessible parking spaces; the athlete bus parking area has 4 minibus drop-off points and 4 coach drop-off points, including 2 accessible drop-off points; the media guest parking area has 3 minibus drop-off points, including 1 accessible drop-off point.

In the Yanqing Olympic/Paralympic Village, there is a walkway that connects all the clusters, with pedestrian trails for people with disabilities meeting the accessibility requirements.

Athletes can take an electric vehicle to reach the underground garages of residential clusters and then take accessible elevators to reach the floors.

4. Operation Functional Layout

The overall functional layout of the Village is divided into the Operational Zone, Plaza, and Residential Zone.

The Operational Zone includes functions of welcome centre, guest pass centre, facility services centre, security centre, technical support, kitchen service, workforce dining hall, waste transfer, transport mall, logistics plaza, Village management office, Village communications centre, and security logistical support.

The Plaza includes functions of media centre, commercial services, and Olympic/Paralympic Family services.

The Residential Zone includes functions of athlete rooms, NOC/NPC offices, main dining hall, casual dining hall, polyclinic, recreational and fitness centre, NOC/NPC services centre, and multi-faith centre.

5. Transition Period

As the scale of the Paralympic Winter Games is smaller than that of the Olympic Winter Games, only one or two clusters are open in the Residential Zone and fewer resources and less infrastructure are required. However, to achieve an efficient and smooth transition, the operational design of the Olympic Winter Games has considered the common venue facilities and reasonably set COVID-19 prevention and security overlays for the Paralympic Winter Games, therefore, no new construction tasks are conducted in the transition period.

6. Post-Games Use

To turn the Yanqing Olympic/Paralympic Village into a leisure resort hotel after the Games, the operational design should, as far as possible, put materials to good use, reduce permanent building demolition and renovation, and use overlays to meet special Games requirements, so as to remove them and open the hotel as soon as possible after the Games.

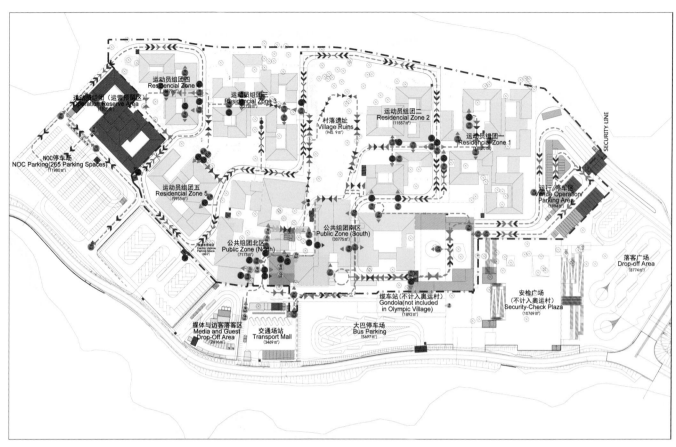

N YVL 总平面图 OB2.1版
YVL Master Plan OB2.1

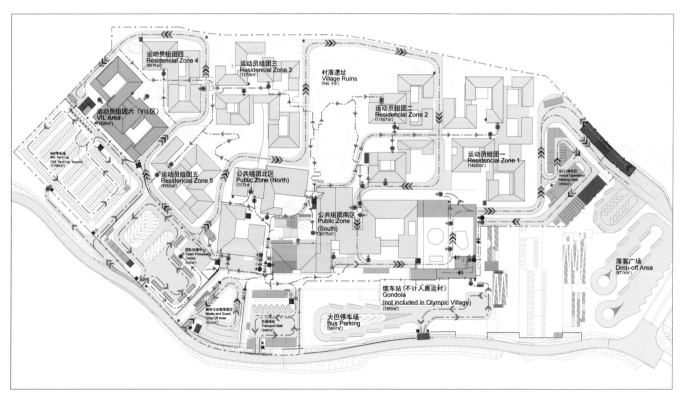

N YVL 总平面图 OB3.0版
YVL Master Plan OB3.0

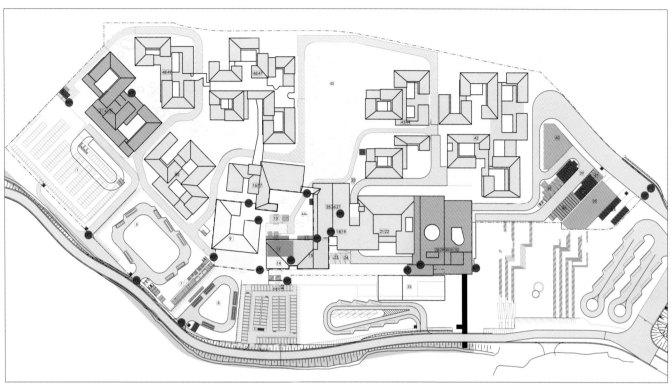

N YVL 总平面图 OB4.0版
YVL Master Plan OB4.0

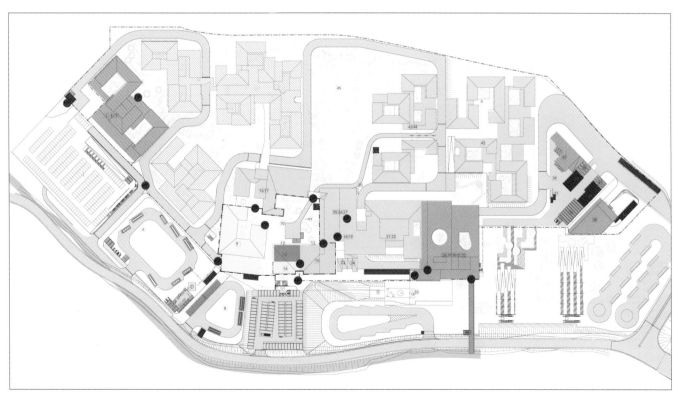

N YVL 总平面图 OB6.0版
YVL Master Plan OB6.0

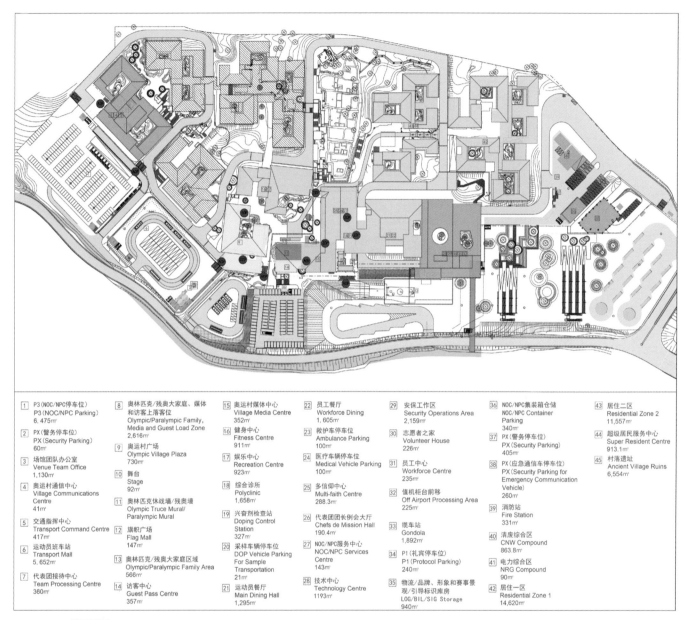

1	P3（NOC/NPC停车位） P3 (NOC/NPC Parking) 6,475㎡	8	奥林匹克/残奥大家庭、媒体 和访客上落客位 Olympic/Paralympic Family, Media and Guest Load Zone 2,616㎡	15	奥运村媒体中心 Village Media Centre 352㎡	22	员工餐厅 Workforce Dining 1,605㎡	29

1	P3（NOC/NPC停车位） P3 (NOC/NPC Parking) 6,475㎡	8	奥林匹克/残奥大家庭、媒体和访客上落客位 Olympic/Paralympic Family, Media and Guest Load Zone 2,616㎡	15	奥运村媒体中心 Village Media Centre 352㎡	22	员工餐厅 Workforce Dining 1,605㎡	29	安保工作区 Security Operations Area 2,159㎡	36	NOC/NPC集装箱仓储 NOC/NPC Container Parking 340㎡	43	居住二区 Residential Zone 2 11,557㎡
2	PX（警务停车位） PX (Security Parking) 60㎡	9	奥运村广场 Olympic Village Plaza 730㎡	16	健身中心 Fitness Centre 911㎡	23	救护车辆停车位 Ambulance Parking 100㎡	30	志愿者之家 Volunteer House 226㎡	37	PX（警务停车位） PX (Security Parking) 405㎡	44	超级居民服务中心 Super Resident Centre 913.1㎡
3	场馆团队办公室 Venue Team Office 1,130㎡	10	舞台 Stage 92㎡	17	娱乐中心 Recreation Centre 923㎡	24	医疗车辆停车位 Medical Vehicle Parking 100㎡	31	员工中心 Workforce Centre 235㎡	38	PX（应急通信停车位） PX (Security Parking for Emergency Communication Vehicle) 260㎡	45	村落遗址 Ancient Village Ruins 6,554㎡
4	奥运村通信中心 Village Communications Centre 41㎡	11	奥林匹克休战墙/残奥墙 Olympic Truce Mural/Paralympic Mural	18	综合诊所 Polyclinic 1,658㎡	25	多信仰中心 Multi-faith Centre 288.3㎡	32	值机柜台前移 Off Airport Processing Area 225㎡	39	消防站 Fire Station 331㎡		
5	交通指挥中心 Transport Command Centre 417㎡	12	旗帜广场 Flag Mall 147㎡	19	兴奋剂检查站 Doping Control Station 327㎡	26	代表团团长例会大厅 Chefs de Mission Hall 190.4㎡	33	缆车站 Gondola 1,892㎡	40	清废综合区 CNW Compound 863.8㎡		
6	运动员班车站 Transport Mall 5,652㎡	13	奥林匹克/残奥大家庭区域 Olympic/Paralympic Family Area 566㎡	20	采样车辆停车位 DOP Vehicle Parking For Sample Transportation 21㎡	27	NOC/NPC服务中心 NOC/NPC Services Centre 143㎡	34	P1（礼宾停车位） P1 (Protocol Parking) 240㎡	41	电力综合区 NRG Compound 90㎡		
7	代表团接待中心 Team Processing Centre 360㎡	14	访客中心 Guest Pass Centre 357㎡	21	运动员餐厅 Main Dining Hall 1,295㎡	28	技术中心 Technology Centre 1193㎡	35	物流/品牌、形象和赛景观/引导标识库房 LOG/BIL/SIG Storage 940㎡	42	居住一区 Residential Zone 1 14,620㎡		

YVL 总平面图 OB7.0版
YVL Master Plan OB7.0

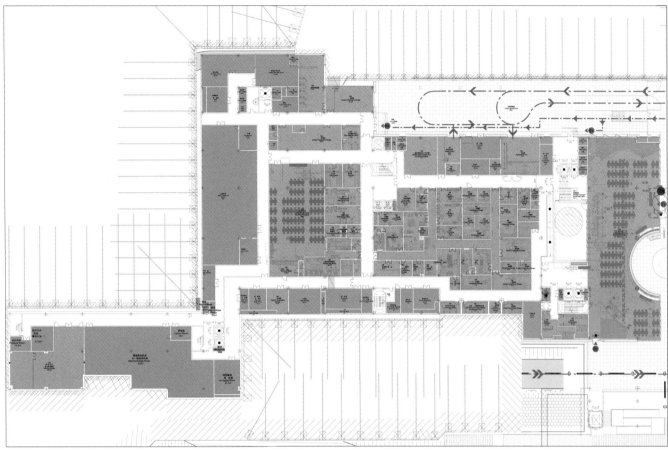

N ⊖ YVL 公共组团南区一层平面图 OB7.0版
YVL Public South Cluster 1F Plan OB7.0

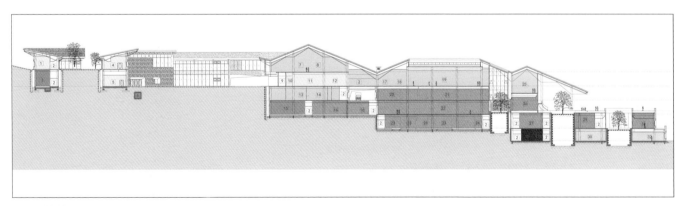

YVL 场地剖面图 OB7.0版
YVL Site Section OB7.0

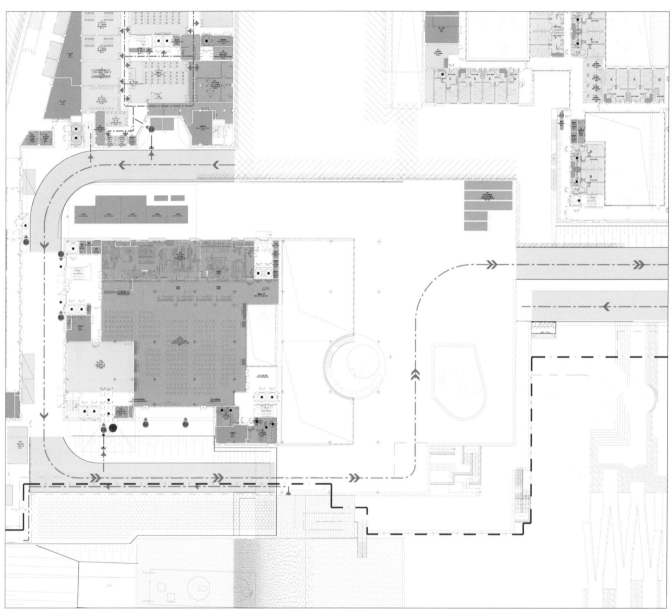

N YVL 公共组团南区二层平面图 OB7.0版
YVL Public South Cluster 2F Plan OB7.0

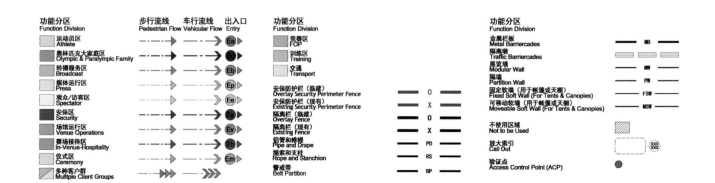

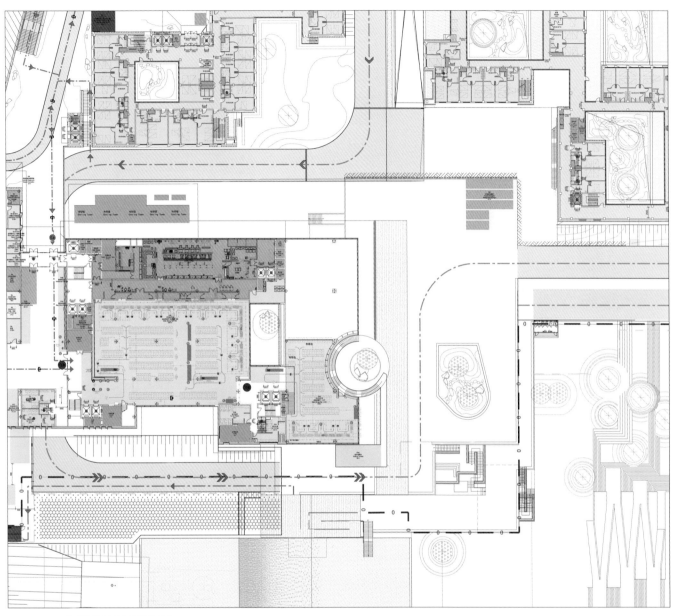

YVL 公共组团南区三层平面图 OB7.0版
YVL Public South Cluster 3F Plan OB7.0

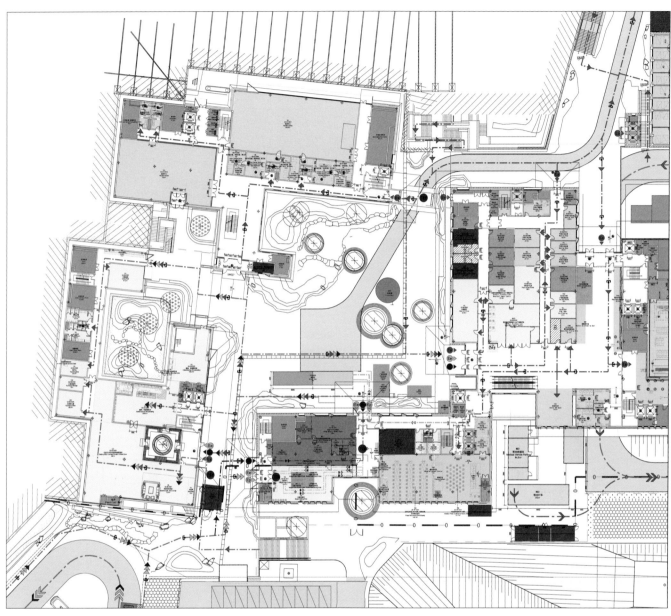

N ⊖ YVL 公共组团北区一层平面图 OB7.0版
YVL Public South Cluster 1F Plan OB7.0

功能分区
Function Division

运动员区
Athlete

奥林匹克大家庭区
Olympic & Paralympic Family

转播服务区
Broadcast

媒体运行区
Press

观众/访客区
Spectator

安保区
Security

场馆运行区
Venue Operations

赛场接待区
In-Venue-Hospitality

仪式区
Ceremony

多种客户群
Multiple Client Groups

步行流线
Pedestrian Flow

车行流线
Vehicular Flow

出入口
Entry

Ea

Eb

Ep

Ee

Ev

Em

功能分区
Function Division

竞赛区
FOP

训练区
Training

交通
Transport

安保防护栏（临建）
Overlay Security Perimeter Fence

安保防护栏（现有）
Existing Security Perimeter Fence

隔离栏（临建）
Overlay Fence

隔离栏（现有）
Existing Fence

铝管和帷幔
Pipe and Drape

绳索和支柱
Rope and Stanchion

警戒带
Belt Partition

O

X

O

X

PD

RS

BP

功能分区
Function Division

金属栏板
Metal Barriercades

隔离墩
Traffic Barriercades

展览墙
Modular Wall

隔墙
Partition Wall

固定软墙（用于帐篷或天棚）
Fixed Soft Wall (For Tents & Canopies)

可移动软墙（用于帐篷或天棚）
Moveable Soft Wall (For Tents & Canopies)

不使用区域
Not to be Used

放大索引
Call Out

验证点
Access Control Point (ACP)

MB

MW

PW

FSW

MSW

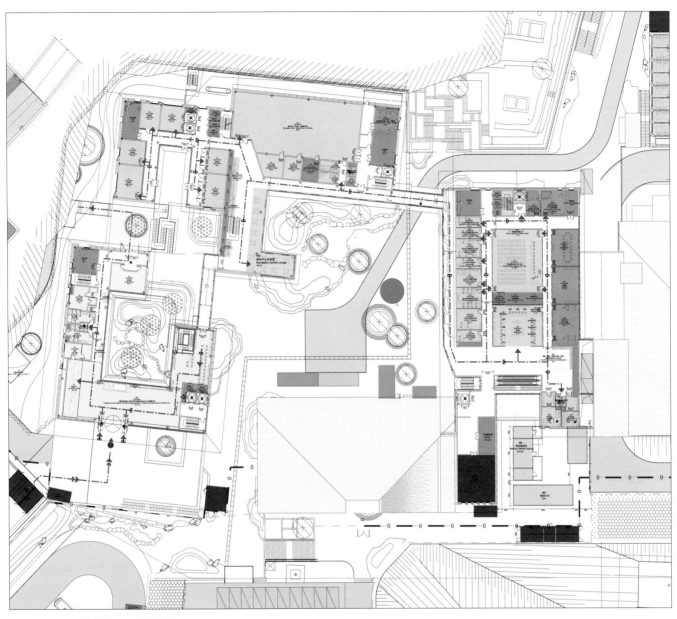

N YVL 公共组团北区二层平面图 OB7.0版
YVL Public South Cluster 2F OB7.0

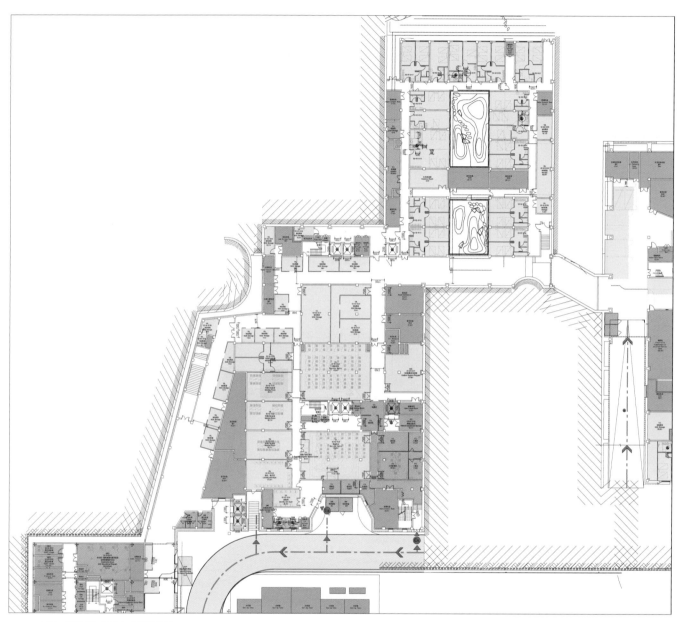

N⊖ YVL 居住组团二区一层平面图 OB7.0版
YVL Residential Zone 2 1F Plan OB7.0

功能分区 Function Division	步行流线 Pedestrian Flow	车行流线 Vehicular Flow	出入口 Entry
运动员区 Athlete			Ea ▶
奥林匹克大家庭区 Olympic & Paralympic Family			● ▶
转播服务区 Broadcast			Eb ▶
媒体运行区 Press			Ep ▶
观众/访客区 Spectator			Ee ▶
安保区 Security			● ▶
场馆运行区 Venue Operations			Ev ▶
赛场接待区 In-Venue-Hospitality			Eh ▶
仪式区 Ceremony			Em ▶
多种客户群 Multiple Client Groups			

功能分区 Function Division	
竞赛区 FOP	
训练区 Training	
交通 Transport	
安保防护栏（临建）Overlay Security Perimeter Fence	O
安保防护栏（现有）Existing Security Perimeter Fence	X
隔离栏（临建）Overlay Fence	O
隔离栏（现有）Existing Fence	X
铝管和帷幕 Pipe and Drape	PD
提索和支柱 Rope and Stanchion	RS
警戒带 Belt Partition	BP

功能分区 Function Division	
金属栏板 Metal Barriercades	MB
隔离墩 Traffic Barriercades	
展览墙 Modular Wall	MW
隔墙 Partition Wall	PW
固定软墙（用于帐篷或天棚）Fixed Soft Wall (For Tents & Canopies)	FSW
可移动软墙（用于帐篷或天棚）Moveable Soft Wall (For Tents & Canopies)	MSW
不使用区域 Not to be Used	
放大索引 Call Out	XXX
验证点 Access Control Point (ACP)	●

YVL 居住组团二区二层平面图 OB7.0版
YVL Residential Zone 2 2F Plan OB7.0

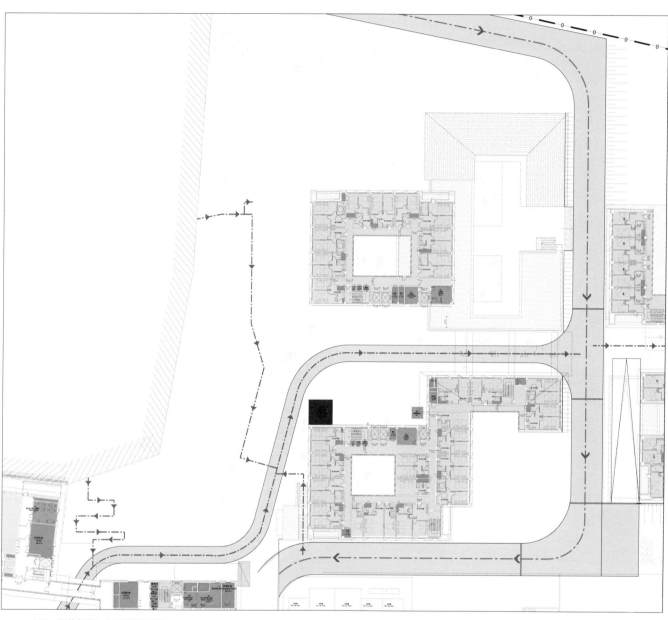

N ⊕ YVL 居住组团二区三层平面图 OB7.0版
YVL Residential Zone 2 3F Plan OB7.0

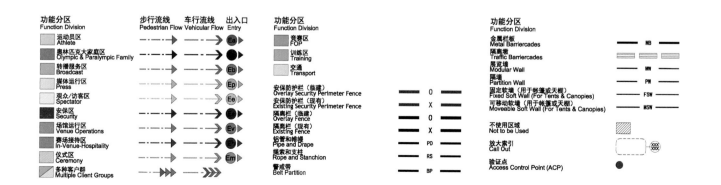

功能分区 Function Division		步行流线 Pedestrian Flow	车行流线 Vehicular Flow	出入口 Entry	功能分区 Function Division		功能分区 Function Division	
	运动员区 Athlete			Ea ▶		竞赛区 FOP	金属栏板 Metal Barriercades	MB
	奥林匹克大家庭区 Olympic & Paralympic Family			● ▶		训练区 Training	隔离墩 Traffic Barriercades	
	转播服务区 Broadcast			Eb ▶		交通 Transport	展览墙 Modular Wall	MW
	媒体运行区 Press			Ep ▶	安保防护栏（临建） Overlay Security Perimeter Fence	0	隔墙 Partition Wall	PW
	观众/访客区 Spectator			Ee ▶	安保防护栏（现有） Existing Security Perimeter Fence	X	固定软墙（用于帐篷或天棚） Fixed Soft Wall (For Tents & Canopies)	FSW
	安保区 Security			● ▶	隔离栏（临建） Overlay Fence	0	可移动软墙（用于帐篷或天棚） Moveable Soft Wall (For Tents & Canopies)	MSW
	场馆运行区 Venue Operations			Ev ▶	隔离栏（现有） Existing Fence	X		
	赛事接待区 In-Venue-Hospitality			● ▶	铝管和帷幔 Pipe and Drape	PD	不使用区域 Not to be Used	
	仪式区 Ceremony			Em ▶	揽索和支柱 Rope and Stanchion	RS	放大索引 Call Out	
	多种客户群 Multiple Client Groups				警戒带 Belt Partition	BP	验证点 Access Control Point (ACP)	●

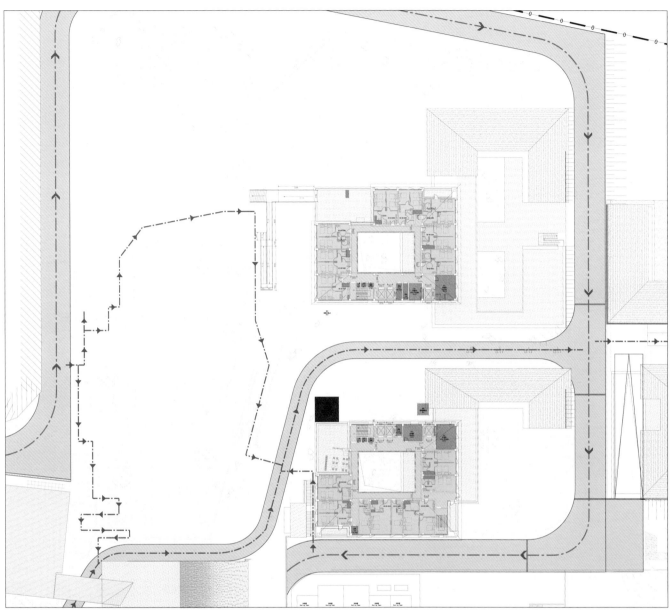

YVL 居住组团二区四层平面图 OB7.0版
YVL Residential Zone 2 4F Plan OB7.0

N

北京冬奥组委 提供
Provide by BOCOG

延庆赛区核心区公共区

Yanqing Zone Core Public Area

延庆赛区核心区公共区位于北京延庆区西北部小海坨山区域，用地面积799.13hm²，总建筑面积26.0万m²，包含国家高山滑雪中心、国家雪车雪橇中心、延庆冬奥村/冬残奥村等3个场馆。

公共区包括赛区核心区枢纽二、三、四号地及赛区指挥及监控中心、海陀收费站、赛区展示中心、西大庄科村、西大庄科服务中心、奥运村和海陀110千伏变电站、赛区垃圾转运站、赛区污水处理厂等功能设施。各交通场地及功能设施由延庆赛区连接线及赛区1至6号路联系起来，并串联运行广场、核心区交通枢纽和山地缆车系统等，为赛时交通提供保障。

延庆赛区核心区公共区围绕"山林场馆生态冬奥"的理念，建设山林掩映中的场馆群，践行了绿色生态、可持续的冬奥会理念。

Located in the Xiaohaituo Mountain area in the northwest of Yanqing District, Beijing, Yanqing Zone Core Public Area covers an area of 799.13 hectares, has a total floor area of 260,000m², and includes the three venues of National Alpine Skiing Centre, National Sliding Centre, and Yanqing Olympic/Paralympic Village.

Yanqing Zone Core Public Area consists of No.2, No.3 and No.4 Land of the Core Area Hub as well as functional facilities such as competition zone command and monitoring centre, Haituo Tollgate, competition zone exhibition centre, Xidazhuangke Village, Xidazhuangke Service Centre, Olympic/Paralympic Village, Haituo 110kV substation, competition zone waste transfer station, and competition zone sewage treatment plant. The transport sites and functional facilities are connected by Yanqing Zone connecting lines and No.1 to No.6 Roads with the operational plaza, core area transport hubs, mountain gondola system, etc. to support Games-time transport.

Yanqing Zone Core Public Area nestled in mountains and forests embraces the concepts of eco-friendly Olympic venues and sustainable Games.

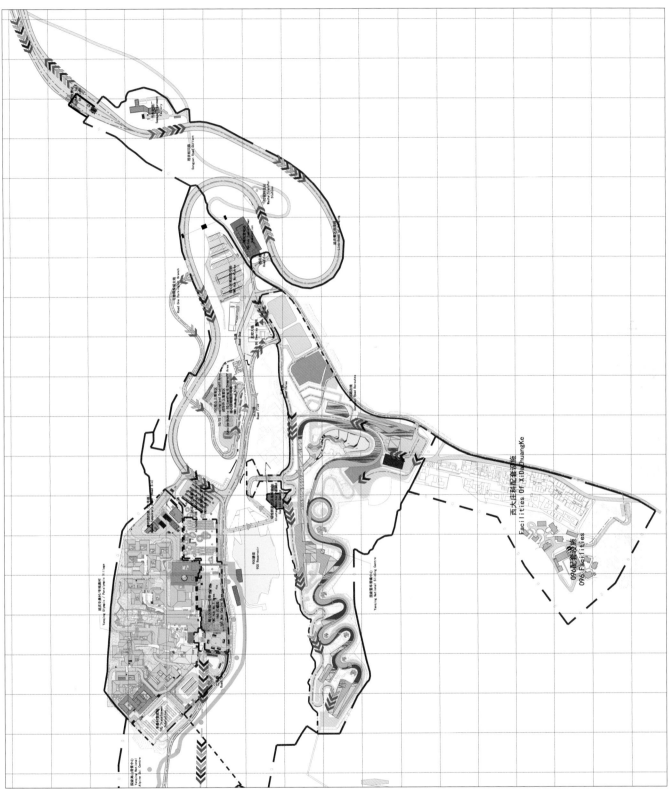

延庆赛区核心区公共区总平面图 OB7.0版
Yanqing Zone Core Public Area Master Plan OB7.0

253

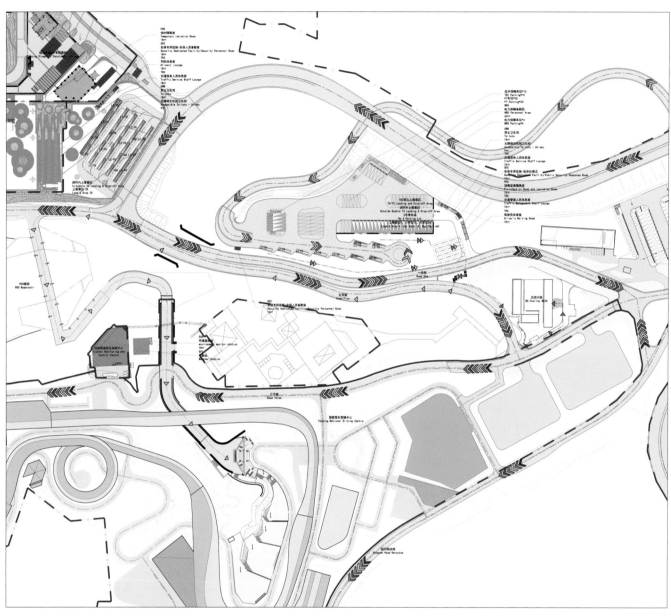

延庆赛区核心区公共区放大平面图一 OB7.0版
Yanqing Zone Core Public Area Enlarged Plan 1 OB7.0

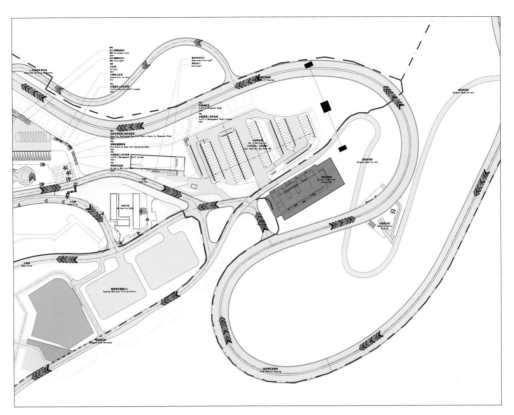

N 延庆赛区核心区公共区放大平面图二 OB7.0版
Yanqing Zone Core Public Area Enlarged Plan 2 OB7.0

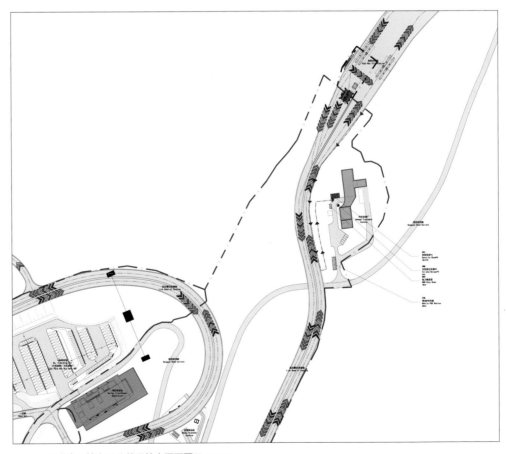

N 延庆赛区核心区公共区放大平面图三 OB7.0版
Yanqing Zone Core Public Area Enlarged Plan 3 OB7.0

阪泉综合服务中心 [YBS]

Yanqing Banquan Service Centre

阪泉综合服务中心位于延庆区北部,京礼高速53.5km处,距离延庆赛区核心区约17km,是北京冬奥及冬残奥会延庆赛区的门户,占地面积16.7万m²,总建筑面积约6000m²。作为非竞赛场馆,在赛时承担两个竞赛场馆(高山滑雪中心和雪车雪橇中心)和非竞赛场馆(延庆冬奥村/冬残奥村)的远端安检、观众检票验票、多客户群交通换乘、运动员抵达安检、环内证件激活等重要功能,同时也是延庆赛区交通综合指挥中心。

阪泉综合服务中心西侧为闭环外区域,赛时观众乘坐TS班车进入、经由1号口到达阪泉综合服务中心,经过安检和验票后进入安保封闭线内,换乘TS班车前往延庆赛区各竞赛场馆观赛。

阪泉综合服务中心根据防疫要求,在安保封闭线内外分别设置了闭环内区域和闭环外区域,分四个象限区域布置,并设置观众安检通道、转播及媒体通道、运动员通道、技术官员通道以及车辆安检通道。

Located in the northern part of Yanqing District, 53.5km from the Beijing-Chongli Expressway and about 17km from the core area of the Yanqing Zone, the Banquan Service Centre is the gateway to the Yanqing Zone of the Olympic and Paralympic Winter Games Beijing 2022, covering an area of 167,000m² and having a total floor area of about 6,000m².

The Banquan Service Centre, as a non-competition venue, performs vital functions during the Games, including remote security checks, spectator ticket checking, client groups transport transfer, athlete security checks upon arrival, and intra-loop pass validation for the 2 competition venues (National Alpine Skiing Centre and National Sliding Centre) and 1 non-competition venue (Yanqing Olympic/Paralympic Village), and also serves as the comprehensive transport command centre of the Yanqing Zone.

The area outside the closed loop is on the west side of the Banquan Service Centre. During the Games, spectators take TS shuttle buses to enter No.1 Entrance to the Banquan Service Centre; after passing through security checks and ticket checking, they enter the secure perimeter to transfer to TS shuttle buses to watch competitions at competition venues in the Yanqing Zone.

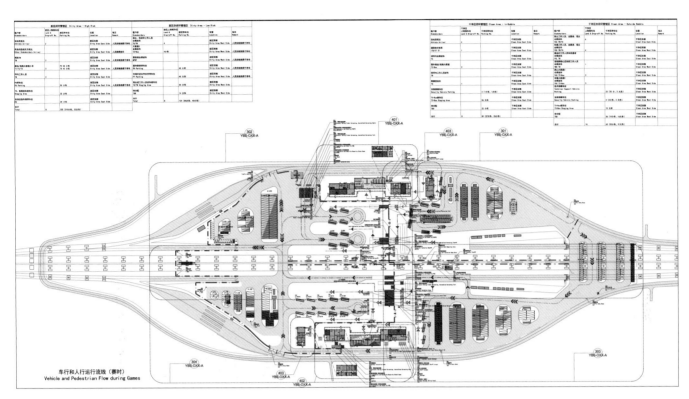

YBS 总平面图 OB7.0版
YBS Master Plan OB7.0

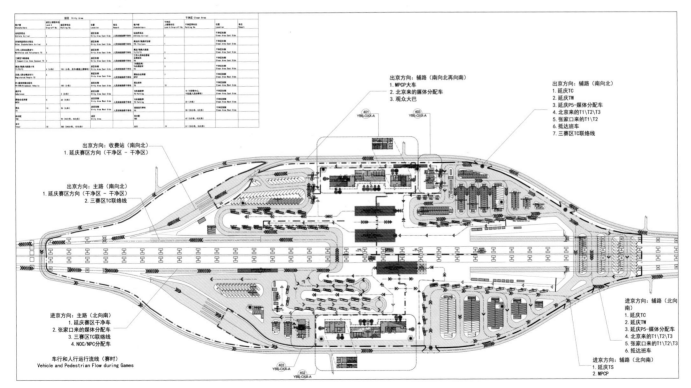

YBS 总平面图 OB6.0版
YBS Master Plan OB6.0

延庆制服和注册分中心 [YUA]

Yanqing Uniform Distribution and Accreditation Centre

延庆制服和注册分中心位于北京延庆区八达岭国际会展中心C馆，承担北京2022年冬奥会和冬残奥会期间延庆赛区工作人员、技术官员、志愿者等客户群的证件注册办理、制服装备发放的工作。

延庆制服和注册分中心在八达岭会展中心现有建筑基础之上改造而成，分为安保隔离区、安检区、注册业务区、制服业务区、仓储区、合署办公区、电力运行区、餐饮综合区等，场馆使用面积约8600m²。

延庆制服与注册分中心分为制服区与注册区。制服工作人员由场馆西门进入，安检后由西门进入场馆，在办公区办公并发放制服。注册工作人员由场馆西门进入，安检后由中门进入场馆，在办公区办公并发放注册卡。

访客由场馆西门进入，安检后进入场馆领取制服、进行注册。

场馆南端集中设置了临时设施，主要为场馆提供安保服务，包括车检大棚、安保岗亭等。

Located in Hall C, Badaling International Convention and Exhibition Centre, Yanqing District, Beijing, the Yanqing Uniform Distribution and Accreditation Centre is responsible for processing accreditation and passes for and distributing uniforms and equipment to client groups such as workforce, technical officials, and volunteers in the Yanqing Zone during the Beijing 2022 Olympic and Paralympic Winter Games.

Renovated from an existing building of the Badaling International Convention and Exhibition Centre, the Yanqing Uniform Distribution and Accreditation Centre is divided into a security isolation area, a screening area, an accreditation area, a uniform area, a storage area, an office area, an energy operations area, and a food and beverage compound, with a usable area of about 8,600m².

There is a uniform area and an accreditation area in the Yanqing Uniform Distribution and Accreditation Centre. The uniform workforce enters from the venue's west gate and, after passing security checks, enters the venue from the west gate to work and distribute uniforms in their office area. The accreditation workforce enters from the venue's west gate and, after passing security checks, enters the venue from the middle gate to work and issue accreditation cards in their office area.

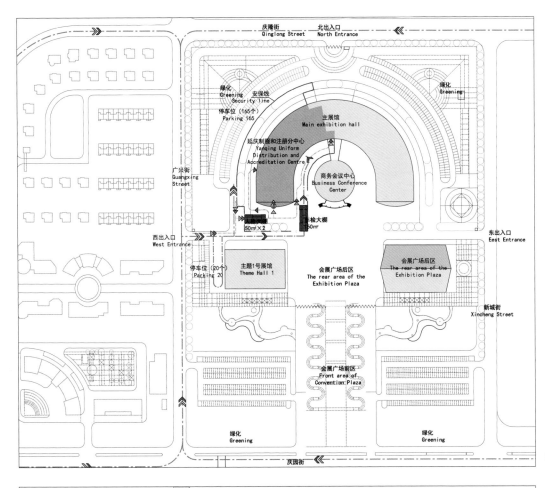

N YUA 总平面图 OB5.0版
YUA Master Plan OB5.0

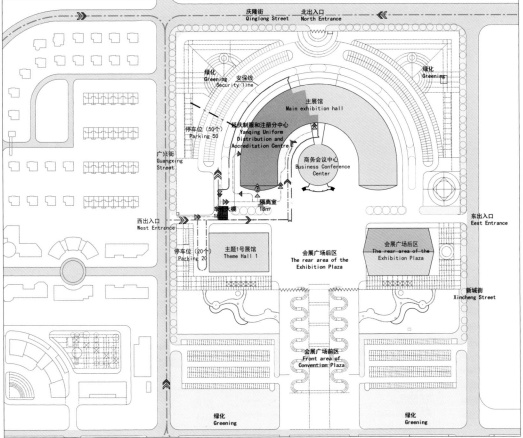

N YUA 总平面图 OB6.0版
YUA Master Plan OB6.0

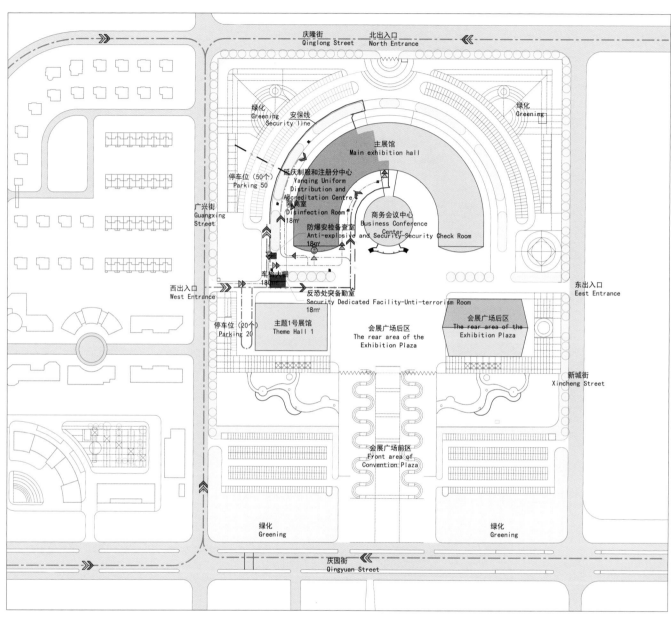

庆隆街
Qinglong Street

北出入口
North Entrance

绿化
Greening　安保线
Security line

主展馆
Main exhibition hall

绿化
Greening

停车位（50个）
Parking 50

延庆制服和注册分中心
Yanqing Uniform
Distribution and
Accreditation Centre
隔离室
Disinfection Room
18㎡

商务会议中心
Business Conference
Center
防爆安检备查室
Anti-explosive and Security-Security Check Room
18㎡

广兴街
Guangxing
Street

东出入口
Eest Entrance

车棚大棚
180㎡

反恐处突备勤室
Security Dedicated Facility-Unti-terrorism Room
18㎡

西出入口
West Entrance

停车位（20个）
Parking 20

主题1号展馆
Theme Hall 1

会展广场后区
The rear area of the
Exhibition Plaza

会展广场后区
The rear area of the
Exhibition Plaza

新城街
Xincheng Street

会展广场前区
Front area of
Convention Plaza

绿化
Greening

绿化
Greening

庆园街
Qingyuan Street

YUA 总平面图 OB7.0版
YUA Master Plan OB7.0

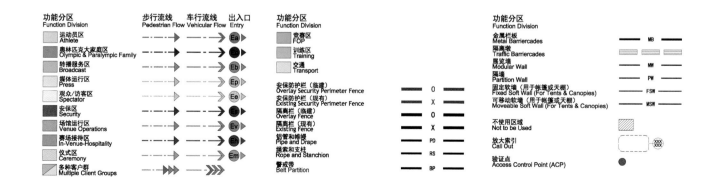

功能分区
Function Division

运动员区 Athlete	
奥林匹克大家庭区 Olympic & Paralympic Family	
转播服务区 Broadcast	
媒体运行区 Press	
观众/访客区 Spectator	
安保区 Security	
场馆运行区 Venue Operations	
赛场接待区 In-Venue-Hospitality	
仪式区 Ceremony	
多种客户群 Multiple Client Groups	

步行流线
Pedestrian Flow

车行流线
Vehicular Flow

出入口
Entry

Ea
Eh
Eb
Ep
Ee
Et
Ev
En
Em

功能分区
Function Division

竞赛区 FOP
训练区 Training
交通 Transport

安保防护栏（临建）
Overlay Security Perimeter Fence
安保防护栏（现有）
Existing Security Perimeter Fence
隔离栏（临建）
Overlay Fence
隔离栏（现有）
Existing Fence
铝管和帷幔
Pipe and Drape
提索和支柱
Rope and Stanchion
警戒带
Belt Partition

O
X
O
X
PD
RS
BP

功能分区
Function Division

金属栏板
Metal Barriercades
隔离墩
Traffic Barriercades
展览墙
Modular Wall
隔墙
Partition Wall
固定软墙（用于帐篷或天棚）
Fixed Soft Wall (For Tents & Canopies)
可移动软墙（用于帐篷或天棚）
Moveable Soft Wall (For Tents & Canopies)

MB
MW
PW
FSW
MSW

不使用区域
Not to be Used
放大索引
Call Out
验证点
Access Control Point (ACP)

XXX

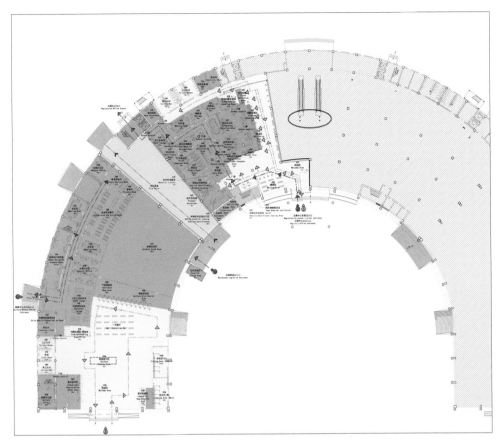

N YUA 一层平面图 OB7.0版
YUA 1F Plan OB7.0

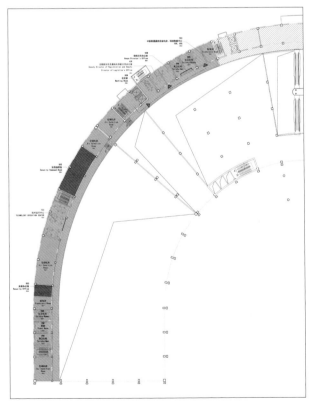

N YUA 夹层平面图 OB7.0版
YUA 1F Mezzanine Plan OB7.0

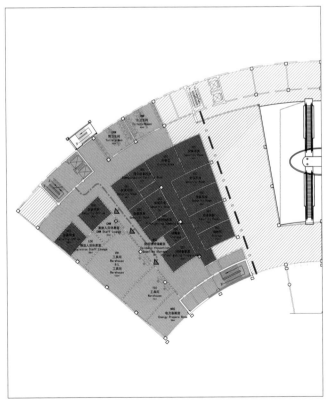

N YUA 二层平面图 OB7.0版
YUA 2F Plan OB7.0

延庆残奥颁奖广场 [YMP]

Yanqing Paralympic Medals Plaza

延庆残奥颁奖广场位于北京市延庆区北京世园公园内，由原世界园艺博览会国际馆改造而成。在北京2022年冬残奥会期间，承担冬残奥会27个比赛项目的奖牌颁发仪式。颁奖演出结合冬残奥竞赛特点，展现残疾人运动员乐观自信、昂扬向上的精神面貌，传递奥运梦想。

延庆残奥颁奖广场包含颁奖舞台、观众观看区、残奥大家庭区、混合采访区、运动员等候区、仪式功能区、场馆媒体中心、后勤办公区、场馆运行区等，总建筑面积约为2.2万m²。

场馆分前后院，前院为观众区、国内贵宾休息区和部分工作人员工作区，其他为后院区。

获奖运动员车辆自世园公园4号安检口进入，经北侧环线道路通过颁奖广场东北角入口，到达B馆东北侧运动员落客区、进入场馆。

大家庭成员车辆从4号安检口进入，通过A馆西北入口落客、进入场馆。媒体和演员车辆从7号安检口进入，通过B馆西侧入口落客、进入场馆。观众车辆从2号安检口进入，通过A馆东入口落客、进入场馆。工作人员车辆从4号安检口进入，通过B馆北侧入口落客、进入场馆。

Located within the Beijing Expo Park, Yanqing District, Beijing, the Yanqing Paralympic Medals Plaza is renovated from the former International Pavilion of International Horticultural Exhibition 2019, Beijing, China.

The Yanqing Paralympic Medals Plaza is responsible for the victory ceremonies of 27 events during the Beijing 2022 Paralympic Winter Games. According to the Paralympic competition characteristics, the victory ceremony performances are designed to show the optimistic, confident and high-spirited outlook of Paralympic athletes and fulfil the Paralympic dream.

The Yanqing Paralympic Medals Plaza consists of a victory ceremony stage, a spectator watching area, a Paralympic Family area, a mixed zone, a medallist waiting area, a ceremony functional zone, a Venue Media Centre, a logistical office area, and a venue operation area, with a total floor area of about 22,000m².

The venue is divided into the Front of House and the Back of House, with the former including the spectator area, domestic dignitary lounge, and some workforce's work area and the latter including the remaining areas.

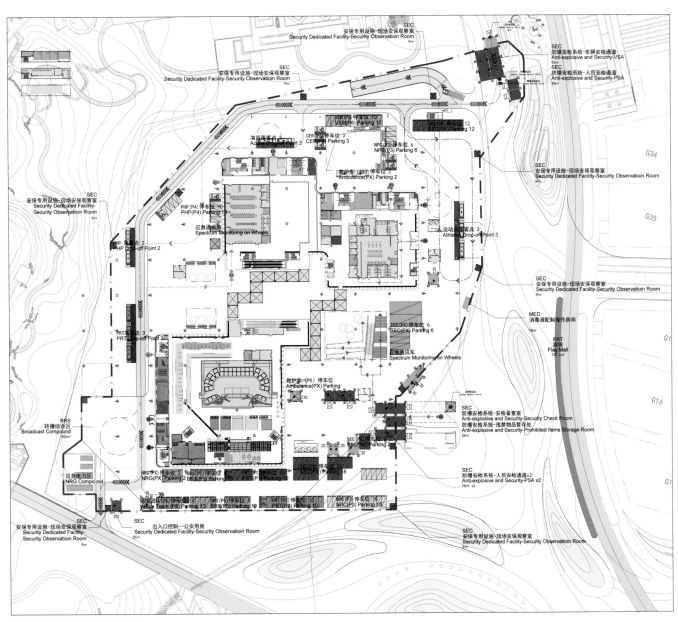

安保专用设施-现场安保观察室
Security Dedicated Facility-Security Observatioin Room

SEC
安保专用设施-现场安保观察室
Security Dedicated Facility-Security Observatioin Room

SEC
防爆安检系统-车辆安检通道
Anti-explosive and Security-VSA
SEC
防爆安检系统-人员安检通道
Anti-explosive and Security-PSA

VEM(H6) Parking 10

演员落客点 3
Actors Drop-off Point 3

CER停车位 3
CER Parking 3

NPC(P3) 停车位 6
NPC(P3) Parking 6

SEC(BK) 停车位 12
SEC(BK) Parking 12

SEC
安保专用设施-现场安保观察室
Security Dedicated Facility-Security Observatioin Room

G34

救护车(PX)停车位 2
Ambulance(PX) Parking 2

G35

SEC
安保专用设施-现场安保观察室
Security Dedicated Facility-Security Observatioin Room

PHP(P4) 停车位 10
PHP(P4) Parking 10

频谱监测车
Spectrum Monitoring on Wheels

运动员落客点 3
Athletes Drop-off Point 3

PHP 落客点 2
PHP Drop-off Point 2

SEC
安保专用设施-现场安保观察室
Security Dedicated Facility-Security Observatioin Room

MED
消毒液配制操作房间

PRT落客点 3
PRT Drop-off Point 3

TEC(PX) 停车位 6
TEC(PX) Parking 6

应急通讯车
Spectrum Monitoring on Wheels

PRT
流车
Flag Mall

G1

救护车(PX) 停车位
Ambulance(PX) Parking

SEC
防爆安检系统-安检备查室
Anti-explosive and Security-Security Check Room
防爆安检系统-违禁物品暂存处
Anti-explosive and Security-Prohibited Items Storage Room

G16

BRS
转播综合区
Broadcast Compound

SEC
SEC(PX) Parking

应急电力区
NRG Compound

SEC
防爆安检系统-人员安检通道x2
Anti-explosive and Security-PSA x2

NRG(PX) 停车位 2
NRG(PX) Parking 2

BRS(P5) 停车位
BRS(P5) Parking

PST(P1) 停车位
PST(P1) Parking 10

G1

场馆团队(P6)停车位 10
Venue Team(P6) Parking 10

BRS(P5)停车位 10
BRS(P5) Parking 10

PRT(P2)停车位 10
PRT(P2) Parking 10

NPC(P3) 停车位 15
NPC(P3) Parking 15

SEC
安保专用设施-现场安保观察室
Security Dedicated Facility-Security Observatioin Room

SEC
出入口控制—公安用房
Security Dedicated Facility-Security Observatioin Room

SEC
安保专用设施-现场安保观察室
Security Dedicated Facility-Security Observatioin Room

N
YMP 总平面图 OB7.0版
YMP Master Plan OB7.0

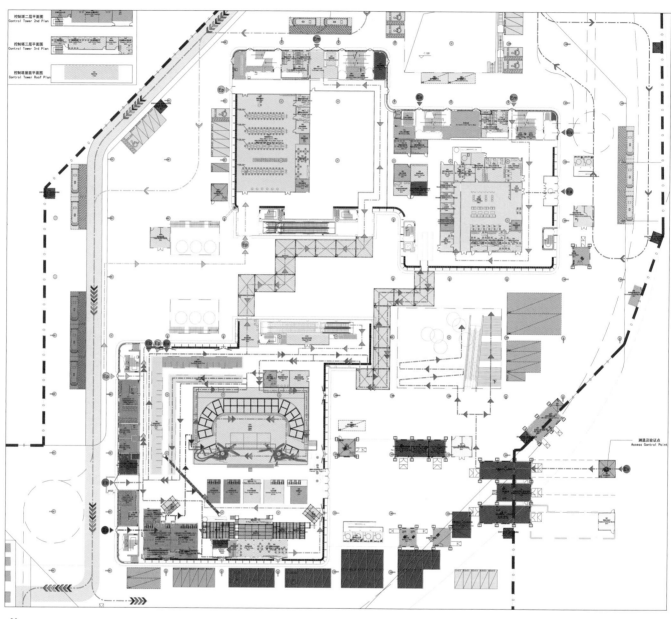

控制塔二层平面图
Control Tower 2nd Plan

控制塔三层平面图
Control Tower 3rd Plan

控制塔屋面平面图
Control Tower Roof Plan

测温及验证点
Access Control Point

N

YMP 一层平面图 OB7.0版
YMP 1F Plan OB7.0

功能分区 Function Division	步行流线 Pedestrian Flow	车行流线 Vehicular Flow	出入口 Entry	功能分区 Function Division	功能分区 Function Division

运动员区
Athlete

奥林匹克大家庭区
Olympic & Paralympic Family

转播服务区
Broadcast

媒体运行区
Press

观众/访客区
Spectator

安保区
Security

场馆运行区
Venue Operations

赛事接待区
In-Venue-Hospitality

仪式区
Ceremony

多种客户群
Multiple Client Groups

Ea
Eb
Ep
Ee
Eh
Ev
Eh
Em

竞赛区
FOP

训练区
Training

交通
Transport

安保防护栏（临建）
Overlay Security Perimeter Fence   O

安保防护栏（现有）
Existing Security Perimeter Fence   X

隔离栏（临建）
Overlay Fence   O

隔离栏（现有）
Existing Fence   X

铝管和维幔
Pipe and Drape   PD

揽索和支柱
Rope and Stanchion   RS

警戒带
Belt Partition   BP

金属栏板
Metal Barricades   MB

隔离墩
Traffic Barricades

展览墙
Modular Wall   MW

隔墙
Partition Wall   PW

固定软墙（用于帐篷或天棚）
Fixed Soft Wall (For Tents & Canopies)   FSW

可移动软墙（用于帐篷或天棚）
Moveable Soft Wall (For Tents & Canopies)   MSW

不使用区域
Not to be Used

放大索引
Call Out

验证点
Access Control Point (ACP)

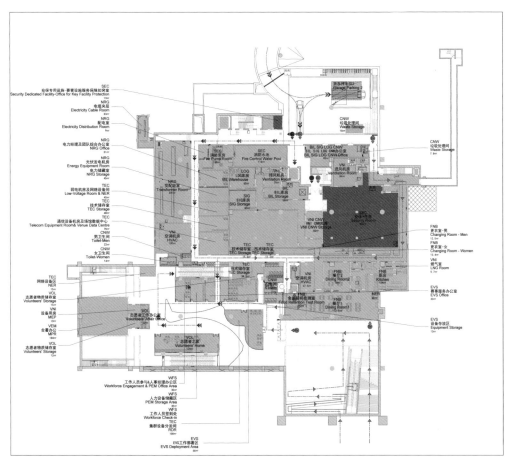

安保专用设施-要赛设施服务保障处突室
Security Dedicated Facility-Office for Key Facility Protection
13㎡

SEC

NRG
电缆夹层
Electricity Cable Room
23㎡

NRG
配电室
Electricity Distribution Room
9㎡

NRG
电力经理及团队综合办公室
NRG Office
91㎡

NRG
光伏发电机房
Energy Equipment Room
NRG
电力储藏室
NRG Storage
46㎡

TEC
弱电机房及网络设备间
Low-Voltage Room & NER
45㎡

TEC
技术储存室
TEC Storage
48㎡

TEC
通信设备机房及场馆数据中心
Telecom Equipment Room& Venue Data Centre

CNW
男卫生间
Toilet-Men
22㎡

CNW
女卫生间
Toilet-Women
14㎡

TEC
网络设备区
NER
15㎡

VOL
志愿者物质储存室
Volunteers' Storage
15㎡

VNI
设备用房
MEP
48㎡

VEM
仓库办公
MPR
18㎡

VOL
志愿者物质储存室
Volunteers' Storage
12㎡

SEC
消防泵房
Fire Pump Room

SEC
消防水池
Fire Control Water Pool

BIL SIG LOG CNW
BIL SIG LOG CNW办公室
BIL SIG LOG CNW Office

CNW
垃圾处理间
Waste Storage
15㎡

CNW
垃圾处理间
Waste Storage
9㎡

LOG
L90库房
BIL Warehouse

VNI
进风机房
Ventilation Room

NRG
变配电室
Transformer Room
33㎡

SIG
SIG库房
SIG Storage

BIL
BIL库房
BIL Storage

VNI
空调机房
HVAC
100㎡

TEC
技术储存室
TEC Storage TEC Storage
15 ㎡

TEC
技术储存室
TEC Storage

VNI
空调机房
HVAC
27.5㎡

CNW
垃圾处理间
CNW

VNI CNW
VNI CNW储间
VNI CNW Storage

VNI
燃气室
LNG Room
5.7㎡

FNB
更衣室-男
Changing Room - Men
12.5㎡

FNB
更衣室-女
Changing Room - Women
11.8㎡

SEC
安保休息室
Security Room

VOL
志愿者工作办公室
Volunteers' Affair Office

VOL
志愿者之家
Volunteers' Home

FNB
餐厅
Dining Room2

FNB
食剩样检查测试
Food Retention Test Room

FNB
餐厅
Dining Room1

FNB
厨房
Kitchen
154㎡

EVS
赛事服务办公室
EVS Office
33㎡

EVS
设备存放区
Equipment Storage
13㎡

NER

WFS
工作人员参与人事经理办公区
Workforce Engagement & PEM Office Area
36㎡

WFS
人力设备储藏区
PEM Storage Area
6㎡

WFS
工作人员签到处
Workforce Check-in
8㎡

TEC
集群设备分发间
RDR
100㎡

EVS
EVS工作部署区
EVS Deployment Area

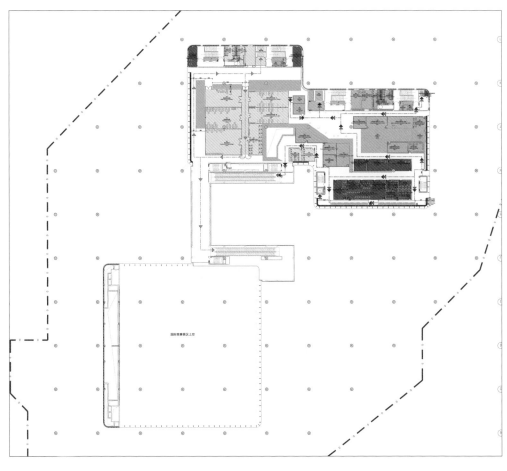

国际赛赛区上空

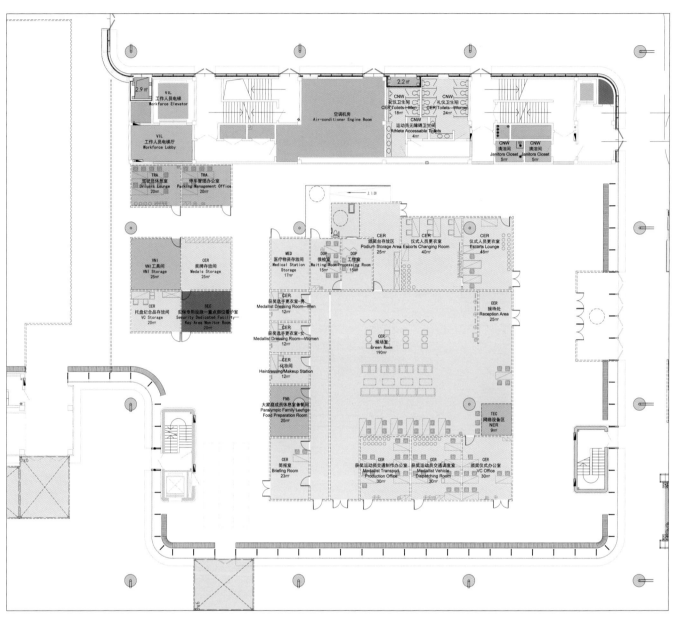

N
YMP 一层放大平面图一 OB7.0版
YMP 1F Enlarged Plan 1 OB7.0

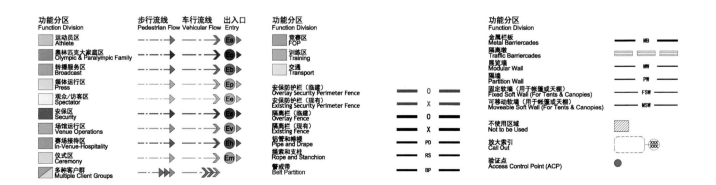

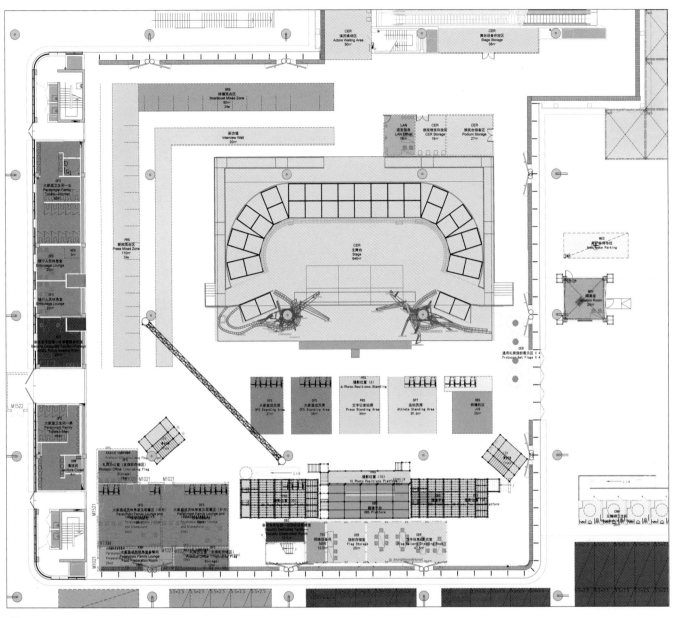

N

YMP 一层放大平面图二 OB7.0版
YMP 1F Enlarged Plan 2 OB7.0

张家口赛区

Zhangjiakou Zone

云顶滑雪公园-Zhangjiakou Genting Snow Park [ZSP]
张家口山地新闻中心-Zhangjiakou Mountain Press Centre [ZPC]
张家口冬奥村/冬残奥村-Zhangjiakou Olympic/Paralympic Village [ZVL]
张家口颁奖广场-Zhangjiakou Medals Plaza [ZMP]
张家口制服及注册分中心-Zhangjiakou Uniform Distribution and Accreditation Centre [ZUA]
张家口古杨树场馆群公共区-Zhangjiakou Guyangshu Cluster Public Area
国家跳台滑雪中心-Zhangjiakou National Ski Jumping Centre [ZSJ]
国家冬季两项中心-Zhangjiakou National Biathlon Centre [ZBT]
国家越野滑雪中心-Zhangjiakou National Cross-Country Centre [ZCC]
张家口山地转播中心-Zhangjiakou Mountain Broadcast Centre [ZBC]

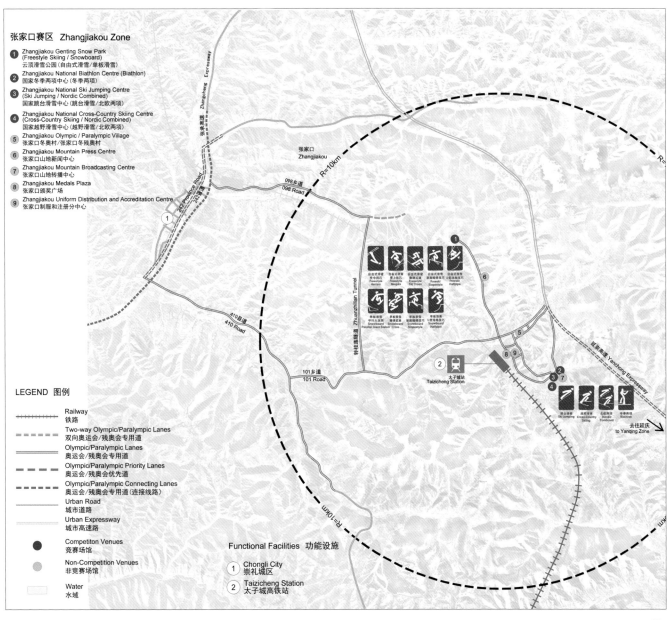

张家口赛区场馆和基础设施布局图
Zhangjiakou Zone Venues and Infrastructure Layout

　　张家口赛区位于张家口市崇礼区太子城区域，冬奥会共有9个场馆，其中竞赛场馆4个、非竞赛场馆5个（冬残奥会共有竞赛场馆2个、非竞赛场馆4个）。张家口赛区共承担2个大项（滑雪、冬季两项）、6个分项（单板滑雪、自由式滑雪、越野滑雪、跳台滑雪、北欧两项、冬季两项）、51个小项的比赛。张家口赛区的场馆布局十分紧凑，集中分布在3个区域：北部的云顶滑雪公园场馆群、中部太子城冰雪小镇和南部的古杨树场馆群。如此紧凑的布局，节省了场馆建设成本，也为赛事组织提供很大的便利条件。

Located in the Taizicheng region in Chongli District, Zhangjiakou Zone contains 9 venues, including 4 competition venues and 5 non-competition venues. It hosted 51 events in 6 disciplines (Snowboard, Freestyle Skiing, Cross-country Skiing, Ski Jumping, Nordic Combined, and Biathlon) across 2 sports (Skiing and Biathlon). Venues are concentrated in 3 areas: the Genting Snow Park venue cluster in the northern region, the Taizicheng Snow Town in the central region, and the Guyangshu venue cluster in the southern region. The concentrated venue clusters saved the cost of venue construction and provided great convenience for the Games operation.

云顶滑雪公园 [ZSP]
Zhangjiakou Genting Snow Park

云顶滑雪公园位于张家口云顶场馆群内，在北京冬奥会期间，承担除大跳台外的其他单板滑雪、自由式滑雪项目的比赛，产生20枚金牌；在冬残奥会期间承担残奥单板滑雪的比赛，产生8枚金牌。场馆充分利用滑雪场的现有设施：雪道、索道、酒店和市政配套设施，赛事运行的功能需求主要通过建设临时设施来实现。

1. 场馆基本情况

云顶场馆群位于狭长的山谷地带，整体落差达488m，场馆群封闭区域总占地面积357hm²，安保边界长度约16km，由入口区、酒店区、运行保障区、竞赛区组成。其中云顶滑雪公园主要使用除酒店区外的3个区域，建筑面积3.3万m²，其中临建2.65万m²，利用现有永久建筑0.69万m²。

2. FOP及相关区域

竞赛区由A、B、C 3个场地组成，设置障碍追逐、平行大回转、坡面障碍技巧、U型场地技巧、空中技巧和雪上技巧6条冬奥赛道，承担着冬奥会自由式滑雪和单板滑雪2个分项20个小项的比赛。6条赛道总长3184m，占地面积11.6m²，每2条赛道共用一个结束区，共计6个出发区、3个结束区。其中障碍追逐赛道长度为1260～1380m，落差164m；平行大回转赛道

Located within the Zhangjiakou Genting Cluster, the Zhangjiakou Genting Snow Park is responsible for hosting Snowboard and Freestyle Skiing events (excluding Big Air events) during the Beijing 2022 Olympic Winter Games, with 20 gold medals won here, and hosting Para Snowboard events during the Beijing 2022 Paralympic Winter Games, with 8 gold medals won here.

1. Venue Overview

The Genting Cluster is in a long and narrow valley area with an overall drop of 488m. The enclosed zone of the cluster covers a total of 357 hectares, and the secure perimeter has a length of about 16km, consisting of an entrance area, a hotel area, an operation support area, and the FOP. The competition venue, the Genting Snow Park, mainly occupies three areas other than the hotel area, with a floor area of 33,000m², including 26,500m² of overlays and 6,900m² of existing permanent buildings.

2. FOP and Relevant Areas

The FOP consists of Fields A, B and C that have six courses in place for Cross, Parallel Giant Slalom, Slopestyle, Halfpipe, Aerials and Moguls events and undertakes 20 events of the 2 disciplines of Freestyle Skiing and Snowboard of the Olympic Winter Games. The 6 courses have an overall length of 3,184m and cover an area

长度560m，落差153m；坡面障碍技巧赛道长度665m，落差181m；U型场地技巧赛道长度265m，落差84m；雪上技巧赛道长度250m，落差116m；空中技巧赛道长度123m，落差49m。竞赛区使用雪场现有的2条索道，同时为赛道区域新建1段吊椅缆车和4段拖牵缆车。

3. 场馆前院区及观众流线

云顶滑雪公园通过机动车道连接入口区及场馆内各个区域。除入口区和竞赛区的观众活动区域外，其他区域为后院区。观众在入口区经过安检后乘坐摆渡车在AB场地和C场地的前院站点落客，经由闭环外通道连接至3个场地的观众服务区，包含取暖、餐饮、卫生等功能，从观众服务区可通过楼梯上至观众看台，或通过无障碍升降梯到达无障碍席位。

4. 场馆后院及注册流线

云顶滑雪公园闭环外区域包括观众区、道路及摆渡车停车区域以及闭环外工作人员使用区域。闭环内区域包括运动员、奥运大家庭、媒体及闭环内工作人员的使用区域。

注册人员从入口区或云顶场馆群内驻地乘坐相应车辆到达运行保障区、媒体区以及3个场地，再步行连接至各功能空间或场地。考虑到转场需求，后院步行流线包含了3个场地之间的连接线路。

（1）运动员流线

运动员及随队官员由冬奥村乘坐班车到达云顶滑雪公园。在打蜡房站，运动员可进入打蜡房或使用索道连接至试蜡区及比赛场地。在AB场地和C场地2个站点，运动员可到达2处运动员休息室。从休息室通过专用通道可到达赛道使用的索道站点，上行至出发区，每条赛道的出发区均设置运动员取暖和热身的空间。比赛结束，运动员通过混采区后，可直接下滑至打蜡房，或返回运动员休息室乘车离场，或由专人专车送至场馆媒体中心的新闻发布厅参加新闻发布会。残奥会期间仅使用A场地的运动员设施，并增设轮椅假肢维修室。

（2）技术官员流线

技术官员乘车到达AB场地和C场地2个站点，分别连接至AB场地共用的NTO和ITO空间，以及C场地的相应空间。

（3）奥林匹克大家庭成员流线

奥林匹克大家庭成员乘坐专用车辆或合成班车到达3个场地的落客点，再步行至3个大家庭休息室。3个场地均设置144m²的休息室及随从用房、观赛平台等配套空间，休息室均位于二层或三层，有专用的无障碍电梯连通。

（4）媒体流线

转播及新闻媒体乘车到达转播综合区和场馆媒体中心站点。转播综合区包含3个平台，供OBS及其持权转播商使用；场馆媒体中心包含记者工作间、媒体休息区和新闻发布厅等用房。由此步行前往3个场地的媒体工作区，工作区包含赛道的摄影摄像点位、混采区、媒体坐席、评论员席等。

5. 场馆坐席

云顶滑雪公园场馆3个场地的总容量分别为1774、2550和1597。其中观众看台坐席容量为1235、1537和1239，媒体看台坐席容量为288、311和267。观赛运动员席位设在站席区。大家庭席位由于设置了观赛平台，仅在A场地看台上为国内贵宾保留60个注册坐席。

of 116,000m², with every two courses sharing a finish area, and a total of 6 start areas and 3 finish areas. The Cross course is 1,260-1,380m long, with a drop of 164m; the Parallel Giant Slalom course is 560m long, with a drop of 153m; the Slopestyle course is 665m long, with a drop of 181m; the Halfpipe course is 265m long, with a drop of 84m; the aerials course is 250m long, with a drop of 116m; and the Moguls course is 123m long, with a drop of 49m. The FOP uses the two existing cableways of the ski resort, with a new section of lift chairs and four new sections of T-bar lifts built for the course area.

3. Front of House and Spectator Flow

After passing through security checks in the entrance area, spectators take shuttle buses to get off at the Front of House (FOH) stations in Field A/B and Field C; then they go to the spectator service area that connects the 3 fields via passages outside the closed loop and has warming, food and beverage and public health related functions, and from the spectator service area, they can go to the spectator stands via the stairs or reach accessible seats via accessible lifts.

4. Back of House and Accreditation Flow

(1) Athlete Flow

Athletes and team officials take shuttle buses from the Olympic Village to the Genting Snow Park. From the wax cabin station, athletes can access the wax cabins or use the ropeways to reach the wax testing area and the FOP. From the two stations in Field A/B and Field C, athletes can reach two athlete lounges. From the lounges, athletes can reach the course cableway station via a dedicated passage to go up to the start areas with warming and warm-up spaces for athletes.

(2) Technical Official Flow

Technical officials take vehicles to the two stations in Field A/B and Field C, where they can go to the NTO and ITO space shared by Fields A/B and the corresponding space in Field C.

(3) Olympic Family Flow

Olympic Family members take dedicated vehicles or shared buses to the drop-off points of the 3 fields and then walk to the 3 Olympic Family lounges.

(4) Media Flow

Broadcast and media personnel take vehicles to the broadcast compound and Venue Media Centre station. The broadcast compound includes three platforms for OBS and other rights-holding broadcasters; the Venue Media Centre includes the press and photographer work rooms, media lounges, and press conference rooms. From the station, they can walk to the media work areas of the three fields, which include course photo/camera positions, mixed zones, press tribunes, and commentary positions.

5. Seating Area

The total capacity of the three fields of the Genting Snow Park is 1,774, 2,550, and 1,597, respectively. The seating capacity of spectator stands is 1,235, 1,537, and 1,239, respectively and that of media stands is 288, 311, and 267, respectively. Spectating athlete seats are in the standing area. As for the Olympic Family seats, owing to the provision of the spectating platforms, only 60 accredited seats are retained for domestic dignitaries in a stand in Field A.

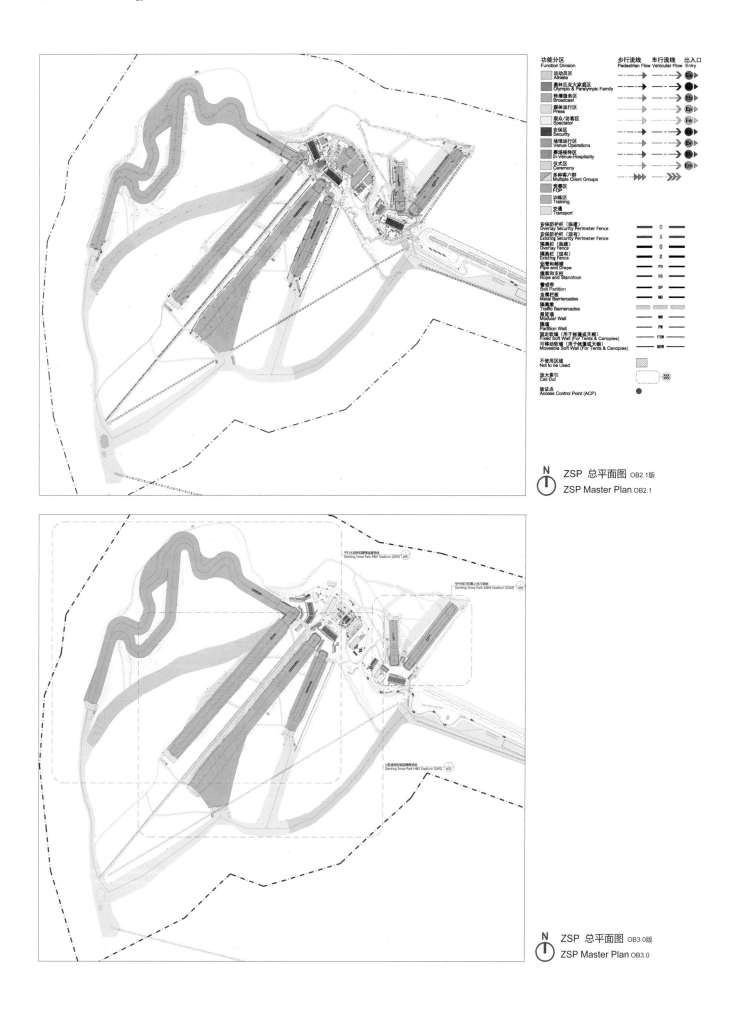

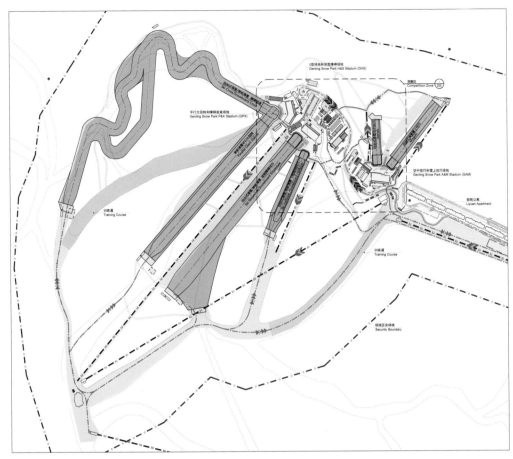

ZSP 总平面图 OB4.0版
ZSP Master Plan OB4.0

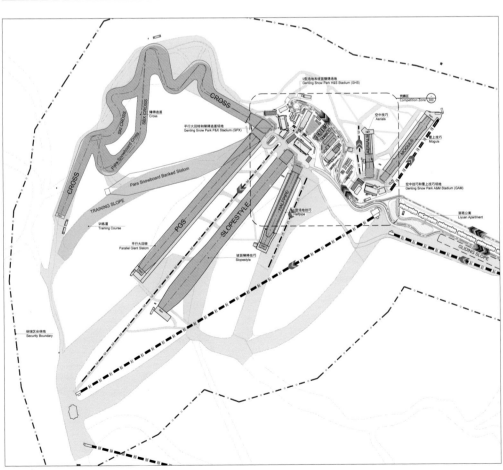

ZSP 总平面图 OB6.0版
ZSP Master Plan OB6.0

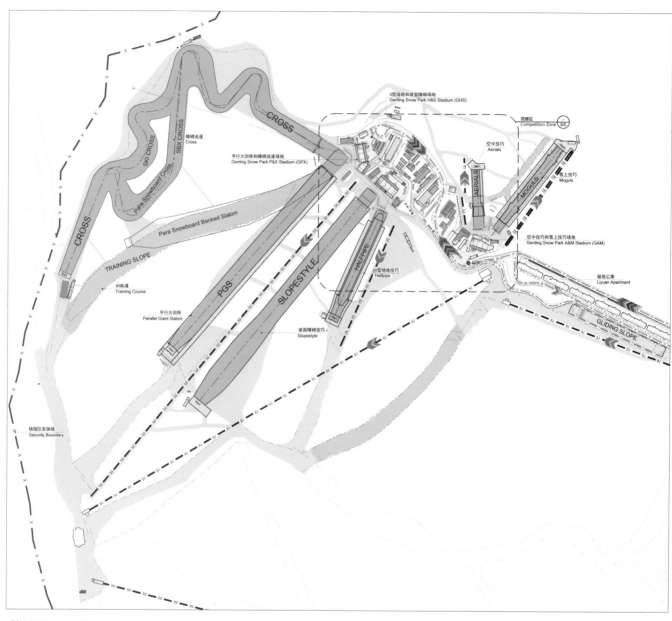

U型场地和坡面障碍场地
Genting Snow Park H&S Stadium (GHS)

竞赛区
Competition Zone 300

空中技巧
Aerials

平行大回转和障碍追逐场地
Genting Snow Park P&X Stadium (GPX)

AERIALS

MOGULS

雪上技巧
Moguls

障碍追逐
Cross

SKI CROSS

SBX CROSS

CROSS

Para Snowboard Cross

空中技巧和雪上技巧场地
Genting Snow Park A&M Stadium (GAM)

Para Snowboard Banked Slalom

CROSS

TRAINING SLOPE

ACP

丽苑公寓
Liyuan Apartment

训练道
Training Course

PGS

SLOPESTYLE

HALFPIPE

U型场地技巧
Halfpipe

GLIDING SLOPE

平行大回转
Parallel Giant Slalom

坡面障碍技巧
Slopestyle

场馆区安保线
Security Boundary

N ZSP 总平面图 OB7.0版
ZSP Master Plan OB7.0

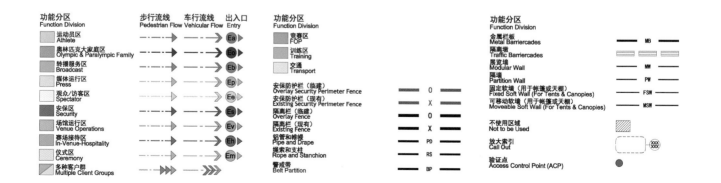

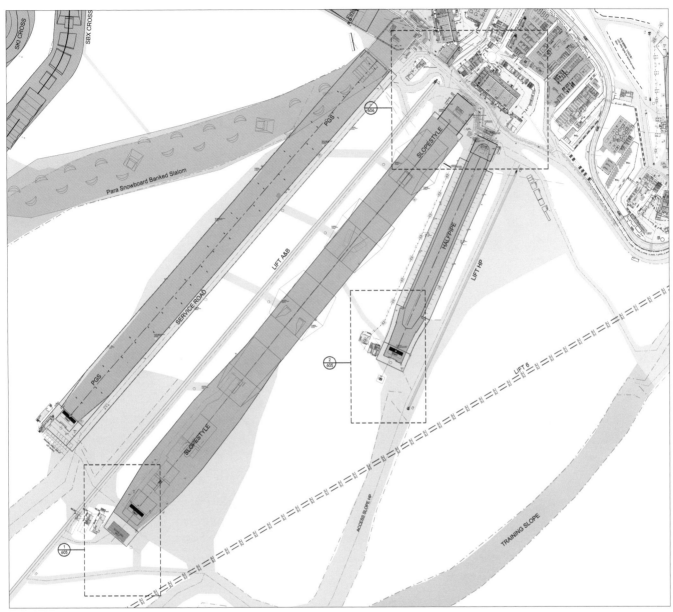

N

ZSP FOP A/B 放大平面图 OB7.0版
ZSP FOP A/B Enlarged Plan OB7.0

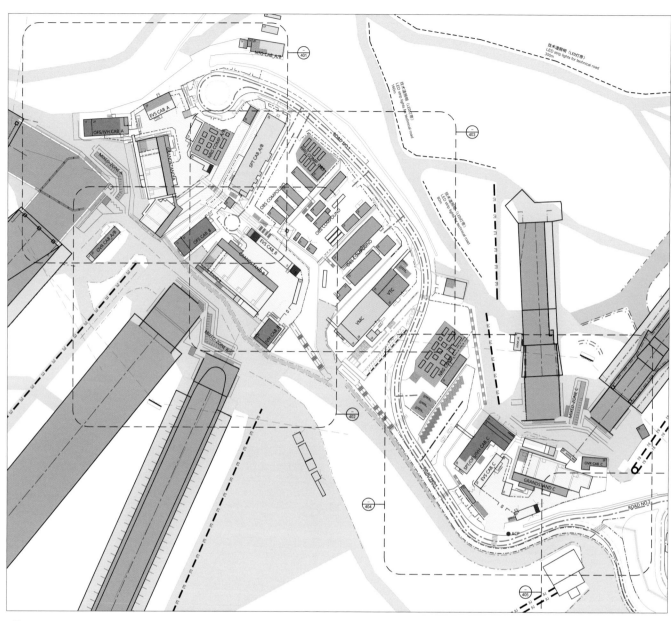

N

ZSP FOP A/B/C放大平面图 OB7.0版
ZSP FOP A/B/C Enlarged Plan OB7.0

功能分区 Function Division	步行流线 Pedestrian Flow	车行流线 Vehicular Flow	出入口 Entry	功能分区 Function Division		功能分区 Function Division	
运动员区 Athlete			Ea	竞赛区 FOP		金属栏板 Metal Barricades	MB
奥林匹克大家庭区 Olympic & Paralympic Family				训练区 Training		隔离墩 Traffic Barricades	
转播服务区 Broadcast			Eb	交通 Transport		展览墙 Modular Wall	MW
媒体运行区 Press			Ep			隔墙 Partition Wall	PW
观众/访客区 Spectator			Ee	安保防护栏（临建） Overlay Security Perimeter Fence	O	固定软墙（用于帐篷或天棚） Fixed Soft Wall (For Tents & Canopies)	FSW
安保区 Security				安保防护栏（现有） Existing Security Perimeter Fence	X	可移动软墙（用于帐篷或天棚） Moveable Soft Wall (For Tents & Canopies)	MSW
场馆运行区 Venue Operations			Ev	隔离栏（临建） Overlay Fence	O		
赛场接待区 In-Venue-Hospitality			Eih	隔离栏（现有） Existing Fence	X	不使用区域 Not to be Used	
仪式区 Ceremony			Em	铝管和帷幔 Pipe and Drape	PD	放大索引 Call Out	XXX
多种客户群 Multiple Client Groups				绳索和支柱 Rope and Stanchion	RS	验证点 Access Control Point (ACP)	●
				警戒带 Belt Partition	BP		

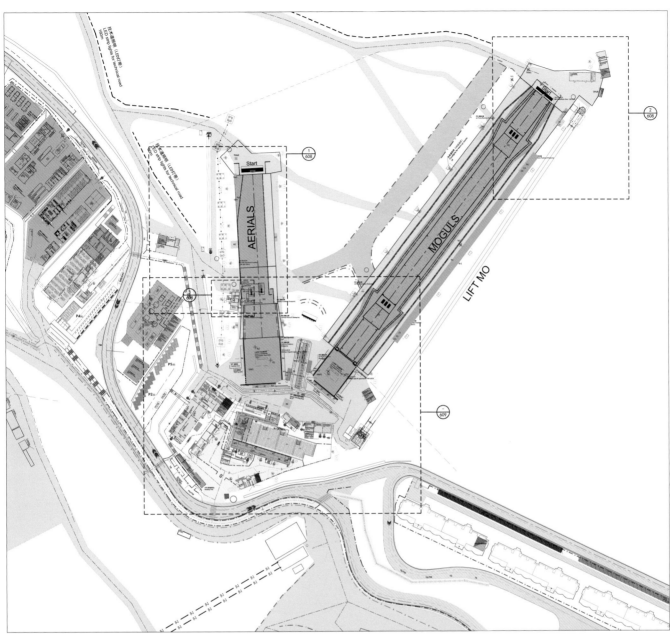

N

ZSP FOP C放大平面图 OB7.0版
ZSP FOP C Enlarged Plan OB7.0

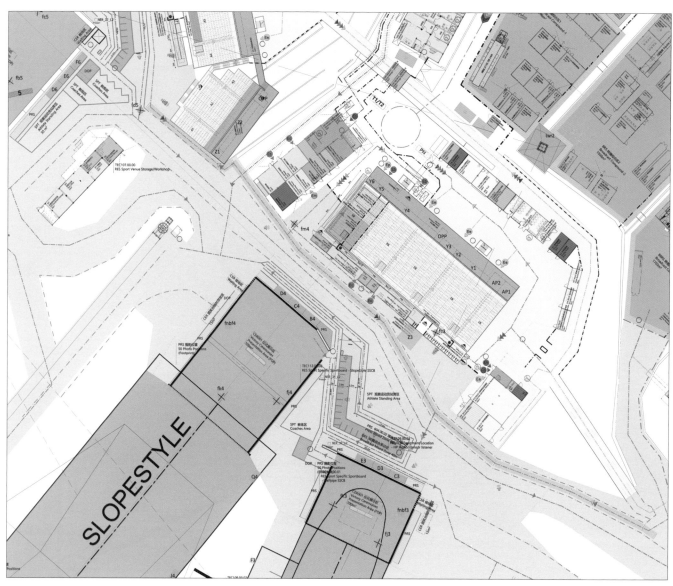

ZSP FOP 放大平面图 OB7.0版
ZSP FOP Enlarged Plan OB7.0

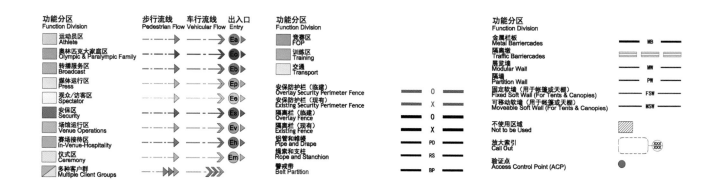

功能分区 Function Division	步行流线 Pedestrian Flow	车行流线 Vehicular Flow	出入口 Entry	功能分区 Function Division	功能分区 Function Division
运动员区 Athlete			Ea	竞赛区 FOP	金属栏板 Metal Barriercades
奥林匹克大家庭区 Olympic & Paralympic Family			Eo	训练区 Training	隔离墩 Traffic Barriercades
转播服务区 Broadcast			Eb	交通 Transport	展览墙 Modular Wall
媒体运行区 Press			Ep		隔墙 Partition Wall
观众/访客区 Spectator			Ee	安保防护栏（临建） Overlay Security Perimeter Fence	固定软墙（用于帐篷或天棚） Fixed Soft Wall (For Tents & Canopies)
安保区 Security			Es	安保防护栏（现有） Existing Security Perimeter Fence	可移动软墙（用于帐篷或天棚） Moveable Soft Wall (For Tents & Canopies)
场馆运行区 Venue Operations			Ev	隔离栏（临建） Overlay Fence	
赛场接待区 In-Venue-Hospitality			Eh	隔离栏（现有） Existing Fence	不使用区域 Not to be Used
仪式区 Ceremony			Em	铝管和帷幕 Pipe and Drape	放大索引 Call Out
多种客户群 Multiple Client Groups				绳索和支柱 Rope and Stanchion	验证点 Access Control Point (ACP)
				警戒带 Belt Partition	

	MB	
	MW	
O	PW	
X	FSW	
O	MSW	
X		
PD		
RS		
BP		

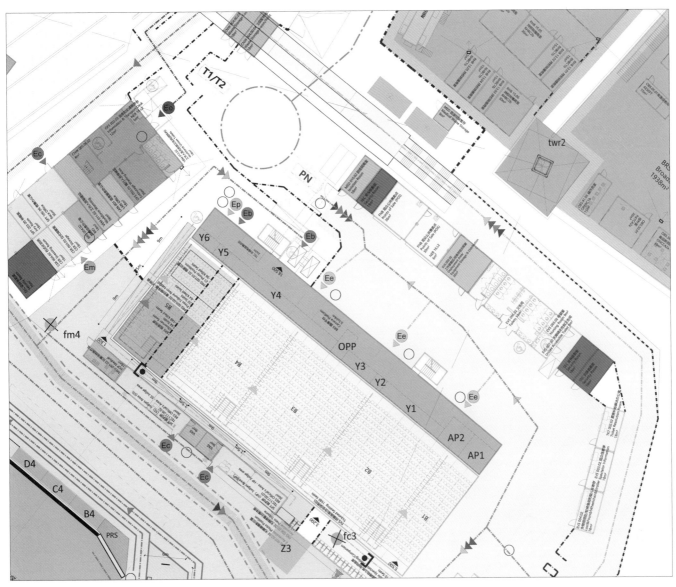

N ZSP 看台平面图一 OB7.0版
ZSP Enlarged Seat Plan 1 OB7.0

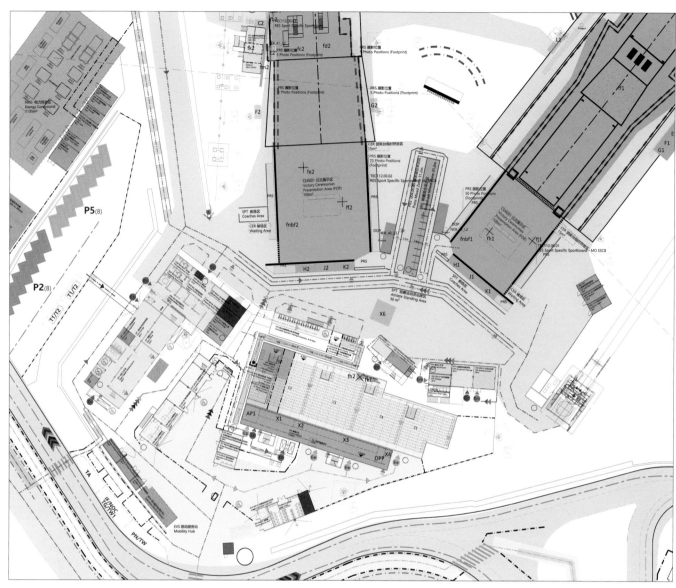

N

ZSP FOP C放大平面图 OB7.0版
ZSP FOP C Enlarged Plan OB7.0

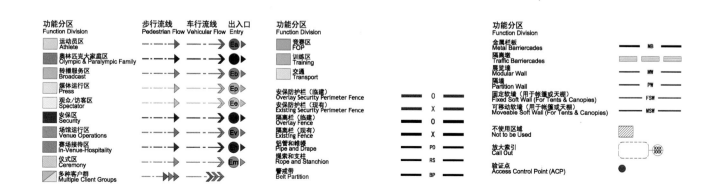

功能分区 Function Division	步行流线 Pedestrian Flow	车行流线 Vehicular Flow	出入口 Entry	功能分区 Function Division		功能分区 Function Division	
运动员区 Athlete			Ea	竞赛区 FOP		金属栏板 Metal Barriercades	MB
奥林匹克大家庭区 Olympic & Paralympic Family				训练区 Training		隔离栏 Traffic Barriercades	
转播服务区 Broadcast			Eb	交通 Transport		展览墙 Modular Wall	MW
媒体运行区 Press			Ep			隔墙 Partition Wall	PW
观众/访客区 Spectator			Ee	安保防护栏（临建） Overlay Security Perimeter Fence	0	固定软墙（用于帐篷或天棚） Fixed Soft Wall (For Tents & Canopies)	FSW
安保区 Security				安保防护栏（现有） Existing Security Perimeter Fence	X	可移动软墙（用于帐篷或天棚） Moveable Soft Wall (For Tents & Canopies)	MSW
场馆运行区 Venue Operations			Ev	隔离栏（临建） Overlay Fence	0		
赛事接待区 In-Venue-Hospitality			Eh	隔离栏（现有） Existing Fence	X	不使用区域 Not to be Used	
仪式区 Ceremony			Em	铝管和帷幕 Pipe and Drape	PD	放大索引 Call Out	XXX
多种客户群 Multiple Client Groups				提索和支柱 Rope and Stanchion	RS		
				警戒带 Belt Partition	BP	验证点 Access Control Point (ACP)	●

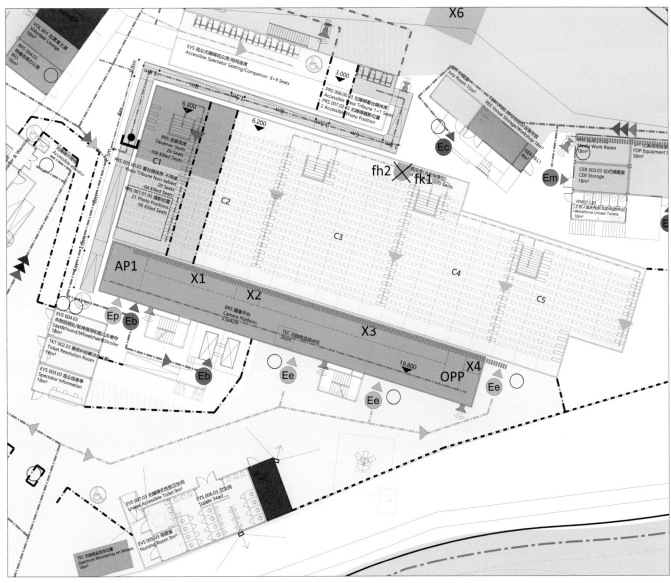

ZSP 看台平面图二 OB7.0版
ZSP FOP Seat Plan 2 OB7.0

清华院 提供
Provide by THAD

清华院 提供
Provide by THAD

场馆业主 提供
Provide by Vunue Owner

清华院 提供
Provide by THAD

张家口山地新闻中心 [ZPC]

Zhangjiakou Mountain Press Centre

张家口山地新闻中心位于张家口云顶场馆群内，利用现有的云顶大酒店会议室、宴会厅、雪具大厅改造而成。在北京2022年冬奥会和冬残奥会期间，张家口山地新闻中心为张家口赛区的文字记者和摄影记者提供集中的工作区域，包括记者工作大厅、新闻发布厅、认证通讯社空间和会议区，以及服务于这些功能的技术、餐饮、商业、物流、安保和医疗等配套设施，赛时场馆使用的总建筑面积约1.3万m²。

Located within the Zhangjiakou Genting Cluster, the Zhangjiakou Mountain Press Centre is renovated from the existing conference room, banquet room and ski equipment hall of Genting Grand. During the Beijing 2022 Olympic and Paralympic Winter Games, the Zhangjiakou Mountain Press Centre serves as a work area of press journalists and photographers in the Zhangjiakou Zone, including a press working hall, a press conference room, accredited agencies spaces, and a conference area as well as supporting facilities for technology, food and beverage, commerce, logistics, security and medical services, with a total floor area of about 13,000m² used during the Games.

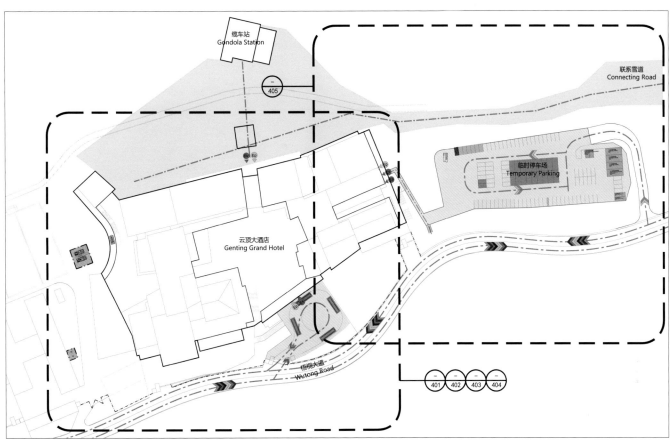

 ZSP 总平面图 OB7.0版
ZSP Master Plan OB7.0

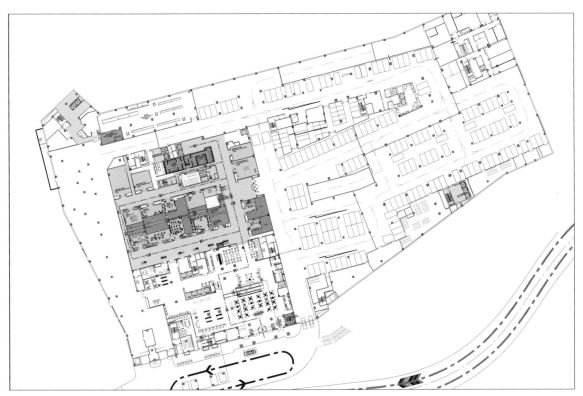

N ZSP 一层平面图 OB7.0版
ZSP 1F Plan OB7.0

◐N ZSP 二层平面图 OB7.0版
ZSP 2F Plan OB7.0

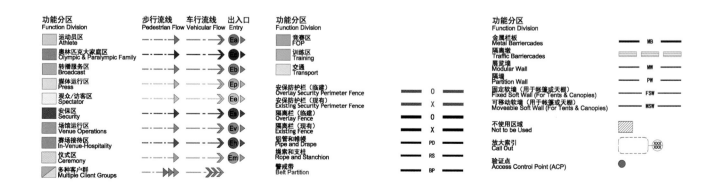

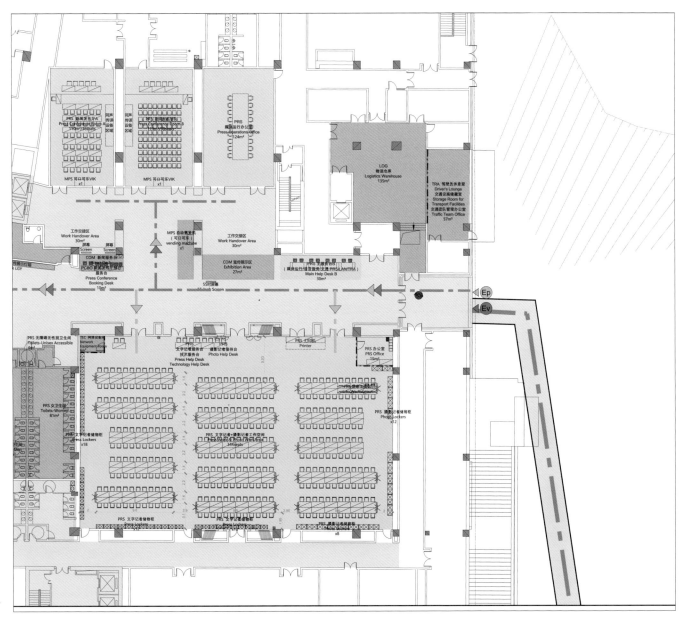

ZSP 二层放大平面图一 OB7.0版
ZSP 2F Enlarged Plan 1 OB7.0

ZSP 二层放大平面图二 OB7.0版
ZSP 2F Enlarged Plan 2 OB7.0

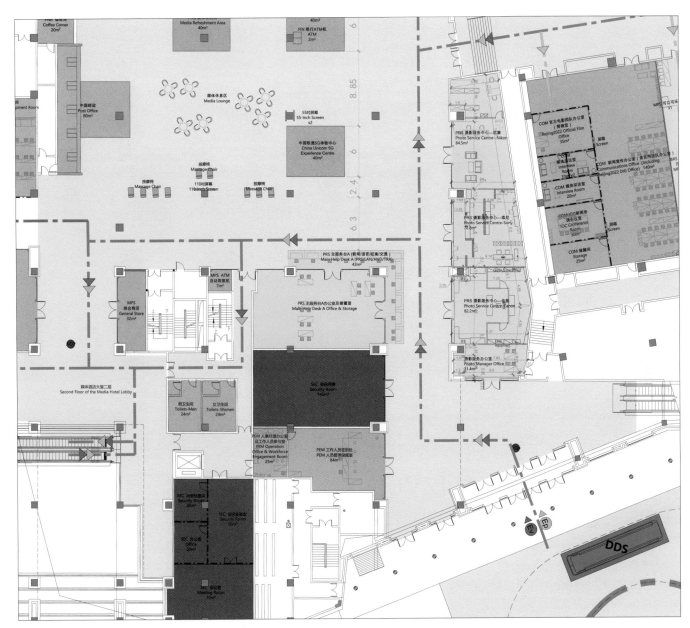

ZSP 二层放大平面图三 OB7.0版
ZSP 2F Enlarged Plan 3 OB7.0

张家口冬奥村/冬残奥村 [ZVL]

Zhangjiakou Olympic/Paralympic Village

张家口冬奥村/冬残奥村位于张家口市崇礼区太子城冰雪小镇，在2022年北京冬奥会和冬残奥会期间，是张家口赛区各国家和地区运动员、教练员及代表团成员的主要居住地，也是各国和地区运动员举行国际交流和休闲活动的场所。

张家口冬奥村/冬残奥村采用院落式布局，内部设置微地形景观。张家口冬奥村/冬残奥村占地19.7hm²，总建筑面积约23.8万m²，共10个组团，31栋楼，以3~4层建筑为主。冬奥会期间可提供1730个房间，2640个床位，冬残奥会期间可提供700个房间，1100个床位。

1. 居住区及流线

居住区包括公寓楼、综合服务中心、综合诊所、兴奋剂检查站、运动员餐厅及班车站等。冬奥会期间全部公寓楼都投入使用，冬残奥会期间北区2、3、4、5号院公寓楼投入使用。运动员入村首先抵达代表团接待中心，经安检及办理入住手续后可直接进入居住区。运动员入住期间在位于居住区东北侧的班车站乘坐各路班车往返各场馆。NOC/NPC车辆在代表团接待中心前设上落客位。居住区工作人员从4、5号院北侧出入口进入地下车库，经地下通道到达各楼宇工作地点。工作车辆从2、3号院北侧出入口进出居住区。

Located in Taizicheng Snow Town, Chongli District, Zhangjiakou City, the Zhangjiakou Olympic/Paralympic Village is the main residence for NOC/NPC athletes, coaches and members in the Zhangjiakou Zone during the Beijing 2022 Olympic and Paralympic Winter Games, and a place for athletes from across the world to have cultural exchanges and leisure activities.

The Zhangjiakou Olympic/Paralympic Village is in a courtyard layout and with landscape elements designed. The Zhangjiakou Olympic/ Paralympic Village covers an area of 19.7 hectares. It has a total floor area of about 238,000m² and a total of 31 buildings (mainly three to four floors) in 10 clusters. A total of 1,730 rooms with 2,640 beds and 700 rooms with 1,100 beds are available during the Olympic Winter Games and the Paralympic Winter Games, respectively.

1. Residential Zone and Flow

The Residential Zone includes the apartment buildings, comprehensive services centre, polyclinic, doping control station, athletes' dining hall, and transport stations. All the apartment buildings are used during the Olympic Winter Games, while apartment buildings in Courtyards 2, 3, 4 and 5 in the north area are used during the Paralympic Winter Games. After entering the Village, athletes first arrive at the Team Processing Centre and can directly enter the Residential Zone after going through security

2. 广场区及流线

广场区包括主入口广场及下沉广场，位于奥运村中心公共区，设有访客中心、媒体中心、混合采访区、奥林匹克大家庭休息室、村长室、冬奥特许商店、发廊、花店、银行、邮局及轮椅假肢维修中心等。访客、媒体及奥林匹克大家庭成员经访客中心进出广场区。广场区与居住区之间设分区围栏，在下沉广场东西两侧分区围栏处设区域控制点，方便居住区运动员进入广场区。

3. 运行区及流线

运行区包括物流、餐饮、电力、清废、安保、交通等综合区，以及员工餐厅、值机柜台前移等区域，主要位于奥运村东侧备用场地。运行区工作人员及车辆经奥运村东路南侧人车同检篷进出运行区。居住区运动员通过班车站南侧区域控制点可前往值机柜台前移区办理归国航班值机及行李托运。

4. 注册分区及防疫分区

奥运村注册分区主要划定居住区（R区）。

防疫分区根据不同人群活动范围进行划分，分为闭环内区域及闭环外区域，两区域独立运行管理。闭环内区域主要为运动员、访客、媒体及相关工作人员活动区域，包含居住区、广场区及运行区内的NOC/NPC停车场、访客停车场、值机柜台前移等区域。闭环外区域主要为非直接接触闭环内人员的其他人员工作区域，主要为运行区内的物流、餐饮、电力、清废、安保等综合区。闭环内及闭环外交界区域设一处物品交换区，位于9号院1号楼南侧，设一处人员交换区，位于7号院2号楼东侧。

checks and checking in. During their stay, athletes can take shuttle buses at the transport mall in the northeast of the Residential Zone to travel between the Village and the venues. There are load zones for NOC/NPC vehicles in front of the Team Processing Centre. The Residential Zone workforce access underground garages from the north entrance/exit of Courtyards 4 and 5 and then reach their workplaces in the buildings via underground passages. Work vehicles access the Residential Zone from the north entrance/exit of Courtyards 2 and 3.

2. Plaza and Flow

The Plaza includes the main entrance plaza and sunken plaza in the central public area of the Village, and there is a Guest Pass Centre, a Media Centre, a mixed zone, an Olympic Family lounge, a Village Mayor office, a Beijing 2022 Licensed Product Official Store, a hair salon, a florist, a bank, a post office, and an orthotic, prosthetic and wheelchair repair centre. Guests, media, and Olympic Family members access the Plaza via the Guest Pass Centre. There are fences between the Plaza and the Residential Zone on the east and west sides of the sunken plaza, with Zone Control Points in place to facilitate athletes from the Residential Zone to access the Plaza.

3. Operational Zone and Flow

Mainly located on a standby site in the east of the Village, the Operational Zone includes logistics, food and beverage, energy, cleaning and waste, security and transport compounds as well as the workforce dining hall and off-airport processing (OAP) area. The Operational Zone workforce and vehicles access the Operational Zone via the pedestrian and vehicle screening tent to the south of Aoyuncun East Road. Residential Zone athletes can process flight check-in and baggage check-in for their departure in the OAP area that can be accessed from the Zone Control Point to the south of the transport mall.

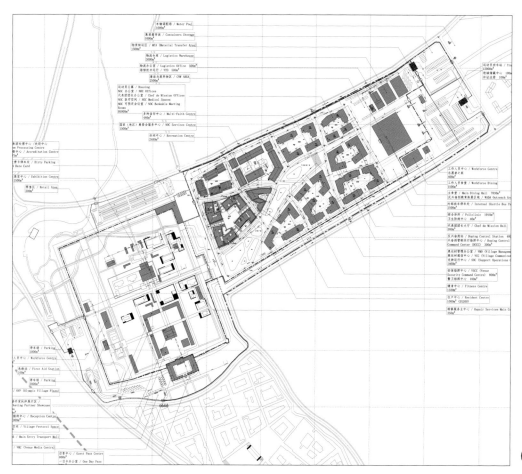

车辆调度库 / Motor Pool
1000m²

集装箱堆放 / Containers Storage
1000m²

物资转运区 / WADA (Material Transfer Area)
1500m²

物流仓库 / Logistics Warehouse
3000m²

物流办公室 / Logistics Office 100m²
验情技术用房 / YTD 100m²

清运与废弃物设区 / CNW AREA
2500m²

运动员公寓 / Housing
NOC 办公室 / NOC Offices
代表团团长办公室 / Chef de Mission Offices
NOC 医疗空间 / NOC Medical Spaces
NOC 可预约会议室 / NOC Bookable Meeting
Rooms
30000m²

多种信仰中心 / Multi-Faith Centre
140m²

国家（地区）奥委会服务中心 / NOC Services Centre
1500m²

休闲中心 / Recreation Centre
2400m²

运动员停车场 / Tran
12000m²
检录缓冲中心 / 100m
许注证室 100m²

热情处理中心 / 欢迎中心
tion Processing Centre
注册中心 / Accreditation Centre
1 Rate Card

脏车停车区 / Dirty Parking

展览室 / Exhibition Centre
1500m²

零售区 / Retail Area
2000m²

工作人员中心 / Workforce Centre
志愿者之家 / Wo
600m²

工作人员餐饮 / Workforce Dining

主餐厅 / Main Dining Hall 7850m²
反兴奋剂教育展览区域 / WADA Outreach Ar
内部班车停车场 / Internal Shuttle Bus Pa
1500m²

综合诊所 / Policlinic 1910m²
卫生防疫站 / 40m²

代表团团长大厅 / Chef de Mission Hall
800m²

反兴奋剂站 / Doping Control Station 40
兴奋剂管制指挥中心 / Doping Control
Command Center (DCCC) 200m²

奥运村管理办公室 / VMO (Village Managem
奥运村通信中心 / VCC (Village Communic
支持运行中心 / SOC (Support Operations C
1800m²

安保指挥中心 / VSCC (Venue
Security Command Centre) 800m²
警卫指挥室 / 100m²

健身中心 / Fitness Centre
1300m²

住户中心 / Resident Centre
1000m² (G&200)

维修服务主中心 / Repair Services Main Ce
350m²

人员中心 / Workforce Centre

急救站 / First Aid Station
100m²

停车场 / Parking
1000m²

OAV Olinmpic Village Plaza)

市场开发展示区
Marketing Partner Showcase

接待中心 / Reception Centre

礼宾 / Village Protocol Space

主入口 / Main Entry Transport Mall

VMC (Venue Media Centre)

访客证件中心 / Guest Pass Centre
800m²
一日卡办证室 / One Day Pass

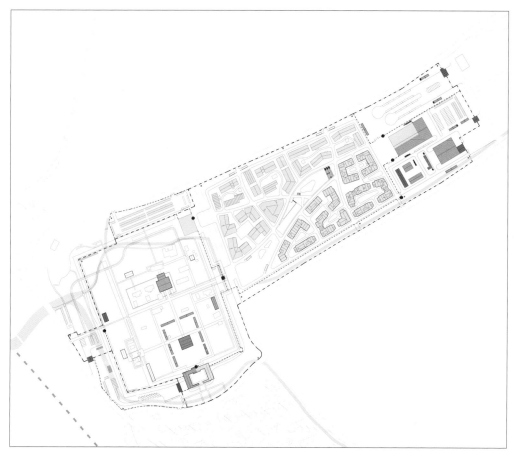

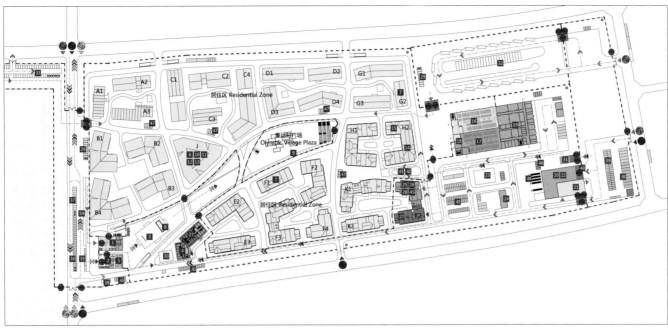

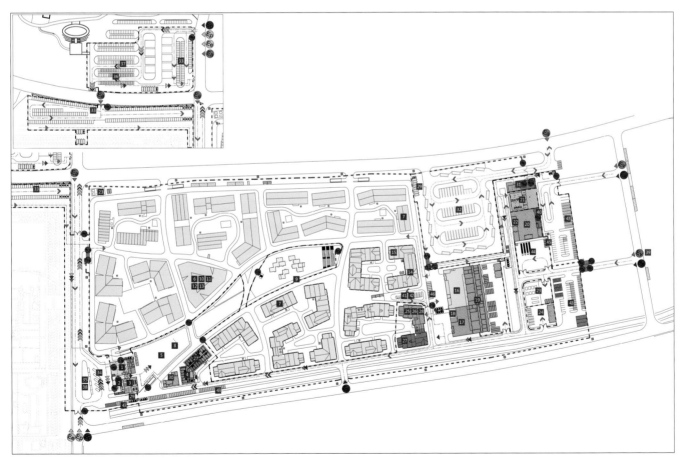

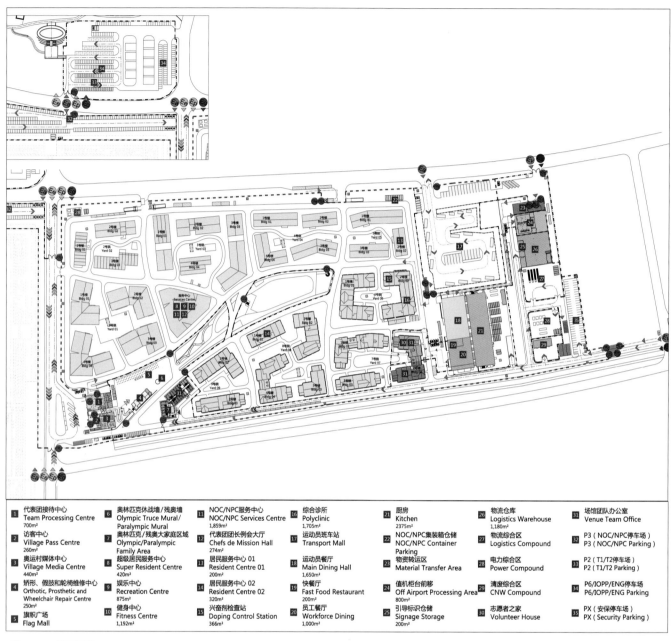

1 代表团接待中心 Team Processing Centre 700m²	**6** 奥林匹克休战墙/残奥墙 Olympic Truce Mural/ Paralympic Mural	**11** NOC/NPC服务中心 NOC/NPC Services Centre 1,859m²	**16** 综合诊所 Polyclinic 1,705m²	**21** 厨房 Kitchen 2375m²	**26** 物流仓库 Logistics Warehouse 1,180m²	**31** 场馆团队办公室 Venue Team Office
2 访客中心 Village Pass Centre 260m²	**7** 奥林匹克/残奥大家庭区域 Olympic/Paralympic Family Area	**12** 代表团团长例会大厅 Chefs de Mission Hall 274m²	**17** 运动员班车站 Transport Mall	**22** NOC/NPC集装箱仓储 NOC/NPC Container Parking	**27** 物流综合区 Logistics Compound	**32** P3（NOC/NPC停车场） P3（NOC/NPC Parking）
3 奥运村媒体中心 Village Media Centre 440m²	**8** 超级居民服务中心 Super Resident Centre 420m²	**13** 居民服务中心 01 Resident Centre 01 200m²	**18** 运动员餐厅 Main Dining Hall 1,650m²	**23** 物资转运区 Material Transfer Area	**28** 电力综合区 Power Compound	**33** P2（T1/T2停车场） P2（T1/T2 Parking）
4 矫形、假肢和轮椅维修中心 Orthotic, Prosthetic and Wheelchair Repair Centre 250m²	**9** 娱乐中心 Recreation Centre 875m²	**14** 居民服务中心 02 Resident Centre 02 320m²	**19** 快餐厅 Fast Food Restaurant 200m²	**24** 值机柜台前移 Off Airport Processing Area 800m²	**29** 清废综合区 CNW Compound	**34** P6/IOPP/ENG停车场 P6/IOPP/ENG Parking
5 旗帜广场 Flag Mall	**10** 健身中心 Fitness Centre 1,192m²	**15** 兴奋剂检查站 Doping Control Station 366m²	**20** 员工餐厅 Workforce Dining 1,000m²	**25** 引导标识仓储 Signage Storage 200m²	**30** 志愿者之家 Volunteer House	**35** PX（安保停车场） PX（Security Parking）

N ZVL 总平面图 OB7.0版
ZVL Master Plan OB7.0

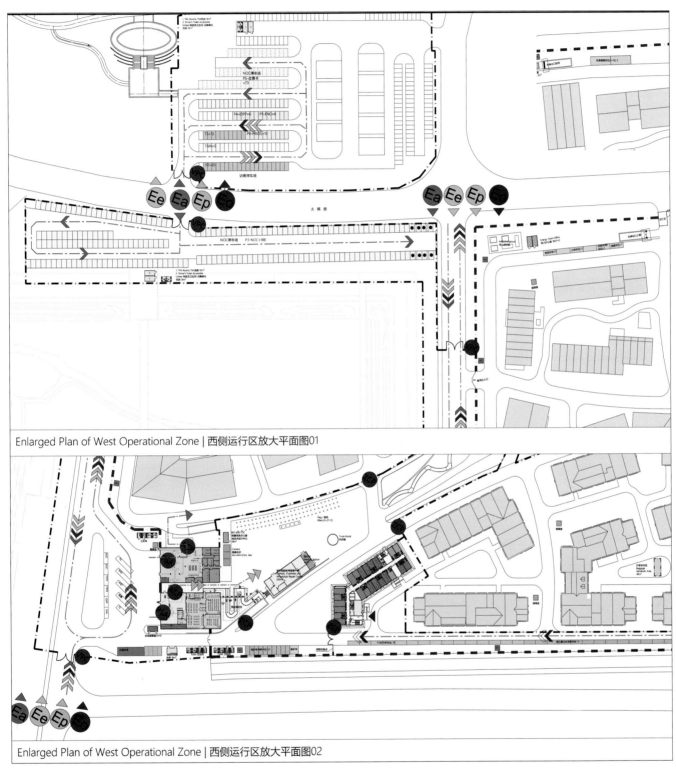

Enlarged Plan of West Operational Zone | 西侧运行区放大平面图01

Enlarged Plan of West Operational Zone | 西侧运行区放大平面图02

N ZVL运行区放大平面图一 OB7.0版
ZVL Operation Zone Enlarged Plan 1 OB7.0

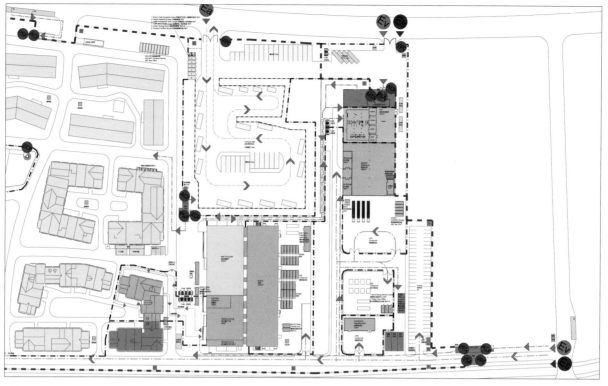

N ZVL 运行区放大平面图二 OB7.0版
ZVL Operation Zone Enlarged Plan 2 OB7.0

N ZVL 广场区放大平面图 OB7.0版
ZVL Olympic Village Plaza Enlarged Plan OB7.0

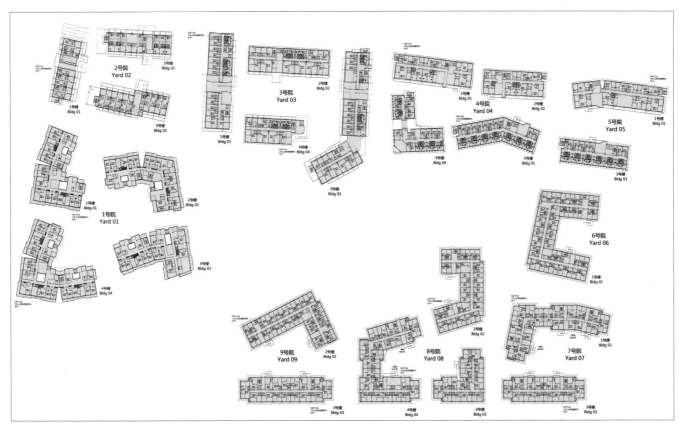

N ZVL 居住区放大平面图 OB7.0版
ZVL Residential Zone Enlarged Plan OB7.0

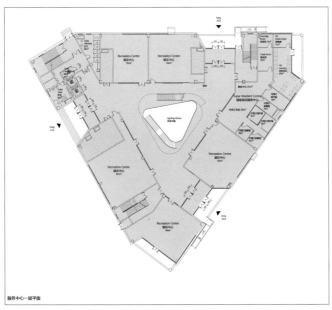

N ZVL 娱乐中心一层平面图 OB7.0版
ZVL Entertainment Building 1F Plan OB7.0

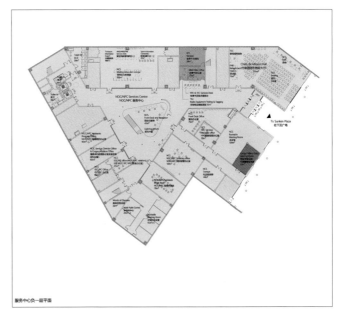

N ZVL 娱乐中心二层平面图 OB7.0版
ZVL Entertainment Building 2F Plan OB7.0

清华院 提供
Provide by THAD

张家口颁奖广场 [ZMP]

Zhangjiakou Medals Plaza

张家口颁奖广场位于张家口市崇礼区太子城冰雪小镇的中心广场，在北京2022年冬奥会和冬残奥会期间，承担张家口赛区比赛项目的颁奖任务。

场馆分为前院区及后院区：前院区主要为颁奖仪式所用，包含颁奖舞台、升旗区、转播服务区及观众区等；后院区主要包括工作人员办公区，运动员候场室，奥林匹克大家庭休息室，志愿者之家，安保和技术设备用房，工作人员餐厅等。场馆占地约1.9万m²。

Located in the central square of Taizicheng Snow Town, Chongli District, Zhangjiakou City, the Zhangjiakou Medals Plaza is responsible for hosting the victory ceremonies of competition events in the Zhangjiakou Zone during the Beijing 2022 Olympic and Paralympic Winter Games.

The venue is divided into the Front of House (FOH) and the Back of House (BOH). The FOH is mainly used for victory ceremonies, including a victory ceremony stage, a flag-raising area, a broadcast service area, and a spectator area; the BOH mainly includes a workforce office area, a green room, an Olympic Family lounge, a volunteers' house, a security and technology equipment room, and a workforce dining hall. The venue covers an area of about 19,000m².

N
ZMP 总平面图 OB6.0版
ZMP Master Plan OB6.0

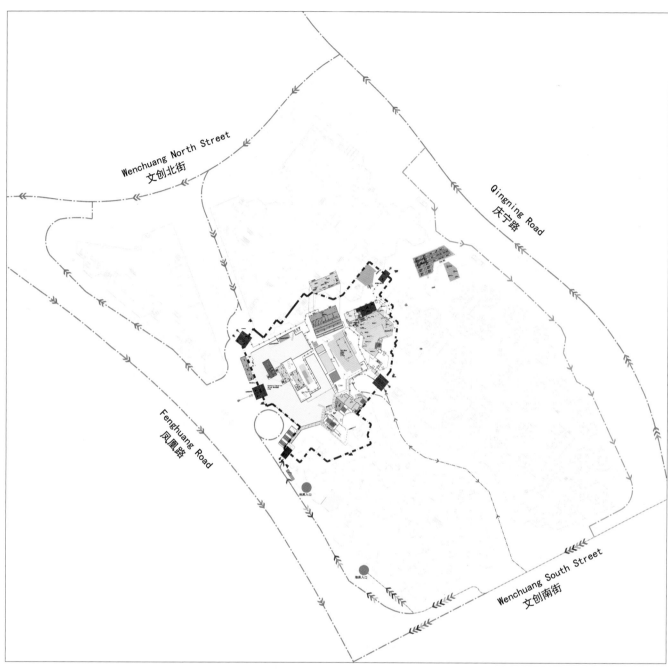

ZMP 总平面图 OB7.0版
ZMP Master Plan OB7.0

颁奖广场地上范围线

小轿车流线

ZMP 地下一层平面图 OB7.0版
ZMP B1 Plan OB7.0

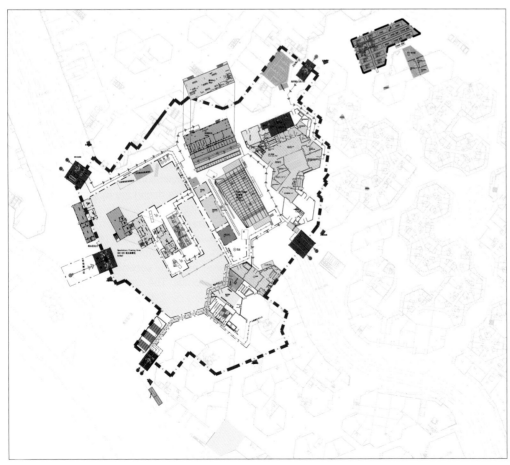

ZMP 一层平面图 OB7.0版
ZMP 1F Plan OB7.0

张家口制服及注册分中心 [ZUA]

Zhangjiakou Uniform Distribution and Accreditation Centre

　　张家口制服和注册分中心位于崇礼太子城冰雪小镇的会展中心内，在北京2022年冬奥会和冬残奥会期间主要承担张家口赛区注册人员身份注册卡的制作核发及工作人员、志愿者、技术官员制服流转发放等工作任务。

　　张家口制服和注册分中心首层为注册、制服及交通服务的对外公共区，以及志愿者、物流及技术工作区，二层及三层为办公区及安保用房，场馆面积约1.8万m²。

Located within the conference and exhibition centre of Taizicheng Snow Town, Chongli, the Zhangjiakou Uniform Distribution and Accreditation Centre is mainly responsible for the production and issuance of OIACs/PIACs of accredited persons in the Zhangjiakou Zone and the transfer and distribution of uniforms for workforce, volunteers and technical officials during the Beijing 2022 Olympic and Paralympic Winter Games.

The first floor of the Zhangjiakou Uniform Distribution and Accreditation Centre includes a public area to provide accreditation, uniform and transport services, and volunteer, logistics and technology work areas, and the second and third floors are office areas and security rooms. The venue has an area of about 18,000m².

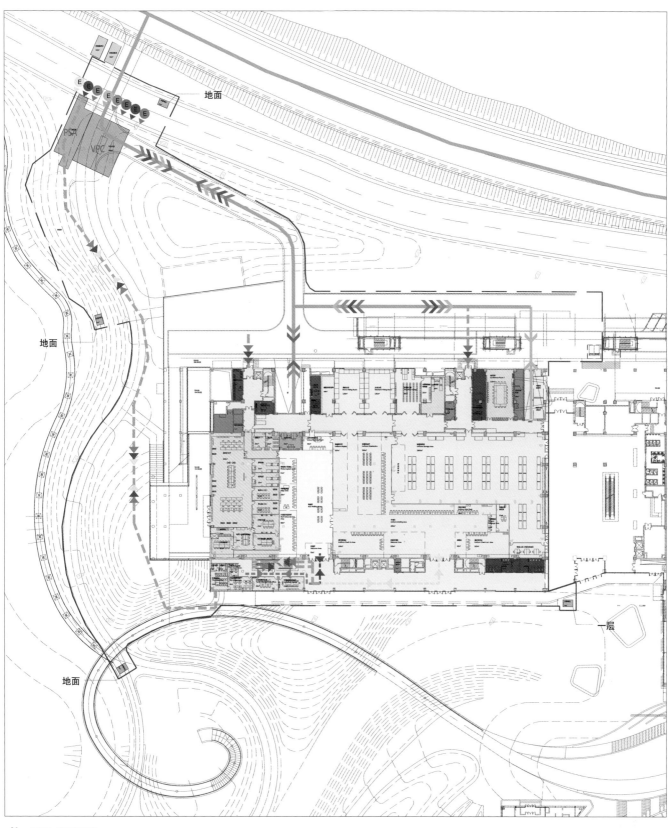

地面

地面

地面

PSA

VPC

一层

N ZUA 总平面图 OB7.0版
ZUA Master Plan OB7.0

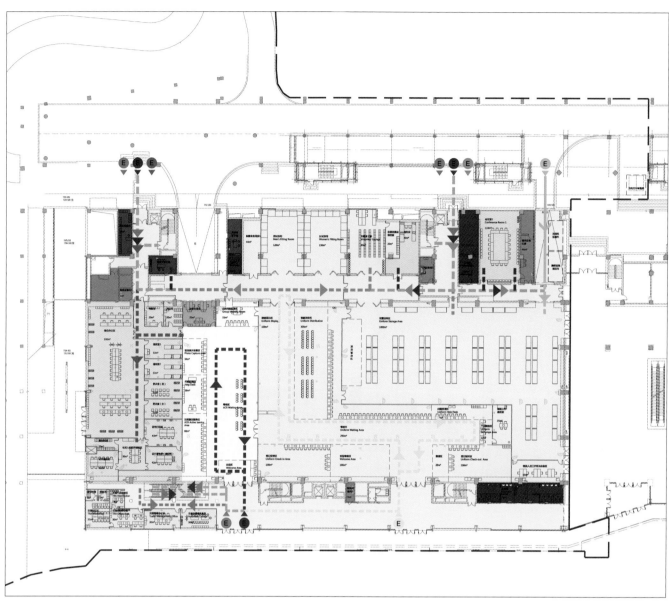

N ZUA 一层平面图 OB7.0版
ZUA 1F Plan OB7.0

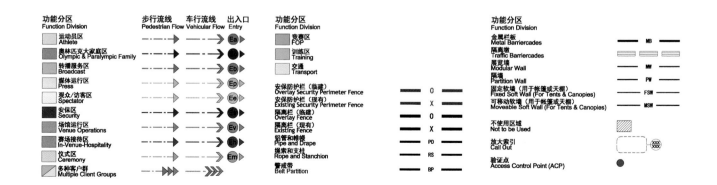

功能分区 Function Division	步行流线 Pedestrian Flow	车行流线 Vehicular Flow	出入口 Entry	功能分区 Function Division	功能分区 Function Division
运动员区 Athlete			Ea	竞赛区 FOP	金属栏板 Metal Barriercades
奥林匹克大家庭区 Olympic & Paralympic Family				训练区 Training	隔离墩 Traffic Barriercades
转播服务区 Broadcast			Eb	交通 Transport	展览墙 Modular Wall
媒体运行区 Press			Ep		隔墙 Partition Wall
观众/访客区 Spectator			Ee	安保防护栏（临建） Overlay Security Perimeter Fence	固定软墙（用于帐篷或天棚） Fixed Soft Wall (For Tents & Canopies)
安保区 Security				安保防护栏（现有） Existing Security Perimeter Fence	可移动软墙（用于帐篷或天棚） Moveable Soft Wall (For Tents & Canopies)
场馆运行区 Venue Operations			Ev	隔离栏（临建） Overlay Fence	不使用区域 Not to be Used
赛后接待区 In-Venue-Hospitality			Eh	隔离栏（现有） Existing Fence	放大索引 Call Out
仪式区 Ceremony			Em	铝管和维幔 Pipe and Drape	验证点 Access Control Point (ACP)
多种客户群 Multiple Client Groups				绳索和支柱 Rope and Stanchion	
				警戒带 Belt Partition	

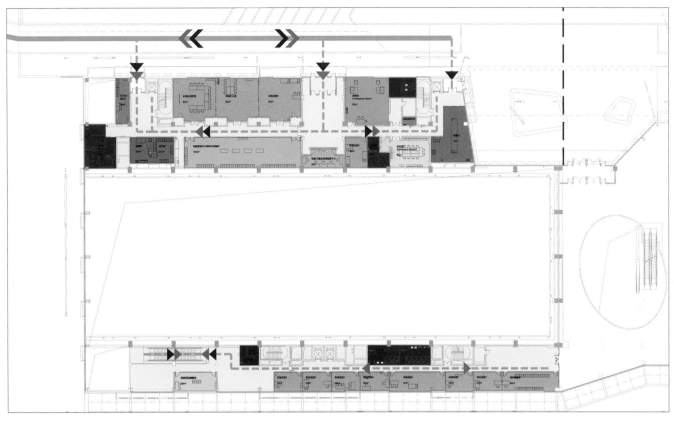

N ZUA 二层平面图 OB7.0版
ZUA 2F Plan OB7.0

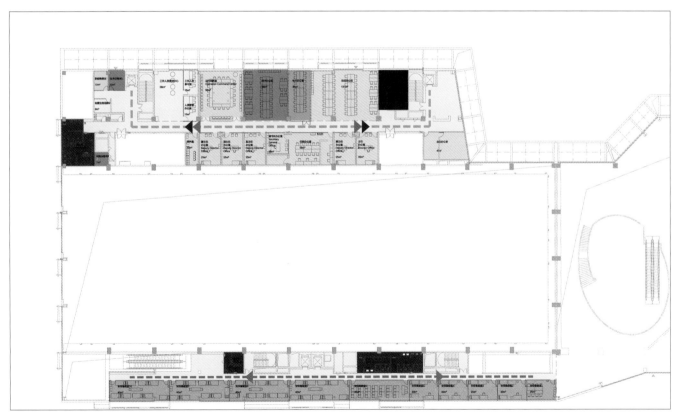

N ZUA 三层平面图 OB7.0版
ZUA 3F Plan OB7.0

张家口古杨树场馆群公共区

Zhangjiakou Guyangshu Cluster Public Area

张家口古杨树场馆群公共区位于张家口市崇礼区古杨树区域，距离太子城高铁站2.3km，距离京礼高速棋盘梁高速口2km。场馆群主要包括国家跳台滑雪中心、国家冬季两项中心、国家越野滑雪中心3个新建竞赛场馆，张家口山地转播中心1个非竞赛场馆，以及两处酒店设施。

公共区内建设了一个长约3km的弧形通道"冰玉环"，将各个场馆连接起来，通道西半环为功能区，上层为观众通道，地面层为赛事运行工作区，赛后可作为张家口崇礼奥林匹克公园附属配套设施。

Located within Guyangshu, Chongli District, Zhangjiakou City, the Zhangjiakou Guyangshu Cluster Public Area ("Public Area") is 2.3km from Taizicheng High-speed Railway Station and 2km from the Qipanliang Entry of the Beijing-Chongli Expressway. The Guyangshu Cluster mainly includes 3 new competition venues, i.e., the National Ski Jumping Centre, the National Biathlon Centre, and the National Cross-Country Skiing Centre, one non-competition venue, i.e., the Zhangjiakou Mountain Broadcast Centre, and 2 hotel facilities.

A curved passage of about 3km long has been built in the Public Area, called the Ice Jade Ring, which connects all the venues. The west half ring is a functional zone, with the upper level being the spectator passage and the ground level being the Games operations area. The Ice Jade Ring can be used as a supporting facility of the Zhangjiakou-Chongli Olympic Park after the Games.

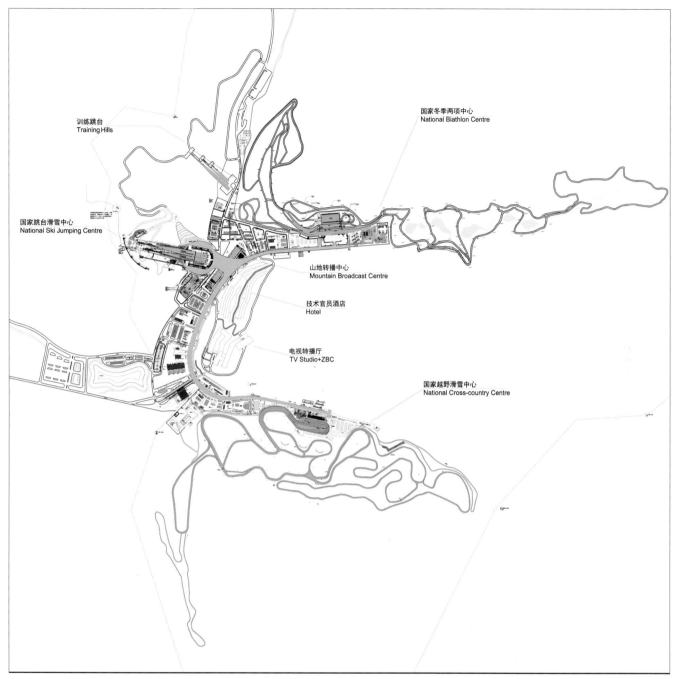

训练跳台
Training Hills

国家冬季两项中心
National Biathlon Centre

国家跳台滑雪中心
National Ski Jumping Centre

山地转播中心
Mountain Broadcast Centre

技术官员酒店
Hotel

电视转播厅
TV Studio+ZBC

国家越野滑雪中心
National Cross-country Centre

N 张家口古杨树场馆群公共区总平面图 OB7.0版
Guyangshu Cluster Public Area Master Plan OB7.0

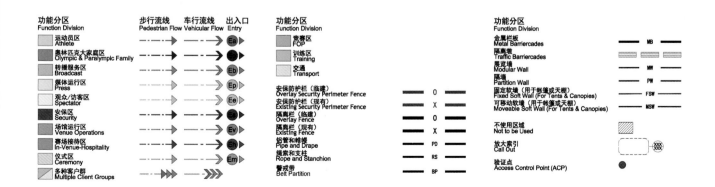

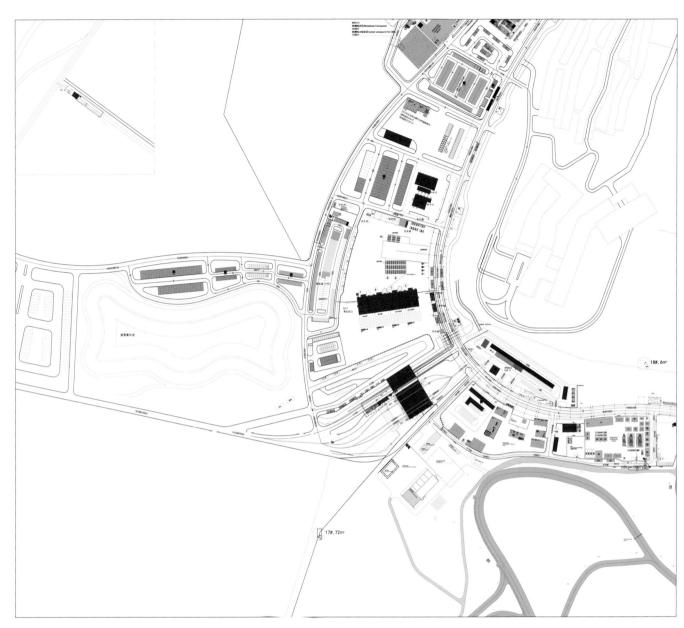

N

张家口古杨树场馆群公共区放大平面图 OB7.0版
Guyangshu Cluster Public Area Enlarged Plan OB7.0

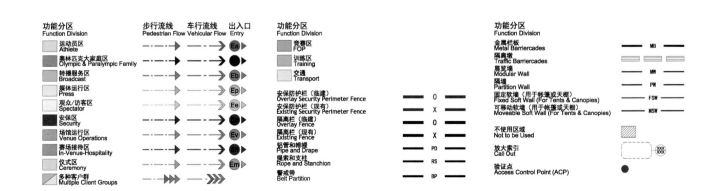

功能分区 Function Division	步行流线 Pedestrian Flow	车行流线 Vehicular Flow	出入口 Entry
运动员区 Athlete			Ea
奥林匹克大家庭区 Olympic & Paralympic Family			●
转播服务区 Broadcast			Eb
媒体运行区 Press			Ep
观众/访客区 Spectator			Ee
安保区 Security			●
场馆运行区 Venue Operations			Ev
赛场接待区 In-Venue-Hospitality			●
仪式区 Ceremony			Em
多种客户群 Multiple Client Groups			

功能分区 Function Division	
竞赛区 FOP	
训练区 Training	
交通 Transport	
安保防护栏（临建） Overlay Security Perimeter Fence	O
安保防护栏（现有） Existing Security Perimeter Fence	X
隔离栏（临建） Overlay Fence	O
隔离栏（现有） Existing Fence	X
铝管和帷幔 Pipe and Drape	PD
提索和支柱 Rope and Stanchion	RS
警戒带 Belt Partition	BP

功能分区 Function Division	
金属栏板 Metal Barricades	MB
隔离墩 Traffic Barricades	
展览墙 Modular Wall	MW
隔墙 Partition Wall	PW
固定软墙（用于帐篷或天棚） Fixed Soft Wall (For Tents & Canopies)	FSW
可移动软墙（用于帐篷或天棚） Moveable Soft Wall (For Tents & Canopies)	MSW
不使用区域 Not to be Used	
放大索引 Call Out	
验证点 Access Control Point (ACP)	●

N

张家口古杨树场馆群公共区主入口广场平面图 OB7.0版
Guyangshu Cluster Public Area Plaza Plan OB7.0

清华院 提供
Provide by THAD

国家跳台滑雪中心 [ZSJ]

Zhangjiakou National Ski Jumping Centre

1. 场馆基本情况

　　国家跳台滑雪中心位于张家口古杨树场馆群内，在冬奥会期间承担跳台滑雪和北欧两项的比赛，产生5枚金牌。

　　国家跳台滑雪中心主要包括山上"顶峰俱乐部"、山下看台、竞赛区以及综合区等，总建筑面积约2.4万m²。跳台剖面的S形曲线与中国传统吉祥物件"如意"的造型相契合，昵称"雪如意"。

2. FOP及相关区域区

　　竞赛区由大跳台（HS140）与标准跳台（HS106）两条赛道组成：大跳台出发区与结束区高程落差136m，标准跳台出发区与结束区高程落差114m。赛道分为助滑道及着陆坡两部分构成，赛道可四季运营，其中助滑道冬季为冰面赛道、夏季为陶瓷赛道，着陆坡冬季为雪面赛道，夏季为人工草皮赛道。在着陆坡南侧K点附近，有900m²左右裁判塔，赛时为裁判员、仲裁员、计时计分技术官员用房，完成对于运动员成绩的评定。

　　运动员赛时活动区域主要为"顶峰俱乐部"，其中打蜡房位于顶峰首层，与标准跳台运动员等候区同层。运动员休息大厅位于顶峰三层、四层，运动员均可通过专用电梯到达。顶峰俱乐部观光层，赛后将成为可容纳500人的会议厅和瞰景餐厅。

　　赛道南侧有一条双轨道地轨缆车，长度227m，垂直落差

1. Venue Overview

Located within the Zhangjiakou Guyangshu Cluster, the Zhangjiakou National Ski Jumping Centre is responsible for hosting Ski Jumping and Nordic Combined events during the Beijing 2022 Olympic Winter Games, with five gold medals won here.
The National Ski Jumping Centre mainly consists of the summit club on the mountain and the stands, FOP, and compounds under the mountain, with a total floor area of about 24,000m². The S-shaped curve of the National Ski Jumping Centre profile is in line with the shape of the traditional Chinese auspicious object "*ruyi*", therefore, the venue is nicknamed the "Snow Ruyi".

2. FOP and Relevant Areas

The FOP consists of 2 courses, the large hill (HS140) and the normal hill (HS106). The start area and finish area of the large hill have an elevation difference of 136m, and the start area and finish area of the normal hill have an elevation difference of 114m. Each of the courses consists of an in-run and landing area. The courses can be operated in all seasons. The in-run is an ice track in winter and a porcelain track in summer, while the landing area is a snow course in winter and an artificial turf track in summer. Near the K-point on the south side of the landing area, there is a judge tower of about 900m² for use by judges, arbitrators, and timing and scoring technical officials during the Games to grade athletes.

108m，分为三站，看台站-裁判塔站-顶峰站，赛时为运动员专用电梯。

3. 场馆前院及观众流线

国家跳台滑雪中心通过"冰玉环"完成了前院与后院的空间分隔，前院位于"冰玉环"及看台区。观众乘坐大巴达到落客位之后经过人检大棚便可经过主入口台阶到达"冰玉环"上，步行550m左右便可以到达跳台看台区。"冰玉环"上设置观众配套暖房、卫生间等。

4. 场馆后院及注册流线

古杨树场馆群后院为场馆的地面层。

（1）运动员流线

运动员及随队官员乘坐班车到达通过北入口人车同检广场进入场馆群，经过登山道路抵达运动员标准跳台出发层打蜡房区域。标准跳台赛时运动员步行从打蜡房至出发等候区，然后进行跳台比赛。比赛结束，运动员经过混采区后可以步行至地轨缆车看台站，乘坐地轨缆车回到打蜡房；或者步行至场馆VMC新闻发布厅接受采访之后再经由地轨缆车回到打蜡房。同时地轨缆车看台站附近预留了备用班车，运动员可乘车回到打蜡房区。赛事结束之后运动员在打蜡房候车区乘坐专用大巴经过场馆群主出入口离开场馆群。

大跳台赛时运动员乘坐专用电梯抵达大跳台出发等候区，然后进行跳台比赛，结束路线同标准跳台。

参加北欧两项比赛的运动员在跳台比赛之后乘坐专用大巴经过场馆群内部C环车行道抵达越野滑雪场打蜡房区进行越野比赛。

（2）技术官员流线

技术官员酒店紧邻国家跳台滑雪中心东侧，技术官员赛时可步行到达场馆。

（3）奥林匹克大家庭成员流线

奥林匹克大家庭成员乘坐专用大巴经过车检广场进入场馆群后院到达落客点，然后经过看台南区专用电梯抵达五层大家庭休息室。为获奖运动员颁花时大家庭成员乘坐专用电梯经过首层抵达场院内颁奖等候区。

（4）媒体流线

转播及媒体人群分两部分，一部分位于山地媒体酒店，可以直接步行直接到达VMC及OBS综合区。另一部分人群乘车由场馆外经过车检大棚到达VMC停车区以及OBS综合区场馆，然后步行到达VMC及OBS综合区用房。场馆内转播及媒体从功能区出来之后步行前往混合采访区、摄像点位、评论员席等。

（5）其他注册流线

其他注册人群位于场馆群外均乘坐大巴抵达车检广场或人检广场，经过安检之后进入场馆群，然后乘坐大巴抵达场馆。

（6）室外综合区

国家跳台滑雪中心室外综合区总面积为5000m²左右，主要为位于顶峰的运动员打蜡房、位于看台南区的OBS综合区场院以及位于"冰玉环"层的评论员席、体育展示、观众暖房及卫生间等。

5. 场馆坐席

国家跳台滑雪中心场馆容量为6000席，其中坐席2534个，站席3346个，无障碍及陪同席位120个。

注册席位共293个，其中大家庭席位107个，运动员席位50个，转播席位38个，媒体席位98个。

The summit club is the main activity area of athletes during the Games, with wax cabins on the same first floor of the summit club as the waiting area of normal hill athletes.

On the south side of the course, there is a dual-rail cable car. The rails are 227m long, with a vertical drop of 108m, and are divided into three stations, i.e., the stand station, the judge tower station, and the summit station, used exclusively by athletes during the Games.

3. Front of House and Spectator Flow

The Front of House (FOH) and the Back of House (BOH) of the National Ski Jumping Centre are spatially divided by the Ice Jade Ring. The Ice Jade Ring part and the stand area constitute the FOH. After taking buses to the drop-off points and passing through the pedestrian screening tent, spectators can reach the Ice Jade Ring via the main entrance steps and then walk about 550m to reach the stand area.

4. Back of House and Accreditation Flow

(1) Athlete Flow

Athletes and team officials take shuttle buses to arrive at and pass through the pedestrian and vehicle screening square in front of the north entrance to enter the cluster; then they can go to the wax cabin area in the athlete standard hill start area via the mountaineering road. During the Games, standard hill athletes walk from wax cabins to the start waiting area to participate in ski jumping events. After competitions, athletes can walk to the stand station of the cable car after passing through the mixed zone, to take the cable car back to wax cabins; or they can walk to the press conference room of the VMC to be interviewed and then take the cable car back to wax cabins.

(2) Technical Official Flow

The technical official hotel is next to the east side of the National Ski Jumping Centre, from which technical officials can walk to the venue during the Games.

(3) Olympic Family Flow

Olympic Family members take dedicated buses to enter the cluster BOH via the vehicle screening square to reach the drop-off points, and then take the dedicated elevator in the south area of the stand to reach the Olympic Family lounge on the fifth floor. During the flower ceremonies of medallists, related Olympic Family members take the dedicated elevator to reach the first floor and then go to the victory ceremony waiting area within the yard.

(4) Media Flow

Broadcast and media personnel are divided into two parts: the part staying at the mountain media hotel can directly walk to the VMC and OBS compound, while the other part can take vehicles from outside of the venue to reach the VMC parking area and OBS compound via the vehicle screening tent and then walk to the VMC and OBS compound.

5. Seating Area

The capacity of the National Ski Jumping Centre is 6,000, including 2,534 seats, 3,346 standing positions, and 120 accessible seats and companion seats.

There are a total of 293 accredited seats, including 107 for the Olympic Family, 50 for athletes, 38 for broadcasters, and 98 for media.

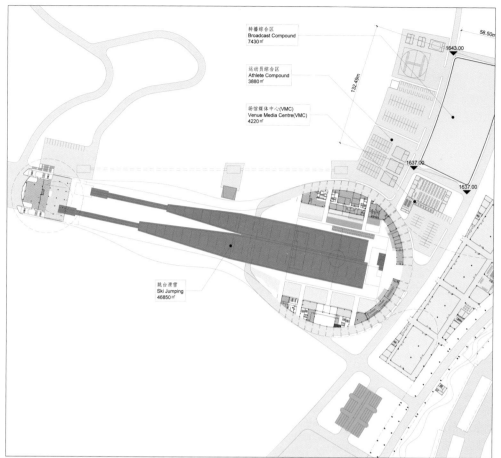

转播综合区
Broadcast Compound
7430㎡

运动员综合区
Athlete Compound
3880㎡

场馆媒体中心(VMC)
Venue Media Centre(VMC)
4220㎡

跳台滑雪
Ski Jumping
46850㎡

58.50m

1643.00

132.49m

1637.00

1637.00

功能分区
Function Division

运动员区
Athlete

奥林匹克大家庭区
Olympic & Paralympic Family

转播服务区
Broadcast

媒体运行区
Press

观众/访客区
Spectator

安保区
Security

场馆运行区
Venue Operations

赛事接待区
In-Venue-Hospitality

仪式区
Ceremony

多种客户群
Multiple Client Groups

竞赛区
FOP

训练区
Training

交通
Transport

步行流线
Pedestrian Flow

车行流线
Vehicular Flow

出入口
Entry

安保防护栏（临建）
Overlay Security Perimeter Fence — 0

安保防护栏（现有）
Existing Security Perimeter Fence — X

隔离栏（临建）
Overlay Fence — 0

隔离栏（现有）
Existing Fence — X

绳索和帷幕
Pipe and Drape — PD

绳索和立柱
Rope and Stanchion — RS

警戒带
Belt Partition — BP

金属栏板
Metal Barricades — MB

隔离墩
Traffic Barricades

展览墙
Modular Wall — MW

隔墙
Partition Wall — PW

固定软墙（用于帐篷或天棚）
Fixed Soft Wall (For Tents & Canopies) — FSW

可移动软墙（用于帐篷或天棚）
Moveable Soft Wall (For Tents & Canopies) — MSW

不使用区域
Not to be Used

放大索引
Call Out

验证点
Access Control Point (ACP)

N

ZSJ 总平面图 OB1.1版
ZSJ Master Plan OB1.1

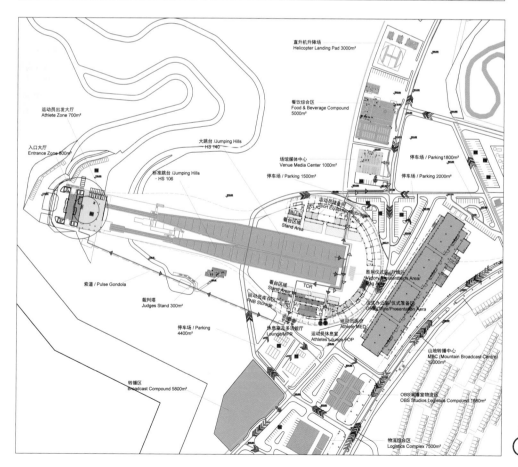

直升机升降场
Helicopter Landing Pad 3000㎡

餐饮综合区
Food & Beverage Compound
5000㎡

运动员出发大厅
Athlete Zone 700㎡

大跳台 /Jumping Hills
HS 140

入口大厅
Entrance Zone 600㎡

标准跳台 /Jumping Hills
HS 106

场馆媒体中心
Venue Media Center 1000㎡

停车场 / Parking 1500㎡

停车场 / Parking 1800㎡

停车场 / Parking 2000㎡

运动员器材存放
Sport Equipment Storage

看台区
Stand Area

索道 / Pulse Gondola

看台区域
Stand Area

TCR

裁判塔
Judges Stand 300㎡

胜利仪式区/颁奖区
Victory Presentation Area

运动员存衣区
RNB Storage

仪式办公室/仪式准备区
Office/Presentation Area

停车场 / Parking
4400㎡

休息室及多功能厅
Lounge/MPR

运动员休息室
Athletes Lounge/POP

运动员医疗
Athlete MED

山地转播中心
MBC (Mountain Broadcast Centre)
12000㎡

转播区
Broadcast Compound 5800㎡

OBS演播室物流区
OBS Studios Logistics Compound 1680㎡

物流综合区
Logistics Complex 7500㎡

N

ZSJ 总平面图 OB2.0版
ZSJ Master Plan OB2.0

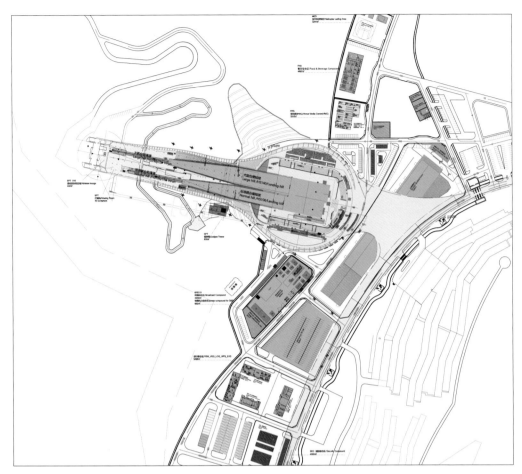

ZSJ 总平面图 OB3.0版
ZSJ Master Plan OB3.0

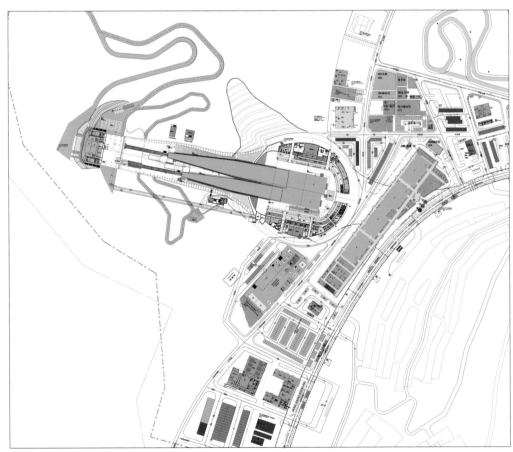

ZSJ 总平面图 OB4.0版
ZSJ Master Plan OB4.0

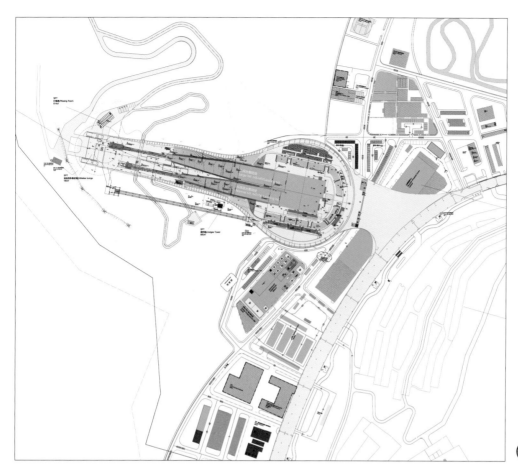

N
ZSJ 总平面图 OB5.0版
ZSJ Master Plan OB5.0

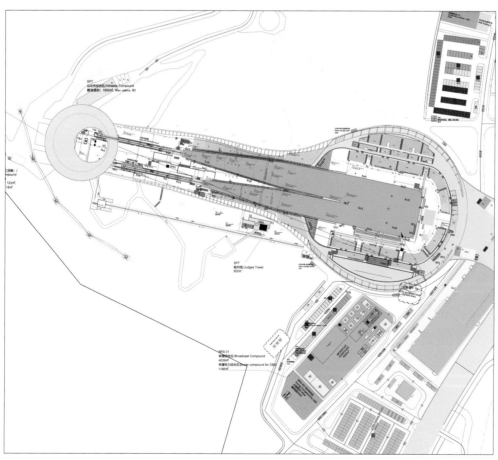

N
ZSJ 总平面图 OB6.0版
ZSJ Master Plan OB6.0

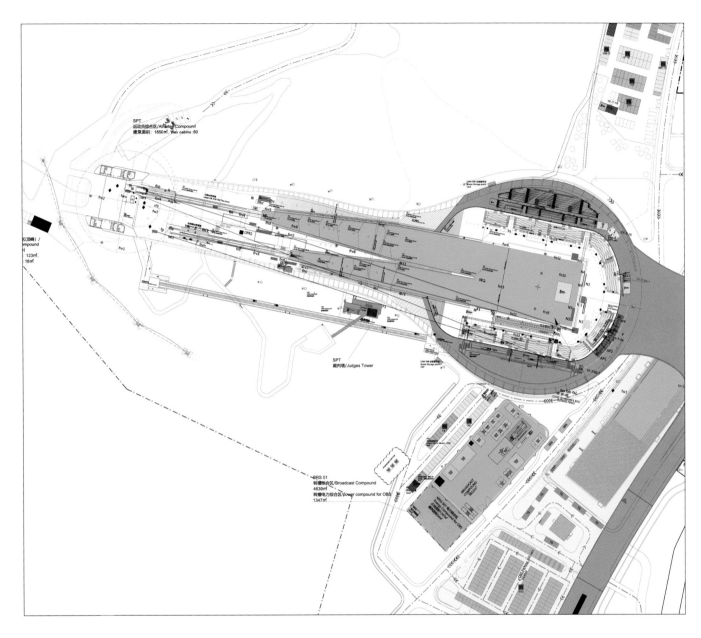

SPT
运动员综合区/Athlete Compound
建筑面积: 1850㎡, Wax cabins: 80

SPT
裁判塔/Judges Tower

BRS 01
转播综合区/Broadcast Compound
4639㎡
转播电力综合区/power compound for OBS
1347㎡

ZSJ 总平面图 OB7.0版
ZSJ Master Plan OB7.0

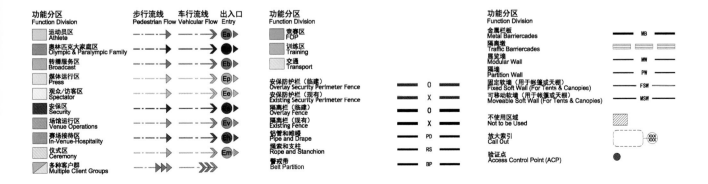

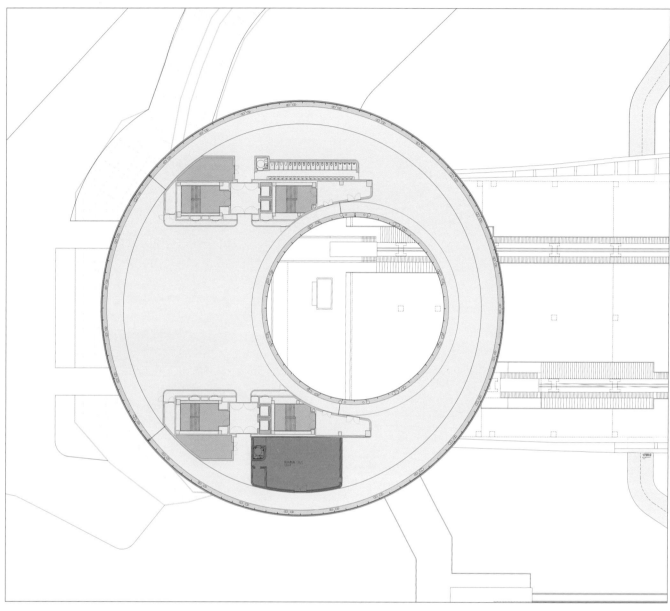

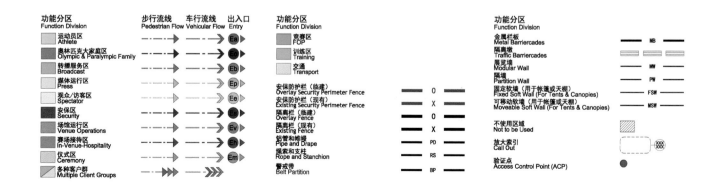

ZSJ 顶峰俱乐部二层平面图 OB7.0版
ZSJ Peak Club 2F Plan OB7.0

功能分区
Function Division

运动员区
Athlete

奥林匹克大家庭区
Olympic & Paralympic Family

转播服务区
Broadcast

媒体运行区
Press

观众/访客区
Spectator

安保区
Security

场馆运行区
Venue Operations

赛场接待区
In-Venue-Hospitality

仪式区
Ceremony

多种客户群
Multiple Client Groups

步行流线
Pedestrian Flow

车行流线
Vehicular Flow

出入口
Entry

Ea
Eo
Eb
Ep
Ee
Es
Ev
Eh
Em

功能分区
Function Division

竞赛区
FOP

训练区
Training

交通
Transport

安保防护栏（临建）
Overlay Security Perimeter Fence

安保防护栏（现有）
Existing Security Perimeter Fence

隔离栏（临建）
Overlay Fence

隔离栏（现有）
Existing Fence

起管和帷幔
Pipe and Drape

绳索和支柱
Rope and Stanchion

警戒带
Belt Partition

O
X
O
X
PD
RS
BP

功能分区
Function Division

金属栏板
Metal Barriercades

隔离墩
Traffic Barriercades

展览墙
Modular Wall

隔墙
Partition Wall

固定软墙（用于帐篷或天棚）
Fixed Soft Wall (For Tents & Canopies)

可移动软墙（用于帐篷或天棚）
Moveable Soft Wall (For Tents & Canopies)

不使用区域
Not to be Used

放大索引
Call Out

验证点
Access Control Point (ACP)

MB
MW
PW
FSW
MSW

XXX

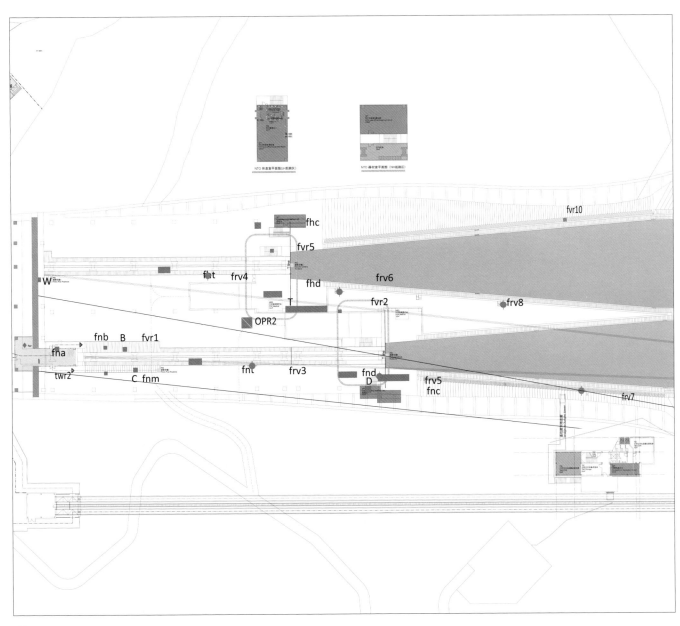

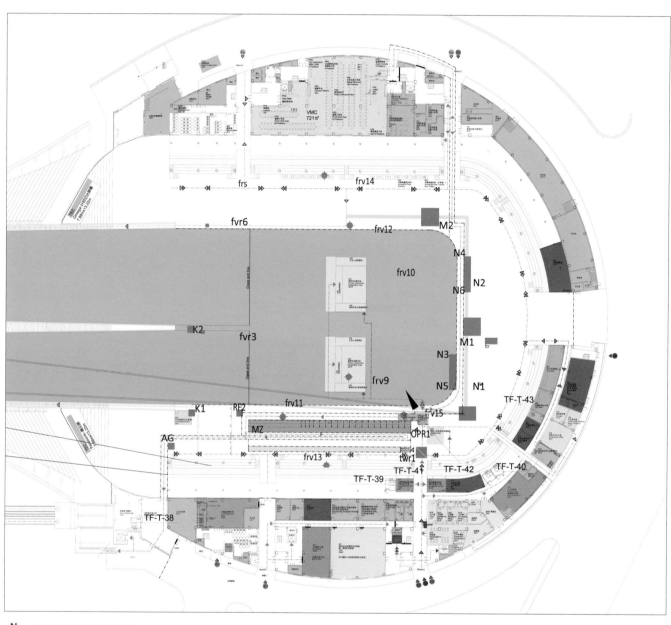

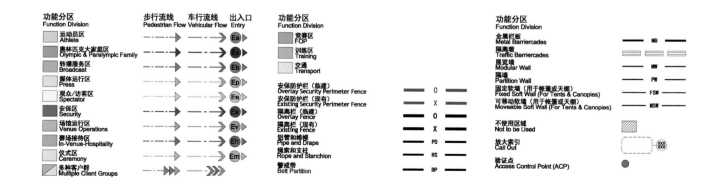

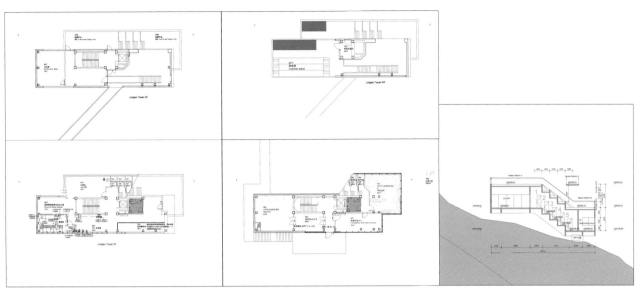

ZSJ 裁判塔平面图、剖面图 OB7.0版
ZSJ Judges Tower and Surrounding Area Plan and Section OB7.0

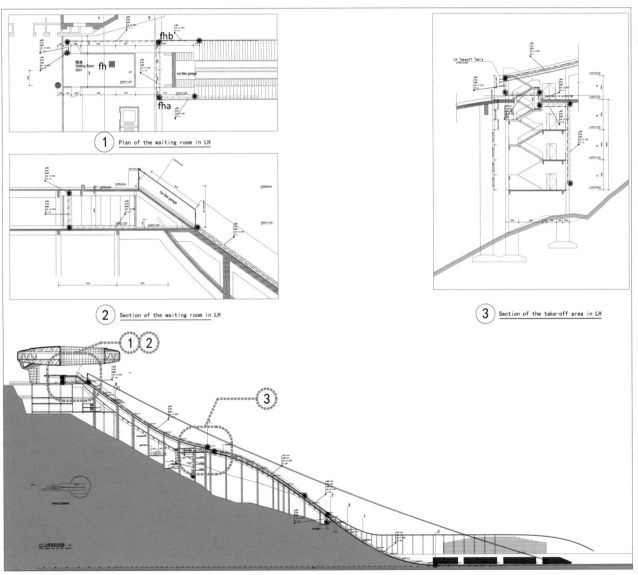

ZSJ 赛道剖面图 OB7.0版
ZSJ LH Section OB7.0

清华院 提供
Provide by THAD

清华院 提供
Provide by THAD

张家口市冬奥办 提供
Provide by ZJK Office

摄影 刘中伟
Photo by Liu Zhongwei

国家冬季两项中心 [ZBT]

Zhangjiakou National Biathlon Centre

1. 场馆基本情况

国家冬季两项中心位于张家口古杨树场馆群北侧山谷内，在冬奥会期间承担冬季两项项目的比赛，产生11枚金牌；在冬残奥会期间承担残奥冬季两项和残奥越野滑雪的比赛，产生38枚金牌。

冬季两项这一运动起源于北欧地区的"雪中狩猎"活动，是一项速度与技术完美结合的运动。国家冬季两项中心结束区的技术楼的设计以运动员举枪瞄准这一动作为灵感，以一条连贯的折线串联建筑屋顶与看台，形成极具张力的造型，建筑面积约5200m²。

2. FOP相关区域

国家冬季两项中心的赛道设计充分结合自然山体而建，最高点海拔1720m，最低点海拔1657m，总长12.3km，包含站姿赛道、坐姿赛道以及训练道等。

核心区有两条地下通道连接FOP与其他区域。其中西侧地下通道为体育专用通道，连接FOP与运动员综合区，运动员在此通道完成验枪后到达出发区进行比赛。东侧地下通道为运行通道，连接FOP与运行区，媒体和转播的运行人员可以通过此通道到达靶场附近的工作点位。

1. Venue Overview

Located within the north valley of the Zhangjiakou Guyangshu Cluster, the Zhangjiakou National Biathlon Centre is responsible for hosting Biathlon events during the Beijing 2022 Olympic Winter Games, with 11 gold medals won here, and hosting Para Biathlon and Para Cross-Country Skiing events during the Beijing 2022 Paralympic Winter Games, with 38 gold medals won here.

2. FOP and Relevant Areas

The courses of the National Biathlon Centre are built according to the shapes of natural mountains, with the highest point at 1,720m and the lowest at 1,657m above sea level and a total length of 12.3km, including standing-position, sitting-position and training courses.

3. Front of House and Spectator Flow

In the Zhangjiakou Guyangshu Cluster, the spectator flow is organised using the elevated spectator walkway, the Ice Jade Ring, which is naturally separated from the ground operations area in space. The Ice Jade Ring part, spectator service area, and spectator stand constitute the Front of House (FOH). During the Games, after passing through security checks from the main entrance in the southeast of the Guyangshu Cluster, spectators walk up the steps or accessible ramp to reach the spectator walkway on the second

3. 场馆前院及观众流线

张家口古杨树场馆群通过高架的观众步道"冰玉环"来组织观众流线，从空间上与地面工作运行区自然分隔。"冰玉环"、观众服务区及观众看台组成场馆前院区。赛时观众从古杨树场馆群东南侧主入口经安检后，通过步行台阶或无障碍坡道到达二层观众步道"冰玉环"，沿着步道向西北方向步行至国家冬季两项中心区域，通过安检门后到达观众服务区，此处为观众设置了餐饮售卖点、观众医疗站、失物招领和卫生间等。观众之后可通过向北的连廊到达技术楼二层的观众活动平台和观众看台观看比赛，比赛结束后通过原路线离开场馆。

4. 场馆后院及注册流线

国家冬季两项中心技术楼一、三、四层和地面综合区为场馆后院区，主要作为运动员打蜡、媒体转播运行、场馆运行及赛事管理区域使用。

（1）运动员流线

运动员由奥运村乘坐班车经张家口古杨树场馆群北入口，到达国家冬季两项运动员综合区内落客。运动员综合区内设置四栋两层打蜡房，共计120个标准房间。另外这个区域还设置了运动员休息室、运动员医疗站等。运动员到达看台下的枪弹库领取枪弹后通过地下通道进入FOP出发区进行比赛，比赛结束后到达终点线东侧的混合采访区，在此处接受转播和媒体的采访，采访后经过看台下部通道返回运动员更衣室。运动员区域充分考虑无障碍设计，残奥会期间可以迅速转换，满足残奥比赛的要求。

（2）技术官员流线

技术官员与运动员一样在运动员综合区落客，运动员综合区设置了NTO休息室及办公室。ITO可通过运动员地下通道到达位于靶场西侧的设备存放区，ITO休息区设置在此区域的一层。

（3）奥林匹克大家庭成员流线

奥林匹克大家庭成员乘坐专用车辆经古杨树场馆群东南侧的主出入口进入场馆群，经玉环路到达国家冬季两项中心技术楼南侧落客位，下车后经2号门进入技术楼，而后可乘坐专用电梯到达位于技术楼二层东侧的大家庭专用休息室、观景台和大家庭看台区。

（4）媒体流线

新闻媒体乘坐媒体班车经古杨树场馆群东南侧的主出入口进入场馆群，经玉环路到达国家冬季两项中心媒体工作区落客位，步行到达场馆媒体中心、媒体看台等区域，场馆媒体中心是集媒体办公与新闻发布厅为一体的大空间办公区，其中设置有新闻发布主席台、文字记者及摄影记者工位、媒体休息区等。媒体工作区紧邻比赛场地、媒体混采区、媒体坐席，可以在最短的时间内抵达各个点位。

（5）其他综合区

除上述区域外，场馆还设置了转播综合区、场馆运行综合区和停车场等区域。

5. 场馆坐席

国家冬季两项中心坐席容量为6024个，其中看台坐席4402个，场地站席1438个。赛时注册坐席包含奥林匹克大家庭坐席、评论员席、观察员席、带桌媒体席、不带桌媒体席、观赛运动员坐席，坐席数量共计310个。各类注册人群均设置了无障碍坐席。

观众席位共计5714个，其中包含87个观众无障碍席位及87个陪同席位。

floor, the Ice Jade Ring; then they walk northwest along the walkway to the National Biathlon Centre area, and after passing through the security gates, they can reach the spectator service area where food and beverage concessions, spectator medical stations, lost and found sites, and toilets are in place for spectators. Then spectators can walk north through the corridor to reach the spectator activity platform and spectator stand on the second floor of the technical building to watch competitions. After competitions, they can leave the venue via the same route.

4. Back of House and Accreditation Flow

(1) Athlete Flow

Athletes take shuttle buses to reach the athletes' compound of the National Biathlon Centre via the north entrance of the Zhangjiakou Guyangshu Cluster. There are a total of 120 standard wax cabins in 4 two-floor buildings inside the athletes' compound, and there are also athlete lounges and athletes medical stations in the compound. After collecting rifles and ammunition in the rifle and ammunition storehouse under the stand, athletes go to the FOP start area via the underground passage to compete; after competitions, they go to the mixed zone on the east side of the finish line to be interviewed by media, and then they return to athlete dressing rooms via the passage under the stand.

(2) Technical Official Flow

Like athletes, technical officials get off in the athletes' compound where there is an NTO lounge and office. ITOs can go via the underground passage for athletes to reach the equipment storage area on the west side of the shooting range, with an ITO lounge provided on the first floor of this area.

(3) Olympic Family Flow

Olympic Family members take dedicated vehicles to enter the cluster via the southeast main entrance of the Guyangshu Cluster and arrive at the drop-off points on the south side of the technical building of National Biathlon Centre via Yuhuan Road; after getting off, they enter the technical building via Gate 2, and then they can take the dedicated elevator to reach the Olympic Family lounge, viewing deck, and Olympic Family stand in the east of the second floor of the technical building.

(4) Media Flow

Media personnel take media shuttle buses to enter the cluster via the southeast main entrance of the Guyangshu Cluster and arrive at the drop-off points in the media work area of the National Biathlon Centre via Yuhuan Road; then they walk to the Venue Media Centre (a large office area that combines a media work space and a press conference room, including a press conference rostrum, press and photographer stations, and a media lounge, etc.), press tribunes, etc.

5. Seating Area

The capacity of the National Biathlon Centre is 6,024, including 4,402 stand seats and 1,438 standing positions. Accredited seats during the Games include Olympic Family seats, commentary positions, observer seats, tabled and non-tabled press tribune seats, and spectating athlete seats, with a total of 310. Accessible seats are provided for various accredited persons.

There are a total of 5,714 spectator seats, including 87 accessible seats and 87 companion seats.

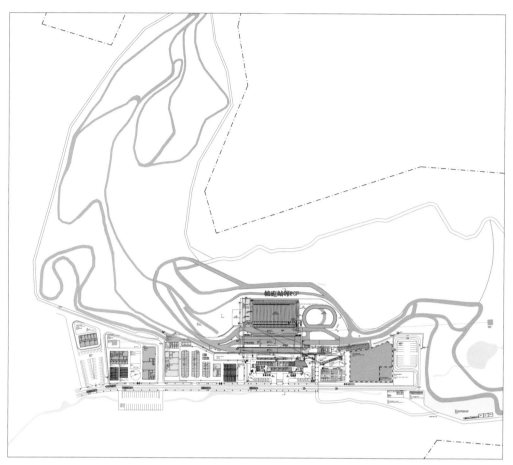

 ZBT 总平面图 OB2.1版
ZBT Master Plan OB2.1

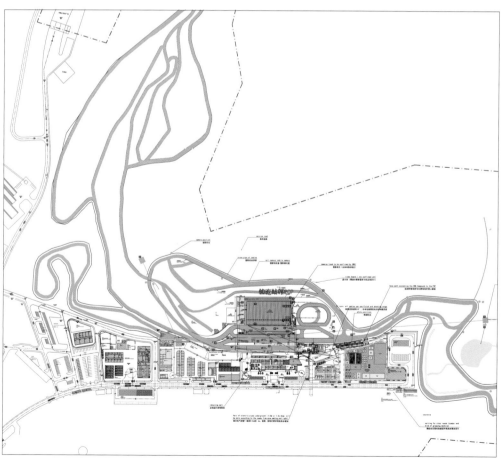

ZBT 总平面图 OB3.0版
ZBT Master Plan OB3.0

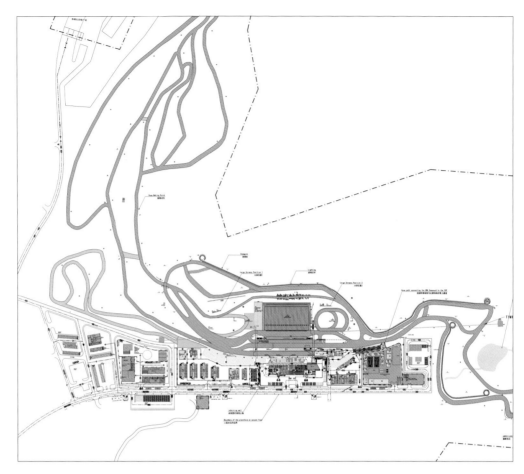

N
ZBT 总平面图 OB5.0版
ZBT Master Plan OB5.0

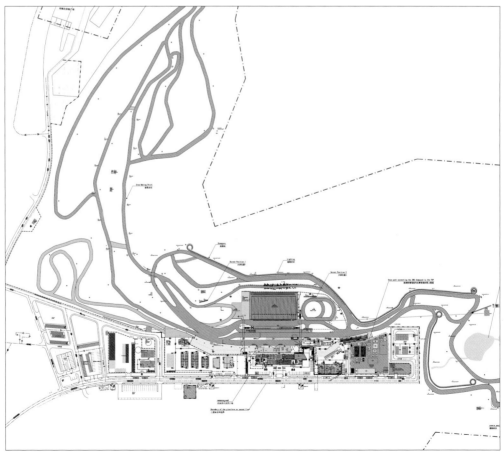

N
ZBT 总平面图 OB6.0版
ZBT Master Plan OB6.0

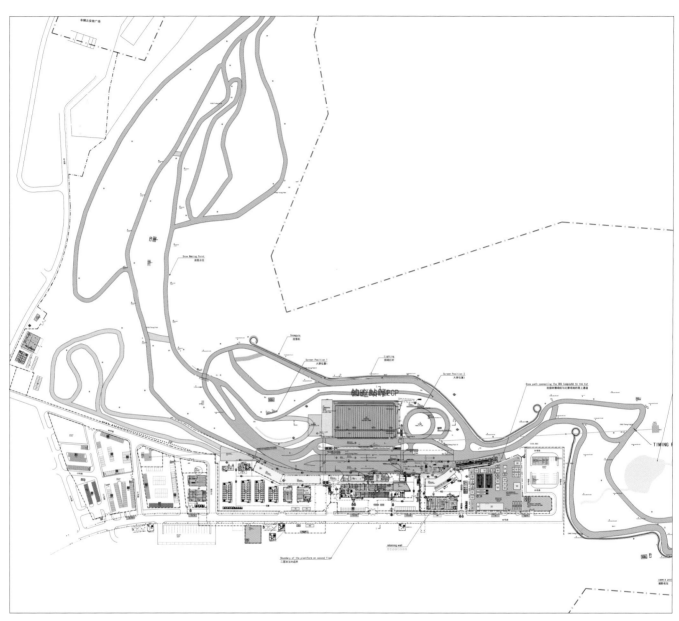

ZBT 总平面图 OB7.0版
ZBT Master Plan OB7.0

功能分区
Function Division

运动员区
Athlete

奥林匹克大家庭区
Olympic & Paralympic Family

转播服务区
Broadcast

媒体运行区
Press

观众/访客区
Spectator

安保区
Security

场馆运行区
Venue Operations

赛场接待区
In-Venue-Hospitality

仪式区
Ceremony

多种客户群
Multiple Client Groups

步行流线
Pedestrian Flow

车行流线
Vehicular Flow

出入口
Entry

Ea
Eo
Eb
Ep
Ee
Es
Ev
Eh
Em

功能分区
Function Division

竞赛区
FOP

训练区
Training

交通
Transport

安保防护栏（临建）
Overlay Security Perimeter Fence

安保防护栏（现有）
Existing Security Perimeter Fence

隔离栏（临建）
Overlay Fence

隔离栏（现有）
Existing Fence

铝管和帷幔
Pipe and Drape

绳索和支柱
Rope and Stanchion

警戒带
Belt Partition

O
X
O
X
PD
RS
BP

功能分区
Function Division

金属栏板
Metal Barricades

隔离墩
Traffic Barricades

展览墙
Modular Wall

隔墙
Partition Wall

固定软墙（用于帐篷或天棚）
Fixed Soft Wall (For Tents & Canopies)

可移动软墙（用于帐篷或天棚）
Moveable Soft Wall (For Tents & Canopies)

不使用区域
Not to be Used

放大索引
Call Out

验证点
Access Control Point (ACP)

MB
MW
PW
FSW
MSW

XXX

330

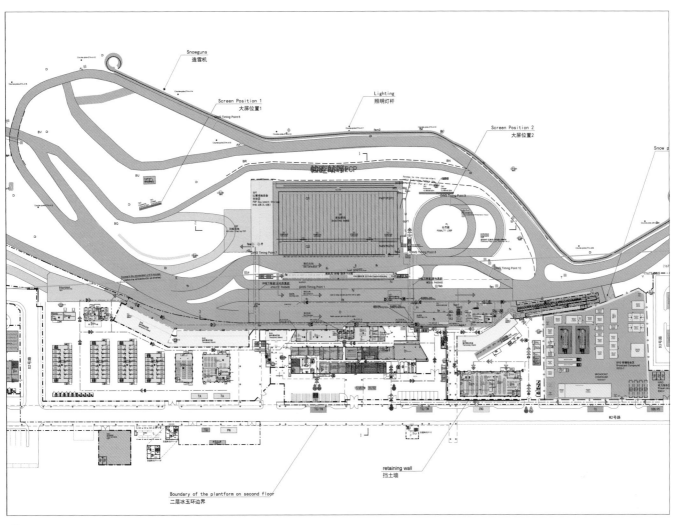

Snowguns
造雪机

Screen Position 1
大屏位置1

Lighting
照明灯杆

Screen Position 2
大屏位置2

Snow p

retaining wall
挡土墙

Boundary of the plantform on second floor
二层冰玉环边界

N

ZBT 核心区放大平面图 OB7.0版
ZBT Core Area Enlarged Plan OB7.0

摄影 魏庆华
Photo by Wei Qinghua

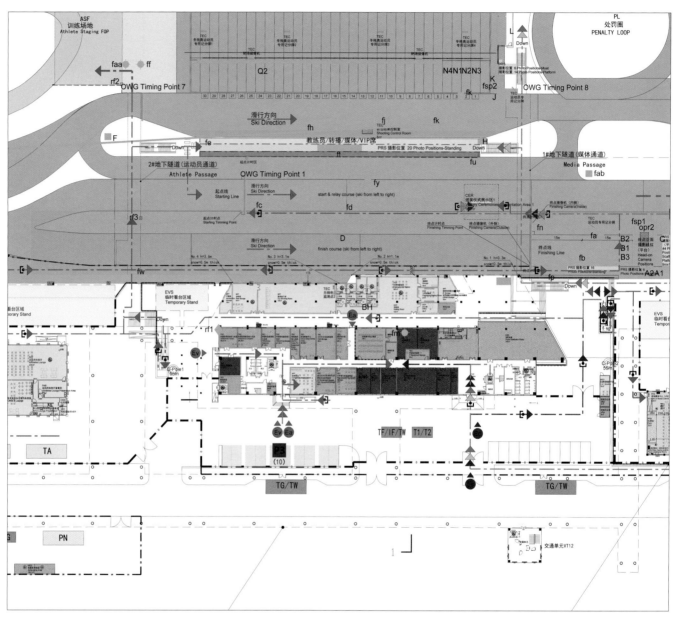

N
ZBT 核心区一层平面图 OB7.0版
ZBT Core Area 1F Plan OB7.0

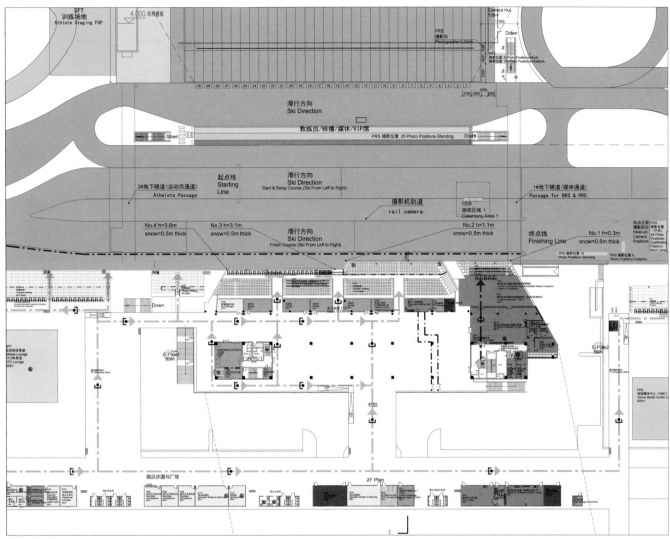

ZBT 核心区二层平面图 OB7.0版
ZBT Core Area 2F Plan OB7.0

摄影 魏庆华
Photo by Wei Qinghua

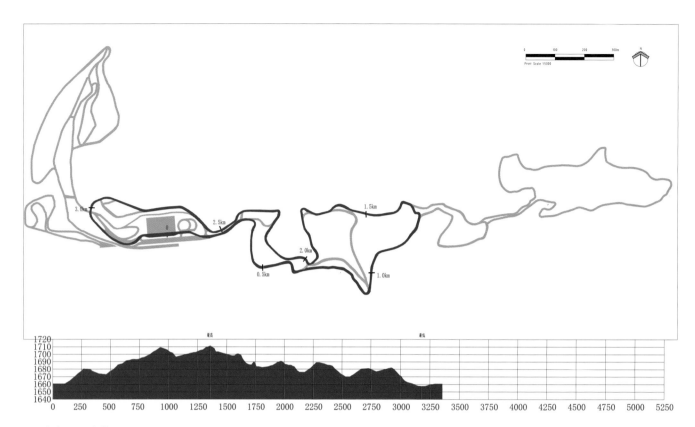

ZBT 冬奥3.3km赛道 OB7.0版
ZBT OWG FOP 3.3km OB7.0

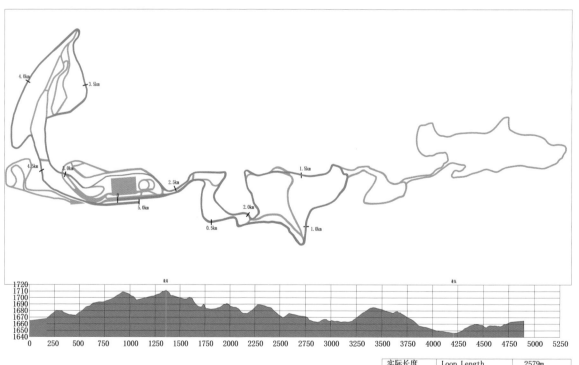

实际长度	Loop Length	2579m
总爬升高度	Total Climb	
最大单次爬升	Maximum Climb	
高程差	Height Difference	39m
最高高程	Highest Point	1685m
最低高程	Lowest Point	1646m
最大上坡	Steepest Upward	
最大下坡	Steepest Downward	

ZBT 冬残奥5.0km站姿赛道 OB7.0版
ZBT PWG FOP 5.0km Standing-Ski Course OB7.0

5.0km赛道数据图 1:10000

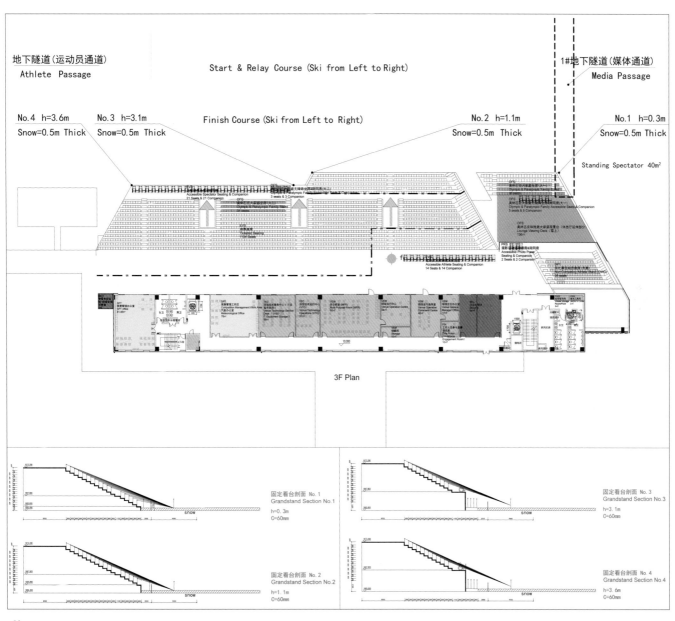

地下隧道（运动员通道）
Athlete Passage

Start & Relay Course (Ski from Left to Right)

1#地下隧道（媒体通道）
Media Passage

No.4 h=3.6m
Snow=0.5m Thick

No.3 h=3.1m
Snow=0.5m Thick

Finish Course (Ski from Left to Right)

No.2 h=1.1m
Snow=0.5m Thick

No.1 h=0.3m
Snow=0.5m Thick

Standing Spectator 40m²

3F Plan

固定看台剖面 No.1
Grandstand Section No.1
h=0.3m
C=60mm

固定看台剖面 No.3
Grandstand Section No.3
h=3.1m
C=60mm

固定看台剖面 No.2
Grandstand Section No.2
h=1.1m
C=60mm

固定看台剖面 No.4
Grandstand Section No.4
h=3.6m
C=60mm

N

ZBT 固定看台平面图、剖面图 OB7.0版
ZBT Grand Stand Plan & Section OB7.0

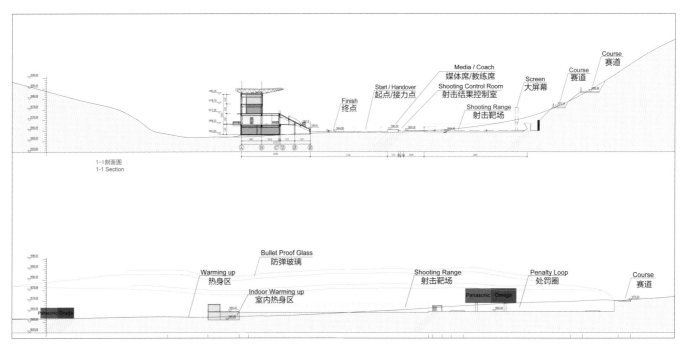

Course 赛道

Course 赛道

Media / Coach 媒体席/教练席
Shooting Control Room 射击结果控制室

Start / Handover 起点/接力点

Screen 大屏幕

Finish 终点

Shooting Range 射击靶场

1-1 剖面图
1-1 Section

Bullet Proof Glass 防弹玻璃

Warming up 热身区

Indoor Warming up 室内热身区

Shooting Range 射击靶场

Penalty Loop 处罚圈

Course 赛道

Panasonic Omega

ZBT 场地剖面图一 OB7.0版
ZBT Site Section 1 OB7.0

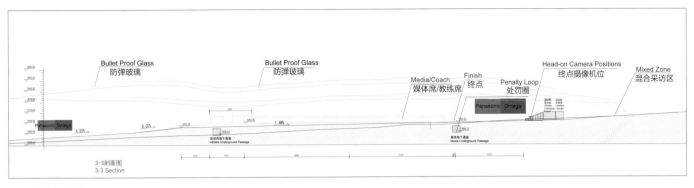

Bullet Proof Glass
防弹玻璃

Bullet Proof Glass
防弹玻璃

Media/Coach
媒体席/教练席

Finish
终点

Head-on Camera Positions
终点摄像机位

Mixed Zone
混合采访区

Penalty Loop
处罚圈

Panasonic Omega

Panasonic Omega

运动员地下通道
Athlete Underground Passage

媒体地下通道
Media Underground Passage

3-3剖面图
3-3 Section

ZBT 场地剖面图二 OB7.0版
ZBT Section 2 OB7.0

国家越野滑雪中心[ZCC]

Zhangjiakou National Cross-Country Centre

1. 场馆基本情况

国家越野滑雪中心位于张家口古杨树场馆群南侧山谷，冬奥会期间承担越野滑雪和北欧两项的比赛，产生15枚金牌。场馆总占地面积106.6hm²，赛道占地面积10.9万m²，结束区的技术楼建筑面积5707m²。国家越野滑雪中心尽量采用临时设施满足冬奥会功能，赛道建设减少人工痕迹对自然的影响，也为赛后利用提供灵活性。

2. FOP相关区域

越野场馆赛道共10条，包括8条比赛赛道、1条热身赛道（含试蜡区）和1条训练赛道，总长度13km。其中比赛赛道总长度9.7km，由1.5km、1.8km、2.5km、3.3km、3.75km、5km、7.5km、8.3km8条赛道组成，占地面积9.4万m²，赛道最高海拔1721.4m，最低海拔1638.8m，高差82.6m。此外，1条热身赛位于FOP区东北部，长度1.5km；1条训练赛道位于FOP区西南部，长度1.8km。

紧邻FOP结束区北侧和西侧，分别设置两处运动员更衣室。其中西侧为小型更衣室，建筑面积27m²，其正上方上设置终点

1. Venue Overview

Located within the south valley of the Zhangjiakou Guyangshu Cluster, the Zhangjiakou National Cross-Country Skiing Centre is responsible for hosting Cross-Country Skiing and Nordic Combined events during the Beijing 2022 Olympic Winter Games, with 15 gold medals won here. The venue covers a total area of 106.6 hectares, with courses covering an area of 109,000m² and the technical building in the finish area having a floor area of 5,707m².

2. FOP and Relevant Areas

The venue has a total of 10 courses, including eight competition courses, one warm-up course (including the wax testing area), and one training course, with an overall length of 13km. Among them, competition courses have an overall length of 9.7km, consist of eight courses of 1.5km, 1.8km, 2.5km, 3.3km, 3.75km, 5km, 7.5km, and 8.3km, respectively, and cover an area of 94,000m², with the highest altitude of 1,721.4m, the lowest altitude of 1,638.8m, and an altitude difference of 82.6m. Furthermore, there is one warm-up course in the northeast of the FOP, with a length of 1.5km; there is one training course in the southwest of the FOP, with a length of 1.8km.

摄影和摄像平台；北侧的为主更衣室，建筑面积165m²，其正上方为混合采访区。

3. 场馆前院及观众流线

国家越野滑雪中心前院主要包括"冰玉环"上、观众看台区、国内贵宾停车场和交通核等区域。

观众从古杨树场馆群的观众大台阶上至"冰玉环"层后，沿"冰玉环"向东步行至技术楼北侧的检票口，由此进入观众区。观众区包括"冰玉环"上的观众取暖棚、观众信息亭和失物招领处、观众售卖点、观众医疗站、卫生间等服务用房以及观众坐席看台等。

国内贵宾乘坐专车至技术楼北，乘坐交通核内电梯抵达"冰玉环"层，随后步行至大家庭休息室2和中方贵宾坐席区。中方贵宾席含60个座席、2个无障碍席和2个陪同席。

4. 场馆后院及注册流线

国家越野滑雪中心场馆内除"冰玉环"层、观众座席区、国内贵宾停车场等区域外，其他均为后院区。

（1）运动员流线

运动员及随队官员从奥运村乘坐大巴出发，经古杨树场馆群北入口进入场馆群，随后抵达运动员综合区。运动员综合区内设置了运动员休息室、更衣室、领队会议室和217间打蜡房等。运动员可通过运动员地下隧道至赛场起点区进行比赛，也可至东部的热身赛道进行热身和试蜡。比赛结束后，运动员可前往混采区或终点摄影摄像平台下方的运动员更衣室，随后，可去混采区接受采访，或至技术楼负一层的兴奋剂检查站进行检查，或步行至场馆媒体中心参加新闻发布会，最后可沿观众看台南侧的运动员通道返回运动员综合区。运动员综合区和训练赛道之间，设置有服务路和摆渡车。

（2）技术官员流线

技术官员乘坐班车抵达技术楼北侧的落客位，其中NTO向东步行至NTO休息室；ITO由技术楼北侧中门进入技术楼，乘坐最东侧电梯抵达四层的裁判室、办公室等空间。

（3）奥林匹克大家庭流线

奥林匹克大家庭成员乘坐专车抵达技术楼北侧落客位进入技术楼一层，随后乘坐专用电梯抵达三层大家庭区域，包括284m²的休息室、咨询台、外方贵宾用房和随从人员休息室等。也可乘坐电梯至二层室外平台，前往坐席区观看比赛。

（4）媒体流线

转播及新闻媒体工作人员乘坐班车至相应落客点，分别抵达转播综合区和场馆媒体中心。其中转播综合区占地面积5733m²，场馆媒体中心建筑面积1135m²。媒体人员可步行至混合采访区、摄影席、看台媒体席、终点摄影平台等区域。

5. 场馆坐席

国家越野滑雪中心总容量为6023个。赛时注册坐席共246个，包括技术楼前的摄影席、看台媒体席、奥林匹克大家庭坐席、运动员及随队官员（同项目）坐席，观众看台后方的评论员席、播报席，观众看台区的中方贵宾席、摄影席和观察员席，以及"冰玉环"东部端头运动员及随队官员（不同项目）坐席。其中，媒体和奥林匹克大家庭两类注册人员设置了无障碍坐席。

赛时观众坐席位于FOP起终点区域北侧，观众坐席数1322个，其中包含28个无障碍坐席及28个陪同席位。

3. Front of House and Spectator Flow

The Front of House (FOH) of the National Cross-Country Skiing Centre mainly includes the Ice Jade Ring part, spectator stand area, domestic dignitary parking area, and transport core.

After going up to the Ice Jade Ring level from the spectator steps of the Guyangshu Cluster, spectators walk east along the Ice Jade Ring to the ticket check point on the north side of the technical building to enter the spectator area. The spectator area consists of a spectator warming tent, spectator information booth and lost and found, spectator concession, spectator medical station, toilets, etc. on the Ice Jade Ring as well as a spectator stand.

4. Back of House and Accreditation Flow

(1) Athlete Flow

Athletes and team officials depart from the Olympic Village by bus to enter the Guyangshu Cluster via the north entrance and then arrive in the athletes' compound. The athletes' compound includes athlete lounges, dressing rooms, team captains' meeting rooms, and 217 wax cabins. Via the underground passage for athletes, athletes can go to the FOP start area to compete or go to the warm-up course in the east for warming up and wax testing. After competitions, athletes can go to the mixed zone or the athlete dressing room under the camera platform at the finish area and then the mixed zone to be interviewed, or go to the doping control station on B1 of the technical building to be tested, or walk to the Venue Media Centre to participate in press conferences, and finally return to the athletes' compound along the athlete passage on the south side of the spectator stand.

(2) Technical Official Flow

Technical officials take shuttle buses to the drop-off points on the north side of the technical building; then NTOs walk east to the NTO lounge, while ITOs enter the technical building from the middle gate in the north of the technical building and take the easternmost elevator to the referee room and office on the fourth floor.

(3) Olympic Family Flow

Olympic Family members take dedicated vehicles to the drop-off points on the north side of the technical building, enter the first floor of the technical building, and then take the dedicated elevator to the Olympic Family area on the third floor, which includes a lounge of 284m², an information desk, an international dignitary room, and an entourage lounge, or they can take the elevator to the outdoor platform on the second floor and then go to the seating area to watch competitions.

(4) Media Flow

Broadcast and media staff members take shuttle buses to the corresponding drop-off points and then go to the broadcast compound and Venue Media Centre. The broadcast compound covers an area of 5,733m², and the Venue Media Centre has a floor area of 1,135m².

5. Seating Area

The total capacity of the National Cross-Country Skiing Centre is 6,023, including 246 accredited seats.

During the Games, 1,322 spectator seats are provided on the north side of the FOP start and finish areas, including 28 accessible seats and 28 companion seats.

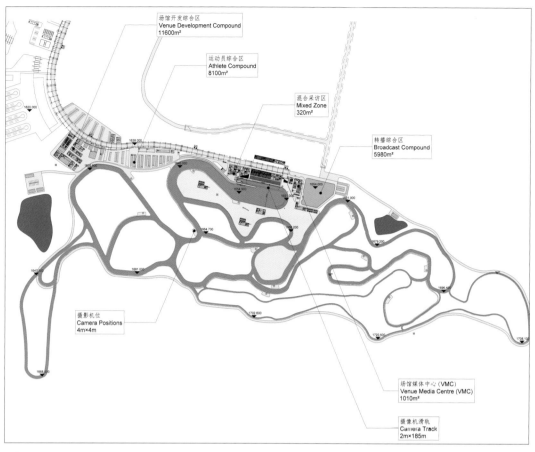

场馆开发综合区
Venue Development Compound
11600m²

运动员综合区
Athlete Compound
8100m²

混合采访区
Mixed Zone
320m²

转播综合区
Broadcast Compound
5980m²

摄影机位
Camera Positions
4m×4m

场馆媒体中心 (VMC)
Venue Media Centre (VMC)
1010m²

摄像机滑轨
Camera Track
2m×185m

N

ZCC 总平面图 OB1.1版
ZCC Master Plan OB1.1

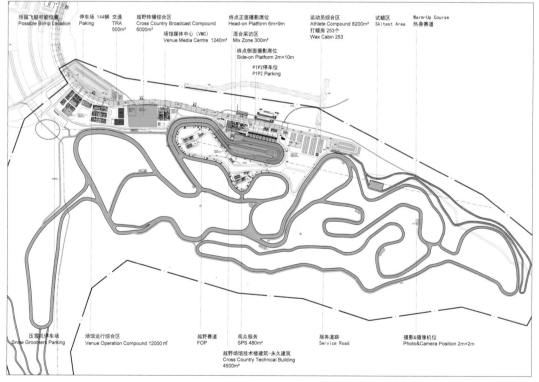

预留飞艇可能位置
Possible Blimp Location

停车场 144辆
Paking

交通
TRA
500m²

越野转播综合区
Cross Country Broadcast Compound
6000m²

场馆媒体中心 (VMC)
Venue Media Centre 1240m²

终点正面摄影席位
Head-on Platform 6m×9m

混合采访区
Mix Zone 300m²

终点侧面摄影席位
Side-on Platform 2m×10m

P1P2停车位
P1P2 Parking

运动员综合区
Athlete Compound 8200m²

打蜡房 253个
Wax Cabin 253

试蜡区
Skitest Area

Warm-Up Course
热身赛道

压雪机停车场
Snow Groomers Parking

场馆运行综合区
Venue Operation Compound 12000㎡

越野赛道
FOP

观众服务
SPS 480m²

越野场馆技术楼建筑-永久建筑
Cross Country Technical Building
4500m²

服务道路
Service Road

摄影&摄像机位
Photo&Camera Position 2m×2m

N

ZCC 总平面图 OB2.1版
ZCC Master Plan OB2.1

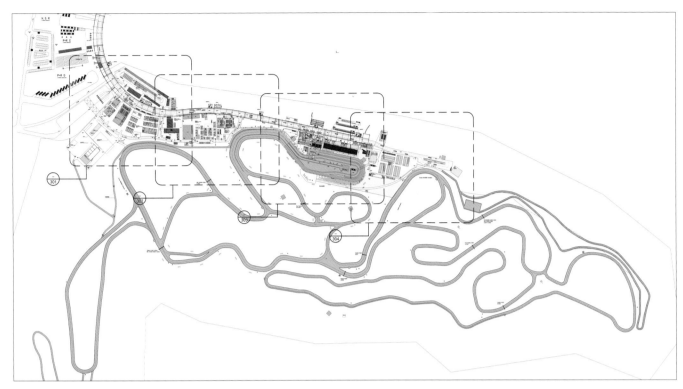

ZCC 总平面图 OB4.0版
ZCC Master Plan OB4.0

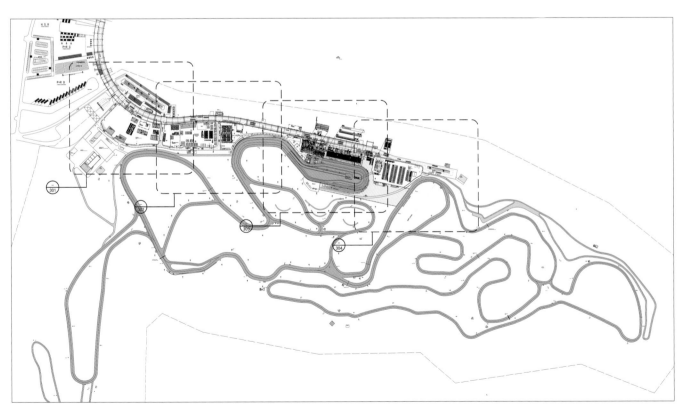

N
ZCC 总平面图 OB6.0版
ZCC Master Plan OB6.0

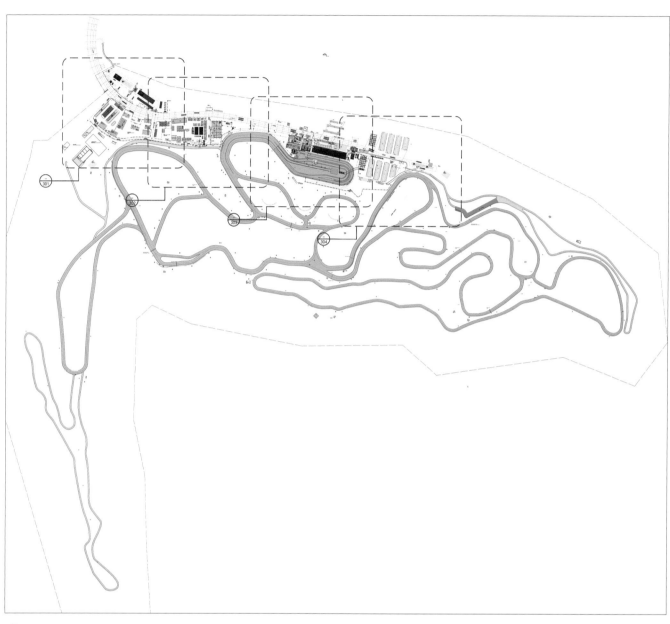

ZCC 总平面图 OB7.0版
ZCC Master Plan OB7.0

功能分区 Function Division	步行流线 Pedestrian Flow	车行流线 Vehicular Flow	出入口 Entry
运动员区 Athlete			Ea
奥林匹克大家庭区 Olympic & Paralympic Family			Eo
转播服务区 Broadcast			Eb
媒体运行区 Press			Ep
观众/访客区 Spectator			Ee
安保区 Security			Es
场馆运行区 Venue Operations			Ev
赛场接待区 In-Venue-Hospitality			Eh
仪式区 Ceremony			Em
多种客户群 Multiple Client Groups			

功能分区 Function Division	
竞赛区 FOP	
训练区 Training	
交通 Transport	
安保防护栏（临建）Overlay Security Perimeter Fence	0
安保防护栏（现有）Existing Security Perimeter Fence	X
隔离栏（临建）Overlay Fence	0
隔离栏（现有）Existing Fence	X
铝管和帷幔 Pipe and Drape	PD
绳索和支柱 Rope and Stanchion	RS
警戒带 Belt Partition	BP

功能分区 Function Division	
金属栏板 Metal Barriercades	MB
隔离墩 Traffic Barriercades	
展览墙 Modular Wall	MW
隔墙 Partition Wall	PW
固定软墙（用于帐篷或天棚）Fixed Soft Wall (For Tents & Canopies)	FSW
可移动软墙（用于帐篷或天棚）Moveable Soft Wall (For Tents & Canopies)	MSW
不使用区域 Not to be Used	
放大索引 Call Out	XXX
验证点 Access Control Point (ACP)	●

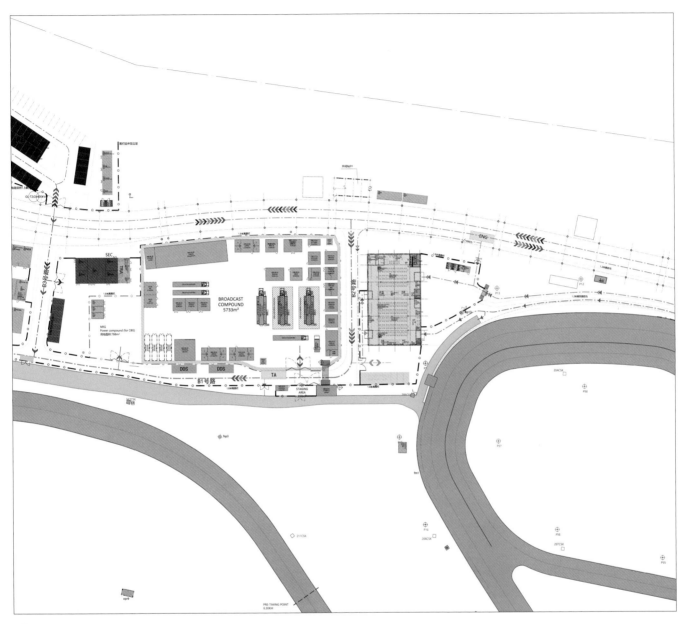

N

ZCC 转播综合区放大平面图 OB7.0版
ZCC Broadcast Compound Enlarged Plan OB7.0

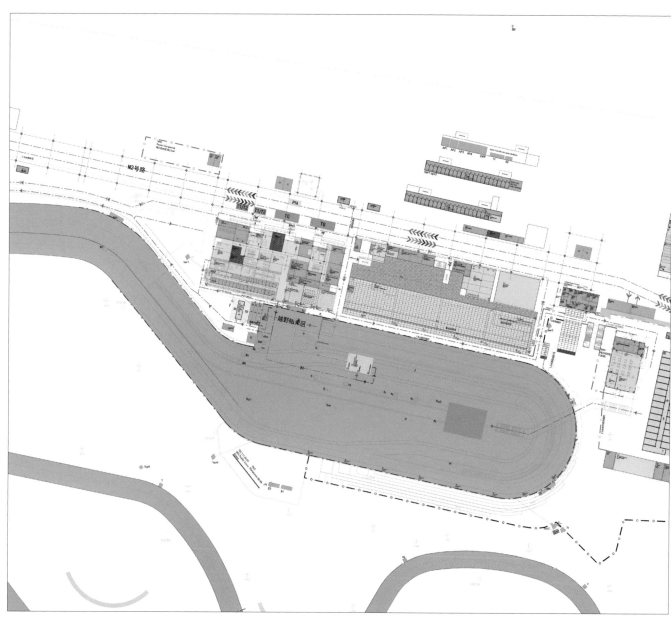

N
ZCC 出发区、结束区放大平面图 OB7.0版
ZCC Start and Finish Area Enlarged Plan OB7.0

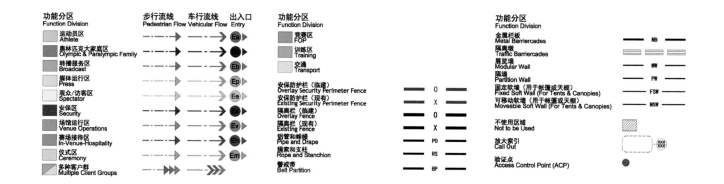

功能分区 Function Division	步行流线 Pedestrian Flow	车行流线 Vehicular Flow	出入口 Entry
运动员区 Athlete			Ea
奥林匹克大家庭区 Olympic & Paralympic Family			●
转播服务区 Broadcast			Eb
媒体运行区 Press			Ep
观众/访客区 Spectator			Ee
安保区 Security			●
场馆运行区 Venue Operations			Ev
赛场接待区 In-Venue-Hospitality			Eh
仪式区 Ceremony			Em
多种客户群 Multiple Client Groups			

功能分区 Function Division
竞赛区 FOP
训练区 Training
交通 Transport

安保防护栏（临建）Overlay Security Perimeter Fence — O
安保防护栏（现有）Existing Security Perimeter Fence — X
隔离栏（临建）Overlay Fence — O
隔离栏（现有）Existing Fence — X
铝管和帷幔 Pipe and Drape — PD
揽索和支柱 Rope and Stanchion — RS
警戒带 Belt Partition — BP

功能分区 Function Division
金属栏板 Metal Barriercades — MB
隔离墩 Traffic Barriercades
展览墙 Modular Wall — MW
隔墙 Partition Wall — PW
固定软墙（用于帐篷或天棚）Fixed Soft Wall (For Tents & Canopies) — FSW
可移动软墙（用于帐篷或天棚）Moveable Soft Wall (For Tents & Canopies) — MSW
不使用区域 Not to be Used
放大索引 Call Out
验证点 Access Control Point (ACP) ●

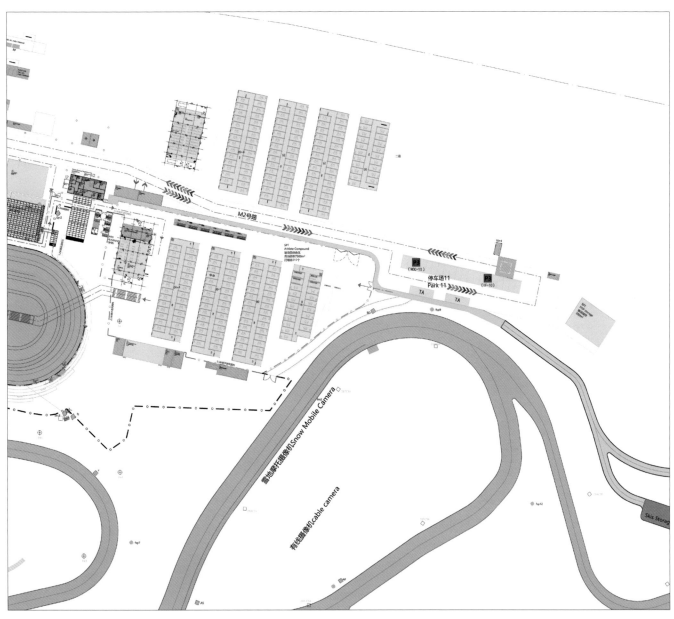

N

ZCC 运动员综合区放大平面图 OB7.0版
ZCC Athlete Compound Enlarged Plan OB7.0

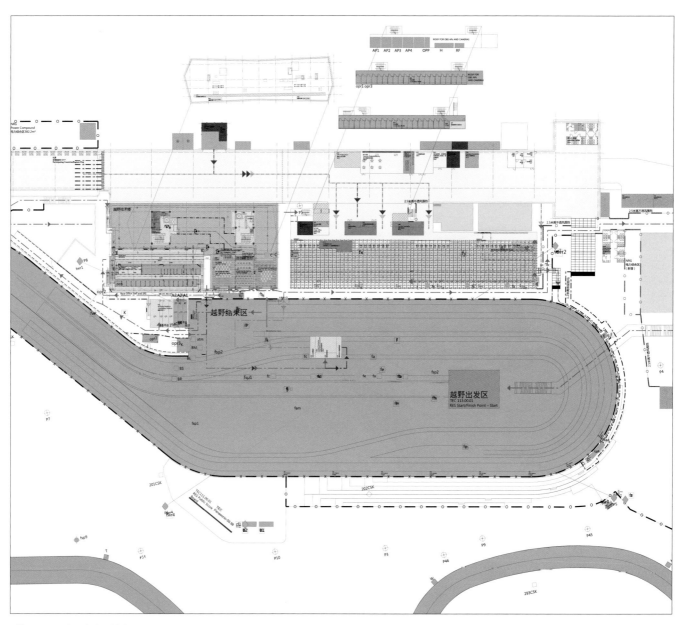

ZCC 注册坐席区放大平面图 OB7.0版
ZCC Accredited Seating Enlarged Plan OB7.0

功能分区 Function Division	步行流线 Pedestrian Flow	车行流线 Vehicular Flow	出入口 Entry
运动员区 Athlete			Ea
奥林匹克大家庭区 Olympic & Paralympic Family			
转播服务区 Broadcast			Eb
媒体运行区 Press			Ep
观众/访客区 Spectator			Ee
安保区 Security			
场馆运行区 Venue Operations			Ev
赛馆接待区 In-Venue-Hospitality			Eh
仪式区 Ceremony			Em
多种客户群 Multiple Client Groups			

功能分区 Function Division	
竞赛区 FOP	
训练区 Training	
交通 Transport	
安保防护栏（临建）Overlay Security Perimeter Fence	O
安保防护栏（现有）Existing Security Perimeter Fence	X
隔离栏（临建）Overlay Fence	O
隔离栏（现有）Existing Fence	X
铝管和帷幔 Pipe and Drape	PD
绳索和支柱 Rope and Stanchion	RS
警戒带 Belt Partition	BP

功能分区 Function Division	
金属栏板 Metal Barriercades	MB
隔离墩 Traffic Barriercades	
展览墙 Modular Wall	MW
隔墙 Partition Wall	PW
固定软墙（用于帐篷或天棚）Fixed Soft Wall (For Tents & Canopies)	FSW
可移动软墙（用于帐篷或天棚）Moveable Soft Wall (For Tents & Canopies)	MSW
不使用区域 Not to be Used	
放大索引 Call Out	XXX
验证点 Access Control Point (ACP)	●

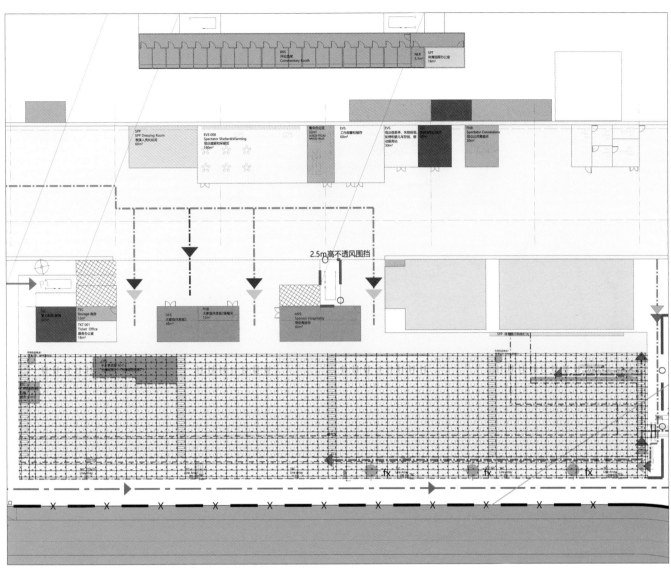

N

ZCC 看台二层平面图 OB7.0版
ZCC Grand Stand 2F Plan OB7.0

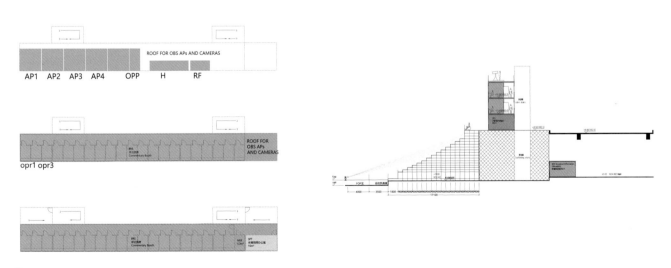

N

ZCC 看台三~五层平面图、剖面图 OB7.0版
ZCC Grand Stand 3F/4F/5F Plan and Section OB7.0

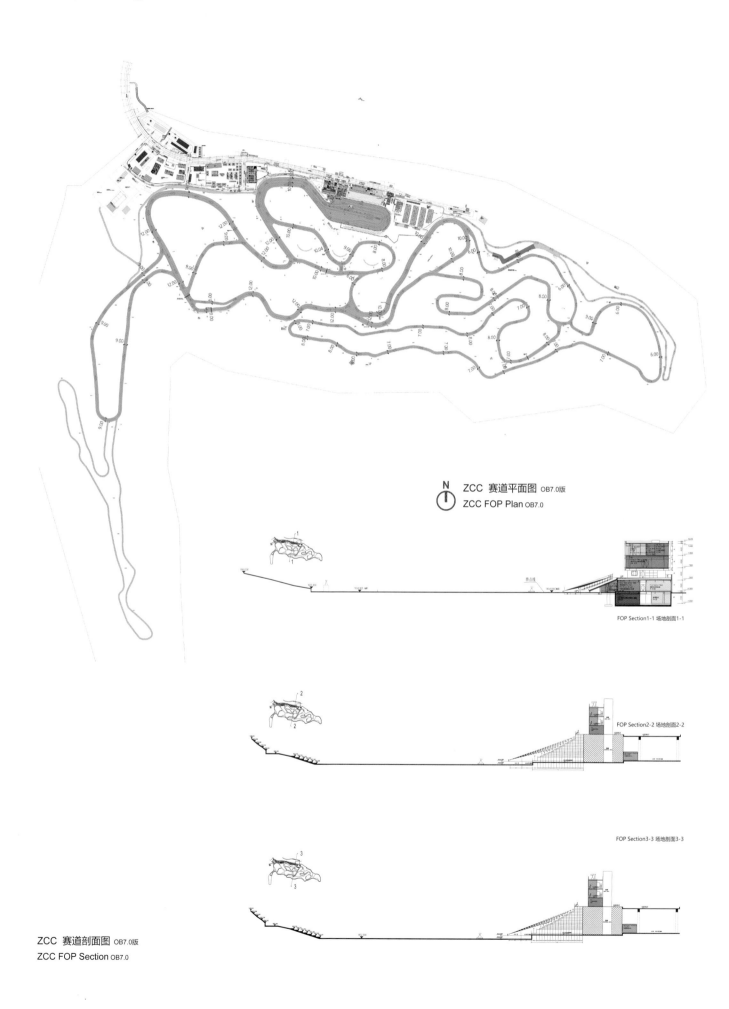

ZCC 赛道平面图 OB7.0版
ZCC FOP Plan OB7.0

FOP Section1-1 场地剖面1-1

FOP Section2-2 场地剖面2-2

FOP Section3-3 场地剖面3-3

ZCC 赛道剖面图 OB7.0版
ZCC FOP Section OB7.0

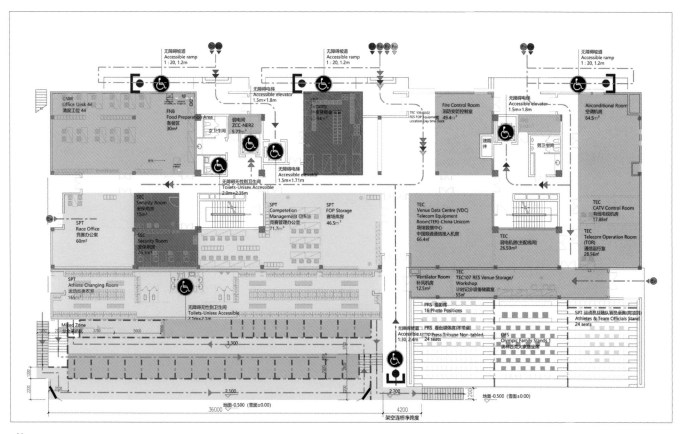

ZCC 技术楼一层平面图 OB7.0版
ZCC Tech-Building 1F Plan OB7.0

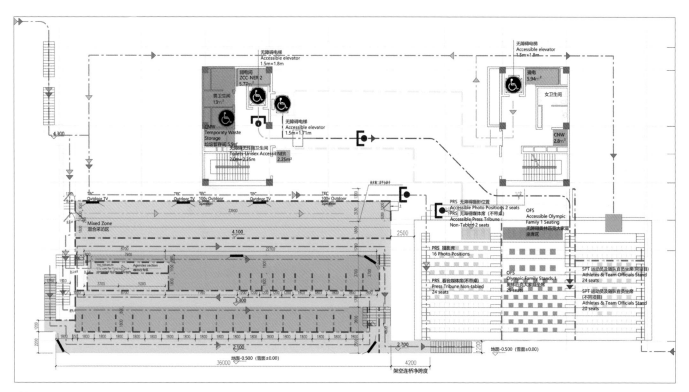

ZCC 技术楼二层平面图 OB7.0版
ZCC Tech-Building 2F Plan OB7.0

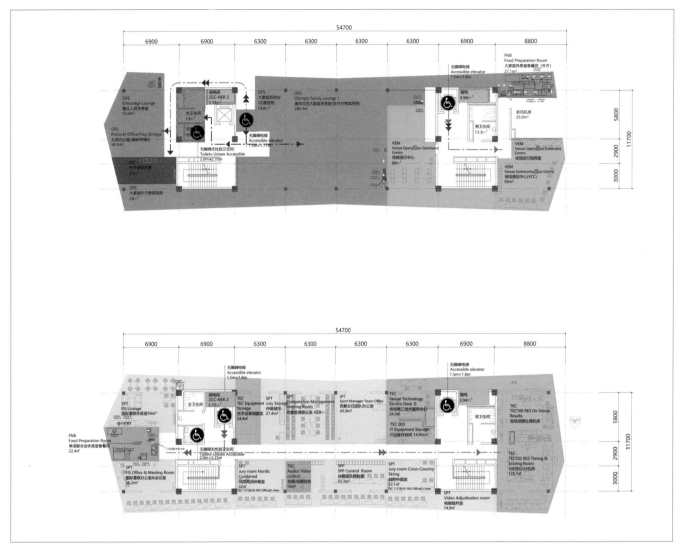

N
ZCC 技术楼三、四层平面图 OB7.0版
ZCC Tech-Building 3F/4F Plan OB7.0

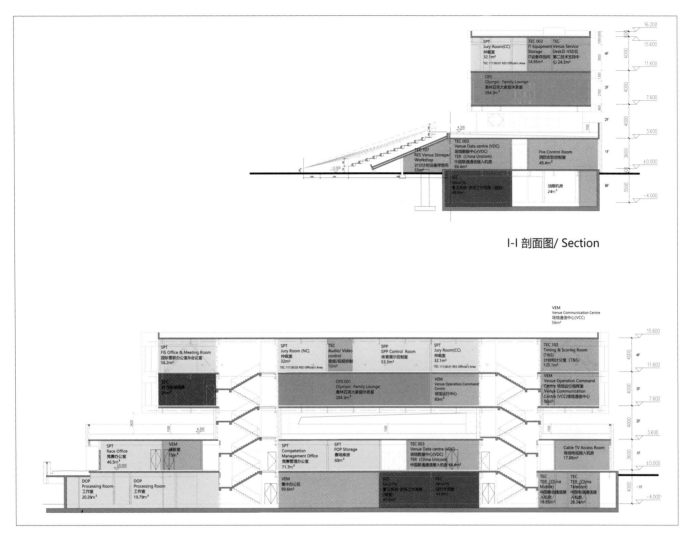

I-I 剖面图/ Section

ZCC 技术楼剖面图 OB7.0版
ZCC Tech-Building Section OB7.0

张家口山地转播中心 [ZBC]

Zhangjiakou Mountain Broadcast Centre

张家口山地转播中心位于张家口古杨树场馆群内，由山地转播中心和电视演播厅两部分组成，在北京2022年冬奥会和冬残奥会期间为OBS和持权转播商提供工作空间和服务设施。

张家口山地转播中心正对国家跳台滑雪中心赛道，呈一字形布置，建筑面积约1.2万m²。电视演播厅位于国家跳台滑雪中心对面的山坡上，电视演播厅的背景中包含有国家跳台滑雪中心赛道、国家冬季两项中心的靶场和远处的长城遗址，是电视转播的绝佳位置，建筑面积为8740m²。

Located within the Zhangjiakou Guyangshu Cluster, the Zhangjiakou Mountain Broadcast Centre consists of a mountain broadcast centre and a TV studio and provides a workspace and service facilities for OBS and rights-holding broadcasters during the Beijing 2022 Olympic and Paralympic Winter Games.

The Zhangjiakou Mountain Broadcast Centre faces directly the courses of the National Ski Jumping Centre and is an I-shaped building with a floor area of about 12,000m². With a floor area of 8,740m², the TV studio is on the hillside opposite the National Ski Jumping Centre, with the National Ski Jumping Centre courses, the National Biathlon Centre shooting range, and the distant Great Wall ruins as its background, making it an ideal location for TV broadcasting.

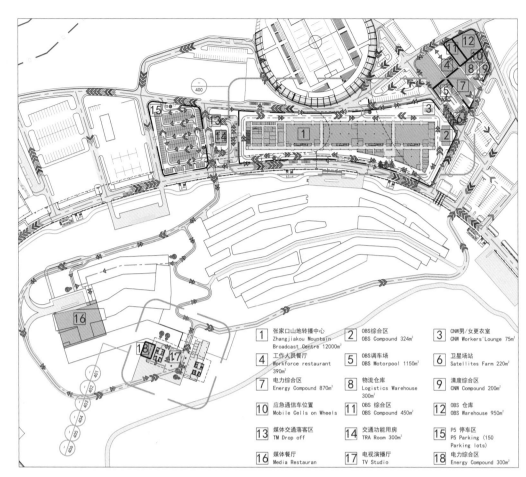

1	张家口山地转播中心 Zhangjiakou Mountain Broadcast Centre 12000m²	2	OBS综合区 OBS Compound 324m²	3	CNW男/女更衣室 CNW Workers'Lounge 75m²
4	工作人员餐厅 Workforce restaurant 390m²	5	OBS调车场 OBS Motorpool 1150m²	6	卫星场站 Satellites Farm 220m²
7	电力综合区 Energy Compound 870m²	8	物流仓库 Logistics Warehouse 300m²	9	清废综合区 CNW Compound 200m²
10	应急通信车位置 Mobile Cells on Wheels	11	OBS 综合区 OBS Compound 450m²	12	OBS 仓库 OBS Warehouse 950m²
13	媒体交通落客区 TM Drop off	14	交通功能用房 TRA Room 300m²	15	P5 停车区 P5 Parking (150 Parking lots)
16	媒体餐厅 Media Restauran	17	电视演播厅 TV Studio	18	电力综合区 Energy Compound 300m²

ZBC 总平面图 OB4.0版
ZBC Master Plan OB4.0

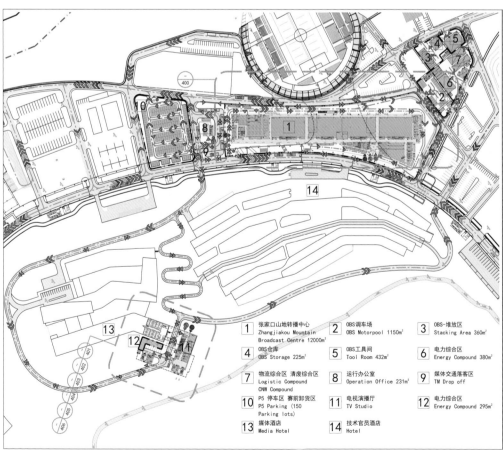

1	张家口山地转播中心 Zhangjiakou Mountain Broadcast Centre 12000m²	2	OBS调车场 OBS Motorpool 1150m²	3	OBS-堆放区 Stacking Area 360m²
4	OBS仓库 OBS Storage 225m²	5	OBS工具间 Tool Room 432m²	6	电力综合区 Energy Compound 380m²
7	物流综合区 清废综合区 Logistic Compound CNW Compound	8	运行办公室 Operation Office 231m²	9	媒体交通落客区 TM Drop off
10	P5 停车区 赛前卸货区 P5 Parking (150 Parking lots)	11	电视演播厅 TV Studio	12	电力综合区 Energy Compound 295m²
13	媒体酒店 Media Hotel	14	技术官员酒店 Hotel		

ZBC 总平面图 OB5.0版
ZBC Master Plan OB5.0

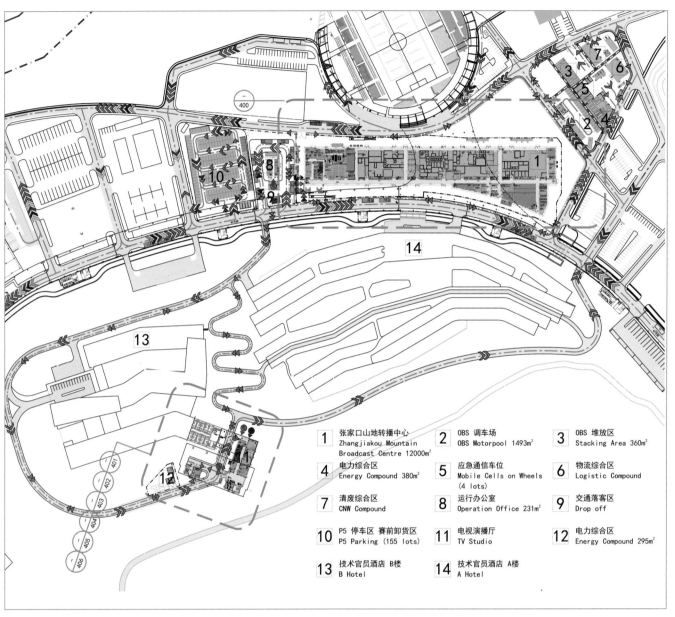

1	张家口山地转播中心 Zhangjiakou Mountain Broadcast Centre 12000m²	**2**	OBS 调车场 OBS Motorpool 1493m²	**3**	OBS 堆放区 Stacking Area 360m²
4	电力综合区 Energy Compound 380m²	**5**	应急通信车位 Mobile Cells on Wheels (4 lots)	**6**	物流综合区 Logistic Compound
7	清废综合区 CNW Compound	**8**	运行办公室 Operation Office 231m²	**9**	交通落客区 Drop off
10	P5 停车区 赛前卸货区 P5 Parking (155 lots)	**11**	电视演播厅 TV Studio	**12**	电力综合区 Energy Compound 295m²
13	技术官员酒店 B楼 B Hotel	**14**	技术官员酒店 A楼 A Hotel		

N ZBC 总平面图 OB7.0版
ZBC Master Plan OB7.0

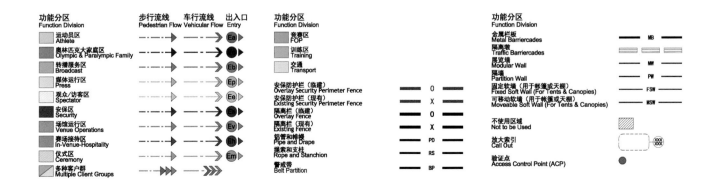

功能分区 Function Division	步行流线 Pedestrian Flow	车行流线 Vehicular Flow	出入口 Entry	功能分区 Function Division	功能分区 Function Division	
运动员区 Athlete			Ea	竞赛区 FOP	金属栏板 Metal Barriercades	MB
奥林匹克大家庭区 Olympic & Paralympic Family				训练区 Training	隔离墩 Traffic Barriercades	
转播服务区 Broadcast			Eb	交通 Transport	展览墙 Modular Wall	MW
媒体运行区 Press			Ep		隔墙 Partition Wall	PW
观众/访客区 Spectator			Ee	安保防护栏（临建） Overlay Security Perimeter Fence	O	固定软墙（用于帐篷或天棚） Fixed Soft Wall (For Tents & Canopies)	FSW
安保区 Security				安保防护栏（现有） Existing Security Perimeter Fence	X	可移动软墙（用于帐篷或天棚） Moveable Soft Wall (For Tents & Canopies)	MSW
场馆运行区 Venue Operations			Ev	隔离栏（临建） Overlay Fence	O	不使用区域 Not to be Used	
赛馆接待区 in-Venue-Hospitality			Eh	隔离栏（现有） Existing Fence	X	放大索引 Call Out	XXX
仪式区 Ceremony			Em	铝管和帷幔 Pipe and Drape	PD	验证点 Access Control Point (ACP)	
多种客户群 Multiple Client Groups				绳索和支柱 Rope and Stanchion	RS		
				警戒带 Belt Partition	BP		

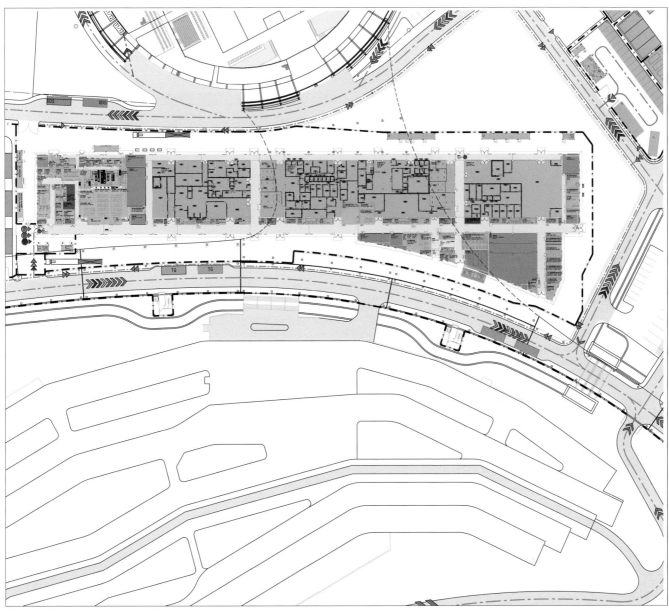

ZBC 一层放大平面图 OB7.0版
ZBC 1F Enlarged Plan OB7.0

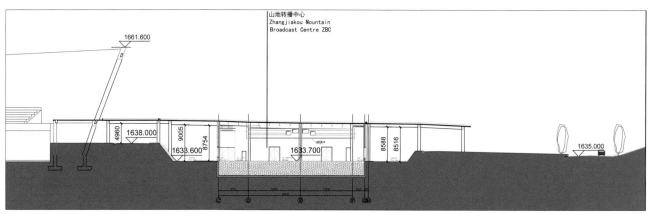

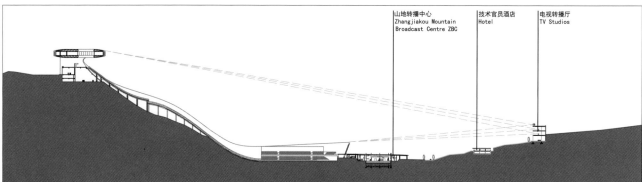

ZBC 场地剖面图 OB7.0版
ZBC Section OB7.0

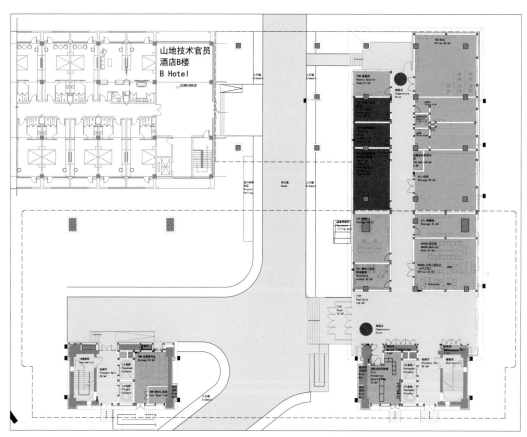

N ZBC 电视演播厅一层平面图 OB7.0版
ZBC TV Studio 1F Plan OB7.0

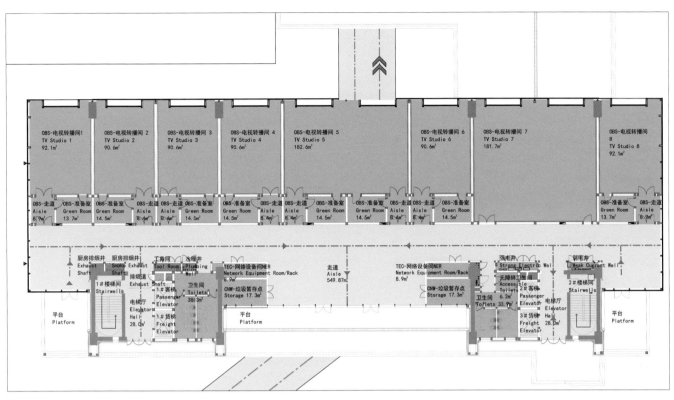

N ZBC 电视演播厅二层平面图 OB7.0版
ZBC TV Studio 2F Plan OB7.0

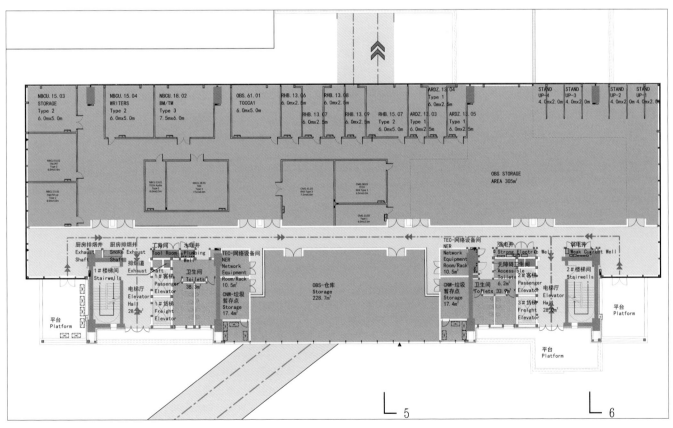

N ZBC 电视演播厅三层平面图 OB7.0版
ZBC TV Studio 3F Plan OB7.0

附录
Appendix

主要撰稿人

场馆总体布局：刘玉民、桂琳、黄雨晨

《场馆设施手册》编制标准及历程：

北京冬奥组委规划建设部：刘玉民、桂琳、杨明、谷鑫

中国城市发展规划设计咨询有限公司、中国建筑设计研究院有限公司：翟长青、董笑岩、李焱、谷婧云、蒋翠、刘宇明、王姝、董文乐

北京市建筑设计研究院有限公司：赵曾辉、李英、赵一凡

《场馆设施手册》问答录：刘玉民、桂琳、赵曾辉、杨明、李英、赵一凡

场馆运行设计简介：

北京冬奥组委规划建设部：桂琳、杨明

北京市建筑设计研究院有限公司：赵曾辉、李英、赵一凡、林志云、冯喆、谢一忱、白惠文、张斯斯、鲍润霞、孙彦亮、盛于蓝

中国建筑设计研究院有限公司：谭泽阳、赖钰辰、袁国茗、范坤仪、谷婧云、梁伟、张若曦

清华大学建筑设计研究院有限公司：张利、王冲、窦光璐、曹婧娴、陈荣钦、党靖然、李月明、潘睿、曲植、王腾、闫梓寒、钟善、周盼

场馆建设、设计单位及运行设计师

1. 国家速滑馆

建设单位：北京国家速滑馆经营有限责任公司

建筑设计单位：北京市建筑设计研究院有限公司（初步设计及施工图）、博普乐勒斯设计有限公司（竞赛方案递交）

运行设计单位：北京市建筑设计研究院有限公司

运行设计师：郑方、孙卫华、林志云、冯喆、张林、闫昊

2. 国家游泳中心

建设单位：北京市国有资产经营有限责任公司

建筑设计单位：北京市建筑设计研究院有限公司（改造）

运行设计单位：北京市建筑设计研究院有限公司

运行设计师：郑方、孙卫华、冯喆、林志云、宋汶凯、张旻娟、任重、王潇潇

3. 国家体育馆

建设单位：北京演艺集团有限责任公司

建筑设计单位：北京市建筑设计研究院有限公司

运行设计单位：北京市建筑设计研究院有限公司

运行设计师：查世旭、赵曾辉、李英、赵宏

4. 首都体育馆

建设单位：国家体育总局冬季运动管理中心

建筑设计单位：北京市建筑设计研究院有限公司

运行设计单位：北京市建筑设计研究院有限公司

运行设计师：谢一忱

5. 首体花样滑冰训练馆

建设单位：国家体育总局冬季运动管理中心

建筑设计单位：北京市建筑设计研究院有限公司

运行设计单位：北京市建筑设计研究院有限公司

运行设计师：谢一忱

6. 首体短道速滑训练馆

建设单位：国家体育总局冬季运动管理中心

建筑设计单位：中国建筑设计研究院有限公司

运行设计单位：中国建筑设计研究院有限公司

运行设计师：彭典勇、张若曦、岳意贺、王秀琴、王朝霞、贺雷刚、赵超

7. 五棵松体育中心

建设单位：北京五棵松文化体育中心有限公司

建筑设计单位：北京市建筑设计研究院有限公司

运行设计单位：北京市建筑设计研究院有限公司

运行设计师：张新宇、白惠文

8. 五棵松冰球训练馆

建设单位：北京五棵松文化体育中心有限公司

建筑设计单位：北京市建筑设计研究院有限公司

运行设计单位：北京市建筑设计研究院有限公司

运行设计师：孙彦亮、景阳、张国书、殷杰

9. 首钢滑雪大跳台

建设单位：北京首奥置业有限公司

建筑设计单位：清华大学建筑设计研究院有限公司、北京戈建建筑设计顾问有限责任公司、杭州中联筑境建筑设计有限公司、北京首钢国际工程技术有限公司

运行设计单位：清华大学建筑设计研究院有限公司

运行设计师：张利、窦光璐

10. 北京冬奥村

建设单位：北京城市副中心投资建设集团有限公司

建筑设计单位：北京市建筑设计研究院有限公司

运行设计单位：北京市建筑设计研究院有限公司

运行设计师：张斯斯

11. 主媒体中心

建设单位：北京北辰会展投资有限公司

建筑设计单位：北京市建筑设计研究院有限公司、法国包赞巴克建筑事务所（方案设计）

运行设计单位：北京市建筑设计研究院有限公司

运行设计师：鲍润霞、滕俊、杨姗、李静

12. 北京颁奖广场

建设单位：北京城市副中心投资建设集团有限公司、北京北奥集团有限责任公司

建筑设计单位：北京市建筑设计研究院有限公司

运行设计单位：北京市建筑设计研究院有限公司

运行设计师：赵一凡

13. 北京奥林匹克公园公共区

建设单位：北京城市副中心投资建设集团有限公司

建筑设计单位：北京市建筑设计研究院有限公司

运行设计单位：北京市建筑设计研究院有限公司

运行设计师：赵曾辉、赵一凡

14. 北京冬奥组委总部

建设单位：北京首钢建设投资有限公司

建筑设计单位：杭州中联筑境建筑设计有限公司、北京首钢筑境国际建筑设计有限公司、北京首钢国际工程技术有限公司、北京华清安地建筑设计有限公司、英国思锐建筑设计有限公司、北京戈建建筑设计顾问有限责任公司、中国建筑设计研究院有限公司

运行设计单位：中国城市发展规划设计咨询有限公司、中国建筑设计研究院有限公司

运行设计师：谷婧云、蒋翠、刘敏跃

15. 运行指挥部调度中心

建设单位：北京首钢建设投资有限公司

建筑设计单位：杭州中联筑境建筑设计有限公司、北京首钢筑境国际建筑设计有限公司、北京首钢国际工程技术有限公司

运行设计单位：中国城市发展规划设计咨询有限公司、中国建筑设计研究院有限公司

运行设计师：梁伟、谷思睿、李焱

16. 制服和注册中心

建设单位：北京京煤集团有限责任公司

建筑设计单位：北京京能建设集团有限公司

运行设计单位：中国城市发展规划设计咨询有限公司、中国建筑设计研究院有限公司

运行设计师：梁伟、谷思睿、董文乐、李焱

17. 国家体育场

建设单位：国家体育场有限责任公司

建筑设计单位：中国建筑设计研究院有限公司（设计联合体牵头人、改造设计单位）、瑞士赫尔佐格和德梅隆设计事务所、奥雅纳工程咨询有限公司（香港）

运行设计单位：中国建筑设计研究院有限公司

运行设计师：谭泽阳、蒋翠、李佳晟、谷婧云

18. 奥林匹克（残奥）大家庭酒店

运行设计单位：北京市建筑设计研究院有限公司

运行设计师：盛于蓝、杜松、张钒、王威

19. 北京首都国际机场

运行设计单位：北京市建筑设计研究院有限公司

运行设计师：王晓群，李春丽、范士兴、胡霄雯、王世博

20. 冬奥交通指挥中心

运行设计单位：中国城市发展规划设计咨询有限公司、中国建筑设计研究院有限公司

运行设计师：蒋翠

21. 冬奥电力运行中心

运行设计单位：中国城市发展规划设计咨询有限公司、中国建筑设计研究院有限公司

运行设计师：蒋翠

22. 主物流中心

运行设计单位：中国城市发展规划设计咨询有限公司、中国建筑设计研究院有限公司

运行设计师：谷婧云

23. 技术运行中心

运行设计单位：中国城市发展规划设计咨询有限公司、中国建筑设计研究院有限公司

运行设计师：梁伟

24. 北京冬奥会兴奋剂检测中心

运行设计单位：中国城市发展规划设计咨询有限公司、中国建筑设计研究院有限公司

运行设计师：谷婧云

25. 清河高铁站

运行设计单位：中国城市发展规划设计咨询有限公司、中国建筑设计研究院有限公司

运行设计师：梁伟

26. 国家高山滑雪中心

建设单位：北京北控京奥建设有限公司

建筑设计单位：中国建筑设计研究院有限公司

运行设计单位：中国建筑设计研究院有限公司

运行设计师：赖钰辰、谭泽阳、谷婧云、蒋翠、邱雪桥、王姝、刘建双、郭倍丞、董笑岩

27. 国家雪车雪橇中心

建设单位：北京北控京奥建设有限公司

建筑设计单位：中国建筑设计研究院有限公司

运行设计单位：中国建筑设计研究院有限公司

运行设计师：袁国茗、赖钰辰、谭泽阳、谷婧云、李玉鹏

28. 延庆冬奥村

建设单位：北京国家高山滑雪有限公司

建筑设计单位：中国建筑设计研究院有限公司

运行设计单位：中国城市发展规划设计咨询有限公司、中国建筑设计研究院有限公司

运行设计师：范坤仪、赖钰辰、袁国茗、谭泽阳、刘宇明

29. 延庆赛区核心区公共区

建设单位：北京北控京奥建设有限公司、北京国家高山滑雪有限公司

建筑设计单位：中国建筑设计研究院有限公司、北京市市政工程设计研究总院有限公司

运行设计单位：中国城市发展规划设计咨询有限公司、中国建筑设计研究院有限公司

运行设计师：赖钰辰、谭泽阳、李佳晟、袁国茗、杨锡为

30. 延庆制服和注册分中心

建设单位：北京八达岭国际会展中心有限公司

建筑设计单位：华诚博远（北京）建筑规划设计有限公司

运行设计单位：中国城市发展规划设计咨询有限公司、中国建筑设计研究院有限公司

运行设计师：袁国茗、赖钰辰、谭泽阳、李玉鹏

31. 阪泉综合服务中心

建设单位：北京市首都公路发展集团有限公司

建筑设计单位：北京市市政工程设计研究总院有限公司、中咨泰克交通工程集团有限公司

运行设计单位：中国城市发展规划设计咨询有限公司、中国建筑设计研究院有限公司

运行设计师：李佳晟、赖钰辰、谭泽阳、杨锡为、刘宇明

32. 延庆残奥颁奖广场

建设单位：北京世园文旅发展有限责任公司

建筑设计单位：北京市建筑设计研究院有限公司

运行设计单位：中国城市发展规划设计咨询有限公司、中国建筑设计研究院有限公司

运行设计师：范坤仪、赖钰辰、谭泽阳

33. 延庆高铁站

运行设计单位：中国城市发展规划设计咨询有限公司、中国建筑设计研究院有限公司

运行设计师：范坤仪

34. 云顶滑雪公园

建设单位：密苑（张家口）旅游胜地有限公司

建筑设计单位：清华大学建筑设计研究院有限公司

运行设计单位：清华大学建筑设计研究院有限公司

运行设计师：张利、陈荣钦、曹婧娴

35. 张家口山地新闻中心

建设单位：密苑（张家口）旅游胜地有限公司

建筑设计单位：清华大学建筑设计研究院有限公司

运行设计单位：清华大学建筑设计研究院有限公司

运行设计师：张利、曹婧娴

36. 张家口古杨树场馆群公共区

建设单位：张家口奥体建设开发有限公司

建筑设计单位：清华大学建筑设计研究院有限公司

运行设计单位：清华大学建筑设计研究院有限公司

运行设计师：张利、王冲

37. 国家冬季两项中心

建设单位：张家口奥体建设开发有限公司

建筑设计单位：清华大学建筑设计研究院有限公司

运行设计单位：清华大学建筑设计研究院有限公司

运行设计师：张利、党靖然

38. 国家跳台滑雪中心

建设单位：张家口奥体建设开发有限公司

建筑设计单位：清华大学建筑设计研究院有限公司

运行设计单位：清华大学建筑设计研究院有限公司

运行设计师：张利、王冲

39. 国家越野滑雪中心

建设单位：张家口奥体建设开发有限公司

建筑设计单位：清华大学建筑设计研究院有限公司

运行设计单位：清华大学建筑设计研究院有限公司

运行设计师：张利、潘睿、周盼

40. 张家口山地转播中心

建设单位：张家口奥体建设开发有限公司

建筑设计单位：清华大学建筑设计研究院有限公司

运行设计单位：清华大学建筑设计研究院有限公司

运行设计师：张利、李月明

41. 张家口冬奥村/（冬残奥村）

建设单位：张家口奥体建设开发有限公司

建筑设计单位：清华大学建筑设计研究院有限公司

运行设计单位：清华大学建筑设计研究院有限公司

运行设计师：张利、钟善

42. 张家口颁奖广场

建设单位：中赫太舞（张家口崇礼）文化旅游有限公司

建筑设计单位：中国建筑设计研究院有限公司、清华大学建筑设计研究院有限公司

运行设计单位：清华大学建筑设计研究院有限公司

运行设计师：张利、阎梓寒、王腾

43. 张家口制服和注册分中心

建设单位：中赫太舞（张家口崇礼）文化旅游有限公司

建筑设计单位：清华大学建筑设计研究院有限公司

运行设计单位：清华大学建筑设计研究院有限公司

运行设计师：张利、阎梓寒、曲植

44. 太子城高铁站

运行设计单位：清华大学建筑设计研究院有限公司

运行设计师：张利、杨琳琳

《场馆设施手册》参与编制单位：

北京2022年冬奥会和冬残奥会组织委员会各部门（中心）、各场馆（群）运行团队

北京2022年冬奥会工程建设指挥部办公室

河北省第24届冬奥会工作领导小组办公室

张家口市筹办冬奥会工作领导小组办公室

北京国家速滑馆经营有限责任公司

北京市国有资产经营有限责任公司

北京演艺集团有限责任公司

国家体育总局冬季运动管理中心

北京五棵松文化体育中心有限公司

北京首奥置业有限公司

北京城市副中心投资建设集团有限公司

北京北辰会展投资有限公司

北京北奥集团有限责任公司

北京首钢建设投资有限公司

北京京煤集团有限责任公司

国家体育场有限责任公司

北京北控京奥建设有限公司

北京国家高山滑雪有限公司

北京八达岭国际会展中心有限公司

北京市首都公路发展集团有限公司

北京世园文旅发展有限责任公司

密苑（张家口）旅游胜地有限公司

张家口奥体建设开发有限公司

中赫太舞（张家口崇礼）文化旅游有限公司

照片提供单位：

北京2022年冬奥会和冬残奥会组织委员会相关部门（中心）、场馆运行团队

张家口市筹办冬奥会工作领导小组办公室

场馆业主单位

北京市建筑设计研究院有限公司（简称北建院，BIAD）

中国建筑设计研究院有限公司（简称中建院，CADG）

清华大学建筑设计研究院有限公司（简称清华院，THAD）

北京冬奥组委照片拍摄：北京水晶石数字科技股份有限公司

其他

英文翻译公司：中译语通科技股份有限公司

英文校对：潘鑫池、刘思琦

页面排版：宇晨

因编录时间有限，以上名录如有疏漏之处，敬请谅解。

索引
Index

北京2022年冬奥会和冬残奥会常用名词缩写

中文名称	英文名称	英文缩写
注册检查点	Accreditation Check-Point	ACP
转播信息办公室	Broadcast Information Office	BIO
场馆后院	Back of House	BOH
体育仲裁法庭	Court of Arbitration for Sport	CAS
解说控制室	Commentary Control Rooms	CCR
解说信息系统	Commentary Information System	CIS
直达专用交通系统	Direct and Dedicated Transportation System	DDS
代表团登记会议	Delegation Registration Meeting	DRM
执行委员会	Executive Board	EB
电子新闻采集	Electronic News Gathering	ENG
业务领域	Functional Area	FA
业务领域运行计划	Functional Area Operating Plan	FAOP
家具、装置与设备	Furniture, Fixtures and Equipment	FF&E
场馆前院	Front of House	FOH
比赛场地	Field of Play	FOP
主转播商	Host Broadcaster	HB
国际广播中心	International Broadcast Centre	IBC
国际单项联合会	International Federation	IF
国际奥委会	International Olympic Committee	IOC
国际奥林匹克照片库	International Olympic Photo Pool	IOPP
国际残奥委会	International Paralympic Committee	IPC
国际残疾人辅助设施标志	International Symbol Of Access	ISA
国际技术官员	International Technical Official	ITO
主新闻中心	Main Press Centre	MPC
国家单项联合会	National Federation	NF
国家/地区奥委会	National Olympic Committee	NOC
国家/地区残奥委会	National Paralympic Committee	NPC
国内技术官员	National Technical Official	NTO
设施手册	Overlay Book	OB

中文名称	英文名称	英文缩写
奥林匹克广播服务公司	Olympic Broadcasting Services	OBS
奥运会组委会（奥组委）	Organising Committee for the Olympic Games	OCOG
奥林匹克身份注册卡	Olympic Identity and Accreditation Card	OIAC
奥林匹克信息服务	Olympic Information Service	OIS
奥运会演播席	Olympic Presentation Position	OPP
奥运会成绩与信息服务	Olympic Results and Information Services	ORIS
奥运村广场	Olympic Village Plaza	OVP
残疾人奥运会（残奥会）	Paralympic Games	PAR
残奥会身份注册卡	Paralympic Identity and Accreditation Card	PIAC
残奥会成绩与信息服务	Paralympic Results and Information Services	PRIS
人行安检口	Person Security Access	PSA
持权转播商	Rights-Holding Broadcaster	RHB
居住区	Residential Zone	RZ
体育信息中心	Sport Information Centre	SIC
票检亭	Ticket Check Peak	TKT
奥林匹克全球合作伙伴	The Olympic Partner	TOP
车辆通行和/或停车证	Vehicle Access and/or Parking Permit	VAPP
车行安检口	Vehicle Security Access	VSA
世界反兴奋剂组织	World Anti-Doping Agency	WADA

2018～2021年，在国际奥委会和北京冬奥组委的共同组织下，北京市建筑设计研究院有限公司、中国建筑设计研究院有限公司、清华大学建筑设计研究院有限公司和中国城市发展规划设计咨询有限公司，联合完成了北京冬奥会和冬残奥会《场馆设施手册》12个版本（包括7个正式版本，5个升级版本）的编制，为赛事的举办提供了重要的建设和运行依据。

为了记录《场馆设施手册》编制历程和主要成果，2022年，四家编制单位将相关内容编辑成书，汇总了北京冬奥会和冬残奥会场馆规划建设概况、《场馆设施手册》编制标准及历程、场馆信息简介和运行设计主要图纸等主要内容，展示了场馆建设的精彩成果和赛时运行的科学缜密性。

《场馆设施手册》编制历时4年，期间得到了北京冬奥组委各部（中心）和各场馆业主的大力支持，唯有大家的携手共进，才能呈现此丰厚的成果和精彩的盛会！

为此，请允许我们向所有参与过《场馆设施手册》编制的单位和个人表示诚挚的感谢！并特别感谢北京冬奥组委规划建设部、感谢刘玉民部长对编制工作的整体统筹和悉心指导，感谢沈瑾、刘江、桂琳、杨永岗、徐典、刘浩冬、王宁、李亮等领导同事给予的大力支持和带动帮助！

最后，要衷心感谢所有在本书策划、撰稿、编辑、摄影、校审、出版、印刷过程中付出辛勤劳动的人，并将此诚挚的谢意送给所有为北京2022年冬奥会和冬残奥会场馆的选址、规划、设计、建设和运行付出过努力的每一个人！

《北京2022年冬奥会和冬残奥会场馆设施手册》编委会
2022年7月31日

Afterword

From 2018 to 2021, organised by the International Olympic Committee and Beijing 2022, Beijing Institute of Architectural Design, China Architecture Design and Research Group, Architectural Design and Research Institute of Tsinghua University and China Urban Development Planning And Design Consulting, jointly completed the Overlay Books for the Olympic and Paralympic Winter Games Beijing 2022 and have produced 12 versions in total, which provides an important basis for the construction and operation of the Games.

In order to record the preparation process and main achievements of Overlay Books, the four units edited the relevant contents into a book in 2022, which summarizes the planning and construction overview of the Beijing 2022 venues, the standards and preparation process of Overlay Books, the profile of the venues and the main drawings of the operation design, showing the wonderful achievements of the venue construction and the scientific meticulousness of the Games-time operation.

The preparation of the Overlay Books took four years, strongly supported by the departments of Beijing 2022 Committee and the venue owners. Only with the joint efforts of everyone can this fruitful and wonderful Games presented!

In this regard, please allow us to express our sincere gratitude to all the units and individuals who have participated in the preparation of the Overlay Books! And special thanks to the Venue Planning and Construction Department of the Beijing 2022 Committee, to Director Liu Yumin for his overall coordination and careful guidance of the preparation work, and to Shen Jin, Liu Jiang, Gui Lin, Yang Yonggang, Xu Dian, Liu Haodong, Wang Ning, Li Liang and other leaders and colleagues for their strong support!

Finally, we are deeply grateful to all people who have helped produce the OBs along the way from planning, contribution, editing, photography, proofreading, to publishing and printing. Our thanks also go to all people who have contributed to those who worked hard on the site selection, planning, design, construction and operation of the venues for the Beijing 2022 Games!

Editorial Board of Beijing 2022 Olympic and Paralympic Winter Games Overlay Books
31 July 2022